WHO SHOT NICK IVIE?

Huey Freeman

ISBN: 978-0-578-68434-5

Printed in the United States

Published by: **Talking Leaves Publishing Co.**
talkingleaves2020@gmail.com

Front cover photograph of Border Patrol Agent Nicholas J. Ivie on his beloved mustang, Mouse, was taken in July 2012 by a friend, who wishes to remain anonymous. Nick Ivie riding across a ridge in the Mule Mountains, looking toward State Route 80.

Book design by Cheryl Taylor
Editing by Rob Siedenburg
Map by Jorge Cazares,
Adept Concept Solutions, Urbana, Illinois

WHO SHOT NICK IVIE?

Huey Freeman

Dedicated to the memory
of U.S. Border Patrol Agent Nicholas J. Ivie,
who served our country with courage and devotion.

Also by Huey Freeman

Judge, Jury and Executioner
Legendary Locals of Decatur (Illinois)

Author's Note

All of the people who are quoted in this book are real people who spoke with the author. The names of some Border Patrol agents and Borderland area residents who contributed to this book have been changed to protect their identities.

Some of the experts who generously shared information on subjects including forensic pathology, crime lab procedures, ballistics, and law also preferred to remain anonymous. Other unnamed individuals contributed valuable resources and tremendous encouragement

Table of Contents

Illustration Index

Unless otherwise stated, all photographs by author

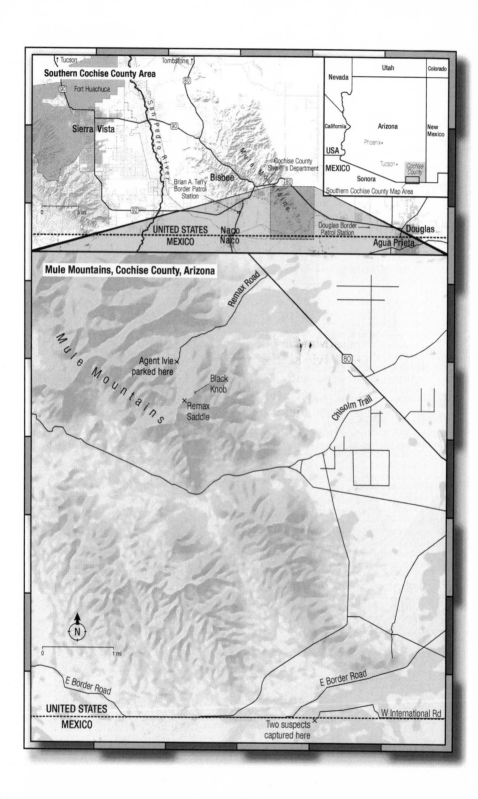

Southern Cochise County Area

↑ Tucson   Tombstone ↑

Fort Huachuca

Sierra Vista

San Pedro River

Bisbee
Brian A. Terry
Border Patrol
Station

Cochise County
Sheriff's Department

UNITED STATES   Naco
MEXICO   Naco

Douglas Border
Patrol Station

Douglas
Agua Prieta

0   5 mi

Nevada   Utah   Colorado

California   Arizona   New Mexico

Phoenix

USA

MEXICO   Tucson   Cochise County

Sonora

Southern Cochise County Map Area

Mule Mountains, Cochise County, Arizona

Remax Road

Mule Mountains

Agent Ivie
parked here

Black
Knob

× Remax
Saddle

80

Chisolm Trail

N

0   1 mi

E Border Road

E Border Road

W International Rd

UNITED STATES
MEXICO

Two suspects
captured here

1

Border Patrol Agent Ivie Responds to Sensor Alarm

"I'm going to be coming from the north—from the north through Remax."

Monday, October 1
Mule Mountain Range, Cochise County, Arizona

The sun set behind the forest-covered Huachuca Mountains on a warm, windless Monday afternoon, as 30-year-old Border Patrol agent Nicholas J. Ivie watched from the sideline, while his wife Christy, 31, practiced with her soccer team.

Ivie was operating on just a few hours' sleep, after rising early that morning to help with their two young daughters, 3-year-old Raigan and 22-month-old Presley. He had arrived home from his work shift shortly before the girls woke up.

When he noticed there were children of other players nearby, in addition to his daughters, Ivie organized a soccer game for them to play, not far from their mothers. Ivie was known by his neighbors in the subdivision where he lived as a friendly, kind-hearted guy, who enjoyed interacting with children.

Ivie, a horse patrol unit member and instructor, who had joined the Border Patrol almost five years earlier, was scheduled to report for duty at 6 p.m. at the station on the north edge of the tiny border town of Naco, Arizona. It normally took him about 35 minutes to make the 30-mile trip from his house in Sierra Vista to his station.

By the time Ivie returned home, changed into his forest green uniform, and prepared to drive to his workplace, he was running late for his scheduled start time.

Ivie enjoyed the home he shared with his family, a ranch-style wood-frame house with a two-car attached garage up front, built just four years earlier in a brand-new subdivision. Several other Border Patrol agents lived nearby, in the neighborhood on the west edge of a sprawling desert.

The Ivie family lived just east of the Huachuca Mountains, a compact, 20-mile-long range, lying mostly within the Coronado National Forest, featuring two of the county's highest peaks, magnificent canyons, and stunning rock formations. The range, which stretches across the Mexican border, is frequently visited by hikers and birdwatchers. Fort Huachuca, which hosts the United States Army Network Enterprise Technology Command, the United States Army Intelligence Center of Excellence, and Libby Army Airfield, is in the northeastern section of the mountain range.

The Huachuca Mountain range wears a deep, dark-green cover following the summer rains and is interspersed with vertical gray granite faces. It is also traversed by smuggling trails, in recent years used almost exclusively by the Sinaloa Cartel.

When Agent Ivie arrived at his workstation, his horse patrol teammates had already left the building to load their steeds onto a trailer and head out to the field in their pickup truck. For the past two years, Ivie had regularly paired up with a senior Border Patrol agent with 16 years of experience, who had served overseas deployments as an Army infantry officer. That agent was off duty on this night.

It was not a serious breach of protocol to start one's patrol shift shortly after the prescribed starting time. In the Border Patrol—the law enforcement unit tasked with protecting the nation from illegal entry by drug smugglers, terrorists, and human traffickers—work shifts were often prolonged at the backend, as chases into desolate wilderness stretched into overtime hours.

The sun had set, with just a few minutes of dwindling daylight left, as Ivie headed out on the evening of October 1, 2012, on a solo patrol in a white pickup truck with a green diagonal slash, the markings found on Border Patrol vehicles, a sight familiar to borderland residents.

Ivie, a six-foot-one-inch tall, 150-pound man with brown hair, hazel eyes, and a quiet, affable personality, treated illegal border crossers with respect and compassion. Ivie once reportedly carried a pregnant woman for a mile and a half across the desert because her bare feet were blistered, and she could no longer walk under her own power.

When a border rancher who was fond of Ivie heard this story of his kind deed, he warned Ivie to be careful while interacting with illegal aliens, lest his compassion interfere with his safety. Carrying a load like that could interfere with his ability to defend himself.[1]

Agent Ivie was respected among his peers for his exceptional work ethic, honesty, and willingness to take on tough assignments. He was a knowledgeable horseman, who had begun riding as a child. He had been sidelined from participating in other sports at the time, so he took up horseback riding—after breaking his jaw in a freak swimming pool accident.

From the moment he started riding, Ivie loved everything about it, especially the friendship with the horses he rode. When he was riding patrol on his Border Patrol horse, he would say that he could not believe he was actually being paid to do what he enjoyed so much. Ivie preferred his horse with him while on duty. Leaving behind Mouse, the wild, speedy Mustang with the rounded ears, which he had trained and named, did not feel right to him.

Ivie was an outstanding horseman and relished riding Mouse. Some of the other agents considered riding Mouse as dangerous as holding a stick of dynamite. After Mouse had been captured in the western wilderness, the agents who tried to train him considered him too unpredictable and tough to handle. Agent Ivie took the challenge and molded the strong and exceptionally intelligent Mouse into an outstanding law enforcement workhorse.[2]

On this cool October night, Ivie kept in touch with his horse patrol partners as he patrolled highways that ran through wide expanses of high desert in the southeast corner of Arizona. This territory was one of the busiest corridors in the nation for illegal border crossers, especially for a continual flow of drug smugglers and human traffickers.

Ivie listened for reports from the dispatchers in the control room at his recently completed station, just north of Naco, a small border town a little west of the Mule Mountain range. Naco, a town of about a thousand inhabitants, contained an elementary school, a century-old 18-hole golf course, a prohibition-era tavern for mostly straight drinkers, called the "Gay 90s Bar," and a port of entry for pedestrian traffic to and from Naco, Sonora, a Mexican border city of 6,000 residents.

The port of entry is used daily by Americans and Mexicans who conduct legal business and visit friends and family in both countries. U.S. Customs and Border Protection (CBP), the agency that oversees the Border Patrol, employs uniformed agents who control the traffic.

The Border Patrol station sits three-and-a-half miles north of the Mexican border, on Naco Highway, just beyond the southwest city limit of Bisbee, a picturesque tourist town with 5,000 residents. It is one of the busiest stations in the nation, covering 32½ miles north of the border, including the Huachuca and Mule mountain ranges, a stretch of desert in between those ranges, two other mountain ranges, a national forest, and several small towns.

The spacious installation with a fenced-off perimeter had been named the *Brian A. Terry Station* a few months earlier. It had replaced a much smaller station that, for decades, had been located right at the border, inside Naco.

The dispatchers at the Brian Terry Border Patrol station, regular field agents serving on a rotating basis, monitored signals from electronic sensors buried throughout the station's vast coverage area. They also watched TV monitor screens, relaying images of movement from cameras set on towers overlooking smuggling corridors. At night, the cameras detect heat and transmit spooky-looking infrared images of individuals walking across rough terrain.

Border Patrol Agent Brian Terry had been killed by illegal border-crossers while on duty with BORTAC, the agency's elite tactical squad. He was gunned down the night of December 13, 2010, in a canyon north of Nogales, the nearest border city west of Naco. His death led to the exposure of the federal government's *Fast and Furious* gunrunning operation, after high-powered semiautomatic rifles connected with the program were found at the scene.

At the time when the Naco Border Patrol station was named for him, Terry, a 40-year-old former U.S. Marine and city police officer in Michigan, had been the most recent Border Patrol agent to be shot to death in the line of duty. On the night when he was killed, Terry and his partners had been under orders to use only bean bag ammunition to initially engage suspects. His killers, illegal alien bandits, who were later tried and convicted of his murder, used live ammunition.

As agents in the busy Tucson Border Patrol Sector, which included Naco and Nogales, patrolled the deserts, mountains, and canyons of the Arizona border on this Monday evening in 2012, two TV networks carried brand-new stories about the Fast and Furious scandal, which first came to the public's attention in February 2011.

An investigation by Univision, a Mexican TV network, had just revealed on Sunday, September 30, that thousands of high-powered firearms sent to Mexican cartels as part of Fast and Furious had resulted in the deaths of hundreds of Mexican civilians, including 14 high school and college students who were attending a birthday party in Ciudad Juarez.[3]

On Monday, Fox News and ABC carried additional stories on the revelation that firearms responsible for the murders of hundreds of Mexican people had been supplied to the killers with the help of the U.S. Bureau of Alcohol, Tobacco, Firearms and Explosives, under the supervision of the U.S. Department of Justice.

American news outlets had previously reported on some of the facts about this bizarre U.S. government program—which had been hidden from Mexican authorities—but the extent of the carnage resulting from those firearms on the south side of the border had not been previously brought to public attention.

The newest revelations in this painstakingly researched story hit the borderland area like a bombshell, because it linked the Obama administration's program to a tremendous increase in violence. The area of the carnage included northern Sonora, just across the line from Arizona. The Sinaloa cartel's takeover of border traffic—through a campaign of extreme violence—coincided closely with the timeline of the government's gunrunning scheme.[4]

As this news broke throughout both nations, President Barack Obama was preparing for his first debate at a sparsely occupied resort hotel in the desert, on the outskirts of Las Vegas, near the Arizona border. The presidential debate against challenger Mitt Romney, the first of the 2012 campaign, was to be held on Wednesday night in Denver.

Monday was a rare day on Obama's campaign calendar, with no public events or meetings scheduled, for the president to focus on cramming for his debate. At a rally at Desert Pines High School the previous evening, Obama told the crowd, "Governor Romney, he's a good debater. I'm just OK."

Obama employed John Kerry, who had lost the 2004 presidential election, to play the part of Romney in mock debates. The race was considered close, with five weeks to go. The president was leading by two to five percentage points, according to various polls.[5]

With the Fast and Furious scandal grabbing new headlines, and the Republicans trying to blame the Obama administration for the murder of four Americans three weeks earlier in Benghazi, Libya, the president needed to win this debate to gain momentum going into the final month of the campaign.

As Agent Ivie headed out for his shift on this momentous news day, the full harvest moon that rose over the Mule Mountains shortly after sundown was unusually bright, making the transition from day to night less stark.

Some Border Patrol agents who worked night shifts preferred the moonlit nights because they could see ahead into the terrain without benefit of artificial lighting and spot illegal aliens who might be cutting across the desert or catching a ride from a vehicle on the side of the road.

But in this century-old game of cat-and-mouse at the international border, the illegal aliens could also get a better look at the agents, as they patrolled in their vehicles, on horseback, or on foot. Many of the border crossers—including smugglers of narcotics, human traffickers, and guides of illegal immigrants—knew the territory as well as or better than the agents.

The Sinaloa Cartel is a sophisticated criminal organization, which ruthlessly punishes competitors. By 2012, there were not many who were so ignorant or desperate that they were willing to risk torture or death to try to make a buck in cartel territory.

The freelance *coyotes*, who for many decades guided illegal immigrants across the desert for much smaller fees, were an endangered species in this territory. The fees charged by the cartel were much higher. Illegal immigrants escorted by the cartel were charged thousands of dollars per person or served as drug smugglers or prostitutes. Illegal immigrants from Central America, the Mideast, Europe, or Asia were charged rates of up to $30,000 per person. Some migrants have been kidnapped and held for ransom, often under horrendous conditions.[6]

Border Patrol agents working the Arizona line were pitted against professional smugglers with tremendous resources. The cartel had operatives working both sides of the border, including bribed law enforcement officers and politicians, as well as sophisticated communication and surveillance equipment, such as satellite phones and night vision scopes.

At about 11:30 p.m., Agent Ivie, nicknamed "Feller" by his fellow agents for his laid-back personality, was alerted by a dispatcher that an underground sensor had been tripped a few miles north of the border.

When Agent Ivie heard the beep signal and saw the message on his computer screen of the triggering of sensor 2453-1, he recognized that this was the sensor he had helped place on Remax Saddle a few weeks earlier. He told the control agent at his station that he would respond.

Agent Ivie had recommended that this sensor be placed on that spot, on a mountain saddle located on federal land, within the boundaries of the Christiansen ranch. He and other agents had found much evidence, including large piles of trash, that this location was heavily used by drug smugglers and other illegal aliens as a layup spot.

The dispatcher said that the electronic sensor, which registered footsteps of people or animals as they moved across the ground in the vicinity, had registered seven hits. That could mean there were as many as seven illegal aliens walking through or resting at the saddle.

Ivie knew that this sensor would be triggered, and that it would most likely result in the arrests of smugglers. There were no Border Patrol cameras monitoring this area at that time, so the sensor would be the key to catching any group that agents might apprehend.

A few hours earlier, Agent Ivie had told two of his horse patrol teammates, Jake McWhorter and Victor Ocejo, that he was on duty but would not be on horseback. The two agents, who were patrolling in a pickup truck with their horses in tow, agreed to stay in touch with him throughout the night.

Horse patrol agents normally worked while "partnered up." Although they did not necessarily stay close to each other while in the field, because that is not the best way to work illegal alien traffic, it was important to have a partner because of the added risk of being on horseback. Besides the risks associated with trying to apprehend criminals, horse riders carry the additional risk of possible horse-related accidents, such as a horse falling and rolling over on the rider. Horse patrol agents also have an advantage when paired up in cases where riders are thrown from horses or are otherwise separated from their steeds. It is easier to chase down a runaway horse on horseback—especially because horses normally desire to be together.

When a partner situation went to an odd number, such as the night Agent Ivie arrived for work after the other horse patrol agents left the station, the odd man out would frequently "go mobile," that is, take out a patrol vehicle. He could have instead taken out a truck and trailer, along with his talented horse Mouse, but he decided to rely on his SUV and his own two legs.

As soon as Agent Ivie heard about the sensor activation, he called Agent Ocejo on his cell phone to tell him and Agent McWhorter that he was going to respond. Agent Ivie said he believed the illegal aliens who triggered the sensor were probably southbound, and because they had already arrived at the saddle—just a short hike from the border—it was unlikely he would catch up to them.

But he would hike up to the saddle—one of his favorite spots in the Mule Mountains because of its magnificent view and its remote setting—on the chance that he would find someone laying up in the area. If they were southbound as he expected, the dope the two-legged mules had smuggled would no longer be with them.

This saddle was one of the most remote points on the cartel's smuggling routes in the area. It was an advantageous location because of its distance from any town, requiring a relatively lengthy response time from Border Patrol agents. The cartel was apparently not yet aware of the sensor that had recently been placed there. When mules realized that a spot was monitored by a sensor, they would avoid it, and then agents would remove the "burned bug."

Agent Ivie began driving east on Highway 80, looking for the familiar unmarked turnoff to Remax Road. This drive to the Remax Saddle trailhead and the subsequent half mile hike to the mountain ridge would probably take him to the end of his shift, just a few hours away, at about 2:30 a.m.

Agent McWhorter pulled the horsemen's green-and-white truck onto Highway 80, then parked a few miles west of the junction with Remax Road, in order to stand by to back up Agent Ivie. The two horse patrol agents sat at the intersection of South Arizona Street and Highway 80, just a quarter mile east of the turnoff to the sheriff's office. The main headquarters for the Cochise County Sheriff's Office, which included the county jail, sat on the eastern edge of Bisbee, a former prominent copper-mining town, which serves as the county seat.

A short time later, McWhorter and Ocejo heard on their radios that agents David G. Johnson, a military veteran, and Graciela "Gracie" Borjas, a former star college athlete, had also told the control agents that they were heading toward the sensor.

Agent Ivie heard the same messages on his radio. Johnson, who had three and a half years with the Border Patrol under his belt, and Borjas, who was nearing her two-year-mark as an agent, prepared to hike up to the saddle from the south side and meet up with Ivie there.

Ivie was not well acquainted with those two agents. There were 400 agents working out of the busy Naco station, and those two agents were not horse patrol members. There were 4,200 Border Patrol agents working in the Tucson Sector—about a fifth of all agents working throughout the nation. The Tucson Sector, covering most of Arizona, was at that time responsible for the highest number of arrests of illegal aliens of any sector.

Agent Ivie activated his radio and called out his star number, 0-225. He asked Agent Borjas where she was located and what route she planned to take to the saddle.[7]

"I'm at Chisolm Trail, waiting for (star number) 341 (Johnson)," Borjas replied.

"OK, I'm going to be coming from the north, from the north through Remax," Ivie said.

"OK. 10-4," Borjas said.

Agent Ivie was glad to hear that he would not be the lone agent working that detail. Although it was not likely he would encounter the illegal aliens who had triggered that sensor, he believed in safety in numbers. Since joining the horse patrol, he had become accustomed to working with a partner. It always seemed strange when he had to be out in the desert alone, let alone relying on his own feet rather than his horse's hooves.

There were other advantages to working on horseback, in addition to working with a partner. Horseback riders chasing suspects cover ground much more quickly than do those on foot. Riding, instead of chasing suspects on foot, conserves an agent's energy. Agents were often outnumbered by large groups of illegal aliens, who might or might not go along with commands from *la Migra* (Spanish slang for Border Patrol).

Horses are also excellent harbingers of danger, because of their superior sensory abilities. A horse's large eyes, mounted on the sides of its elongated head, gain a wide-angle view of almost 360 degrees and can see ahead over long distances. Horses also possess excellent night vision, which can detect tiny motions of potential predators on a dark night.

A horse's mobile, funnel-shaped ears are constantly listening to sounds all around it, detecting the slightest of noises, such as a snake slithering nearby or distant people whispering. Working horses often alert agents to danger—such as smugglers hiding or hiking in the vicinity.

A horse also relies on its acute sense of smell to warn it of potential predators. When horses stop suddenly and are reluctant to continue on a trail, agents know it is time to shift into high alert.

Ivie sped eastbound on State Highway 80 until he reached Remax Road, an unmarked, one-lane dirt road five miles east of the edge of Bisbee. It was not happenstance that there was no sign to mark the road: most vehicles were not equipped to navigate the treacherous route.

The young agent had driven on Remax many times, but it was a challenge to do so at night because of its dangerous terrain, with large rocks embedded in the roadway, and steep drop-offs, which made it impossible to drive at a reasonable rate of speed without severely damaging the vehicle.

At several points, he would have to slow down to about 1 mph to gingerly make forward progress across steep, dry washes that dipped across the roadway.

Even with the bright moonlight, it would be necessary to use headlights. It was too risky to try to drive without artificial light, with the roadway barely wider than his vehicle's wheelbase. One uncalculated move could plunge the SUV into a deep drop-off. One tire dropping off an edge would put the vehicle out of service.

Nobody wanted to suffer the aggravation and embarrassment of disabling his truck and calling for a tow.

With his lights on, any illegal alien at the mountain saddle or on the north side of the ridge would easily spot him approaching. Although he believed the smugglers who triggered the sensor were southbound, there could be others heading his way—toward the highway—to deliver their drug cargo or to be picked up by a cartel-employed vehicle at a prearranged spot.

After Ivie parked his vehicle at a turnaround frequently used by agents patrolling this area, he began to hike the well-marked dirt trail toward the saddle. He could clearly see the outline of the saddle, with a 5,800-foot tall peak protruding from it at a sharp angle toward its left.

Ivie, an excellent marksman, was armed only with his .40 caliber semiautomatic H & K P1000 pistol. He had never fired his weapon while on duty, and he had never been involved in a confrontation with suspects that would necessitate his doing so. He would shoot in self-defense or defense of others, but he understood that it was rare for agents to find themselves in that kind of situation.

If there were any smugglers at the saddle, they could be carefully monitoring the progress of the vehicle heading toward them. They would be fully aware that the approaching headlights belonged to a Border Patrol vehicle. They would know that nobody else regularly used this dead-end road. There were no human habitations or any other kind of structures along its entire length—except for remnants of buildings in the final stages of decay.

Smugglers routinely used this road as the final downhill pathway from the border, over the mountain and down to the well-traveled highway.

The entire journey for a string of human mules, from the border to Highway 80, could be completed in less than two hours. With almost 12 hours of darkness in early October, a turnaround drug load delivery could be made easily during one night by the well-conditioned, sometimes highly drugged mules, from the border to a spot near the highway, then back across the border. Some of the speedy mules possessed the climbing abilities of mountain goats, able to ascend or descend on steep drops that would defy seasoned two-legged mountaineers.

Each mule train is slightly different, but the basic components are five to 10 mules, each carrying about 50 pounds of compressed marijuana on his back, in a burlap-wrapped bundle or backpack. One mule in each train would be packing food for everyone, and another might be carrying an AK-47–style semiautomatic or automatic rifle or other firearms. Some of the armed guards were Mexican military veterans.

The street value of 10 bundles of weed would come to about $50,000. After paying a few hundred dollars to each mule, that would be a nice piece of change for the cartel. Just another tiny drop of cash into the cartel's multi-billion-dollar ocean of untraceable U.S. currency.

The mules and their armed escorts are part of the cartel's highly sophisticated and pervasively corrupting network, which includes scouts looking out for them from their perches on mountain peaks and hilltops on both sides of the border. If Border Patrol agents are nearby, the scouts warn the mule trains of the whereabouts of their adversaries, with guidance on how to avoid them.

There are also spotters cruising the highways—some of whom are young U.S. citizens—to ensure that Border Patrol agents are not around when the smugglers cross a road or meet up with someone. Cartel operatives are armed with the most high-end equipment available, including night vision binoculars, satellite phones, and encrypted two-way radios.

The cartel has developed a close relationship with many members of Mexican police agencies and the Mexican military. The Spanish phrase, *"plata o plomo,"* which translates to "silver or lead," is the catchphrase cartels have been throwing at officers and soldiers, who are then asked to decide between accepting bribes or their own deaths.

The cartel has no shortage of intelligence on the movements of the Border Patrol, including the number of agents on duty during various shifts, shift change schedules, and the habits of some specific agents. In the Cochise County region, the cartel also had an advantage because of a history of corrupt politicians on both sides of the border. With billions of dollars in unaccounted cash in its coffers, the cartel has made lucrative offers to many public officials, and some have not refused.

Agent Ivie parked his patrol vehicle at the grassy turnaround at the end of Remax Road. He decided to leave his body armor behind. He checked his pockets for his vehicle keys and made sure the 12-round magazine was seated in his .40 caliber pistol. He chambered one round.

He made sure he had his two other magazines, 12 cartridges in each, on his duty belt. He did not pack any water, which was his habit while hiking at night. It was unnecessary weight, because he could hike for many hours without becoming thirsty. It was not a tough climb for him.

Soon after he began hiking uphill on the silent trail, climbing steadily while using his flashlight to "cut for sign," Border Patrol slang for seeking signs of illegal aliens, Ivie spotted footprints. The trail, loose soil dotted with rocks, flanked by thorny ocotillo spikes and dwarf mesquite trees, yielded signs only to well-trained eyes.

Ivie called Agent Ocejo's cellphone and informed him of his discovery.

"I've got southbound foot sign headed up toward the saddle," Ivie told Ocejo.

Ocejo told him he believed the footprints might be from the same illegal aliens who had set off the sensor.[8]

Whether or not those tracks were from the individuals who had triggered the sensor a short time earlier, one thing was certain— anyone walking around in this remote border region in the middle of the night was involved in some kind of illegal activity.

Despite the fact that recreational hikers might enjoy the view, it would be rare for anyone to take a moonlight stroll in cartel territory.

As Agent Ivie ascended to the saddle, he stayed in radio contact with the two other agents. He let them know he thought the smugglers who had left those footprints were already "south," across the border and safely back in Mexico, or speedily on their way. If they had already dropped their drug loads and triggered the sensor at the saddle, they would be hightailing it homeward.

As Ivie spoke with his horse patrol partners, he used his full voice because he apparently was unconcerned about the possibility of encountering anyone at the saddle. When agents are concerned about the presence of illegal aliens, they are known to whisper. However, in the quiet expanse where the agents were hiking, even whispers could travel a long way.

Agent Ivie told his horse patrol partners he was going up to the saddle "to check it out," but he was not concerned about encountering anyone. He was not whispering that he was "onto these guys," which would be normal if he believed he was closing in on someone.[9]

If the smugglers who tripped the sensor were southbound, it would be unlikely for them to remain at the highest spot on the trail. On the other hand, if they were northbound, fully loaded with heavy drug bundles, it would make sense to rest on the saddle before descending and releasing their loads.

Ivie and the horse patrol agents who were sitting in their truck a few miles away were operating on the belief that the tracks belonged to southbound mules, who were "hauling ass," sprinting toward the border at a rapid rate.

The mules who worked for the cartel for a living were known to be quick as jackrabbits. They could sprint from the saddle to the border in less than 30 minutes. It was known among agents that the mules did not care whether they tripped sensors as they were closing in on the border. It was unlikely that they would be apprehended as they headed toward Mexico without any contraband.

The wild card in the scenario was that Agents Johnson and Borjas were hiking up toward the saddle from the south. Although Ivie believed the mules were out of the territory as he made his ascent, those who tripped the sensor might not have made it to the border before the other agents began hiking toward them.

As Ivie hiked up the trail, he took his time, checking for footprints or other signs, such as shreds of burlap from smuggler's packs snagged by tree branches or ocotillo stalks, or fresh markers, such as plastic streamers tied to branches. Occasionally agents found women's panties and bras hanging from tree branches, reminders of the ruthless nature of cartel operatives, who were apparently proud of their vile exploitation of the women they were transporting into America.

Agents had to express boldness without fear when confronting illegal border crossers. But they also exercised caution and restraint. There was a deeply ingrained reluctance to use deadly force against anyone—with the exception of someone threatening them with a deadly weapon. Nobody wanted to face possible criminal prosecution, or the wrath of the supporters of illegal border crossers, because of an agent-involved shooting.[10]

There were many area residents—Mexicans, Mexican Americans, and liberal gringos—who loathed the Border Patrol and supported illegal aliens.

With Ivie on his way to the saddle, a place with which McWhorter and Ocejo were also familiar, the two backup agents awaited further instructions to be ready to come to his aid, if necessary. They sat in their parked vehicle adjacent to Highway 80, listening to their radios. They were aware that Ivie and the other two agents would most likely be outnumbered if they encountered a group.

Whether the agents would apprehend any "bodies," BP slang for illegal aliens, round up some of their dope, or strike out altogether, was anybody's guess. Although those who had triggered the sensor might be long gone, there was always the possibility of finding someone else on this heavily used trail. The two agents waiting in reserve could play a key role, especially if the illegals scattered down the north side of the mountain, with agents riding up toward them on horseback, and possibly with pursuing agents behind them.

Ivie, a hunter and skilled tracker, presented himself to the illegal border crossers he met with quiet confidence, believing he could handle whatever he might encounter on any night. He held no ill will toward people, but he was motivated to prevent the smuggling of drugs that were harmful to young people. He was also keenly aware that cartel smugglers were known to traffic women for sex and would sometimes abandon in the desert illegal immigrants who had paid them to provide safe passage.

Ivie was dedicated to protecting the numerous innocent victims of the cartel's activities.

Remax Saddle was a spot Agent Ivie patrolled often. He especially enjoyed looking out from the ridge at the view of the mountain peaks and desert in the daytime or at the sparkling lights of the nearby city of Douglas at night. He found the view magnificent and exhilarating. It was one of the best outlooks from which to see almost 360 degrees of the land below. If he was sitting in Mouse's saddle, the climb was routine and effortless.

Agua Prieta, Sonora, which lies just south of Douglas, is barely visible at night because of a lack of artificial illumination. Those two cities are known as beehives of smuggling activity. It is common with border towns—normally separated by fencing and ports of entry administered by customs agents—for the Mexican town to be several times larger than the one in the United States. The smuggling of drugs, illegal immigrants, sex slaves, firearms, and cash has played a large role in the economy and atmosphere of both cities—for many decades. Families of smugglers have passed down their enterprises to their children and grandchildren—for as many as six generations.

Cartels have employed numerous methods to move their wares, including elaborate tunnels that carried large shipments underneath the two layers of border fences inside the Douglas city limits, as well as cannons firing loads over the fences onto city streets.

Plaza bosses from the cartel manage operations in the cities on both sides of the border. A busy port of entry for vehicles and pedestrians in Douglas allows hundreds of Mexican and U.S. citizens to cross the border legally each day from Agua Prieta, which has about 75,000 residents, to Douglas, with about 15,000.

CBP Agents (CBP includes the Border Patrol) regularly arrest smugglers transporting large shipments of narcotics through the port. Some drug caches are hidden in compartments inside vehicle doors, gas tanks, ceilings, or elsewhere.

A number of CBP agents have been arrested and convicted for taking bribes to allow smugglers to pass through unimpeded. As an example of the level of temptation involved in the cartel's corruption schemes, an honest customs agent in Nogales was offered $50,000 to allow one semitruck free passage through his lane one time. He did allow that vehicle to pass through but notified other authorities: that occurrence led to the arrest a short distance north of the border of smugglers transporting cocaine with a street value of more than $1 million.

A devout Mormon, Ivie served as a counselor in his temple in Sierra Vista. He helped lead a religious service for the first time on Sunday, September 30, the day before this shift began.

Agent Ivie often worked on short sleep hours because he pushed himself out of bed to help care for his daughters when they got up in the morning. His relationships with his wife and two daughters were his highest priorities.

Ivie spoke fluent Spanish and held affection for the Mexican people. He had served two years as a missionary in Mexico City, beginning when he was 19 years old. After returning to the States, Ivie served as an emergency medical technician and volunteer firefighter in Spanish Fork, Utah, before joining the Border Patrol.

His brother Joel, a Border Patrol agent since 2003, helped guide him toward his new career in law enforcement. Nick greatly admired his older brother, who also served a stint as an FBI agent after joining the Border Patrol. But he returned to the Border Patrol, where he was still serving in 2012. Joel, married with five children, was also a private airplane pilot. Joel Ivie was living with his family on the northeast side of Sierra Vista at that time.

The brothers served together for several months in the Naco horse patrol unit, an arrangement believed to be unique throughout the nation's largest law enforcement agency. The Border Patrol employed about 20,000 officers at that time, most of whom served on the southern border, about 1,969 miles long, stretching from California's Pacific coast to the Gulf of Mexico on the Texas shore.

Although smugglers hiking across the border carried mostly marijuana in 2012, another drug was occasionally buried inside the marijuana load. Most of the more potent drugs, such as cocaine, methamphetamine, and heroin, were smuggled in vehicles, including semitrucks, entering through the busy ports of entry. Vehicles carrying drugs and illegal immigrants also drove across the border between ports of entry, often leading to dangerous high-speed chases.

After narcotics bundles were dropped by the human mules, who operated on foot, they would be picked up at a rendezvous point indicated by GPS coordinates, and hoisted onto a vehicle. The smugglers' wares could then be driven from Highway 80 to Interstate 10 in less than an hour. That drug shipment could then be carried west to Phoenix, Los Angeles, or any West Coast city, or east to Texas, and on to Chicago, Detroit, or any East Coast metro area.

Each shipment carried potential death sentences for the drug users or victims of gang warfare, including the innocent bystanders who reside in gang war zones. The distribution network of cartel narcotics operations is one of the main contributors to the epidemics of shooting deaths and drug overdoses throughout the United States.

The mules were mostly men, ranging in age from their teens to midtwenties, hailing from the nearby border towns or farms. Many were illiterate and carried marijuana bundles because this was their best chance to earn something resembling a living wage. They were known to have tremendous stamina, hiking with 50-pound bundles strapped to their backs for 20 miles at a time, sometimes across the desert, under the 100-plus–degree sun.

The mules were reputed to have superior night vision, which came in handy when making a living, mostly after dark, trudging through canyons, and ascending mountains on a regular basis. The mules did not use flashlights or night vision goggles as they furtively hiked through territory that supported numerous plant species sporting painful thorns and needles, including ocotillo, dwarf mesquite trees, and prickly pear cacti. Not to mention the rattlesnakes, scorpions, and tarantulas that also slink and crawl through the desolate mountain range.

The drug mules then returned to Mexico to carry more loads, with the exception of those who carried drugs in exchange for passage into the United States. The mules who returned to Mexico often burglarized ranches, carjacked or stole vehicles, and occasionally attacked, robbed, or kidnapped borderland residents.

A popular local rancher, Rob Krentz, 58, was murdered on his own ranch, about 40 miles east of the Mule Mountains, by a southbound illegal border crosser in March 2010. The killer had stolen a firearm from a truck and burglarized a house before shooting Krentz, who was disabled following surgery. Krentz, a fourth-generation rancher who was married with four children, had stopped his all-terrain vehicle to help the man, whom he believed to be in distress. The killer also shot and killed Krentz's dog.[11]

The death of Rob Krentz led to an outcry in the region for better border control. That death lead to a controversial Arizona state law, SB 1070, which required law enforcement officers to check the immigration status of any person they had reasonable suspicion of being in the country illegally. That law was actively opposed by the Obama administration, which failed to prevent it from being enacted.

One of the most active proponents of the law was Cochise County Sheriff Larry Dever, who died in a one-vehicle accident on September 18, 2012. That was the same day there was a dedication for the Brian A. Terry Border Patrol Station, which received widespread news coverage. Dever decided not to attend because of a family camping outing.[12]

Dever's death was ruled an accident, with a finding of a high blood alcohol level. But there were suspicious circumstances, including witnesses who disagreed with the possibility that Dever was intoxicated. Dever believed his life was in danger at that time. Immediately before the accident, he said he was being closely followed, and several official findings were at odds with observations by officers and acquaintances.[13]

Those two events—the opening of a brand-new Border Patrol station named after a man whose death had sparked a scandal that rocked the Obama administration, and the suspicious death of a man who went toe-to-toe with that administration on its border policies— would both play roles in the story that would unfold in the days following Agent Ivie's fateful encounter at the mountain saddle.

But for Nick Ivie, October 2, 2012, was just another night on patrol.

2

Two Agents Ascend Mile-high
Mountain from Border Side

"This is going to be good." Border Patrol agent Borjas, on what she thought
when she heard a sensor on a smuggling trail had been triggered seven times.

Monday, October 1, 11:30 p.m.
Mule Mountain Range, 3½ miles north of the line

Graciela Borjas, 29, a Border Patrol agent for nearly two years, was a fluent Spanish speaker who grew up near the border in the El Paso, Texas, area. Short of stature, but unfazed by the challenges of working as an officer on a nearly all-male force, Borjas was willing to confront a group of smugglers by herself, if necessary.

That was the nature of the job she had taken on a few years after graduating from the University of Texas, El Paso, where she excelled in the classroom as an education major and as the shortstop on the softball team. One of her brothers, also a law enforcement officer, had challenged her to join the Border Patrol.

After checking her e-mails for about 10 minutes in the quiet room at the Brian Terry Station, Agent Borjas joined about 40 other line agents at the 10 p.m. muster, to receive her shift assignment. Borjas was assigned to patrol Grid 7A, a territory in the Mule Mountains east of Bisbee that stretches down to the border. Borjas's assignment was to work as a "tac," or tactical agent, to patrol several miles north of the border and work the illegal traffic from there. She was told during the muster that there was some smuggling traffic going on in the area, so "they might bring the dope down to 7." In other words, 7A could be a hot spot that night—which was not unusual.[1]

The Mule Mountain range is about 30 miles long, northwest to southeast, and 10 miles wide at its widest point, appearing from the sky as a swirling funnel cloud that dips its southern tip a few miles into Mexico. Nestled into the center of this range is Bisbee, a picturesque city that boasts the best climate in America. Bisbee, which attracts many tourists to its eclectic shops, hotels, and museums was built around one of the world's most productive copper mines. Its residents tend to have a liberal bent toward border security, evident by their proud flying of a Mexican flag next to an American flag on the edge of its bustling downtown.

This mountain group lies just east and south of the vast Sonoran Desert, where hundreds of illegal border-crossers have died from the brutally hot conditions, the unavailability of water, and the cruel indifference of their "coyotes" to their fate. The Mule Mountain route, crisscrossed by numerous trails, offers consistently cooler temperatures than the lowland desert, a shorter distance between the border and a major highway, and numerous canyons and washes to help conceal movements.

Borjas and the 400 other agents working out of the Brian Terry station were just getting used to the brand-new facility. In place of the small, aging station where Borjas and thousands of other agents had begun their careers, this was a sprawling, state of the art, $34 million facility, set on more than 40 acres. It included a heliport, horse stable, indoor shooting range, spacious control room, and detention center to house illegal border-crossers.

Construction had begun shortly before the shooting death of Agent Brian A. Terry. An act of Congress had named the facility after Terry in May 2012. This was only the second Border Patrol station named after a slain agent. Naming the new facility after Terry the previous month had led to some national publicity about the station's dedication ceremony.[2, 3]

Before heading out on patrol, Borjas retrieved her H & K P2000 semiautomatic pistol. She seated the 12-shot magazine in her pistol, chambered a round, then topped off the magazine, as she would later tell investigators. She always carried one additional full magazine. During the muster, she wrote in her pocket notebook the star numbers of the other agents assigned to Grid 7 that night, including O-341, the star number for David G. Johnson.

Shortly after she began her shift, Borjas drove on Border Road toward Mesquite Ridge, within the Mule Mountain Range, about a mile north of the border and one and a half miles southeast of the Bisbee Municipal Airport. It is a remote area, with a smattering of spread-out rural houses near Arizona Street, a paved road that empties into Highway 80 a few miles to the north.

Borjas had heard on her radio that Robert Kristinsson and another agent, star number O-125, were involved with a group of illegal aliens in the area.[4]

She activated her radio and asked them, "Do you need me to go anywhere to assist?"

"No, we're just backtracking a group from this morning," Kristinsson replied. That meant that they were not pursuing a group, but only investigating where the group they had just pursued had crossed the border. They might have to repair a fence that had been cut or readjust camera surveillance if they discovered a blind spot. It was important to know the locations the cartel was using to breach the line.

Just as Agent Kristinsson was turning down her offer for assistance, Agent Borjas heard on her radio that a sensor had been triggered. She checked the sensor number on her chart and immediately realized it was right smack in the middle of Grid 7.

She heard that the sensor had registered seven hits and thought: "This is going to be good."

She called her station's control room on her radio and announced, "I am going to check out that sensor."[5]

Borjas was suffering from an injured knee that night, which might present a challenge if it did come down to a foot chase.

Even when she was in perfect health, she could never be certain that she would be able to bring illegal aliens into custody. Some of the mules who hauled 40- to 80-pound bundles of marijuana on their backs on a regular basis seemed to possess supernatural abilities. Mules were known for feats of athletic prowess, such as leaping from some serious heights—especially when trying to elude BP agents.

Borjas liked to be where the action was. The agents in the field, overwhelmingly male—by a ratio of about 19 to 1—mostly did not treat her as an equal. But she was just as smart as or smarter than most of them, was a fluent Spanish speaker, and was more focused on performing well than a lot of her fellow agents.

Agent Johnson, a military veteran with three-and-a half years' experience as a Border Patrol line agent, also volunteered to respond to the sensor hit, after hearing on his radio that Borjas was going to hike to the saddle by herself.

Johnson had been assigned that night to "work the line," the agency's term for patrolling the border. He knew there was another male agent stationed to cover the line, in Section 7 Alpha, one of the sections of Grid 7. If he left the border area to meet up with Borjas, the line would still be covered.[8]

An agent serving in a line position is stationed right on the border, on or near the roadway just north of the border fences. If an individual or group jumps the fence, the line agent moves to apprehend them. Line agents are routinely involved in chases with illegal border-crossers and apprehensions in which the aliens surrender without fleeing.[7]

At the 10 p.m. muster at the Brian Terry Station, Johnson and another male agent had been assigned to patrol 7 Alpha, in the vicinity of the junction of International Road, which runs parallel to the border fence, and Border Road, which winds down from just south of Highway 80, near a large limestone quarry on Paul Spur Road.

After muster, Johnson walked to the armory building, checked out his M4 rifle, then walked outside to the ammunition loading barrel. He stuck the barrel of his rifle into the barrel, racked it to make sure it was clear of ammunition, and flipped the safety on. He checked his EOTech rifle sight, closed its dust cover, and walked over to his vehicle.

Johnson also carried an H&K P2000 semiautomatic .40 caliber handgun, with a 12-cartridge magazine. He did not carry spare magazines for either weapon.

Both Johnson and Borjas were designated "line agents" as their general agent category. Line agents, differentiated from specialty agents, such as members of the horse patrol, rotated through various assignments. That included patrol shifts in an assortment of geographical areas within their station's area of responsibility, as well as stints as dispatchers in the control room and as guards who processed inmates in the holding facilities.

There are other assignments, called *Hard X*, in which agents are ordered to remain in one spot, not budging, even if border-crossers are spotted nearby. In places where Hard X agents are on duty, such as in the town of Naco, Hard X assignments are designed to prevent floods of illegal crossers, who would quickly disappear into houses inside the border town, if they did not see a uniformed agent.

It might sound redundant for a line agent to be assigned line duty on a particular shift, but this is clearly understood within the Border Patrol. In his assignment to line duty, Johnson had some flexibility. He could decide for himself whether to leave the line in order to chase border-crossers—or remain close to the border, as agents farther north chased groups toward him.

Agent Johnson thought it would be a good idea if another agent, perhaps another tac agent, would volunteer to hike up the mountain with Borjas. If someone else volunteered, he would remain at his position on the line.

After waiting awhile to see whether anybody else volunteered to go up with her to respond to the sensor, Johnson called her cell phone.

Borjas told him she was planning to go up by herself.

"I'll go with you," Johnson told her.[8]

Johnson was not well acquainted with Borjas, but he had noticed her at their duty station for some time. Everybody noticed when a female officer arrived on the scene—especially if she happened to be attractive and young, like Gracie. There were just a few female agents at the Naco station, and they were rarely assigned to work in the field on the midnight shift.

The two agents arranged to meet at the junction of State Highway 80 and Chisolm Trail Road, about 17 miles northeast of their duty station. That intersection, marked by a common blue street sign on a pole, lies about halfway between Bisbee and Douglas.

Johnson drove the Border Road, a two-lane dirt-and-rock road that wound past an empty ranch house on the right, then headed toward an industrial complex that processed lime from an excavated hillside. He turned onto the paved Paul Spur Road, which quickly took him to Highway 80, the main east-west thoroughfare of southeast Arizona.

When Johnson determined that the triggered sensor was in the Remax area, just south of Highway 80 and east of Bisbee, he realized he was not familiar with that terrain.

On the way to Chisolm Trail, Johnson asked a dispatcher at the station to give him GPS coordinates for the sensor. The dispatcher gave him the coordinates, as well as "the best route to take up to the sensor."[9]

Borjas drove west on Border Road toward Arizona Street, then headed a few miles north to Highway 80. At the stop sign, she turned right, heading east toward Douglas for five minutes until she spotted the familiar sign for North Chisolm Trail. She pulled off the Highway, crossed the cattle guard, and parked near the group of rural mailboxes by the roadway. Borjas arrived at the agents' rendezvous point first.

She heard Agent Ivie call out his star number on the radio and ask what route she was taking. She said she was waiting for 341 (Johnson) and didn't know exactly what route they would be taking up to the saddle. Ivie told her he would be coming up from Remax Road.

Johnson rolled up in his patrol vehicle, stopping next to Borjas's SUV. "Did you hear 225 (Ivie) on the radio?" Borjas asked Johnson.

"Yeah, I did," Johnson said, adding that he had the GPS coordinates for the trail to the saddle.

Johnson put his patrol vehicle in gear, heading south on Chisolm Trail, a dirt road with a few scattered residences on either side. Borjas stayed close to Johnson's taillights, despite the cloud of dust and occasional stones that were kicking up into her windshield. They turned west on Hidden Trail Road—also known as Gravel Pit Road. They drove past tall piles of gravel at their left until Johnson found a spot to park near the head of Dead Girl trail, about a mile from Highway 80.

They would have to ascend about 1,000 feet from where they parked their vehicles. Although Borjas was also unfamiliar with that territory, they were both seasoned climbers, with many hours of hiking under their belts in similar conditions.

They were confident they could arrive at their destination without any trouble, especially with the help of a full moon, clear skies and the GPS map.

Regular duty agents were rotated from one border section to another, changing beats as frequently as every two weeks. In that way the agents were expected to gain a general knowledge of a wide range of territory. It was nothing new for either of these agents to venture out into an unfamiliar location in search of illegal aliens.

They had a clear view of the ridgeline to their north, where the plateau known as Remax Saddle was silhouetted between a distinct peak at its right and a more gradual rise to the left.

The network of roads connecting with Chisolm Trail was known as a frequent loading point for smugglers hauling dope from the border. A driver could enter from Highway 80, pick up a load that had been dropped there, and be on the highway within a few minutes.

For the next eight minutes, the two agents retreived from their vehicles the gear they would carry with them on their late-night hike.

Johnson always carried his semi-automatic M4 rifle with him. He never wanted to face a group of smugglers with less firepower than they had. His M4, holding a 14.5-inch-long barrel, weighed about seven pounds. It contained 28 soft point .223 cartridges in his magazine. The M4 is similar to the M16, formerly a standard U.S. Army weapon, but with a shorter barrel. It has the capability of shooting on fully automatic, something agents mostly ignore, because it is less accurate in the quicker mode and the magazine is emptied at lightning speed.

As stated earlier, Agent Johnson was also carrying his H&K P2000 semiautomatic .40 caliber pistol, with an extra 12-cartridge magazine containing hollow point bullets. The hollow point bullet, which expands on impact, is favored by many law enforcement agencies because it has outstanding stopping power and tends to not penetrate. This reduces the risk of damage from bullets that could strike unintended victims, after exiting their intended targets.

Johnson grabbed some extra batteries for his flashlight, punched the sensor coordinates into his GPS, and checked to be sure he hadn't locked his keys in his vehicle.[10]

He left his body armor in his vehicle. Agents often choose to leave their vests behind when hiking up mountain trails because they are heavy and increase body heat. The vests constrict movement and can

This image of four smugglers was captured by a trail camera near Dead Girl Trail as they carry marijuana and possibly other drugs into the United States from Mexico. This spot is near the point where Agents Borjas and Johnson began their ascent to Remax Saddle the night of the shooting.

make breathing more difficult and even noisy. Wearing a heavy vest is also an enormous handicap in the event of a foot chase. Wearing vests—highly recommended for safety—can slow down an agent and prevent him from reaching his destination quietly and efficiently.

It was eerily quiet, with practically no wind, and the lightly traveled nearby highway was far enough away that not even the occasional semitruck would be heard.

When they exited their vehicles, Borjas got on her radio and told Ivie, "We are going up through Dead Girl Trail."

"Ten-four," Ivie replied.[11]

It was a good sign that they were hearing each other on their radios, even when they were at low points, on opposite sides of the mountain. The calm weather and cloudless skies played a positive role in their clear communication.

Johnson was in the lead. Borjas, who had been a speedy college athlete just a few years earlier, was having trouble keeping up with him because of her sore knee. Johnson would hike ahead of her, realize she was falling behind, then wait for her to catch up. At one point, he backtracked to her so they could stay together.

"So I'd go up, I'd stop, and she'd catch up," Johnson said later, during a postincident interview. "And we did the whole accordion thing up the side of the hill."

While Ivie was ascending at a slow, steady pace in order to continually check for signs, the other agents were also moving slowly, partly because of Borjas's injured knee.

Agents Johnson and Borjas would periodically turn on their flashlights to "cut for sign," but they walked on the trail, mostly solely by moonlight.

"So, we continued on the trail, occasionally cutting," Johnson said. "We'd turn on our lights only here and there. I'd put my hand over my light because I didn't want to give away our position, because the smugglers have an advantage at night."

The trick was to cup your hand around the business end of the flashlight, reducing the beam to a thin line, just enough to be able to spot a footprint on the ground.

"So, you try to use it to your advantage to sneak up to where you got to go, cut around, and then go from there. Because if they see your light, they're gone. You're never going to catch them."

The moonlight was sufficient for staying on the trail.

"You could see the ground," Johnson said. "Every once in a while, you could see Ivie's light in the distance. He was coming up."[12]

Although they were trying to keep their lights to a minimum, they repeatedly spotted Ivie on the northern mountain slope, as he lit up the ground with his light, once they were all on high ground, converging on the saddle. Ivie was apparently operating on the belief that the smugglers were long gone.

But if there were any illegal aliens on the saddle or elsewhere on high ground, they would spot Agent Ivie's light. There was a good chance they would also see the lights of the other two agents, despite their efforts to conceal their beams.

Regardless of the consequences of using their flashlights, if the illegals were still in the area, they would certainly have seen the agents approaching the trailheads in their vehicles.

There was no way agents could sneak up on a group of illegal aliens that night, if the aliens held the higher ground and were awake. From the vantage point of the saddle, the border-crossers could have seen for miles in almost every direction, including the trails the agents were taking and some of the roads on which they had driven to the trailheads.

The cartel had scouts, regularly stationed in high places on both sides of the border, who would alert traveling groups by radio or cell phone when Border Patrol agents were approaching.[13]

But, despite the unceasing efforts of the cartel operatives, there was always the possibility that the illegal aliens or their dope could be apprehended. It was not unusual for smugglers to drop packs weighing 50 pounds or more and take off running. It was considered a victory to just recover the dope.

A Border Patrol tactic in confronting smuggling groups was to send agents from two opposite points to hem them in. Illegal aliens tended to scatter, or "quail," when being confronted by agents from one direction. But, if they were approached from two directions, they tended to stay together, and they were thus more likely to be apprehended as a group. Good luck to agents who were trying to apprehend a group of 20, who were simultaneously heading for every point on the compass.

Tactics of the cartel would change time after time to thwart Border Patrol efforts—and law enforcement tactics would adjust accordingly to those changes.

The smugglers usually avoided confrontations. It was not an everyday occurrence for illegal aliens to pose a serious threat to agents. The cartel preferred to go about its business stealthily, like the variety of poisonous snakes that slithered on their bellies near the cartel's web of smuggling trails.

The cartel did not want to bring unnecessary attention because of a trigger-happy "mule" or "coyote." The agile young men who did the cartel's dirty work were dispensable tools of the organization, insulated from knowledge of the leadership ranks by several layers of contacts. But the underlings were keenly aware that anything they did that displeased their unknown masters could result in severe punishment.

This was the cartel that was directed by drug lord Joaquin "El Chapo" Guzmán, who would be sentenced to life plus 30 years in federal prison, after he was convicted Feb. 12, 2019 on 10 criminal counts. His charges included being the principal operator of a criminal enterprise that committed conspiracy to commit murder, as well as numerous narcotics violations.

At his three-month trial in Brooklyn, New York, witnesses revealed details of Guzmán's personal involvement in torture and his murder of members of rival drug gangs, including burning them in bonfires and burying them alive. One former associate accused Guzmán of drugging and raping many girls as young as 13 years of age. Guzmán had been an inmate in several high security prisons in Mexico— from which he famously escaped—after his 1993 conviction for the assassination of a Roman Catholic cardinal.[14]

There have been numerous authenticated stories about the sadistic brutality of the cartel—including beheadings with chain saws, kidnappings and murders of women and children, sex-trafficking, and torture methods rivaling the atrocities of the German Nazis in the 1930s and 1940s. At his three-month-long trial, it emerged that Guzmán had earned about $13 billion dollars from his enterprise, while bribing officials at the highest level of the Mexican government. At his July 17, 2019, sentence hearing, Guzmán claimed he had not received a fair trial.[15]

The Mule Mountain region was at the epicenter of the operation of the cartel, which has not slowed down its worldwide operations since Guzmán's arrest and conviction. At his trial, evidence was presented that one of the largest cash hauls by law enforcement in the cartel's money laundering operation was $1.26 million, seized from a truck driven by Guzmán's brother in Douglas, Arizona, in 1989.

However, despite the cartel's violent operation and the recent murder by illegal border-crossers of Agent Brian Terry, Border Patrol agents generally operated on the bold premise that they had the upper hand whenever they encountered any illegal border-crossers. The three agents who were hiking toward Remax saddle on their regular shifts were not overly concerned about the possibility of facing danger.

3

Approaching the Smugglers' Lair

"10-4. We're about one tenth of a mile away," Borjas told Ivie, as she and Johnson approached the saddle where the sensor was located.

After hiking for an hour on the winding trail, Johnson reached a mountain ridge. When Borjas did not arrive shortly afterward, he went back down the mountain to look for her.

"I waited for her. She was taking longer than expected, so I went down to look for her," Johnson would later tell investigators.

After they reconnected, they walked along the north side of the ridge overlooking Remax Road.

"There was a ton of trails, and I looked at my GPS. I have a topographical map on my GPS, and the mountain went way around," Johnson said.

Johnson decided that the trail they had originally set out on was taking too much time. He decided to ascend toward another ridgeline, then hike east on the south side of the mountain.

The two agents were aware that Agent 225 was heading toward the ridge from Remax Road.

The ascent from Ivie's turnaround parking place at the end of Remax Road was a fairly easy climb on the narrow trail. There were plenty of leaves on dense branches on the mesquite trees and creosote shrubs alongside the trail. Ivie's long-sleeved uniform would occasionally brush up against the thorny spikes of the tall ocotillo plants.

At about 1:00 a.m., less than half an hour before arriving at the saddle, Ivie transmitted to his fellow agents, "I am still working my way up the saddle. I was checking some of the washes down below. Haven't come up with anything yet."

"10-4," Borjas replied.[1]

The hike from the north was straightforward, on a trail that led down into a wash that was not very deep, then a steady, gradual climb of about 650 feet.

When Johnson and Ivie were about a mile apart, Johnson clearly saw Ivie, with his flashlight directed toward the ground.

As they all hiked steadily toward the saddle, Ivie reported over his radio that he "had sign for two," but he "wasn't sure if it was new, if it was good, if it was new or old." Whether the sign was for those who were nearby or long gone, it was important to share the information. If those were recent footprints, they were heading toward the saddle, and possibly toward Agents Borjas and Johnson immediately afterward. Borjas heard him and relayed his report to Johnson.

Johnson's radio was "acting up," so he took the battery out, replaced it, and it began working again.

As Johnson walked point, carrying his rifle, Borjas talked to Ivie by radio, freeing Johnson to focus on his surroundings.

As Johnson and Borjas closed in on the saddle, while walking along the ridge, Ivie was continuing to cut for sign with his flashlight. Borjas spotted him again, when he was just about 200 or 300 yards away, the equivalent of about one city block.

"He's over there. I saw his flashlight," Borjas told Johnson.

"Yeah, I see his flashlight," Johnson said.[2]

Those two agents did not have their flashlights turned on at the time. Borjas had her flashlight in her hand, but she used it only when Johnson used his, which was sparingly. As they closed in on their destination, they approached the saddle as stealthily as possible.

The hike from the south was more challenging than the northern route, with several ascents and descents along the way, as well as more cacti to dodge and other thorny plants intruding on the trail. Even with leather gloves and boots, as well as uniform trousers with reinforced knees, a slip or fall into a cactus could produce painful injuries, as needles could penetrate clothing, and some stubbornly resisted extraction.

As they walked along a ridgeline running from northwest to southeast, within one half mile of the saddle, the two agents came upon a steep descent followed by a steep ascent.

Agents Johnson and Borjas gazed at the challenge before them. They were not feeling as fresh as when they had left their vehicles.

"If I have to go back up that, I'm not going to," Johnson said.

Borjas chuckled at the remark. Then Johnson suggested they take an easier route.

They found a ridgeline that circumvented the steep chasm, and that met up with a north-south ridgeline that would take them through a saddle, over a peak, and through another saddle.

Ivie was well acquainted with the challenging climb the two agents were making from the other side of the mountain. Dead Girl trail—so named because a body had been found there more than 20 years earlier—was not a walk in the park at any time. He realized the two agents would have to ascend, descend, and re-ascend because of the ridges and canyons that stood between their parking spot and the saddle where the sensor was buried.

Although radio contact could be challenging at times in mountainous terrain, under circumstances such as traveling on opposite sides of a mountain, the agents were enjoying relatively clear communication as they approached the saddle, each within a few minutes of arriving. They were all close to the same elevation, a little more than one mile above sea level, 1,100 feet higher than the border line.

The border fence, which had various configurations and heights in this area, was three-and-a-half miles away. Whether the border-crossers had found the wide opening created to allow flood water to come through or had chosen a slatted bollard-style fence they could easily shimmy over, there was no major obstacle preventing them from entering the United States.

Once they were north of the line, the mules—who were sometimes pumped up with stimulant drugs such as methamphetamine—had a short, quick trek across uninhabited land, covered with dense brush. If there were no signs of *La Migra*, this would be the fastest route to hustle from the fence to the mountains. The temperature stayed at about 60 degrees throughout the night, with almost zero breeze—excellent trekking conditions.

The saddle was a couple of miles or so from the closest residences, about a dozen homes connected by a network of well-graded dirt roads connected to Chisolm Trail, which fed into Highway 80.

Every sound or light of civilization seemed far off in the distance from high up in the mountains. The combination of dead silence and occasional human voices would help anyone who might be present at the saddle to keep track of the agents as they approached.

With Johnson in the lead and Borjas trailing about 10 feet behind him, they heard a transmission from Ivie when the saddle was directly in front of them.

Johnson was the only one of the three agents who was carrying a long firearm. Johnson *always* carried his M4 with him when he was pursuing illegal aliens. In a firefight, he would be at a disadvantage if he encountered "bodies" with AK-47s—which can be fired on full auto—while he was armed only with his pistol. In addition to his rifle, Johnson wore his service pistol on his hip.

Ivie did not carry a rifle, partly because long firearms tended to get in the way as horses galloped across territory that included narrow passages through thick brush. Although he was not on horseback this night, he also did not carry a long arm when he "went mobile." Agents were permitted to use their own judgment as to which weapons they used.

As they closed in on the mountain saddle, Borjas caught a glimpse of Agent Ivie's flashlight once more.

"Oh, we're almost there," Borjas said to Johnson.

She stopped for a moment to place her flashlight into her CamelBak pack, so her hands would be free in case they encountered illegal aliens.

With Johnson in the lead and Borjas trailing just behind and to his left, they heard a transmission from Ivie, with the saddle straight ahead of them.

Ivie asked the agents where they were and "10-18?" That was the Border Patrol code to inquire whether they had encountered any illegal alien traffic and whether they were OK.[4]

Borjas told them they had not seen anyone and were fine.

"Hey, what's your guys' location?" Ivie asked the other two agents.

Johnson looked at his GPS and said to Borjas, "We're a tenth of a mile out."

Borjas relayed Johnson's information to Ivie.[5]

"10-4. We're about one tenth of a mile away," Borjas told Ivie, indicating the distance from the sensor on Remax Saddle.[6]

"Ten-four. I just made it up to the saddle," Ivie responded. It was 1:21 a.m.[7]

"So we continued up," Johnson said in his postincident interview. "We're at the ridgeline where we hit the saddle. We started making our way up the peak. As we're coming down the peak, normally what happens is, when an agent cuts sign, you see a light. We came up; I didn't see any light."

At 1:24 a.m., Ivie told the other agents on his radio that **he saw the foot signs of two suspects at the saddle**, which appeared to be the same as the signs he had seen in the canyon below a short time earlier.[3]

Because Ivie had said just a few minutes earlier on the radio that he had seen signs of two illegals at the saddle, Johnson expected to see Ivie there with his flashlight, casting a beam at the ground. Ivie had not said anything about seeing any "bodies" there, just footprints.[8]

If Ivie was there, doing what he normally did, Johnson and Borjas would also hit their lights and scour the saddle floor with him. They would be looking for possible clues as to which way the smugglers had gone from there.

Ivie did not indicate that anything was wrong. He was there.

"We came up. I didn't see any light. I thought that maybe he was further north of us," Johnson said.

Ivie had arrived a few minutes before the other two agents.

Borjas would later say she did not think Ivie had arrived at the saddle when they got there.

As the two other agents reached the edge of the saddle, Johnson felt uneasy.

He did not see any light. Here was the saddle, a flat, rocky stretch of ground, dotted with thickly foliated, stunted mesquite trees. The ground area was large enough to accommodate a host of illegal aliens. Johnson could see why this would be a popular layup spot.

But when the saddle came into view, Johnson did not see a flashlight beam or any other sign of Agent 225. Where was that agent?

One moment everything was quiet and still. Ivie's tone of voice over the radio had been normal, unconcerned, apparently unaware of any danger lurking nearby.

It was not surprising that the illegal aliens who triggered the sensor were not there. But finding their tracks could reveal important information, including how many were there.

Because of the vegetation throughout the saddle, leaving no clear lines of sight for anyone to see the entire area, each agent was seeing a different picture.

Borjas, who was about ten feet behind Johnson and to his left, saw Ivie's light as they approached their destination.[9]

"I had seen Ivie's flashlight when we came around, and I said, 'Oh, we're almost there,'" Borjas would later tell investigators.[10]

Johnson was at the saddle a moment later.

He saw something that put him on alert. He had been "kind of relaxed" as he approached the saddle, because he expected to see Ivie there and nobody else.

But something totally different caught his eye while he had his guard down—it was the silhouette of a person to his left. He was wearing a cube-shaped smuggler's pack on his back, a typical burlap-wrapped parcel containing compressed marijuana.

"It didn't look right," he would later say in his FBI interview.

Seeing a man carrying this kind of pack was very familiar to the seasoned agent—yet so out of place here at this moment.

Where was Agent 225?

Johnson held his M4 at the low ready position, pointed toward the ground, and started walking toward the silhouette.

The man with the smuggler's pack on his back shoved a blanket off his shoulders. Johnson advanced toward the moonlit silhouette.

Several men jumped out from behind the thick brush, grabbing Agent Ivie's forearms and wrestling him to his knees. He saw his two fellow agents approaching and yelled with all his strength. He fought to keep his pistol in its holster by holding fast to the grip and pushing downward.

The stillness of the night was suddenly shattered by Agent Ivie's scream, followed closely by gunshots. The sky lit up with bright flashes from the muzzle of a long firearm. Johnson froze in place, stunned by the unexpected gunfire. Who was shooting?

A bullet penetrated Nick Ivie's forehead—and he was gone. He fell face forward, his flashlight dropping from his left hand.

Agent Borjas heard and saw the horrifying commotion as the night exploded in front of her. She drew her black semiautomatic service pistol from her holster and aimed it toward the shooters, with her index finger on the trigger.

She was behind Johnson and to his left, as she suddenly heard a yell, followed by a sudden storm of muzzle flashes from a long arm, the bullets flying in the direction of her and her partner. She also caught a glimpse of flashes from a handgun, with a reflection of the shiny weapon in the moonlight.

The shooters seemed to be just 5 or 10 feet in front of her. Everything was happening so fast. She was trying to fire her weapon toward the shooters. [11]

As soon as Johnson took a step or two toward the smuggler, he heard gunshots ringing out and saw muzzle flashes. Johnson later said he was about 15 or 20 feet away from the muzzle flashes when the shooting began. The shell casings found at the scene would confirm the accuracy of his statement.

"And it was by the third shot I realized I was getting shot," Johnson would later say. "It was the first three shots. It was a shock. By the third shot I realized I was getting shot at."

He was blinded by the muzzle flashes. In his mind, an instant earlier, Agent Ivie had been there all alone. But instead, there was now a smuggler's silhouette and incoming fire.

After the short burst of three shots, Johnson tensed up and hoped the shooting would stop.

"Hey, hey, hey, hey!" Johnson yelled.

He was trying to tell the shooter to stop shooting. Everything was happening so fast. No whiff of any danger, then this.

Just a moment before, he had thought only 225 was there. Then someone else was there. If it was 225 who was there—then he couldn't fire.

He just stood there frozen for a moment.

In the few seconds between expecting to see Agent Ivie there by himself and suddenly taking fire from an unknown shooter, Johnson was struggling to understand what was going on.

He couldn't just open fire. Where was 225?

Johnson could focus only on the muzzle flashes. He didn't hear the first three shots, but just saw the explosions from the ends of the gun barrel.

He was still standing there when "they just started shooting again."

Nothing made sense. Someone was firing, but why? Where was Agent 225? Who was shooting at them?

He saw and heard about seven more shots after he yelled, "Hey, hey, hey, hey!" More muzzle flashes exploded in the night, keeping him from seeing anything else.

Johnson felt rocks hitting his shins, kicked up from the bullets, as they impacted the ground. He did not know who was shooting, so he just wanted to get away. An agent is under orders to not shoot at unknown targets. Period.

"And then I got hit in the ankle (by a bullet), and then my focus went back to my ankle. At that point I turned, and I think I got hit in the buttocks. I took a step or two, and then I turned around and engaged."

The moment Johnson was hit, he knew he had to return fire.

He told himself: You know what? You'd better do something, or you're going to get killed up here.

Johnson lifted the rifle stock to his right shoulder, gripped the barrel with his left hand, peered through his rifle sight, saw no target, and pulled the trigger. He fired rapidly six times in the direction of the muzzle flashes.

"When I brought my weapon up, it just seemed like forever. I sighted in, and I just started shooting," Johnson would later say. "I brought it up; I couldn't see anything. I have an EOTech (rifle sight), and I could just see the circle with the dot in the middle. It was dark. And I brought it up, and I just started firing towards where the muzzle flashes were coming from."

Johnson did not see any additional muzzle flashes as he fired shots, while peering through his rifle sight. He was firing in the general direction of the muzzle flashes that he had seen just moments earlier.[12]

He rapidly pulled the trigger of his semiautomatic rifle six times. His burst of gunfire lasted for about one second.

It was suppressive fire, a military tactic he had learned during basic training to pin down the enemy and prevent them from performing in battle. Johnson hoped it would intimidate the shooters and prevent them from firing their weapons.

Everything went quiet. Johnson didn't think he had hit anything. His tactic had apparently worked. For now.

"I don't know how many rounds I shot," Johnson would later say in his interview. "When I was shooting, I could barely hear my M4 going off, and then all of a sudden it just got loud, like *boom, boom, boom, boom*! And then it just went low again."

Johnson stopped shooting as soon as he realized nobody was shooting at him anymore.

He knew the shooters could open fire again at any moment. He turned back away from the shooters, to retreat and regroup.

"I looked to my right and I seen Borjas. She was already going in the direction we came. I took three or four steps, and I felt it was like a Charlie horse in my buttocks," Johnson would later tell FBI interviewers. "And I could just feel the blood gushing out."

Johnson told himself: "You're hit. You've got to get down."

"I kind of blacked out a little bit because the shock of being hit. Knowing that I was hit, I kind of blacked out. I hit the ground."

Borjas, who did not realize that Johnson had fired toward their attackers, turned around and looked for cover.

She saw a rock down the slope and toward her right and ran toward it. "Shots fired," she said on her radio, right before taking cover behind the rock.

Then she heard Johnson say, "Shots fired. I'm hit."

As Borjas sat behind the rock, everything became quiet. She heard people talking and thought that they were coming toward her. She turned off her radio, because she realized that, if she could hear people, they would be able to hear her. She did not want to confront an unknown number of smugglers who had just opened fire on her and her partner.

"I was just sitting there with my gun out," Borjas said.[13]

"So I stayed there," she would tell investigators a few hours later. "I tried to calm myself down." She made a little noise in the brush when she moved, but she tried to stay as quiet as possible.

Right after she had settled in her hiding place, two or more suspects began whispering nearby. She believed they were speaking Spanish. She could not make out what they were saying at first.

Then she understood that they wanted to complete their ambush, to kill the surviving agents. She was not sure where Agent Johnson was, or whether he was still alive.[14]

The young agent clutched her service pistol and decided she would fire it if she were discovered by suspects. Although she was outnumbered, perhaps she would be able to shoot her way out if she shot at them first. They were cold-blooded killers, so there was no other way for her to survive.

After those suspects left the area, she relayed the message over her radio that suspects were hunting for agents. Some suspects ran past her, down the mountainside toward the border. She didn't know if any remained nearby.

After a few minutes, she decided to try to make her way toward Agent Johnson. She ran eastward on the slope. Then she sat down and listened for any indication of where the shooters might be.

"I was trying to be quiet, trying to hear if they were coming my way, where they were going. I didn't hear anything at that point. I sat there for a while, and I could see the agents on Highway 80. I could see a bunch of vehicles with their lights on, with their overheads on."[15]

Borjas tried to remain perfectly still and silent in her hiding place. She could feel her heart thumping rapidly and struggled to control her breathing, to prevent any sound from giving away her position.

Not only was she concerned about her own welfare, because she was in danger of being shot to death, but she also had this dreadful thought that the gunmen might find her and force her to lead them to her partner. Then they would kill both of them.[16]

4

Shots Fired

"Shots fired," both agents radioed, sending hundreds of officers from many agencies to the Mule Mountains.

Johnson took a few steps away from the shooters.

After his momentary blackout, Johnson regained consciousness, sprang to his feet, retreated down the side of the mountain a few yards, and sat down and took a defensive position, with a firm grip on his M4 and his finger on the trigger.

Johnson checked the GPS coordinates on his phone for his location, as he sat on the mountain slope, watching and listening for movement from those who might move or shoot in his direction. He needed to know exactly where he was when he called for help.

He grabbed his radio from its shoulder clip and dropped it on the ground. He lost it, then found it and picked it up. Johnson pushed open the radio mic.

"Three forty-one," he said, reporting his own star number to dispatchers and other agents who might be listening.

"Shots fired," he announced, throwing every agent within earshot into high alert. Then he reported his location, using his GPS coordinates.

"Shots fired," Johnson heard his own voice emanating from a radio down the slope and to the west. It had to be from Borjas's radio. That was the direction he had seen her take off.

Then he heard Borjas also report "shots fired." First, he heard her directly, coming right from the spot where he had just heard her radio. Then he heard the same report over his radio.[1]

It was 1:28 a.m., just four minutes after a healthy Nick Ivie had reported his arrival at the saddle and some suspicious footprints.[2]

Then there was absolute, eerie silence. But that didn't mean that the bodies who had shot at them weren't still around. The illegal aliens were as good as mice at sound discipline. They could be hiding nearby, possibly still at the saddle, just a few yards away.

Johnson did not know exactly where Borjas was, but he knew her general position. They were partners for that assignment, and he wanted her closer to him. They were supposed to be working closely with each other, covering for each other. He could not make his way over to her because he would lose more blood. He had to stay put for now.

He looked in her direction but could not see her. She was probably hunkered down. She would be better off with him, but there was no way he could make that happen. He didn't waste much time trying to spot her. He had to focus on where the enemy shooters might come from. Their point of attack was his target.

If they went after her, he would have to go over there and try to intervene. It would be a mess, trying to shoot at bodies with her in the mix.

The smugglers weren't stupid. They might charge him from several different points. But they might not know where he was—just as he had no idea where they were. And they probably didn't know he was wounded. Even if they charged from several points, he would shoot as many of them as he could.

He gripped his rifle again and aimed it toward the point at the saddle where he thought he could see the smugglers first if they attacked. He was ready for them. He did not know how many cartridges were left in his magazine, but he also had his pistol at hand if his rifle ran out of ammo.

He would tend to his wounds later. Sitting down seemed to slow the blood flow. He did not want to let go of his rifle to bother with his wounds. He hoped he would not black out from the loss of blood.

That could cost him his life, if the bodies attacked again.

He believed there could be a large number of border-crossers nearby. It was not unusual for groups of 10 or 20 smugglers to use this remote route through the rugged mountain range, with relatively quick access to a main highway, just a few miles from the border.

Johnson had no way of knowing whether any smugglers were still around, just as he hadn't known they were there a few minutes earlier. Border Patrol had no cameras surveilling that area, and no other way of detecting illegals there—other than the sensors.

And the sensors gave only limited information. Someone had triggered this sensor at such-and-such a time. Whether the person or persons were still there or long gone was anybody's guess, after the initial hits. They might trigger it again, or they might be far enough from the sensitive ground to keep the sensor silent after the initial hits.

It was not unusual to find illegals hiding anywhere—but this had been the shock of his lifetime.

The smugglers knew exactly where the three agents were as they were advancing. This was the perfect time and place for an ambush. One of the smugglers decided he didn't want to run or hide—and he apparently thought shooting his way out was the best strategy.

Johnson hoped they would be tracked and busted soon. He wanted to see the guys who almost killed him—and see them put away for a long time in prison. Or maybe they would die that night in a shootout with other agents.

As Johnson returned fire, Borjas either pulled the trigger on her .40 caliber semiautomatic pistol, or thought she was pulling the trigger. She believed she was shooting in the direction of the shooters. It would later be revealed that she had not fired her weapon.

Perhaps she had failed to chamber a round after inserting her magazine, which would have caused her to pull the trigger without firing. Or else she just thought she was firing rounds, while her finger was outside the trigger guard, or frozen in place.

With all the noise and muzzle flashes—in her face like a nightmarish personal thunderstorm—perhaps she did not know exactly what her trigger finger was doing. Nothing in her training or in the past 23 months on the border force had prepared her for that ambush.

Borjas witnessed the suspects firing a long arm. She also believed she saw firing from a pistol. This would prove to be important eyewitness evidence, as Ivie was armed only with his service pistol. At least one of the smugglers firing toward the agents was using a long arm. She clearly saw that.[3]

Then she heard smugglers nearby. They were whispering. It sounded like they were trying to find her and Johnson. When she thought they were just far enough away, she took a chance and quietly reported on the radio what was happening.

When other agents heard on the radio the surreal report of agents being hunted, the search for the suspects quickly reached another level of intensity. A helicopter was hovering above them within about 15 minutes.

In the ensuing hours, the area was flooded with hundreds of federal and local law enforcement officers, including agents in Customs and Border Protection helicopters, and an unmanned aircraft.

After Johnson first hit the ground, he knew he had to change his position. He was too close to an unknown number of shooters. He did not know how much ammunition was left in his magazine. He had loaded twenty-eight shots in the mag when he set out. How many rounds had he fired? 10? 12? 15?

"I jumped up, and I went south, down the hill a little bit. I took a defensive position, and I sat there. I was waiting for someone to come over the ridgeline. I was waiting for anybody else to come over," Johnson would later say at his interview.

"I didn't know how many people were there: it could have been 50 people. I don't know. I just went down. I got shot. I went down. I held my position to make sure that nobody else was following down. I was waiting for somebody to come over the ridgeline. Waiting for someone to follow up, and it never happened."

He removed his magazine from his rifle to make sure he still had some rounds in it. Then he quickly shoved it back into his weapon. He had been ambushed, but he was now on full alert. He would empty his magazine into any bodies that appeared.

Johnson activated his radio and called out "225," hoping to hear from Agent Ivie.

There was no response.

Then he called out "358," hoping to hear from Agent Borjas.

Johnson did not know whether she was in the same spot as when he had heard her radio. She might still be up on the mountain, or she might have headed down to her vehicle.

Agent Johnson decided he needed to do something quickly to knock down the bleeding from his butt. He hurriedly cut fabric from his green uniform pants, loosened his belt and applied the piece of cloth to his bullet wound.[4]

Johnson knew he was fortunate to be alive. He was not going to take any more chances. Someone who was shooting at him was a bad shot, and he was still alive. Not many people could say they had been shot at about 10 times at close range—and lived to tell about it.

He also felt a sharp pain in his ankle, but it didn't seem as critical. He thought it was better to leave his boot on, because his ankle didn't seem to be bleeding too much, and it would probably just cause more pain to remove it. If he had to stand up to get out of there or fire from a standing position, the boot would serve him better if it stayed where it was.

Johnson wondered about Agent 225. Where was he?

Agents were supposed to identify themselves—in all situations. But when he got there, right where Ivie was supposed to be, nobody said a word.

No words. Just shooting.

An agent never just opened fire on anyone without identifying himself or issuing some kind of warning. Nobody ever just opened fire on another agent. Who ever heard of anything like that happening?

If agents see someone who is a threat, they are trained to identify themselves and be ready to defend themselves.

But agents are also trained to hold their fire until they identify themselves as Border Patrol agents—except for cases in which their lives or the lives of others are in immediate danger.

The possible consequences of opening fire on someone without the certainty of an immediate deadly threat were too great.

Shoot a body in the dark—and become the center of a nationwide controversy. Your job could be gone, and you could end up in prison.

Johnson just stood there while someone fired at him. He followed the rules, and amazingly, he survived. He demonstrated phenomenal courage in the face of almost certain death.

It all happened so fast. Someone opened fire on him without saying a word—as he stood out in the open. And he was still alive.

By holding fire because he believed Ivie was there somewhere, Johnson could easily have been killed. But there was no way he would just open fire toward a fellow agent.

Maybe somebody had been shot on the saddle—but not by him. He had just squeezed off some rounds of suppressive fire. If he hit someone, he would have known about it.

Maybe his partner shot someone. He saw her pointing her gun toward the shooters.

Johnson was not going to return to the saddle. It was still close by, but that could be an instant suicide mission—especially while he was compromised.

He wanted to go check out what was up there. That was what agents did. But that would not be a smart move while he was wounded. He wanted to confront the threat, and he wanted to see what else might be up there.

Just standing up again could cause him to pass out. He would have to stay put until help arrived.

They were supposed to meet Ivie there. Ivie was supposed to be there. He said he was there and saw signs of bodies. But where was he?

After the shots were fired, Agent David T. Woodbury, a Border Patrol agent on duty in the Brian Terry Station control room, called the cell phones of agents Ivie, Borjas, and Johnson.[5]

Johnson took his call. The other agents did not respond.

Help was already on its way on the ground at the time at 1:48 a.m., less than 20 minutes after the first shots were fired—but had not yet arrived.

"I know control called me to see how I was doing," Johnson recalled during his FBI interview.

Johnson said he asked control whether they had heard from Ivie, and the agent in the control room said he had not.

When the control agent told Johnson he was unable to reach Ivie, Johnson told him, "I think this might be green on green."

He was using the common police phrase for an accidental law enforcement shooting, "blue on blue," but substituted the color of the Border Patrol uniform.

"Green on green" is not a common expression, because Border Patrol agents do not shoot at each other. There was no record of any prior "green on green" incident in the 88-year history of the agency.

Johnson told the control room agent he was losing a lot of blood.

But Johnson "seemed to be calm," Agent Woodbury would later recall in his FBI interview.

It was possible Johnson believed that Agent Borjas might have fired shots toward Agent Ivie. During his FBI interview two days after the incident, he said he thought it possible that Ivie was shot by a fellow agent, but he didn't know.

"It was a chaotic situation," he said.

The entire shooting incident—from first to last shot—occurred within a very short time. All the shots were likely fired within one or two minutes.

Johnson's actions undoubtedly saved the lives of Agent Borjas and himself. When he unleashed a volley of rifle fire toward the smugglers, they had no response.

He believed that help would be on the ground with him soon.

Nick Ivie's Partners Rush to the Scene

Agents Victor Ocejo and Jake McWhorter were standing by in their truck, nearly five miles west of Remax Road, when they heard the calls of "shots fired" over their radios at about 1:30 a.m. The location of the shooting was given as near mile marker 350 on Highway 80.

Horse patrol agents were responding rapidly because of their teammate, Agent Ivie.

When horse patrol agents are on duty, they are members of a brotherhood. After Agent Ivie told them he was going out by himself in a vehicle, the other agents knew at all times where he was.

They had been sitting in their truck cab with their horses in tow since Agent Ivie told them he was going up to Remax Saddle to check the sensor. They were just a quarter mile east of the Cochise County Sheriff's Office, which was sending a contingent of deputies rushing to the scene from throughout the area.

"As soon as we heard that shots were fired, I immediately activated my emergency equipment and drove east on Highway 80," Agent McWhorter would later write in his incident report.[6]

McWhorter slowed down when he saw the highway guardrail at his right that preceded the entrance to Remax Road, which had no other marking to indicate its presence. He made a sharp right turn and immediately braked to make the transition from smooth asphalt to the rocky, narrow roadway.

The horse trailer swayed and clanged as McWhorter pushed his truck to its limit. He knew there was no way he could take the rig all the way to the end of this treacherous road without causing serious damage to the vehicle or causing the trailer to drop off a ledge.

When the truck slowed down to a maximum speed of just a few miles per hour, McWhorter realized the horses would get them to Remax Saddle much faster from there. He stopped the truck, and the agents unloaded their horses and mounted up.

McWhorter and Ocejo heard another radio call, reporting that an agent was injured. They did not hear anything about that agent's identity. They hoped their friend was unhurt. Ocejo called Nick's cell phone. It went right to voicemail.

"Agent Ocejo and I then deployed on horseback, rode south to the end of Remax Road, and continued southeast towards the Remax saddle, where we believed the injured agent to be," Agent McWhorter later wrote in his report.

As Johnson gripped his rifle and awaited another possible attack, he heard the hoofbeats of horses somewhere on the other side of the mountain—certainly Border Patrol Horse Patrol agents were nearby. Cartel smugglers did not generally ride around on horseback north of the border.

The cavalry was arriving! Johnson felt an enormous wave of relief. The tension throughout his body began to loosen.

But then the horse hoofbeats suddenly stopped.

As the two skilled riders rapidly approached the saddle, they were told by a dispatcher to remain in place.

"As we were about 50 yards from the Remax saddle on the trail, our radio dispatch informed us via radio to stand by until air support arrived," Ocejo wrote in his report. "At that time Agent McWhorter and I stopped riding and awaited further instructions."

Just 20 minutes or so after the first group of agents had been greeted by a storm of gunfire, Border Patrol officials did not want two more agents riding into another deadly ambush. Although the horsemen were eager to find their friend and the other agents, they understood that air support could save their lives.

"At that time Agent McWhorter and I stopped riding and waited for further instructions," Agent Ocejo wrote. "Minutes later, we saw the lights of the Air and Marine helicopter coming over the Remax saddle sweeping the area with its spotlight."

With the helicopter spotlighting the mountainside, Johnson knew his ordeal was coming to an end. There was no way anybody would attack him now. They would be busy trying to hide from the chopper if they were still nearby. The guys in the helicopter would be aware of what had occurred. They might open fire on the shooters if they spotted anyone with a weapon.[7]

When the helicopter arrived, the two Horse Patrol agents resumed their urgent mission to aid their comrades.

"Agent McWhorter and I then proceeded to ride the rest of the trail to the top," Agent Ocejo would later write in his report.

Then Johnson heard the unmistakable popping sounds of helicopter rotors slashing through the sky, a series of sonic booms in rapid succession. He sat up straight and turned his eyes toward the sky. The Black Hawk chopper's wide spotlight illuminated the saddle, its light spilling onto the slopes on either side.

Johnson thought he heard hoofbeats again. It was hard to tell, with the overwhelming noise from the chopper's powerful engines.

5

A Heartbreaking Discovery

"I asked him where the shooters had been when he was shot," first responding agent to the wounded agent after finding him on the mountainside.

When their horses reached the crest of the saddle, Agents Ocejo and McWhorter made a startling discovery.

They believed their close friend and teammate Nick Ivie would be somewhere nearby—and would possibly be wounded. But they were not prepared for the sight on the ground a few yards ahead.

"As we approached the saddle, I saw a Border Patrol agent lying face down on the north side of the saddle. I dismounted and ran to help the Agent and as I turned him over, I recognized him as Agent Nicholas Ivie," Agent McWhorter wrote. "I searched for a wound and discovered he was deceased due to what appeared to be a gunshot wound to the front of the head."

He and Agent Ocejo were witnessing a scene every law enforcement officer dreads—the loss of a brother or sister officer.

Both men were shocked by the sight, yet they knew they had to perform their duties according to their training. They were in a remote place, with an unknown number of hostile shooters and agent casualties.

This was the beginning of a soul-wracking nightmare for the two agents who found his body, as well as for the two surviving agents and many other fellow agents. Of course, the cataclysmic impact of Agent Nick Ivie's death would be borne chiefly by his wife, daughters, parents, siblings, and friends, who loved and admired him.

Agent Ocejo wrote in his report about the horrific scene he encountered that night:

"As Agent McWhorter and I reached the scene, I shined my flashlight to my right and spotted Border Patrol Agent Nicholas Ivie lying on the ground and appeared to be unconscious. After conducting a quick survey of the area, Agent McWhorter and I dismounted our horses and approached Agent Ivie.

"McWhorter then grabbed Agent Ivie and turned him face up and held him in a propped-up position as I continued to hold our horses and survey the area."

Ocejo's account matched McWhorter's. He wrote that he dismounted and ran to help an agent who was lying face down on the north side of the saddle.

"As I turned him over, I recognized him as Agent Nicholas Ivie," McWhorter wrote in his report. "I searched for a wound and discovered he was deceased due to what appeared to be a gunshot wound to the front of his head.

"I retrieved Nick's service pistol, which was lying on the ground near his flashlight, and scanned the immediate area for any threats."

Then Agent McWhorter "grabbed Agent Ivie and turned him face up and held him in a propped-up position as I continued to hold the horses and survey the area," Ocejo wrote.

This explains why the crime scene map shows Agent Ivie lying faceup, with a large pool of blood to the right of his body's position, mostly between the area of his hips and knees. If he had just been rolled over toward his right hand, from facedown to faceup, the pool of blood would have been more confined to the area next to his head, because he was bleeding only from his head.

But because Agent McWhorter "held him in a propped-up position," before placing him back on the ground parallel to where he was originally found, his head was two or three feet farther to the south than its original position.

Although the repositioning of the body has no special significance, nor does it raise any suspicion, it does call attention to the fact that Agent Ivie's head was originally found on the ground, five to ten feet northeast of the shell casings from his pistol.

This evidence tends to eliminate him as the one who was shooting his pistol immediately before he was killed. The shell casings were not found in a place that fits with a narrative of him shooting his pistol before he was killed. There is no evidence that Agent Ivie ever fired his pistol—but there is evidence that his pistol was fired.

It is significant that Agent McWhorter wrote in his report that he retrieved Agent Ivie's service pistol, which was lying on the ground near his flashlight. Then he "scanned the immediate area for threats."

Ordinarily law enforcement officers who arrive before the crime scene investigators will not touch anything at a crime scene, especially firearms. But in this case, it was appropriate to secure Agent Ivie's pistol.

Leaving it on the ground could have opened the door for a suspect to pick the weapon up and turn it against the agents. There was still the possibility that a suspect, perhaps wounded or even unconscious, was lying or hiding somewhere in the vicinity.

The horse patrol agents were aware of that possibility.

The crime scene was being treated like an active shooter scenario—not as a secured crime scene.

The fact that Agent McWhorter picked up Agent Ivie's pistol explains why it was later found in a different place from where it had been prior to his arrival on the scene. The crime scene map placed the pistol in an altogether different place—just north of Agent Ivie's feet. This was different from where Agent McWhorter found it and where he said he later placed it back on the ground.

The two horse patrol agents stood near their friend's body, on high alert regarding another possible attack.

"As Agent Ocejo and I scanned the area for any threats, we heard someone yelling from the south side of the saddle," Agent McWhorter wrote.

He told the man, who was outside his line of sight, to identify himself.

"He identified himself as 'Johnson' and stated that he had been shot and couldn't walk," McWhorter wrote in his report. "I then dropped Nick's service pistol by his side and left Agent Ocejo to hold the horses so that I could help Agent Johnson."

Agent McWhorter apparently felt that the immediate scene was now secure enough to return the pistol to the ground, as soon as it was determined that Agent Ocejo would remain at the scene. There was also at least one helicopter overhead, and there were possibly more.

Agent Ocejo's account of discovering the wounded agent matched his partner's.

"Agent McWhorter and I heard a voice coming from the south side of the Remax Saddle. Agent McWhorter and I asked the individual to identify himself," Agent Ocejo wrote in his report. "He responded that he was Agent Johnson. Agent McWhorter laid Agent Ivie back on the ground and went to assist the other agent, as I stood close to Agent Ivie and continued to take care of the horses and secure the area."

When Agent McWhorter found Agent Johnson, "he was lying on the ground, holding his M4. He told me he had been shot in the ankle and the buttocks. I took his M4 (serial #W344027), and as I did, he told me there may not be many rounds left in the magazine," McWhorter wrote in his report.

Johnson had discharged just six of his 28 bullets, but he did not yet know how many shots he had fired. When a shooter is firing rapidly, as many as six bullets can be fired per second.

Responding Agent Concerned About Another Possible Attack

"I asked him where the shooters had been when he was shot and he responded by saying 'right there' and pointed towards some bushes approximately 10 yards to his west," McWhorter wrote. "I scanned the immediate area for some threats."

The same agent who had just discovered that Agent Ivie was dead was now directing his attention to his surroundings because he was concerned about a possible threat.

This was immediately after he had spoken with Agent Johnson.

According to McWhorter's report, when he asked Agent Johnson where the *shooters* had been, Johnson pointed toward where his assailants had been when they fired at him.

If McWhorter's report is accurate, Johnson did *not* say anything to refute any part of this question, such as, "I think there was *only one shooter*."

A key element of the investigation into this case is whether there had been one or more armed illegal aliens on the scene. It is noteworthy that one of the first two law enforcement officers to arrive on the scene asked the wounded officer—one of only two known eyewitnesses— where the *shooters* were. And the officer who was there when the shooting took place responded without correcting him.

In his report, McWhorter wrote, "When I got to Agent Johnson, he was lying on the ground holding his M4. He told me he had been shot in the ankle and the buttocks."

In Johnson's interview two days later, Johnson said he did not know the name of the Border Patrol agent who first contacted him, but he believed his star number was 190.

Part of what Johnson said on the encounter matches what was written in McWhorter's report, whereas another part tends to contradict the McWhorter account. That issue will be explored later in the chapter on the FBI interview with Agent McWhorter.

When later questioned by an FBI agent, Johnson said he responded to the newly arrived agent by saying, "I'm over here."

The agent then asked him, "Who's this?"

After Johnson told him his star number and name, the agent advanced toward him, with the bright beam of his flashlight seeking the injured agent.

"They were looking around for a while actually, before they actually got to me," Johnson recalled during his interview.

Then the agent who was seeking him on the hillside said, "Can you come here?"

"No, I'm hit," Johnson responded.

The agent approached Johnson. He rolled him over to treat him for his wound. He cut a strip off Johnson's shirt and applied the fabric to his wound. The bandage Johnson had made from his pants was already soaked with his blood.

"And then he took my M4," Johnson told the interviewer.

During Johnson's interview, he was asked whether the Border Patrol agent who aided him on the hillside had asked him what had happened.

"No," Johnson replied.

"Or where the threat was?" the FBI agent asked.

Johnson did not respond directly to the question of whether the first responding agent had asked him where the threat was. The way Johnson remembered the interaction, he then asked the first responder a question.

"I think I asked him where 225 (Ivie) was," Johnson replied.[1]

Both agents agreed that McWhorter did not ask Johnson what had occurred. But Johnson apparently did not recall whether McWhorter had asked him "where the threat was."

So instead of responding to the question by the FBI agent, Johnson said he had asked McWhorter where 225 (Ivie) was.

"OK, and what did he say?" the FBI agent asked Johnson.

"I think he just nonchalantly pointed over the hill," Johnson said.

At some point, while Johnson was sitting on the mountainside after he was wounded, he heard that a Border Patrol agent was down. He also learned that O-225, the agent he had planned to meet, had not been in communication with the control room after the shooting.

McWhorter was the one who delivered the news to Johnson that the slain agent was the one he had planned to meet at the saddle.

"Agent Johnson asked me if the deceased agent was 0-225 (Agent Ivie) and I told him it was," McWhorter would later write in his report.

McWhorter held on to Johnson's rifle—to continue to guard against another possible attack—until two other horse patrol agents, Brandon Gilbreth and Shane Ebert, arrived about 10 minutes later.

"Agent Brandon Gilbreth arrived, and I gave the M4 to him so that I could examine Agent Johnson's wounds," McWhorter wrote.[2]

Then Agent Gilbreth and Agent Ebert stood guard on the perimeter of the saddle.

McWhorter administered further treatment to the injured agent, now that they had security against another attack. "I exposed the wound on his left buttock and cut a piece of his shirt to use as a bandage to control the bleeding," McWhorter wrote.

Johnson had been losing blood—enough that he would later say that he "could feel the blood pouring out," and he "kind of blacked out and hit the ground." But he considered it a greater priority to stand watch against shooters, with his rifle in his hands, than to focus entirely on his wounds. After he went to the ground for the second time, he was confident that he would survive the wound.

But he was not certain that he would survive a second attack.

Crime Scene Treated as Possible Active Shooter Situation

Agent Johnson did not know how many smugglers were involved in that ambush, or where they went afterward. From experience with groups in that area, he believed the small group of agents could be outnumbered if the smugglers were in hiding nearby.

McWhorter looked into Johnson's boot to assess his ankle injury.

"I could not see the wound on his ankle as it appeared to be covered by his boot but observed there was minimal bleeding," McWhorter wrote.

It was likely that Johnson's boot helped protect his ankle from receiving a more serious wound. The bleeding from Johnson's buttock wound had slowed down considerably.

"I assured Agent Johnson that the wound on his buttock was not bleeding badly and handed him his duty belt, which had been removed before I arrived, so that he had his service pistol with him if needed," McWhorter wrote in his report.

Because of the possibility of another attack by an unknown number of assailants, it was important for the injured agent—who could not even walk without assistance—to continue to be armed. Some of the smugglers who were involved in the shooting could still be hiding nearby—perhaps frozen in the vicinity by the quick response from multiple law enforcement officers. The agents knew they had to exercise extreme caution.

As other agents were guiding a Customs and Border Protection helicopter to make a landing about 200 yards to the west, at a suitable spot on the ridge, McWhorter stayed with Johnson until it landed.[3]

At the time when Agent McWhorter handed Agent Johnson his fully loaded pistol, there were already many agents in the vicinity, in addition to air support overhead.

But they had no way of knowing how much firepower the smugglers were packing.

What would a killer or killers of a Border Patrol agent have to lose by shooting at another group of agents? If they were bold enough to shoot it out with three agents, what would they have to lose by jumping out of another hiding place and shooting again? The general rule was that smugglers who committed crimes north of the border would be safe from criminal prosecution if they could return safely to Mexico. If they could shoot their way out in the dark and scamper back across the border, all could be well for them.

Johnson never saw Agent Ivie at the scene. He had expected to see him at the saddle, after Ivie said he was there—when Johnson and Borjas were just a few minutes away.

But when Johnson arrived, he saw instead the silhouette of a man throwing off a blanket, revealing a smuggling pack underneath. Then all hell broke loose, which caught him off guard. He was suddenly, unexpectedly, under fire. He stood there trying to decide what action to take, until a couple of bullets struck him.

Agent Johnson had many reasons to acknowledge that it was amazing that he was still alive, including the fact that he was not wearing his body armor. Although he had no protection, none of the bullets fired in his direction had hit vital organs or severed critical blood vessels.

There is no feeling in the world quite like being fired upon at close range and escaping without being killed or disabled.

It was exhilarating to be alive after taking direct hits, but that feeling was tinged with dread and gloom because his fellow agent had been killed. Everything had happened so fast—and without warning. One moment he was approaching his destination somewhat relaxed, because he had a false assurance that no smugglers were there. The next moment he was taking fire from shooters at close range.

He had been through a lifetime of adventures and hairy situations during his three and a half years patrolling the desert and mountains of Southern Arizona. But nothing like this.

Agent Johnson wondered who shot Agent Ivie, and how that came about. It seemed possible that Agent Borjas shot him, because she pulled her gun out and might have been shooting. He didn't think there was any way he shot him, because he was just shooting suppressive fire in their direction. He had no target. The shooters were not in sight when he fired. They had scattered, hit the ground, or otherwise taken cover by the time he opened fire.

If he had landed a direct hit on a fellow agent—or anyone—he would have known about it. He would have seen or heard something as he peered through his sight while pulling his trigger. But there was no indication his bullets had struck anybody.

There had been instant chaos involving an unknown number of armed smugglers, and he did his best to respond to the deadly situation. A well-executed ambush. Zero warning. Like a dangerous lightning storm striking on a calm, sunny day.

There was nobody there in his rifle sight when he opened fire. He heard that Agent Ivie had taken a head shot. Strange things happen during shootouts, but there was no way any of his shots could have landed on Agent Ivie's head.

How do you land a shot like that on someone you never even saw?

Johnson laid down suppressive fire, and it worked. It stopped the enemy from firing again at him and his partner. He was trained to fire toward the enemy when attacked at close range. Suppressive fire is designed to move the needle on enemy fighters from an offensive position to retreating or taking cover. His firing worked well. The bodies went silent after that.

Agent Johnson did not know why the smugglers were shooting at him and the other agents, but he was glad they did not follow through and attack again after he was wounded.

The border-crossers knew exactly where the three agents were when they approached and arrived at the saddle. They held their fire until the agents were right there.

But the agents had no idea that there were any smugglers there — until shots were fired that almost killed all of them.

Agent McWhorter stayed with Agent Johnson until the helicopter landed on the ridge, just west of the saddle. Then Robert Edwards, an acting supervisory agent, and another agent helped Agent Johnson walk to the helicopter.

Agent Ocejo remained at the saddle, protecting the crime scene, where Agent Ivie's body would remain until after noon that day.

6

Agent Saw Three or Four Suspects and Long Firearm

"Agent Borjas told me she saw three—four individuals in the group and she saw one longarm and was not sure which direction they fled."

Tuesday, October 2, 2:10 a.m.
South slope, below Remax Saddle

Robert Edwards Jr., acting BP supervisor, was assigned to Grid 7 that night, the patrol district that included the shooting scene. When he heard the radio call of "shots fired," he was assisting other agents in the Hunter Canyon area, in the Mule Mountains, about 35 miles west of Remax Saddle.[1]

He activated his emergency lights and siren and sped to the Chisolm Trail turnoff. Edwards, who was familiar with the territory, drove toward the border on the well-graded dirt road, past a few houses scattered on either side, then turned west on Hidden Trail Road, past the gravel pit that was being set up as a law enforcement command post.

Edwards parked at the Dead Girl trailhead, where he met up with several other Border Patrol agents. The agents then hiked up the same trail agents Johnson and Borjas had used a short time earlier.

Edwards would later write in his report that he met up with six agents, and then some of them hiked up the trail with him. Another Border Patrol agent wrote that there were four agents hiking together in the Edwards group.

"I informed each agent of the plan to take the Dead Girl Trail to the ridgeline and once on the ridgeline head southeast towards the shooting scene," Edwards wrote. "Once we got on the ridgeline, we headed southeast towards the area of the sensor activation and last known area of the agents."

As Edwards closed in on the mountain ridge, he heard on his radio that Agent Borjas was contacting a Customs and Border Patrol helicopter, which was flying overhead. She informed the crew of her position on the side of the mountain.

Borjas was greatly relieved when she was suddenly bathed in the bright glow of the chopper's intense spotlight. With timing befitting a Hollywood movie script, the Edwards group appeared almost simultaneously, and stepped into the light.

"As the Omaha Unit found Agent Borjas in their spotlight, I approached Agent Borjas and asked her of her condition," Edwards wrote. "She told me she was ok and unharmed." (The Border Patrol uses the code word "Omaha" to refer to helicopters and other supporting aircraft.)

After ascertaining that she was unharmed, Edwards asked Borjas where the other agents were who were involved in the shooting incident.

"She pointed to the Remax saddle approximately 150 yards northeast of her position," Edwards wrote in his report.

Edwards then "asked Agent Borjas approximately how many suspected illegal aliens were in the group, if any were armed, and if she saw which direction they fled."

Borjas gave him information that hopefully would aid in the capture of the suspects.

"Agent Borjas told me she saw three–four individuals in the group, and she saw one longarm and was not sure which direction they fled," Edwards wrote.

This is what Agent Borjas said about 40 minutes after the shooting, when everything was fresh in her mind. Her story would be corroborated by much of the evidence discovered in the hours and days that followed.

There has never been any evidence presented to the press or the public that contradicts this significant statement.

Despite the facts that Borjas was never accused of dishonesty and that her testimony matched all the evidence, FBI agents would later try to coerce Borjas into recanting this important statement.

Edwards relayed the information Borjas gave him to other agents via radio.

By this time, the Cochise County Sheriff's office had dozens of officers responding to the scene. Those officers, who often worked closely with the Border Patrol, were tuned in to the federal agency's radio frequency. Sheriff's Commander Marc Denney heard the report that the agents "had come under fire from three or four people."[2]

Agent Borjas told Edwards that she fired some shots from her pistol, according to his report. Edwards directed her to replace the magazine in her weapon with a fully loaded magazine, "since the scene was still insecure." Replacing a magazine from her pistol with a fully loaded magazine was an indication that Edwards believed the agents at the scene could need every possible bullet if another ambush erupted.

Once again, we see an experienced agent who had just arrived on the scene, who was intensely focused on preventing another possible attack. Everyone on or near the scene was on high alert.

It was important for all the law enforcement officers who were streaming into the area to know there were at least three or four suspects involved in the homicide of one Border Patrol agent and the wounding of another agent. All agents on duty or on subsequent shifts from nearby Border Patrol stations were sent to the grids of the Mule Mountains from the moment of the report of *shots fired* and throughout the nighttime and morning hours to come.

There were also indications that Mexican law enforcement officers and military personnel were being deployed south of the border to try to apprehend the smugglers who shot the agents. Photographs of officers south of the border, taken that morning by news photographers, indicated that municipal police in Sonora were participating in the manhunt.[3]

If apprehended, all of the smugglers involved in the incident would likely face charges of first-degree murder and attempted first-degree murder, for their involvement in criminal activity related to the shooting of the agents.

Although the cooperation of Mexican authorities was often unreliable or even treacherous, there were times when they did cooperate in the apprehension and extradition of criminals who had committed serious crimes on American soil. This was one case in which U.S. officials could apply maximum pressure on Mexican authorities—and could possibly obtain assistance in an investigation leading to the conviction of the gunmen who murdered Agent Ivie.

North of the border, the law enforcement officers who were rushing to the scene were from numerous federal and local agencies, including the U.S. Customs and Border Protection, the U.S. Bureau of Alcohol, Tobacco, Firearms and Explosives, the F.B.I., the U.S. Drug Enforcement Administration, and the Bisbee Police Department.

With Borjas reporting that she had seen three or four suspects, federal agents and other law enforcement officers were hoping to apprehend at least that many individuals.

Border Patrol agents were keenly aware of their *plus one rule*. After determining the number of people involved, they would seek to find at least one more person. Experience had taught them that the initial head count by agents often fell short of the actual number in a group.

After one of the worst attacks in Border Patrol history, they were not going to lose another agent to some lone suspect who had escaped capture.

If Borjas saw three or four suspects, then they would try to locate at least five. Agents are trained to keep their heads on swivels, to expect another possible ambush following any attack.[4]

Edwards reported that Borjas said she had fired her service pistol. During her interview later that morning, she said she had drawn her gun but was not sure whether she had fired it. It was later determined that she had *not* fired her weapon. One possibility was that she had failed to chamber a round after loading a magazine into her pistol. If she had not racked the slide to place a round in her weapon's chamber, it would not have discharged a projectile when she pulled the trigger.[5] No shell casings from her service pistol were found at the scene.

Although she was shaken up by her near-death experience, Borjas appeared to the on-scene supervisor to be competent to perform her duties. Edwards made sure that she was well armed in case of further trouble, with the maximum amount of ammunition. There was no indication at the scene that she was unduly upset by what had occurred, or that her mental faculties were compromised. Because she said she had discharged her weapon, Edwards made sure she was fully armed.

There was nothing in the report by Supervisory Agent Edwards to indicate that he thought anything Agent Borjas said was incorrect or untrue.

Edwards wrote that he had been involved in identifying a place for a helicopter to land, in order to evacuate the surviving agents.

"After all Agents were accounted for, I advised Omaha Unit of a good landing zone to the west of the Remax Saddle," Edwards would later write in his report.

After the Black Hawk helicopter landed on the mountain ridge, a pilot told Edwards the helicopter had room for two passengers.

Edwards and Borjas hiked uphill in a northeast direction toward the ridge. While they were en route, Agent Joshua Garza met up with them. Garza was one of the agents who had hiked to the scene with Edwards, along with agents Kyle Babbie and Rogelio Velasco.[6]

"I advised Agent Garza to take Agent Borjas to the top of the ridgeline where we had set up a landing zone for the Omaha Unit. I advised Agent Garza to remain with Agent Borjas and to not let her come into the Remax Saddle where the shooting had taken place," Edwards wrote.

As Agent Borjas was escorted toward the helicopter landing zone to be evacuated from the mountain, Agent Edwards hiked toward the saddle "where the agents were shot."

The saddle was being protected as a crime scene. There was no reason for Agent Borjas to return to the saddle. Instead, she was evacuated, to return to her station to be interviewed.

Agent Borjas was not aware at this time that an agent had been killed. It is possible that Edwards did not want Agent Borjas to see the terrible sight of a fallen agent.

Before he arrived at the saddle, Edwards had heard the news over his radio that Agent Ivie, referred to as "O-225," was "10-7," police code for *out of service,* or *deceased.* Edwards was still on the south slope of the mountain, just below the saddle, when he spotted the other agents on the scene.

His account meshes with many of the details recorded by other agents: "As I approached, I noticed that Horse Patrol Agent Jake McWhorter was rendering aid to Border Patrol Agent David Johnson and that Agent Brandon Gilbreth was standing nearby with an M4 rifle," Edwards wrote.

"I immediately asked where Horse Patrol Agent Nick Ivie was, and Agent McWhorter pointed in a northern direction and told me that he was deceased. I approached Agent Ivie and from about 10–15 feet observed a mortal wound that he had sustained in his face."

Edwards asked the wounded agent about his condition, to which he replied that "he was OK." Edwards wrote that he "observed that Agent Johnson had been shot in his buttocks and ankle.

"I then radioed in, via my service radio, Agent Johnson and Borjas' condition [sic] to the command post on Gravel Pit Road."

Agent Johnson, suffering from the two gunshot wounds and a loss of blood, was supported by Supervisory Agent Edwards and another agent, as they slowly hiked together toward the chopper.

As Agent Johnson departed, his loaded firearms remained at the scene. The scene was still considered hot, even 45 minutes after the shots were fired.

"I also took custody of Agent Johnson's entire gun belt to include his service weapon, and Agent Gilbreth was using Agent Johnson's assigned M4 to enhance security of our perimeter," Edwards wrote in his report.

"Both agents Johnson and Borjas where [sic] extracted from the scene around 2:15 a.m.," Edwards wrote.

There was nothing in the report by Supervisor Edwards on what Johnson said at the scene about what had occurred. If Edwards did garner information from Johnson on the shooting incident, it was not included in the report that he later filed and signed.

There were already agents guarding the saddle when Acting Supervisor Edwards took command of the crime scene, but Edwards wanted to extend the perimeter, to prevent contamination of a larger area.

"After the Agents involved in the shooting were extracted from the scene, I returned to the area of Agent Ivie and began setting up a perimeter," Edwards wrote. "I left Douglas Border Patrol Agent Velasco at the landing zone and advised him that no one else was to continue eastbound down the ridgeline to the Remax Saddle without my expressed permission."

Edwards noted that the agents at the saddle at that time were Horse Patrol Agents Victor Ocejo and Shane Ebert, as well as Agents Joshua Garza and Jason Nelson. He advised the agents "to set up a 360-degree perimeter around Agent Ivie," while also instructing them to "stay clear of the immediate area around Agent Ivie so we could limit contamination of the scene.

"The scene was secure and perimeter set up by around 2:20 a.m. I advised the command post of our status and what Agents where [sic] on the scene."

The murder of a law enforcement officer had occurred, and every officer on the scene was going to do everything in his power to ensure that this investigation was not compromised. The scene would be carefully guarded against contamination, and every detail surrounding this homicide would be carefully documented. Every officer on the scene was keenly aware that he was playing a role in bringing Agent Ivie's killers to justice.

When the helicopter landed near the command post at about 2:44 a.m., Agent Johnson was loaded onto an ambulance, where he would be treated for his wounds.

Then he was flown by Medevac Helicopter to the University of Arizona Medical Center (UAMC). The Tucson hospital contained the only Level I trauma center in Southern Arizona. In order to receive that highest level of designation, a trauma center had to fulfill a long list of qualifications, including 24-hour coverage by a variety of specialized surgeons.

The UAMC had been in the public spotlight nearly two years earlier. U.S. Rep. Gabrielle Giffords, D-Tucson, was treated there, along with 10 other shooting victims, on January 8, 2011, after a crazed gunman opened fire at an event in Tucson where Giffords was meeting with constituents. Six people were killed, including a 9-year-old girl and a federal judge. Giffords, who was shot in the head and partially paralyzed, represented the Congressional district that included Cochise County.

The FBI investigated that case, under the supervision of then FBI director Robert S. Mueller III, who flew to Tucson "at Mr. Obama's request," said a *New York Times* story posted on January 9, 2011. Mueller said an intensive investigation was seeking to determine "why someone would commit such a heinous act and whether anyone else was involved," the *Times* story said.[7]

Although the FBI also investigated the Ivie murder while Mueller was FBI director, there is no record of the director's personal involvement in that case. He did not fly to Arizona to find out why anyone would commit the heinous act of shooting two Border Patrol agents, nor did he announce that he would try to find out whether anyone else was involved.

In stark contrast to the public announcement of Mueller's involvement in the Tucson shooting, there was no public record of FBI Director Mueller's involvement in the investigation of the shooting death of Agent Ivie. Because of its high profile—and implications in the reelection of the president who worked closely with Mueller—it would seem likely that Mueller *was* involved in this investigation. But Mueller had learned long ago—during his extended 12-year tenure as FBI director—to remain in the background of cases that had political implications.

The shooter in the heinous Tucson case was apprehended on the spot. Yet Obama had thought it was important to send the FBI director to Arizona, for various reasons—none of which involved apprehending suspects.

When a Border Patrol agent was shot to death and another injured the following year, the suspects were *not* immediately apprehended. There were two to five suspects taken into custody in connection with this shooting incident. But there was no announcement that the FBI director would fly to Arizona to oversee this investigation.

A case involving smugglers who worked for a prominent drug cartel—who shot to death a federal agent, would seem to be a prime case for attention by the FBI director. Wouldn't he be the perfect person to work with Mexican authorities at a high level to try to obtain justice for the slain and wounded agents?

If Obama did ask Mueller to get involved in this investigation, he kept that information to himself. There was no *New York Times* story to announce that Director Mueller was going to oversee this case.

Deputies Help Medics Aid Wounded Agent, Discover Southbound Tracks

"The gunfire was from an apparent ambush, and not an accidental discharge." Border Patrol agent to a sheriff's deputy, while responding to the scene shortly after the shooting occurred.

October 2, 1:30 to 3:00 a.m.
Vicinity of Remax Saddle

Deputy Arthur Estrada of the Cochise County Sheriff's Office was working the overnight shift, along with Deputy Guy Hudson. They were close to each other, in their parked patrol vehicles, on the east side of Douglas, about 12 miles east of the Mule Mountains.

At about 1:30 a.m. October 2, Estrada's computer screen lit up with the word "ASSAULT," and then he saw that "Border Patrol was requesting assistance for one of their agents was shot in leg and buttocks."

Estrada, a 10-year law enforcement veteran, tailed Hudson, as they sped in their patrol vehicles, emergency lights flashing and sirens blaring, toward Highway 80, then 14 miles west to the Chisolm Trail Road turnoff.

Deputy Estrada saw many Border Patrol vehicles pouring into the area south of the highway. When he spotted BP Agent Erick Cazarez, with whom he was familiar, he motioned to him to pull over as he turned into Chisolm Trail.

They stopped at the same spot where BP agents Borjas and Johnson had met before they hiked up the mountain a couple hours earlier.

Agent Cazarez, who worked out of the Brian Terry station, told the deputy that two agents had been shot and that he was familiar with the area where those agents would be located.

While he was talking with Cazarez, Estrada saw two ambulances from Bisbee with flashing emergency lights driving east on 80, speeding right past the Chisolm Trail turnoff. Believing that they were assigned to render aid to injured agents, Estrada activated his emergency lights and gave chase, to stop the Bisbee medics and direct them to a rendezvous point in order to help the injured agent.[8]

Deputy Estrada requested that Deputy Hudson follow Agent Cazarez to the shooting scene.

Hudson tailed Agent Cazarez, as he headed south on Chisolm Trail, then turned west onto Hidden Trail Road. Hudson remained behind the Border Patrol vehicle as Cazarez drove past the gravel pit, a well-known area landmark, and "up a rocky, uphill dirt road," Hudson would write later in his report. They parked their vehicles behind other Border Patrol vehicles, just south of the mountain saddle where the shooting incident occurred.[9]

"I asked Agent Cazarez what he knew of the situation," Hudson wrote. **"He stated the gunfire was from an apparent ambush and not an 'AD' (accidental discharge).** He stated he believed two agents had been injured due to gunshot wounds and one was unresponsive."

Hudson relayed that information to a dispatcher at the sheriff's office and advised that it should be passed on to the command officers.

As the deputy and the Border Patrol agent prepared to hike to the saddle, Hudson donned his SWAT vest, "capable of defeating rifle rounds," and his "load-bearing vest," which contained his CamelBak hydration system.

"I grabbed my AR 15 (semiautomatic rifle) and three additional 30-round magazines," Hudson wrote.

Then the two law enforcement officers began the arduous hike to the saddle, setting out at about 2:08 a.m. They were heavily armed, in order to possibly confront ruthless killers.

While Hudson followed Casarez's SUV toward the trailhead, Deputy Estrada stopped the Bisbee ambulances on Highway 80 and told the drivers to turn around and follow him.

When Estrada returned to Chisolm Trail and sped onto the graded dirt road, he hoped to catch up with the two other law enforcement vehicles heading toward the trail head. But they were already far ahead of him, and he could not see where they were. They had already driven past the main dirt roads and onto narrower, bumpier side roads.

In his rush to catch up with Cazarez and Hudson in the maze of roads south of Highway 80, Estrada left the ambulances behind. He stopped to let the ambulances catch up with him, to ensure that they would be in the best location to meet the injured agent when the chopper landed.

Estrada saw that many more Border Patrol agents were "piling in" to the area in their vehicles and beginning to set up a command post near the spot where he was waiting. Estrada stopped the ambulances in the vicinity of the new command post. As the medical personnel waited for the wounded agent, Estrada helped the BP agents establish the post.

Deputies Estrada and Hudson stayed in touch via cell phone.

Deputy Hudson told Estrada that he and Agent Cazarez were going to climb the mountain toward the shooting scene.

Estrada heard on his radio's Border Patrol frequency the voice of a female agent, as she was trying to direct a helicopter that was flying over the mountain near her location. She said that she was close to the shooting scene. Estrada believed that this female agent could be the third agent who had been involved in the shooting.

The deputy then heard that "one agent had been shot and killed." Estrada knew many of the Border Patrol agents who worked out of the Brian Terry station. He wondered who the fallen agent was.

Deputy Photographs Shoe Prints

While hiking up a trail to the scene, Deputy Hudson and Agent Cazarez located shoe impressions of individuals heading southwest toward the border. Hudson took photos of the shoe prints with his cellphone camera at about 3:00 a.m.

Hudson wrote in his report the GPS coordinates of the location of the shoe impressions on the trail.

"One shoe impression which was the most obvious in rocky terrain was that commonly described as a 'thicker running W' type pattern," Hudson would write in his report.

He forwarded his photos to Deputy Estrada, as officers from several different departments continued to converge at the command post in the gravel pit area. Officers at the post or at the border could possibly use those photos to inform them about suspects, especially if they encountered anyone wearing shoes with similar tread patterns.

The images of the sole patterns could also possibly be used as evidence in the case. Matching shoe impressions to shoes found on a suspect could help place him in the vicinity of the shooting scene.

The officers at the scene were focused on trying to find the shooting suspects and evidence, in order to apprehend the shooters and assist in their prosecution. There is no higher priority for a law enforcement officer than helping to bring a cop killer to justice.

While hiking to the scene, Hudson saw a helicopter flying "really low" to the area of the shooting scene.

"I also copied [heard] over radio traffic from USBP that one agent was unresponsive and deceased," Hudson wrote. "The other with wounds was conscious and being loaded into the helicopter."

As Agent Borjas and Agent Johnson rode down to Highway 80 in the Black Hawk helicopter, they remained silent. They were given earplugs to muffle the roaring of the two powerful engines and the continuous popping from the whirling rotor blades. The helicopter, which carried up to 11 passengers and four crew members, was loaded with heavily armed agents.

A short time later, a Lifeline II air ambulance landed on Highway 80, as deputies held back the few vehicles traveling on the roadway. Agent Johnson was loaded onto the medevac helicopter and whisked to the Tucson's University of Arizona Medical Center, where he would undergo surgery.

He was treated and released from the hospital later that day.

No information about Johnson's injuries has ever been released to the public, except that he was wounded in the buttock and ankle. Nothing was ever released about evidence connecting his wounds to any specific shooter or firearm.

Deputy Hudson arrived at a location near the shooting scene at about 4 a.m., "approximately 100 yards to the south, on a high rise, with abilities to see over the scene. From our vantage point, we could ensure no one came from any direction to the scene," he wrote in his report.

Hudson remained at that "scene security" station until 7:30 a.m. He made a list of those who accompanied him at that station during the hours just before and after sunrise. They were nine Border Patrol agents, eight from the Brian Terry Station, and one from Douglas. The agents standing watch included some of the men mentioned earlier: Agents Cazares, Babbie, and Kristinsson.

"Shortly after 700 hours, a Black Hawk helicopter dropped off two FBI agents to the south of where our security line was set," Hudson wrote. "Shortly thereafter, the helicopter began to transport other investigators to the scene."[10]

The Worst Possible News
October 2, 4 a.m.
The Ivie residence, Sierra Vista, Arizona

Christy Ivie was accustomed to her husband coming home from work in the wee hours, but she was startled when she heard a knock at her door.

When she opened the door, she immediately knew there was something seriously wrong. There were four agents standing there. They informed Christy that her beloved husband had passed away while performing his duties on a nearby mountain.[11]

When she heard an agent say that Nick had been shot and killed, she went into a state of shock.

"No, no, no, no," Christy said over and over again.[12]

7

"These Guys are from the FBI" — Interview of Female Agent

"We didn't see him face to face. And never got to see him before or after."
Agent Borjas on not seeing Agent Ivie at Remax Saddle

Detective Sergeant Gijanto, of the Cochise County Sheriff's Office (CCSO), was at home when he received a call from a dispatcher at 1:46 a.m., informing him about a Border Patrol–involved shooting, with one agent possibly dead.[1]

When he arrived at the command post on Hidden Trail Road, Sergeant Gijanto contacted Deputy Art Estrada, who told him that Border Patrol agents were securing the scene on the mountain ridge. He also learned that Deputy Guy Hudson was hiking to the scene with a Border Patrol agent.

As other Border Patrol agents and law enforcement officers from several agencies reported to the command post, Gijanto and Border Patrol Supervisor Joe Serino were detailed to the Brian Terry Station to participate in the interview of Agent Borjas.

At about 5:00 a.m., Border Patrol Agent Graciela Borjas was interviewed at the station in a room occupied by two FBI agents, a supervisor of the Border Patrol Critical Incident Team (CIT), Sergeant Gijanto from the Cochise County Sheriff's Office, and two other Border Patrol agents.

She had no legal or union representation as she underwent an interview about the most traumatic event of her life.

Agent Borjas had always striven to do her best and had been highly regarded throughout her life as an outstanding student and athlete. Now she was uncertain whether her career as a Border Patrol agent had just ended. She wondered what would happen to her, now that she had run for cover when she ran into bad guys who tried to kill her.

Sergeant Gijanto would later write a report about the interview. His report—which clashed with some of the later assertions of the official investigation—would become an important element that would lead to my reporting on this case.

The interview was recorded on Sergeant Gijanto's Puma tape recorder. It would later be transcribed by a secretary at the sheriff's office. Sergeant Gijanto would proofread and edit the interview transcript.

Gijanto wrote that the interview of Agent Borjas was administrative in nature.

CIT (Supervisor) Joe Serino read off of a card which had eight questions, which Agent Borjas was required to answer.

The Cochise County Sheriff's Office was a key player in the early stages of this investigation. It had 15 detectives in its investigative division, including three sergeants and a lieutenant. Sergeant Gijanto, who at the time had 15 years under his belt with the sheriff's department, would be promoted to lieutenant shortly after completing work on this case.

Near the end of the 35-minute interview, FBI Special Agent Marjoe Jennings told Agent Borjas, "Just so you are aware, we are investigating the assault on you guys. That's our jurisdiction on this; it's not like we are investigating you."

Before that statement was made by the FBI agent, it is not clear whether Agent Borjas understood what the purpose of the interview was.

It was certainly an unnerving experience for the young agent, to answer to the FBI and Border Patrol about a shooting incident involving the death of a fellow agent.

This was another upsetting experience, on top of the initial shock. The ambush had been the shock of her lifetime. Having to talk about it again in front of all these important men felt like another ambush. She was struggling to control her emotions as the men grilled her about that horrifying attack.

During her interview, Borjas said that she was distraught. After undergoing a near-death experience, here she was in a room with four investigators peppering her with questions.

The horrific nightmare on the mountain was closely followed by this new nightmare. She understood that she had information they wanted, but it all seemed cold and hard. She let them know she was not in any shape to undergo this interrogation.

Agent Borjas had already told a supervisor important details about what happened while she was on the mountain. What else did they need from her? If they caught the border-crossers who almost killed her, she would be glad to testify and help put them away.

She had just passed her probationary period 11 months earlier, and she had hoped to have a long career in federal law enforcement, which offered excellent pay, benefits, room for advancement, and adventure.

Borjas had attended the University of Texas, El Paso (UTEP), on an athletic scholarship, earning a bachelor's in education degree in 2006, with honors for her academic and athletic performance. Borjas was a member of UTEP's first NCAA softball team when it was founded in 2004. She was the sole representative of her softball team to receive the school's academic all-conference award, and one of only five athletes to receive that award on the entire campus. A speedy shortstop and third baseman, she broke the school's single-season stolen base record.

A native of Canutillo, Texas, an El Paso suburb 10 miles north of the Mexican border, Borjas attended El Paso Community College, where she also excelled on the softball team. In her freshman year, she was honored as the school's National Junior College Athletic Association outstanding defensive player.

Just two months after graduating from UTEP, Borjas was visited by tragedy. Her family home and her possessions were destroyed by floodwaters from the Rio Grande River in August 2006. Her former teammates at both of her colleges held a fundraising rally to help Borjas and her family recover.

The rally included a scrimmage between the softball teams of the two schools, which was held in October 2006 on the university's home field. The fact that both colleges worked together to help Borjas in her time of need was a testimony of the high esteem in which she was held by those who knew her. She was displaced from her home, but she was invited to stay with a former softball teammate in the wake of the flood.

Borjas began her career with the Border Patrol on November 1, 2010, after accepting a challenge from her brother, a law enforcement officer. She underwent 12 weeks of training at the Border Patrol Academy in nearby Artesia, New Mexico, which does not have diverse standards for women. She succeeded in passing all the physical and academic qualifications—which were all set for men.

Borjas joined the federal law enforcement agency that had the lowest percentage of female officers. Fewer than one out of 20 Border Patrol agents are women.

Border Patrol Supervisor Serino was the chief interviewer at the postincident session at her station. She was also questioned by FBI Special Agents Marjoe Jennings and Chad Edlund, as well as by Sergeant Gijanto. Two unidentified people were sitting in the back of the room, believed by Sergeant Gijanto to be Border Patrol agents. When the interview was nearly concluded, one of those individuals offered to retrieve another pistol for Borjas, to replace the one she had possessed during the shooting incident.

There had been some conversation between Agent Borjas and other members of the Border Patrol before the formal interview began. One of the first questions asked of her during the interview was whether she had spoken earlier with someone named Jim. The last name of Jim was transcribed as "inaudible" in the interview transcript.

The interview was mandated by a Border Patrol regulation, which states that an employee must report on a shooting incident involving an agent within one hour of that incident, Serino told Borjas. Before the formal interview began, she was informed that there would be eight specific questions she would have to answer.

BP Supervisor Serino began the interview by telling her, "To the best you know, the best that you can recall, you know, to the best of your knowledge, try to help us out with the understanding of what happened."

Agent Borjas responded by asking about the other men in the room.

"These guys are from the FBI," Serino responded.

Agent Borjas responded to questions about her name and the start date of her Border Patrol service.

Serino read the regulation that states that any service employee who participated in "a reportable shooting incident that defines [sic] in sub-section 38 shall orally report the incident to a supervisor."

"The report shall be made within one hour of the time of the incident, of the time the incident occurs, or within one hour of the time the employee becomes aware of the incident," Serino told Borjas.

As she considered the idea that she was late in complying with this regulation, Serino began going through the list of questions.

"Uh, the date, time, and location of the shooting incident," he said.

"October first, and uh, I don't know the time," she responded.

"OK, do you have any idea proximately [sic]?" Serino asked.

FBI Agent Chad Edlund interrupted, to nail down the detail of the date the shooting occurred.

"Today is the second," Edlund said. "So it happened yesterday?"

"No, it happened this morning, I believe. . . . I, I'm not sure how long ago it happened. . . . I don't know how long it took us to get in place and . . .," Borjas stammered.

"OK," Serino said, moving to the next question on his list. "The identity and current location of any danger or deceased persons including an assessment of the extent of the injuries."

"I don't know their names," Borjas said. "I know their star numbers. . . . I'm fairly new, so I don't know them. It was Oscar 341. . . Who was with me, and 225, I believe." Oscar [for the letter O] is the designation for the Naco/Brian Terry Station. Stations are assigned letters associated with their locations. In this case, N was already taken by nearby Nogales.

"Any suspects, deceased or injured?" Serino asked.

"I don't know," Borjas said.

"Don't know?" Serino followed up.

"Nuhm," Borjas said, according to the transcript.

"The identity, physical description, and current location of any individuals known to be involved in or to have witnessed the incidents, including suspects who are at large?" Serino said, reading off his question sheet.

"The only ones that witnessed it?" Borjas asked, in response to the lengthy question. "Just myself and 341 (Johnson) and I don't know where 225 (Ivie) was. I, we weren't together."

"OK, How many suspects did you see?"

"Maybe three, four, I'm not too sure," Borjas said.

This is the second documented time that Borjas said she saw three or four suspects. She told the same thing to the supervisory Border Patrol agent who found her on the side of the mountain about 20 minutes after the shooting.

Borjas was then asked to describe the incident, to give a synopsis of what occurred.

Borjas said that she responded to a call on her radio, which reported that there had been a sensor hit. She did not know what time she heard that call. She said that, when she heard that a sensor went off, she called in to dispatch and said, "10-4," that she was going to go up there.[2]

She drove to the area in her patrol vehicle and met another agent, whom she identified only as O-341. They both parked near the "Dead Trail" and hiked from there.

The two agents knew that another agent, O-225, was also responding to the triggering of the sensor. Borjas and O-341 would be hiking toward the sensor from the south, while O-225 was coming in from the north.

Agent Borjas said that she and O-341 were in radio contact with O-225. She and 341 got together and went up there together.

"And as we walked up there, he was the lead agent the whole time," Borjas said.

Serino asked her how long it took them to get up there and she said she wasn't sure.

"How did everything just start?" Serino asked, cutting straight to the shooting incident.

"From what I remember, we were walking the trail, and I was behind 341, and all of a sudden I just heard like yelling and shot guns," Borjas said.

"You said shotguns?" FBI Agent Edlund asked.

"Uh hum, just rounds going off," Borjas said. "Like shots fired, sorry."

"OK. You said you heard yelling?" Serino asked.

She said she heard yelling, but she couldn't remember what was said.

"It was English, Spanish?" Edlund asked her.

"Umm," Borjas said, apparently thinking about it.

"Not sure?" Edlund asked.

"I don't recall. I'm just so distraught right now," Borjas said.

FBI Agent Jennings asked if it was 225 (Ivie) that was yelling.

Borjas said she believed it was 341 (Johnson) who was yelling.

"Uhm, you know what I'm not sure who was yelling, to tell you the truth," Borjas said. "Right after I heard just the yelling, and I just heard gunshots, and I saw the gunshots."

"You saw the muzzle flash?" Serino asked.

"Yes, uh hum, the muzzle, I just saw it," Borjas said.

"Do you recall like how many times or . . .?" Serino asked

"I don't remember," she said. "Everything was just so fast."

In response to a question from Sheriff's Sergeant Gijanto about where Ivie was located, Borjas said, "He came up from the north. We actually came up from the south."

When Serino asked a question about the "operational activity," Borjas replied that the agents were just responding to the triggering of a sensor. There was no report of the Border Patrol having any information from surveillance cameras.

Then Serino offered another routine question—triggering a response that would prove to be of paramount importance regarding the facts of this case.

"The type of firearms used, the number of shots fired, and the current location of all the firearms used in the incident?" Serino asked.

"Three-four-one was carrying an M4, and that's what he used," Borjas said. "And from what I kept seeing **from how [unintelligible] they were, the rounds were coming, that they had a long arm also,"** she said.

Borjas reiterated that important detail, that she saw one of the suspects firing a long arm. She had also told this to the supervisory agent who first found her shortly after the incident. **Note that she said** *"also," referring to the fact that Johnson also had a longarm.*

Ivie was not carrying a long arm, so if Borjas was correct—and we have no reason to believe she was not—there was a suspect shooting a rifle or shotgun at the scene, just a short distance in front of Borjas.

Edlund asked if there was more than one long arm, and she said it was a single longarm.

"Did you see any other weapon?" Serino asked.

Ah, when I took cover, I might of seen like a little flash of a pistol. But I can't exactly say I saw . . . I kind of saw like a shiny part, so what I saw like specifically was a long arm from the way it was coming out, the rounds were coming out.

Borjas and Johnson both said that Borjas took cover after the gunfire stopped. If she saw a pistol that was shiny when she took cover, that would have been a suspect's weapon. The Border Patrol pistols are black and have no shiny parts. However, it is not clear exactly what the "flash of a pistol" was indicating. It could have meant a muzzle flash. Or it could have meant something else, like a reflection of moonlight off the pistol.

In response to a question about the gunfire being loud, Borjas said it was rapid gunfire, and she made sounds resembling "tatatatata."

She was asked if it was automatic gunfire.

"I don't know. It was quick; everything was just fast," Borjas said.

When asked if she fired any rounds, she said she drew her gun, but didn't remember whether she fired it.

Serino asked Borjas whether she had any information that could assist law enforcement in the search they were conducting in the vicinity of the shooting scene.

"I have no information 'cause I went and took cover. I don't know where they ran," she said.

This was almost four hours after the shooting. She had no idea where the suspects would be at this time. The important detail here is that she was talking about actual suspects, some of whom she knew had fled the scene.

"You say that you saw maybe three or four?" Serino asked.

"Yes," Borjas said.

This was a detail that was obviously seared into her mind. She came upon the saddle, her destination. At the saddle, instead of finding Agent Ivie there by himself, she saw three or four people—as one or more suspects immediately opened fire on her and her partner.

This testimony was obviously important evidence to indicate that there was an ambush by smugglers, which she had also previously related to a supervisor. A massive manhunt was already underway.

Nobody questioned the validity of her statement in the hours and days following the shooting incident, according to all the numerous reports written by the Border Patrol agents and Cochise County Sheriff's officers who responded to the scene.

With the eight administrative Border Patrol questions completed, FBI Agent Jennings took over the interview. He questioned Borjas on other aspects of her experience, to get a fuller picture of what had occurred.

"Where did you guys start at?" Jennings asked.

"We parked at the Dead Trail," Borjas said. "It was my first time going up there."

The trail is commonly known as "Dead Girl Trail," by ranchers and law enforcement officers who work in the area. The name was attached to the trail near "Dead Girl Wash" after a body was found in the area. Borjas, who was not familiar with the area, called it by an abbreviated name.

Borjas said she exited Highway 80 at Chisolm Trail and met up with 341. She parked her vehicle near the base of the mountain and hiked on the ascending trail for about a mile.

She knew that the other agent was heading up from the north side. She did not know whether Ivie was hiking up by himself or with another agent.

Sergeant Gijanto also asked some questions.

"So before the shooting, you didn't see him?" Gijanto asked.

"No, I didn't see him before the shooting; like, we copied [slang for saw] **his light but I, we didn't see him face to face. And never got to see him before or after,"** she responded.

"So how did you know he was involved?" Gijanto asked.

"Because he was on the radio," Borjas said.

FBI Agent Jennings asked if she went up there because the sensor went off.

Borjas said the sensor was triggered for seven hits. The sensor sent a signal directly to the control room. Then an agent in the control room put out the information to agents.

"So you mean seven people probably stepped on it?" Jennings asked.

"Yeah," Borjas said.

Serino interjected that "it can be people, or it can be animals, it could be any, any other number of things that can set off a sensor."

This was followed by an interchange between Serino and Jennings, in which Serino explained that the Border Patrol had a network of sensors, small boxes, "out there all over the place," and whenever one of them was triggered, the agents were able to respond because they knew the location of that sensor.

The FBI agent asked Serino if he had the exact location of that sensor and the times it was triggered. Serino said he could retrieve that information for the FBI.

Jennings asked Borjas if she knew what time the sensor was triggered. She said she did not know.

In response to another question from an FBI agent, she told him she was working the midnight shift, 10 p.m. to 6 a.m.

Jennings asked if the three agents were all working the same shift. She said she was not sure whether Ivie was working the same shift or a different shift.

The FBI agent asked for her phone number and birth date, which she supplied. He told her, "We appreciate your assistance on this. . . . I know it's pretty hard right now."

"After the news . . ." she said, apparently referring to the death of her fellow agent. Then she was overcome by emotion.

BP Supervisor Serino asked the FBI agents if "you guys are going to want to take her weapon as well?"

That sparked a question from FBI Agent Jennings to Borjas about the handling of her weapon during the incident.

"You dropped it on the ground, and you picked it back up?" Jennings asked.

"No, I never dropped it, I drew it out," Borjas said.

This is an odd question. Borjas was a Border Patrol agent who had just undergone a shooting incident in which she had almost been killed. Considering that she had never dropped her pistol—but had instead withstood a storm of gunfire at close range with her weapon in her hand— one wonders why an interviewer would ask that question.

"You drew it, OK. I got you. You drew it, and you don't know if you shot it?" Jennings said.

The response by Borjas to that question is recorded as "inaudible" on the interview tape transcript.

The FBI agent then asked Serino if his "CIT (Critical Incident Team) guys can take that (her service pistol) and do your checks on it?"

Serino said he would take it.

FBI Agent Chad Edlund took over the questioning.

He asked Agent Borjas what happened once the shooting stopped.

She said she ran toward the right, as Agent 341 (Johnson) "went toward the left." She ran toward the bottom of the mountain slope.

"I was trying to make my way down so they wouldn't see me," she said, referring to the suspects she just saw at the saddle.

"This is while the shooting is happening?" Edlund asked.

No. It had already stopped. And Agent 341 "had called it in."

She said she was heading down to the bottom of the ridge because she heard Agent 341 on the radio "and he said he got hit."

"I was trying to make my way down to the ridge to make my way up to him to see if he was OK," Borjas explained, adding that she took cover "in that rock" and she was "trying not to make noise."

Borjas calculated that by descending on the south side of the ridge, she would have a better, safer path back to Johnson. She was keenly aware the suspects could still be nearby. Walking up near the saddle seemed to be dangerous. She believed that there was nobody below her on the south slope. It would be safer to approach from a point farther down from the saddle.

"So it was taking me awhile," she said. "And then at that point that's when I just heard Omaha so then I got on the radio and told them my location."

This appears to be an honest statement from a young woman who had just faced the most momentous scenario of her life. She admitted that she ran for cover. That is something of which she undoubtedly would not be proud. Everything she said would mesh with the testimony of her fellow agent and much of the evidence collected later. Nothing she said would clash with any of the evidence.

"After the shooting stopped, and you were trying to maneuver to go assist with the agent, did you, did you hear or see any of the suspects?" FBI Agent Edlund asked.

"I could hear them like whispering but I couldn't make out anything, I was, I mean, I was probably in shock," Borjas said.

"So if you heard them whispering, so they weren't too far away from you?" FBI Agent Jennings asked.

"Yeah, I guess not, 'cause I could hear them, so that was why I was trying to go way down," Borjas said.

"Was it Spanish or English?" Jennings asked.

"I don't know; I couldn't figure it out," Borjas said. "The shooting just happened, so I was, I was trying to calm myself down and calm my breathing down so I wouldn't make noise."

Apparently responding to Borjas's distraught emotional state, Serino said to the other interviewers, "I think, oh crap, I think we have enough information right now, right?"

"Yeah," an unidentified interviewer said.

Serino said that maybe Agent Borjas could set up a session with a counselor from the Employee Assistance Program.

"He came in earlier," Borjas said.

Jennings asked Serino if the Border Patrol would take her weapon and run checks on it. Serino said he would take it.

Sergeant Gijanto told Agent Borjas that typically "a lot of people in critical incidents" might recall events with more detail 48 to 72 hours later. He said that because "your brain kind of goes into self-defense mode" at the time of the incident, typically she should remember more details later.

"Yes, sir," Borjas said.

"OK, please feel free to come forward and contact somebody and provide that information, even if you are not sure you know what's real information," Gijanto said.

The detective sergeant urged her to bring more facts forward, even if she was unsure about them, and to let investigators "sort it out with the facts that we find on the scene."

He told her that in two or three days she might remember some details differently. She should not be afraid of possibly having conflicting statements. It was normal to remember things differently after a short passage of time.

"It happens with every officer-involved shooting I've been involved with," Gijanto said. "You know, typically people change their statements. They remember different things. So don't think that's unusual or that somebody is going to question you 'cause your statements are changing. OK?"

Borjas responded affirmatively.

But the FBI was in charge of the investigation, and they would not interview her again for nine more days. That would be after they had reached a conclusion that contradicted her testimony.

As the FBI agents had almost completed their portion of the interview with Borjas, the officers from the various agencies exchanged contact information and engaged in conversation about new FBI supervisors in the area.

BP Supervisor Serino said that he thought that four Border Patrol agents would be coming over from Tucson, the agency's section headquarters. Those arriving agents would bring with them equipment to process and map the shooting scene. Serino told the FBI agents that his Critical Incident Team (CIT) had usually processed crime scenes in the past for a specific FBI supervisory agent who worked in the Bureau's Tucson office.

FBI Agent Jennings said he wanted to know why the job of processing this crime scene was assigned to the Border Patrol.

"I did. I told them to," FBI Agent Edlund said.

Serino asked the FBI agents if they had heard any updates on the condition of Agent Johnson.

"Last thing I heard he was going into surgery . . . minutes ago," an unknown person responded.

Sergeant Gijanto then asked Borjas if she had seen the other agents or their injuries after the shooting.

"No. Well, I flew with 341, and he was just holding himself . . . his butt cheeks," Borjas said.

Summary of the First Borjas Interview

Three and a half hours after the shooting incident, Borjas told interviewers, including two FBI agents, her recollection of what had just occurred. She said she heard yelling as she approached the saddle, followed by shooting. She saw muzzle flashes from a long firearm, which one of the suspects was shooting in front of her. Agent Borjas saw three or four suspects at the scene. She never saw Agent Ivie at the scene, before or after the gunfire. She said she saw his light as he approached the saddle, but "didn't see him face to face."

After the shooting stopped, she ran down the slope, away from the saddle. She heard people whispering, but she was not sure whether it was in Spanish or English. She could not hear what they said. She tried to be as quiet as possible, trying to calm her breathing in order not to make any sounds that might lead to detection by the suspects.

When she heard on her radio that her partner had been shot, she ran farther down the mountain, hoping to make her way back to help him from a lower elevation. She hid behind a rock on the mountain.

When she heard a helicopter overhead, she contacted it by radio and told the crew where she was located. That helicopter landed nearby on the ridge and evacuated her and Agent Johnson from the mountain.

The two FBI agents, the Border Patrol supervisor, and the sheriff's sergeant all heard eyewitness testimony that placed several unknown suspects at the shooting scene, one of whom was firing a long firearm. Agent Borjas never expressed any doubt as to what she saw and heard regarding the several suspects and the one who was firing a long weapon.

Her testimony during the interview was consistent with what she told the Border Patrol supervisor who found her on the mountain shortly after the shooting.

An FBI Agent Puts a Slant on Agent Borjas's Interview

After the interview was completed, and after it was transcribed at the Cochise County Sheriff's Office the following day, FBI Special Agent Chad Richard Edlund, one of the two FBI agents in the room when Agent Borjas was interviewed, filed a report that inaccurately represented what Borjas had said.[3]

The FBI report turned her testimony from something crystal clear, involving three or four suspects she saw, one of whom brandished a long firearm, to a watered-down mess. If the suspects who shot Agent Ivie were to be apprehended and tried for their crimes, Agent Edlund's report could be used by a defense attorney to try to confuse jurors.

According to Edlund's witness statement, a *302* in FBI parlance, "BORJAS said **she may have heard** three or four people whispering at that point (after the gunfire stopped). **She never saw anyone** and could not tell if the suspects were speaking English or Spanish."

It is true that Borjas heard suspects whispering after the gunfire stopped.

But **she never at any time said she *heard* three or four suspects.**

In fact, **Agent Borjas twice said she *saw* three or four suspects.**

"How many suspects did you see?" BP Agent Serino had asked her during her interview.

"Uh, maybe three or four, I'm not too sure," she replied.

A couple of minutes later, Serino asked for information that might help in the search for suspects.

"You say that you saw maybe three or four?" Serino asked.

"Yes, uh hum," Borjas replied.

Why in the world would an FBI agent omit this from his synopsis of the interview? **Instead of reporting that she said—and reiterated—that she *saw* three or four suspects, he falsely reported that she "said she may have *heard* three or four whispering."**

We could accept this as an innocent error if this were the only glaring mistake in this report.

However, another important detail is distorted in exactly the same way.

Remember how Agent Borjas said that the suspects had a long arm and possibly a pistol? That also was very important, especially considering that suspects would be arrested a few hours after her interview with a rifle and a revolver.

"And **from what I kept seeing** from how the [sic], they were the rounds were coming, that **they had a long arm also**," Borjas said.

FBI Agent Edlund was paying close attention at this time during the interview, because he jumped in with a question.

"Multiple or single?" Edlund asked.

"Uhm, a **single long arm**," Borjas said. "I think, I just, we didn't have our lights on, so (inaudible)."

"Did you see any other weapon?" Serino asked.

"Ah, when I took cover uhm, I might of [sic] seen like a little flash like a pistol," Borjas said. "But I can't exactly say I saw like . . . I kind of saw like a shiny part so, so what I saw specifically was a long arm from the way it was coming out, the rounds were coming out."

A trained, honest law enforcement officer would naturally include in a summary of this interview that the Border Patrol agent said she saw three or four suspects and saw them firing a long arm and possibly also saw someone with a pistol.

But instead, **this FBI agent** *omitted* **any mention of her** *seeing* **any suspects as well as her** *seeing* **suspects firing a long firearm and possibly also brandishing a handgun.**

When Agent Edlund's report did mention something about a long firearm, the way it was written would carry no evidentiary value in a criminal case.

"Borjas believed a long gun was used due to the rapid succession of gunfire, and based on her previous training with firearms," Edlund wrote.

Once again, he failed to mention what Agent Borjas reported that **she** *saw* **the long firearm.**

She never said she believed it was a long gun based on the rapidity of the bullets firing toward her or because she had training that taught her to differentiate firearms by the sounds they made while being shot at from close range.

FBI Agent Edlund did not report the truth—that Agent Borjas said she *saw* **a long firearm—but instead that she** *believed* **it was a firearm based on some nonexistent training.**

Agent Borjas was never asked about what kind of firearm **it sounded like** during her interview. She had **positively identified one weapon by sight,** while stating that she possibly also saw another weapon. It was apparent that she was being honest when she said she saw a long arm—with a degree of certainty—yet she admitted that she was not certain about the glimpse she caught of a shiny pistol.

Let's summarize this twisting of Agent Borjas's testimony into something unrecognizable: **The FBI agent did not report on the two most important things she said: that she** *saw* **three or four suspects, and that she** *saw* **one shooting a long firearm and another possibly brandishing a pistol.**

He also failed to report another extremely important element of her interview—that she said she *heard* **suspects whispering:**

"I could hear them like whispering, but I couldn't make out anything, I was, I mean, I was probably in shock," Borjas said.

Instead Agent Edlund wrote that she *may* **have heard three or four suspects whispering and** *believed* **a long gun had been shot.**

The FBI agent turned her from a reliable *eye*witness into an unreliable *ear*witness. The young Border Patrol Agent would not be qualified by a courtroom judge to testify as an expert witness in identifying firearms by the sounds they make. No competent defense attorney would let pass, without objection, testimony about identifying a specific firearm by hearing alone—while being fired upon during an ambush at close range.

When a witness testifies in court, it is important that she have some degree of certainty about what she saw or heard. If the suspects were to be caught and prosecuted, this FBI report would serve only to help the defense.

There is much solid eyewitness testimony in Agent Borjas's interview—but none of it is reflected in the FBI report.

Why not just report what she actually said?

What Agent Borjas actually reported sharply contradicted the narrative the FBI would release to the public three days after the shooting—the same day this FBI report was filed.

Was it just a coincidence that this report shows her as an ineffective witness, who was not certain about anything, **an agent who attempted to identify a firearm by its sound** instead of sight, and **never saw anyone**?

In all fairness to the agent who wrote this report, it is unclear whether the final draft report was the work of the agent—or whether it had been edited by an FBI supervisor.

8

Treasure Trove of
Evidence of Smugglers

"Two Mexican currency coins were discovered amid the area where the .40 caliber casings were located," Sheriff's Detective John Monroe wrote in his incident report. "The coins, one with a nickel finish and one with a copper finish, did not appear to show any signs of weathering."

Monday, October 2, 7:00 a.m.
Remax Saddle, Mule Mountains

A contingent of Border Patrol officers and sheriff's deputies stood watch over the crime scene through the brightly moonlit early morning hours. They waited patiently for daybreak, when they would be relieved of their guard duty by crime scene investigators.

It was a solemn watch, with the body of their fallen comrade lying on the ground during all those hours, right next to where he had fallen forward when slain.

At the command post near the gravel pit, just south of Remax Saddle, Ray Vogt, leader of the BP Critical Incident Team, announced the members of the team who were selected to process the crime scene and take over scene security: FBI Agent Brent Templeton, BP Critical Incident Team (CIT) agents Carey Daniel and Brian Levin, and CCSO Detective John Monroe.

Their assignment was to gather physical evidence, take photographs, and create maps, in order to help other investigators, prosecutors, family members, and the general public understand what occurred early that morning. These men were well-trained, diligent investigators who sifted through the terrain and produced documents essential to the discovery of the facts of the shooting incident.

Before the crime scene team began its work, an elite Border Patrol tactical (BORTAC) squad arrived by helicopter to ensure that no more dangerous assailants were in the area.

There were already several BP agents and sheriff's deputies standing guard on a perimeter, which extended to the helicopter landing zone west of Remax Saddle, established to evacuate the surviving agents. Now that the sun had brought light to the mountain ridge, one more intensive sweep was in order, just in case there still remained some dangerous smugglers hiding nearby.

After the BORTAC agents completed their sweep, the officers who had kept watch as moonlight gave way to sunrise, shortly after 6:00 a.m., were relieved of their duties, just as a Black Hawk helicopter brought the crime scene investigators to the mile-high ridge.

BP Acting Supervisor Robert Edwards had been on the mountain since about 2:00 a.m. He documented the arrival of the first wave of replacements.

"At about 7:00 a.m., a team of BORTAC Agents were dropped off in the landing zone and conducted a search of the area around the scene to ensure it was safe for the investigation team," Edwards wrote in his report. "With the BORTAC team there was a Critical Incident Team (CIT) member and an F.B.I Agent.

"The CIT agent and F.B.I. agent approached our position around 7:15 a.m. and began asking questions about the scene. We gave the CIT agent our names and star number [sic] and gave a summary of what we saw as we arrived.

"Sometime soon thereafter additional investigators arrived on the scene along with CIT Supervisor Raymond Vogt. Agent Vogt again asked for a brief summary of the scene and took custody of all weapons involved in the incident."

The weapons remaining at the scene were the H&K P 2000 service pistols of Agent Ivie and Agent Johnson, as well as Agent Johnson's M4 carbine.

A contingent of law enforcement officers worked diligently to document every piece of evidence that would help tell the story of what occurred when the three courageous Border Patrol agents encountered the stealthy smugglers on the silent mountain ridge. The officers were dedicated to performing their important roles in this tragic event, which resulted in the loss of life of one of their highly esteemed brothers.

Detective John Monroe of the Cochise County Sheriff's Office wrote a detailed account of what the crime scene investigators discovered. In addition to his important written document on the scene, he contributed to the incident record by taking photographs of the scene and the surrounding environment.

Monroe wrote that he was contacted by phone at about 2:25 a.m. on October 2 and told that Detective Sergeant Gijanto wanted him to stand by while information was being gathered on a "possible ambush of U.S. Border Patrol agents."[1]

When he arrived at the command post at about 4:30 a.m., Monroe was informed on the details of the shooting of the agents. He was also told that an uninjured agent was being debriefed at the Naco Border Patrol station. A fellow sheriff's detective told Detective Monroe that BP agents were patrolling the general area "and tracking foot sign heading south."

The most skilled Border Patrol trackers in the area had been brought in to track the killers.

When the crime scene investigators arrived at the scene, they asked the officers who had been guarding the scene "if any of them had done anything, deliberately or accidentally, to alter the scene," Monroe wrote in his report.

They were told that Agent Ivie "had been found face down and had been rolled, left to right, to check on his condition. When it became apparent he had died, they left him in that position (face up)."

The only other change reported to the team was that Agent Johnson's duty belt was secured when the agents set up the perimeter because his sidearm was in the holster.

A major change at the crime scene that was apparently not reported to the investigative team was that Agent Ivie's pistol was moved from where it had been found by BP Agent McWhorter. It is understandable that it was moved from its original place, because it would not have been advisable to leave it there for anybody to pick up at that time. However, I could not find in the written record an explanation as to why it was moved from the spot Agent McWhorter said he placed it to where it was found when the crime scene was later mapped.

Information regarding Agent Ivie's service pistol is critical to the complete understanding of what occurred. There is ample evidence that his pistol was fired, but no evidence has been uncovered that proved that Agent Ivie ever fired his pistol.

Border Patrol agents were ordered to write up reports on their involvement with this important investigation.

"All departing agents were advised by (BP CIT) Agent Vogt that they would have to provide memos of their actions from arrival to departure of the scene," Monroe wrote in his report.

One staging area was set up on the high ground near the west side of the saddle, which is roughly the length of a football field, and two-thirds of its width. Another position for surveillance was established on the rise just east of the site.

"From these positions they were able to view approaches from the west and east of the saddle, as well as uphill approaches from the north and south," Monroe wrote.

Six hours after the ambush, there was still a sense of uneasiness on the mountain ridge. Was this an isolated incident, or was that ambush the beginning of a new phase of extreme violence against the Border Patrol by the cartel?

There were frequent threats of assassinations of agents, designed to intimidate them. Occasionally cartels would announce bounties for killing specific federal agents. Agents were keenly aware that they were interacting on a regular basis with individuals associated with ruthless mass murderers. Although most of the cartel violence occurred south of the border, there were plenty of violent crimes committed throughout the United States by individuals associated with the Mexican cartels and their illegal enterprises.

Plastic Water Jugs were Dropped Recently

The Remax Saddle shooting scene was divided into three sections, Monroe wrote. The "process team" began its initial sweep at the southeast corner, searching for evidence from there to the western edge of the saddle.

In the section identified as the "southern third," there were multiple items found, "consistent with a smuggling route/bed-down area," including empty drink bottles, food wrappers, and empty metal containers.

There was a "heavily used trail running north/south, which passes through the middle of the saddle." The officers also found "a lesser used trail, possibly older, which ran southwest/northeast up to the saddle."

This section, which included the adjoining southern slope of the mountain, included trails leading to the international border.

The "middle third" section contained a great deal of potential forensic evidence, including spent shell casings, possibly from Agent Johnson's rifle, and **shoe prints identified as not belonging to law enforcement.**

Three plastic drink bottles with blood on them were found along a trail of blood, which was believed to be from an individual descending in a southerly direction.

The bottles were consistent with those used by illegal border-crossers—and never used by Border Patrol agents. The blood trail was consistent with the route Agent Johnson took between when he was shot and when he took his final defensive position. Those water bottles were likely hurriedly dropped by the smugglers, along the same route Johnson used to retreat after he was shot.

Items found in the middle section were also "consistent with a smuggling route/bed-down area," as were the items found in both of the other sections. **Items found in the middle and northern section appeared to be "fresh," or recently left at the scene,** Monroe wrote in his report.

"Some of these items, drink bottles and food wrappers, appeared fresh, as the bottles contained liquid/condensation and the wrappers showed no signs of exposure to the elements."

In other words, the bottles were almost certainly dropped there after sundown—by the smugglers involved in the ambush of the three agents. They still contained liquid, which would not be left in a bottle by smugglers— unless they left the scene in a hurry. Every drop of water was precious in the desert. If the bottles were from an earlier time frame, the liquid would have evaporated by then.

For the bottles to be in the exact spot where Johnson could have tripped over them would tend to indicate they had been dropped on the trail just shortly before Johnson retreated in that direction.

It is possible that the smugglers were heading south toward the border— when they saw the two agents approaching. Perhaps they then retreated toward the saddle, dropping their nearly empty water jugs along the way.

The number of jugs also coincides with the approximate number of suspects seen by Agent Borjas.

Monroe's report says that a black nylon "under belt," used with a patrol duty belt, with four black nylon keepers (used to clip the under belt to the duty belt), and a pair of black gloves were found in the "middle section" of the shooting scene.

"It was learned these items belonged to Agent Johnson," Monroe wrote.

There was a blood trail that ran north to south between near the high ground of the saddle to where the under belt was observed.

"The blood drops are small at the north end of the trail and grow larger as the trail goes down the slope to the under belt location. Splatter patterns on some of the blood drops indicate source was moving (south) down the hill."

This blood trail corroborates the account Agent Johnson would later give the FBI.

The three plastic bottles with blood on them were from the area of the blood trail and the under belt.

Agent Johnson's green Border Patrol uniform hat was found near his under belt.

Six spent rifle casings, believed to be .223 caliber, were found on the ground. Three were clustered about five feet east of the under belt. The other three spent casings were in a line east of and parallel to the blood trail running north and south. Those casings were about five or 10 feet from the blood trail.

The placement of the shell casings tended to affirm that Johnson had been shooting south to north, as other evidence also tended to indicate. His weapon ejected shell casings to the right.

Examination of Johnson's rifle showed one round in the chamber and 21 rounds in the magazine, Monroe wrote.

Shoe Prints Could be the Ones Agent Ivie Saw

At the scene were found "several shoe prints that we were not able to identify as from a responder. **One print was of higher interest because the sole pattern was not associated with any type of footwear worn by responders.**"

Agent Ivie reported on his radio shortly before he was killed that he had just seen signs that could have been from the same suspects as the signs he had seen on the trail below. The footprints seen at the saddle by the crime scene investigators were possibly the same ones Ivie had seen a few hours earlier.

The crime scene team found evidence that marijuana smugglers had been at the saddle.

Officers found three areas where indentations were made by "heavy rectangular objects that had been set down," Monroe wrote.

"These indentations were consistent with double bundles of marijuana, commonly used by smugglers in the area," he wrote in his report. "Two locations were on the opposite sides of a medium-sized bush. The third was at the base of a small tree."

Monroe wrote that it is "common practice to hide bundles while smugglers rest nearby. This is most common in saddles and ridge tops as the smugglers rest from walking up before going down the other side."

Each of the indentation locations had "a long stick which appeared to be used as markers for hidden bundles. These sticks were observed at each indentation location and were placed nearby, and parallel to, the indentation spots."

Had Agent Ivie seen these sticks? If so, it is possible he shone his flashlight into one of the hiding places, discovering a bundle, a smuggler, or both. Three sticks standing up at the saddle would have been a dead giveaway for ongoing or recent smuggling activity, which Ivie might have seen.

Here is one possible scenario: The smugglers had lain up at the saddle with the dope some hours earlier, then dropped it down near the highway, leaving the marking sticks in place. They were hiking back toward the border when they saw agents coming toward them from the south. Then they retreated to the saddle, dropping their near-empty jugs just below it. When they arrived at the saddle, they realized they were being squeezed by an agent approaching from the north. Then they went into hiding.

During a second sweep through the shooting scene, Monroe "observed a small mesquite tree with an apparent bullet hole in one of its branches." It appeared to be a small hole, possibly a .223 caliber.

The tree was in between the location where Ivie was found and "the north end of the blood trail."

It is believed that Johnson was wounded at the north end of the blood trail. "Based on lead streaking in the hole from the round, it appeared the round had traveled from south to north," Monroe wrote.

This was a possible indicator of the trajectory of one of the shots fired by Agent Johnson. Some or all of the shots fired toward Agent Johnson likely originated near Agent Ivie's body. It makes perfect sense that Agent Johnson was shooting toward muzzle flashes originating close to the location of Agent Ivie's body.

Members of the Border Patrol Critical Incident Team mapped the scene, using the *Total Station* system. That is an electronic instrument that surveys a scene to assist in mapping it out. After a map was made of the terrain, the team recorded the location of each item that had been marked by the processing team, Monroe wrote.

One Fatal Shot to Agent Ivie's Forehead

The body of Agent Ivie was lying in the northern section of the saddle, on the side of the saddle nearest to Remax Trail, which he had used during his ascent.

When the crime scene investigators arrived, the body of Agent Ivie was face up, "with his head pointing south and feet pointing north," Monroe wrote. "His left hand was in a position of an open grip as if holding an object. . . . His right arm was straight out to his side perpendicular to body axis. His right hand was also in a position of an open grip. His flashlight was next to his right hand.

"Agent Ivie had one small diameter entrance hole in the middle of his forehead, just above the eyebrow line. Blood appeared to have come out of his ears, nose and mouth. No other injuries were observable."

Later in the day, Agent Ivie's body was rolled onto his side "so we could examine his back side and the ground beneath," Monroe wrote. "No exit wound was observed on the back of his head, nor was there any other injury observed on the back side of his body."

Investigators did not find any evidence beneath his body.

Agent Ivie suffered one fatal bullet wound to the middle of his forehead. Although crime scene investigators did not annotate any other injuries on his fully clothed body, several other injuries were later discovered at the medical examiner's office.

During the first sweep through the crime scene, "after Agent Ivie had been visually examined and aerial photography had been accomplished, we cleared his body for removal," Monroe wrote.

Randy Wilson, a detective with the sheriff's office, obtained clearance with the Pima County Medical Examiner's Office to transport the body to its office in Tucson.

It was not noted in this report what time the body was "cleared for removal." It was written elsewhere that Agent Ivie's body remained in place at the saddle until about 12:30 p.m.—11 hours after the agent's death.

There was no explanation in this report—or in any other document I examined—as to why the body remained at the saddle for that length of time. It is abnormal to leave the body of any homicide victim in place for many extra hours after it has been photographed and all evidence processed.

Agent Ivie's body "was placed in a body bag and then strapped into a Stokes litter," Monroe's report said. "Agent Ivie was carried by team members to the helicopter landing zone and placed on the helicopter. Agent Ivie was then flown to the Pima County Medical Examiner's Office."

Both of Agent Ivie's spare pistol magazines were found in their pouches on his duty belt. The magazines were later examined and shown to each contain the full capacity of 12 rounds.

The only items that were not "in their holders" were his flashlight and service pistol.

"His radio was still on and operating," Monroe wrote.

About two feet east of Agent Ivie's head there was a "large pool of congealing blood."

"This location was consistent with where his head would have been prior to responding agents rolling him," Monroe wrote.

"Approximately ten spent .40 caliber shell casings were located south/southwest of Agent Ivie's head. These spent casings were clustered in an approximate three-foot by three-foot area.

"This would have placed the casings approximately 4–5 feet west/ southwest from his original position."

To clarify this important detail, the shell casings found on the ground near Agent Ivie were four to five feet away from the original position of his head, when he was found face down. They were in front of and to the right side of his head, as his head was facing down, where he had fallen forward. His head was toward the south, his feet toward the north.

The location of the shell casings, and what was found with them, are two important clues as to what occurred. His service pistol would have ejected shell casings backward and to the right.

"Two Mexican currency coins were discovered amid the area where the .40 caliber casings were located," Monroe wrote in his incident report. "The coins, one with a nickel finish and one with a copper finish, did not appear to show any signs of weathering."

When Ivie's service pistol and magazine were examined later, one cartridge was in the pistol's chamber and two were in the magazine.

"These rounds plus the ten spent .40 caliber casings found near Agent Ivie's body complete the 37-round compliment [sic] USBP agents normally field," Monroe wrote.

The 10 shell casings found in front of Ivie's body were likely ejected from his weapon during the incident. However, no evidence has been presented to establish the identity of the shooter of his pistol.

Evidence such as the position of the shell casings in relation to his body and circumstances surrounding his murder tend to point in another direction. If Agent Ivie was shot to death at the outset of this incident, it is unlikely that he ever fired his pistol.

If Agent Ivie had been firing his pistol from the place in which he was standing or kneeling before he was shot in the head, the shell casings would not have been found in front of his head.

One of the injuries Agent Ivie sustained on his hand indicated a possible struggle for his weapon. Some of the evidence suggests that one of the smugglers fired Ivie's service pistol from near Agent Ivie's body, after wresting it away from him.

During a second sweep of the scene, to search for more possible evidence and assist in the production of crime scene maps, an FBI Evidence Recovery Team (ERT), led by Agent Scott Hunter, established an area for processing evidence within the staging area. Hunter was briefed by Agent Vogt and Sergeant Gijanto on what had occurred before he arrived.

"After the ERT (Evidence Recovery Team) had completed setting up in the staging area, they began to collect the evidence we had marked," Monroe wrote, adding that Total Station is used to survey a scene to produce maps. "No marked evidence was collected without ensuring it had been photographed and mapped first."

During this phase of the investigation, "CIT members began mapping the scene using a 'Total Station' system," Monroe wrote, adding that *Total Station* is an electronic, optical instrument used to survey a scene in order to produce maps.

The CIT members first established the basic outline of the scene, including the locations of stationery items, such as trees. Then the evidentiary items—such as shell casings, water bottles, and items left behind by Agent Johnson—were added to the maps. As those items were located, their locations were recorded, to be mapped by the crime scene-processing team.

After every item of evidence had been photographed where it was found and its location recorded for placement on maps, the items were taken to the evidence processing area. Once the removable evidence had been collected, the scene was cleared of all individuals, so a third sweep could be made by the original scene-processing team.

"This sweep consisted of ensuring all previously marked pieces of evidence had been collected and, using visual scanning and a metal detector, ensuring no other evidence/items of interest had been missed," Monroe wrote.

No other evidence was found during the third and final sweep.

K-9 Team Deployed to Hunt for Guns and Shell Casings

As the agents returned to the staging area to retrieve their personal gear before departing, another special Border Patrol unit arrived on the scene to search the southern slope of the mountain, just below the saddle. This was the area where the two surviving agents had been found after the shooting incident.

A K-9 team, trained in detection of weapons and ammunition, was deployed by this unit, Monroe wrote in his report. The K-9 team was employed by the police department of Oro Valley, a northern Tucson suburb.

After the FBI Evidence Recovery Team completed the process of bagging and tagging the evidence, those involved in the crime scene investigation proceeded to the landing zone. They were then transported by helicopters to the command post.

Evidence collected from the scene, according to the FBI evidence report, included two Mexican coins, two empty Powerade bottles, a cut corner baggie (normally used for drug possession), a cigarette butt, and seven empty plastic bottles, three of which had a "red substance" on them. There were food package items, including an empty Jumex (Mexican drink) can, a potato chip bag, and yellow and pink snack wrappers.

A tree branch with a hole in it was entered into evidence. Six .223 caliber shell casings (from Agent Johnson's rifle) and 10 .40 caliber shell casings (from Agent Ivie's pistol) were recovered.

Impressions of three ground depressions made by marijuana bundles were made, as well as two boot impressions and one shoe impression.

The thoroughness of the evidence collection showed that the crime scene investigators hoped to connect those items to possible suspects, a critical element in a case that could result in the conviction of the killers. This is something that is normally done in every homicide investigation.

9

Daring Capture of Armed Suspects in Mexico

"We watched the BORTAC helicopter land in Mexico. They got permission very quickly to land in Mexico and to hold the suspects there until the Mexican officials got there."—An eyewitness account of the capture of armed suspects.

Tuesday, October 2, about 9 a.m.
South of the border fence, near the shooting scene

As FBI agents conducted the crime scene investigation on the Remax Saddle, an unusual scene was unfolding just beyond the international border fence, three-and-a-half miles to the south.

Two armed Mexican suspects, residents of Agua Prieta, were taken into custody by BORTAC agents, who made a dramatic helicopter landing just south of the border fence.

It is rare for U.S. Border Patrol agents to make an incursion into Mexican territory in pursuit of suspects, so agents who were stationed nearby were surprised to witness this event as it unfolded.

The account by an agent on the scene—the first eyewitness account to be published of this important event—was largely verified by reports in several media outlets.

However, those media accounts lack the details provided to this author by an eyewitness. The majority of agents and officers who were on the scene during the hours following the shooting have chosen to remain silent about what they saw and heard. There were certainly many others keenly aware of this monumental development in the case—something the FBI has never publicly acknowledged.

There was immediate suppression of the speech of federal officers by their supervisors, under penalty of disciplinary action and possible criminal prosecution for anyone who spoke out about the case—except to back the government version.

But local, national, and international media outlets reported on the story of the arrest of these two suspects, confirming some of the details provided by this agent.

A Mexican news outlet based in the nearby Sonoran city of Cananea would refer to the arrested suspects as the "killers of the Naco Border Patrol agent." A story by a British newspaper, which covered the arrest of the Mexican suspects, carried a headline that said that Agent Ivie had been shot by a drug cartel. The *Los Angeles Times* published a story that included details of the specific firearms seized on or near those suspects.

Border Patrol Agent Andrew Carlton was deployed near the border, along with his partner, about four hours after the shooting incident. Carlton was a friend of Nick Ivie's. Carlton and his partner were deployed near the line to try to locate possible suspects who might still be in the area, trying to make their way back to Mexico.

"Naco had its entire horse patrol out there. They had us spread out over as much of that area as we could cover," Carlton said of the saturation coverage by law enforcement the morning of the shooting.

There was a line of Border Patrol agents all along the border, some on foot and others in vehicles.

Agents, including expert trackers, were seeking signs, such as footprints in the area.

"They were tracking sign from the saddle Nick was shot in, and it was headed west by southwest," Carlton said, referring to fresh footprints on a trail. "They were trying to get us south of them and set up. They didn't know how far behind they were on the sign."

It was impossible to know exactly when those tracks were made, but agents were sent to the border in case the individuals who made them were still up north.

In the early morning hours, immediately following the shooting, the sky was filled with aircraft deployed to find the suspects who had shot the agents.

"One of the high-flying, fixed-wing aircrafts, I think it was a Predator (drone), got a visual of a couple of bodies in Mexico," Carlton said.

Normally Border Patrol agents do not enter Mexico, but this was not a normal operation.

"We watched the BORTAC helicopter land in Mexico," Carlton said. "They got permission very quickly to land in Mexico and hold the subjects there until the Mexican officials got there. The guys we were with in the field even said, 'Wow, that got approved very quickly.' That is not a decision they can make at the station level."

Carlton was standing in the bed of his pickup truck, about 50 yards north of the border, when the helicopter landed on the other side of the 12-foot-tall, slatted metal border fence.

"We were out in Grid Seven," Carlton recalled, identifying the border area, which includes the saddle where the agents were shot. "It's the smuggler's tunnel area; it's just a landmark. It's by where the railbed goes through. We were up on the two tracks, west of the Christiansen house."

The Christiansen ranch house was unoccupied at that time. It sits about a quarter mile north of the border, southeast of the saddle. There were numerous easy crossing points in the vicinity, including some low fences and periodically wide-open flood gates.

Even the highest fences in the area were climbed easily by cartel mules. Some smugglers could shimmy up one side and drop down the other within a matter of seconds. Others would use portable rope ladders, if necessary.

Carlton and other agents were standing at elevated positions, peering through high-powered binoculars, because Border Patrol supervisors had told them that members of the group that had attacked the three agents were still at large.

"They just didn't know which way they went," Carlton said. "So, we were scanning around, looking with our binoculars. And we were in the bed of our truck to get higher elevation."

But when the helicopter made its landing beyond the slatted fence, Carlton and his partners put down their binoculars.

"We weren't using binoculars to watch the helicopter. We were close enough that we were just watching it. So it wasn't very far into Mexico at all."

Carlton said that it was a short time, just about 15 or 20 minutes, between the time the drone surveilled the suspects on the other side of the fence and the order was given to the helicopter crew carrying the tactical Border Patrol agents to "Go get them."

"Somebody at a very high level was paying attention to what was going on," Carlton said. "That is not normally allowed. That is not any kind of normal situation. It had to be coordinated between someone who was at a very high level in the United States and approval from Mexico."

Border Patrol officials work with Mexican authorities on a regular basis, Carlton said. It normally takes weeks just to get routine operations approved and scheduled. So, it was stunning to the agents who witnessed the helicopter landing that permission was given so rapidly to cross into Mexican territory in order to apprehend suspects.

"Even if you wanted to take liaison officers and get them on the south side of the fence, with an escort, to go do a fence inspection, that takes a long time, and that's something that is done on a fairly regular basis," Carlton said. "It takes time to get that coordinated and to get it approved.

"So, for armed helicopters to go into Mexico (chuckles), and land in Mexico, somebody was paying attention to what was going on from the very beginning, somebody at an incredibly high level, to get that pushed through in that time frame."

Carlton said there was no way that even the section chief in Tucson, a prestigious position because of the strategic location of that duty station, would have had the authority to order an armed incursion into Mexico.

"They don't have any authority to fly into international air space like that," Carlton said. "I think they may have been coordinating with someone in D.C. But historically, the Border Patrol is kind of a nonentity as far as politics go. They're not political movers, they're not climbers. It's not one of your D.C. sexy jobs. You're a desert rat. That's what we've always been.

"And we don't have any kind of political pull. The big thing is not just that a helicopter went into Mexico. Because they do that. American aircraft have the ability to fly into Mexico a certain distance, without registering anything with Mexico."

Aircraft at the nearby Douglas Municipal Airport routinely use Mexican airspace for takeoffs and landings.

"But the people on board being armed is a huge deal. That's the part that had to have approval. And you can't just call, like a Border Patrol section chief can't call his counterpart in Mexico and get approval. That has to come from a much higher level.

"To go down and detain people in Mexico, armed. The scale of that is astronomical, when you see the other political red tape we have to go through for anything."

Because Americans are accustomed to seeing armed law enforcement officers arresting people, it might not seem like anything unusual that Border Patrol agents would apprehend people just across the border after the killing of an agent, Carlton said.

"But to do that on an international scale and crossing a border, that's a big deal. And for that to get approved in a very short time, as it was happening, is a very big deal."

Border Patrol supervisors later told Carlton and other agents that "A helicopter never went into Mexico," Carlton said.

"We watched it," the agents told their supervisors.

The BORTAC agents who landed in Mexico were approved to apprehend two suspects, search them, and turn them over to Mexican authorities. That is exactly what they did, Carlton said.

"But they were specifically prohibited from collecting evidence," Carlton said, adding that he heard those orders on his radio, along with other communications.

The BORTAC agents ignored those orders.

"When the helicopter lifted off and returned back to the U.S. side, they said, 'Oh, we happened to collect some electronic evidence. Who do we turn it over to?'" Carlton recalled.

Carlton and the other agents who were stationed just north of the border, were glad that the tactical agents did collect evidence, as they followed those developments on their radios.

"We kind of got a kick out of it, that they were specifically told not to and that they did anyways," Carlton said, adding he believed they possibly retrieved cell phones. "We have no idea who they turned it over to."

Carlton said Border Patrol supervisors initially told agents, including himself, that there were illegal aliens at the shooting scene.

That accounted for the massive deployment, which included law enforcement officers from several other federal and local agencies.

But supervisors later informed the agents that "There were never any bodies up there," and "the bodies they caught in Mexico weren't the correct bodies."

Carlton was referring to those two suspects whose apprehension he and other agents witnessed.

Border Patrol officials later "completely denied" to the line agents and horse patrol agents that any evidence was collected from the suspects who were arrested.

"In our muster meetings, where they were giving us updates on the case, they just flat out said, 'That never happened.' It was the most blatant, obvious thing I can remember," Carlton said.

Carlton recalled that he challenged a supervisor during one meeting.

"I said, 'I was in the field. I know it happened.'"

"They said, 'Oh no. It didn't.'"

Carlton said he was aware that there was something unusual about the way this case was being handled—as early as the day of the shooting.

The two suspects were apprehended, turned over to the Mexican military, then remanded to the custody of Mexican civilian authorities and held in a jail in Hermosillo, the capital city of Sonora. News reports said the suspects were arrested with firearms and narcotics.

The agent said that after the BORTAC agents apprehended the suspects, they were turned over to Mexican officials.

"Our station management told us they were being interviewed by U.S. officials," the agent said.

Because the FBI was responsible for investigating all shootings involving federal agencies, the agent said he believed it was most likely that the Bureau was the agency that interviewed the suspects in Mexico.

Another agent who knew Agent Ivie also told me that he heard from agents on the scene that the arrest of the two suspects had occurred.

"Border Patrol agents in a helicopter landed in Mexico," that agent said in an interview in June 2017. "They apprehended the two suspects, turned them over to the Mexican Army. They had a rifle and a handgun."

The FBI subsequently interviewed the two suspects and collected DNA and fingerprint evidence from them. The arrests of the two men were reported in the U.S. media, but the fact that the FBI interviewed them was never released to the media or to the public in any official statement. The names of those suspects were never reported by any U.S. media outlets, but one Mexican news outlet published their names.

A controversial 2013 article credited to former Border Patrol official Ron Coburn, stated that **three other suspects were arrested on the U.S. side of the border, one-and-a-half miles south of the shooting scene, a few hours after the shooting occurred.**[1]

No other information on the arrests of those three suspects has surfaced in the numerous media or law enforcement reports I have seen.

If the smugglers crossed the border directly south of the saddle, this is what they would have seen as they looked toward their layup spot. Traveling mostly at night, smugglers can cover the distance, 4.3 miles as the crow flies, in about an hour. They carry marijuana packs of 40 to 80 pounds. Photo by author.

No information has ever been released to the public by the FBI or by any other U.S. law enforcement agency about any of the suspects arrested in connection with the shooting death of Agent Ivie. The head of the FBI's Arizona division repeatedly declined to answer questions about the two suspects arrested in Mexico.

Border-crossing traffickers could have triggered shooting

Lydia Antonio, spokeswoman at the Mexican Embassy in Washington D.C., confirmed the arrests of the two suspects to several news outlets, on October 2 and afterward.

In a statement carried in an Arizona Republic news story, Antonio said in a statement, "two persons presumably involved in cross-border trafficking could have triggered the shooting."[2]

With their arrests reported by several national, international and local news reports, why did the FBI remain silent about those suspects?

Almost all of the facts about this case were buried by government officials under a thick blanket of silence and disinformation.

Additional information has been recently uncovered about those two suspects. They were held in custody in Mexico for at least 11 days, long after the FBI released its narrative about what occurred. Despite the circumstances of their arrest—which pointed to possible involvement—and the fact that ATF agents believed they were suspects in the Ivie shooting—the FBI would quietly exonerate them within a few days.

More details on those suspects, including the handling of their firearms by a federal law enforcement agency, are covered in a latter chapter.

10

Homicide Victim's Body
Remains in Place for 11 Hours

"Once inside the helicopter, I observed an American Flag draped over a litter basket." Sheriff's detective, documenting the handling of Agent Ivie's body.

Tuesday, October 2, 12:30 p.m.
Remax Saddle to University of Arizona Medical Center, Tucson

Detective Randal "Randy" Wilson, a 13-year veteran of the Cochise County Sheriff's Office, was assigned to make arrangements for Agent Ivie's autopsy.

By a standing arrangement between the two adjoining counties, the Pima County Medical Examiner's Office performed autopsies on victims of homicides that occurred in Cochise County.

After inquiring about the details of the case from other sheriff's officers at the command post, Wilson contacted the medical examiner's office in Tucson and spoke with Investigations Officer Jimmy Rosario.

"I advised Jimmy we were investigating the death of a Border Patrol agent, and the Agent's body would be transported to the Medical Examiner's Office, either by ground or air transport," Wilson, the lead detective from the sheriff's office in this homicide case, wrote in his incident report.[1]

In almost all homicide cases, after photographs are taken, and notations are made about the position of the body and other essential observations, the body is removed from the scene.

In this case, Agent Ivie's body was left on the mountain ridge for about 11 hours—more than six hours after sunrise and more than 10 hours after a helicopter extracted the two surviving agents from the scene.

BORTAC agents and crime scene investigators were airlifted to the scene between 7:00 and 8:00 a.m. There were plenty of opportunities for the body of Agent Ivie to be carried off the mountain during that time period, if officials were waiting for daylight before removing the deceased agent's body.

Why would FBI supervisors allow the body of a fallen federal agent to lie on the ground for 11 hours? Could they have been told to await further instructions from FBI leaders in Washington? Were top FBI officials huddling with their politically appointed superiors because of the political implications of this case? This is one of the many mysteries surrounding this unusual case.

Once it was decided that it was time to transport the body, there was apparently a disagreement as to how the body should be transported.

"It was determined by Border Patrol Supervisors and the USBP Honor Guard that the body would be airlifted to Tucson, however moments later the decision was made for a ground transport," Wilson wrote in his report.

Wilson was first sent to the Border Patrol station to await the arrival of the body. He was planning to ride along from the border area to Tucson in a hearse. Then the ground transport decision was overturned.

"Once at the station, I was contacted and advised the body of Agent Ivie would be flown to Tucson via helicopter, and the helicopter would pick me up at the Naco BP helipad," Wilson wrote.

The helicopter carrying the agent's body arrived at the Brian Terry station at about 12:30 p.m. Detective Wilson boarded the helicopter.

"Once inside the helicopter, I observed an American Flag draped over a litter basket," Wilson wrote. "I was advised the body of Agent Ivie was inside the litter basket."

Two other law enforcement officers were in the helicopter along with Wilson, FBI Special Agent Gabriel Maxwell and BP Honor Guard Supervisor Frank Ayala. The flight to the University of Arizona Medical Center South (Kino) took about 45 minutes.

When the Black Hawk helicopter landed, the litter was carried to a gurney, then placed in a vehicle belonging to the Pima County Medical Examiner's Office. Maxwell and Ayala rode with the body to the office.

One of Detective Wilson's tasks was to observe and record details regarding the handling of the body.

"Once the body of Agent Ivie was at the Medical Examiner's Office, I was advised by Special Agent Maxwell he had placed an evidentiary seal of tape across the zipper of the body bag," Wilson wrote in his report. "I removed a portion of the flag from the foot portion of the body bag and observed a clear piece of tape over the zippered portions of the body bag. I advised Agent Maxwell the bag was sealed."[2]

The helicopter landed on the roof of a building on the south campus of the medical center.

Agent Ivie's body was then transported by a vehicle to the medical examiner's office on the campus. A contingent of Border Patrol agents lined the street between the heliport and the office building.

"The body of Nicholas Ivie was then turned over to the Pima County Medical Examiner's Office at approximately 13:40 hours (1:40 p.m.)," Wilson wrote in his report.

FBI Agent Maxwell "completed the Medical Examiner's paperwork" at the office. The agents were then told the autopsy would be performed at 8:30 a.m. the following day.

11

Ivie Case Connected to Fast and Furious

President Barack Obama to Nick Ivie's family: His administration was "doing everything it could to locate those responsible for this tragic event."

Just five weeks ahead of the presidential election, the campaigns of President Barack Obama and Republican candidate Mitt Romney were in high gear.

National media outlets were busy cranking out great numbers of stories on the first presidential debate, scheduled to begin in Denver on Wednesday night.

Obama heard about the slaying of Agent Ivie the day before the first debate of his reelection campaign.

President Barack Obama with FBI director Robert Mueller in 2009. Photograph by Saul Loeb/AFP/Getty Images.

On Sunday night, the day before Agent Ivie hiked the mountain trail to the Remax Saddle, Obama arrived at the Westin Lake Las Vegas Resort, Henderson, Nevada, nine miles west of the Arizona Border. He had two and a half days to complete his preparation for the debate.

On the evening he arrived, Obama spoke to a crowd of about 11,000 at an outdoor rally at Desert Pines High School, a public school on the east side of Las Vegas, about 10 miles from the resort hotel where he would be staying.

Although he was focused on preparing for that debate, which would be watched by millions of voters nationwide and had the potential to help swing the election in either direction, Obama took time out from his schedule to make sure the public knew he was concerned about the young Border Patrol agent's death.

According to a statement released the day of the shooting, Obama called the Ivie family to express his sadness for their loss and express his gratitude for Ivie's "selfless service to his nation."[1]

"The President told the family they are in his thoughts and prayers and made clear that **his administration was doing everything it could to locate those responsible for this tragic event,**" the White House statement said.[2]

Just 18 days earlier, Obama had issued a similar statement when confronted with another situation that threatened to embarrass his administration.

"We will bring to justice those who took them from us," Obama told the relatives of four slain American men—an ambassador, foreign service worker, and two diplomatic security officers—who lost their lives during a terrorist attack in Benghazi, Libya. This statement was made by the president at a ceremony in a hangar at Andrews Air Force Base, Maryland, after the bodies of the slain men were removed from an airplane.[3]

On the same day that Obama met with family members of the Benghazi victims, the president underwent his last in a series of mock debates in Washington, D.C., to prepare for the debate in Denver.[4] In between the Benghazi terrorist attack, which lasted about 13 hours, and the return of the bodies to America, Obama attended fundraising campaign events in Las Vegas and Colorado.

Ivie Killing Follows Two of Obama's Worst Scandals

There are several similarities between the cases of four Americans killed in Libya and the Border Patrol agent killed near the Mexican border. In both cases, Americans were killed while serving their country, shortly before the presidential election. In both cases, the Obama administration created policies that endangered the murder victims. In both cases, all stops would be pulled out to conceal what actually occurred.

In the Ivie case, Obama's policies enabled smugglers and human traffickers to cross the border at will. His administration was involved in an operation in which more than 2,000 high-powered firearms were sent to the Sinaloa Cartel, the controlling force for illegal traffic crossing at the Arizona–Sonora border. The weapons that the U.S. government purposely sent to the cartel helped the organization to exert power over other cartels and innocent people.

Despite the unbridled illegal border-crossing traffic—which was the source of much misery to borderland residents—Obama insisted the border was secure. He exerted executive privilege to conceal documents about the gunrunning operation and took no responsibility for the consequences of Fast and Furious. Obama also failed to take responsibility for the deaths of four Americans during the terrorist attack in Benghazi.

In Benghazi, security measures were low, despite urgent requests for more protection from foreign service workers. When the terrorists attacked, no help was sent from outside Libya, despite full knowledge by the Obama administration of military units nearby and total awareness by high ranking officials of what was taking place as the attack progressed.

Obama tried to deceive the families of the victims and the public by claiming that the murder of American government workers in Libya was the result of a spontaneous demonstration against an anti-Islam video. But Obama and all the members of his administration that met to address the situation as it unfolded had full knowledge that the attack was a planned action by terrorists, who greatly outnumbered the armed security forces in Benghazi.

After the four Americans were killed in Benghazi, U.N. ambassador Susan Rice, in the role of Obama administration spokeswoman, told a national audience on a Sunday talk show on Sept. 16, 2012, that the best information available on that day was that "it was not a preplanned, premeditated attack. . . . It was a spontaneous reaction to what had just transpired in Cairo as a consequence of the video." Rice implied that this information—which was known by administration and military leaders to be false on the day the attack occurred—came as a result of an FBI investigation. The FBI, which had not reached that conclusion, failed to publicly contradict this false statement. [4]

The difference between the murderous attack in Northern Africa on September 11, 2012, and the ambush three weeks later in

Southern Arizona, was that four men died in Benghazi, whereas one died serving near Bisbee. In Benghazi, the brave efforts of several diplomatic security agents saved the lives of about 30 people. On Remax Saddle, the courageous effort of a Border Patrol agent saved the lives of two agents.

As Obama and his debate preparation team were settling in to their upscale digs out in the desert, just two weeks after Rice made her rounds of the Sunday talk shows to mislead the public about the Benghazi terrorist attack, they had no idea they were about to be confronted with another story of the murder of an American public servant.

While the flames of the Benghazi story were being fanned by his political opponents, the Ivie murder story couldn't have exploded in Obama's face at a worse time.

And this story was potentially even more damaging to the reelection hopes of the president, because it was closely tied to one of the worst scandals of his presidency—the government's Fast and Furious gunrunning operation. The idea that the Obama administration helped arm a brutal cartel would not sit well with most voters.

This is how former federal prosecutor Andrew McCarthy described it in his 2019 book, "Ball of Collusion": "The 'Fast and Furious" scandal involved a blatant Obama administration politicization of law enforcement: to wit, a 'gun-walking' investigation in which thousands of firearms were allowed to be transferred illegally to Mexico. This cockamamie scheme was designed to serve a political narrative about the evils of American gun commerce, concocted to promote the progressive agenda of restricting Second Amendment rights."[5]

The Fast and Furious gunrunning operation led to the murders of hundreds of people. Benghazi was seen by Obama's political opponents as the result of incompetence, whereas Fast and Furious was understood as something far worse—an unprecedented, cynical scheme to arm a brutal cartel in order to promote an antigun agenda.

What a nightmare it must have been for Obama and his campaign prep team to wake up the day before the debate to headlines such as this one on the ABC News Web site: **"Slain Border Agent Identified, Drug Traffickers Suspected."** If the Republicans used the Ivie slaying to pour gasoline on the smoldering Fast and Furious scandal, the fallout could send Obama's reelection hopes into a tailspin.[6]

Stories on major TV networks and in prominent newspapers were busy fanning the dying embers of the Fast and Furious scandal into a potential new firestorm. The story of this bizarre government operation, already being resurrected on TV sets and at newsstands right *before* the Ivie killing, was now bringing out a louder chorus, also shouting about the broader failure of Obama's border policies.

Obama, who was leading by about eight percentage points in nationwide polls, took time out from his debate preparation in the Las Vegas area to call the Ivie family. He offered his condolences privately to family members and sent out that press release that said his administration was doing everything it could to locate the shooters.

There was just one problem with that grand-sounding idea of locating the killers of Agent Ivie and bringing them to justice.

If Agent Ivie's killers were arrested, identified, and charged, then all of the publicity surrounding their cases would be a major distraction from the Obama campaign's official narrative—that the border was secure.

There had to be a better way to deal with this situation, to make the Ivie murder case disappear from public view.

The victims of the terrorist attack in Libya were a U.S. ambassador— the first one killed in the line of duty since 1979—two diplomatic security agents, and a foreign service employee.

Now that there was another possible blemish on the carefully crafted image of a president who was never involved in a scandal, it was once again important to win over the relatives of a murder victim.

Homeland Security Director Janet Napolitano, an Obama appointee and former Democratic governor of Arizona, would be sent from Washington, D.C., to Southern Arizona to meet with the family and oversee the Border Patrol's role in the investigation.

She also issued a statement on the day of the Ivie slaying.

"I am deeply saddened by the death of Border Patrol Agent Nicholas J. Ivie and the attack on another Border Patrol Agent early this morning," Napolitano's statement said. **"Both agents were on patrol near Bisbee, Arizona, when they came under fire from an unknown assailant. . . . We are working closely with our federal, state, and local law enforcement partners to track down those responsible for this inexcusable crime, and to bring them to justice."**

Those were strong words. The head of the federal agency charged with protecting our nation from terrorists, drug smugglers, and human traffickers was crying out to bring "an unknown assailant" to justice.

Her statement initially referred to *one* assailant, followed closely by an indication that she was working with others to find *multiple* assailants. She and her partners would "track down *those* responsible" and "bring *them* to justice." It is not clear why her statement referred to one assailant, but then acknowledged that several suspects were involved.

Putting aside the number of assailants, Napolitano delivered a clear, tough-sounding message, based on facts that were widely believed and disseminated the day of the incident. As Homeland Security director, Napolitano would immediately have the inside word on what occurred. She certainly would not release a public statement about tracking down perpetrators of an inexcusable crime if she did not believe the crime had occurred.

However, her initial expression of bringing justice to the killers of Agent Ivie would turn out to be just another emission of empty words. There were much more important considerations than bringing to justice the killers of an unknown border agent on an obscure mountain ridge. There was an election to win, and there was no way another failure of the Obama administration would be allowed to become a big story with long legs.

With Obama and Napolitano intimately involved in the aftermath of this crime, reporters from national media outlets—many of whom had covered other stories related to the heated issue of illegal immigration—flocked to Southern Arizona to report on the most recent fatality in the Border Wars.

First news conference reveals that Agent Ivie "died at the hands of criminals."

"As (the three agents) headed up a desert hill, someone fired right at them, in what is being described as an ambush. The agents work in the very Naco, Arizona station named just two weeks ago for Brian Terry, the last Border Patrol agent shot on duty."[6] "World News with Diane Sawyer," National News Broadcast on ABC.

Tuesday, October 2, 1:30 p.m.
Brian A. Terry Border Patrol Station, near Naco

A news conference held at the Brian A. Terry Border Patrol station early in the afternoon was attended by officials of the primary law enforcement agencies involved in the investigation.

During the press conference the day of the shooting, **Jeff Self, U.S. Customs and Border Protection Joint Field Commander for Arizona, said Ivie died "at the hands of criminals" operating near the border.**

"First and foremost, our thoughts and prayers are with Agent Ivie's family during this terrible time," Self said. "This is a tragic loss for Customs and Border Protection. **We have an unwavering commitment to pursue and bring the perpetrators of this heinous act to justice."**

James Turgal, FBI Special Agent in Charge of the Phoenix Division, was asked whether two suspects in the case were arrested in Mexico.

"I'm not going to talk about any issues regarding suspects at this time," Turgal said.[7]

But during the conference, Turgal practically admitted that he had knowledge of the arrest on the south side of the border.

"I'm not going to talk any further about those issues," Turgal said. "It's way too early, and I don't want to prejudice anything that either us or the military in Mexico or the Mexican government is working on right now."[8]

However, Acting Cochise County Sheriff Rod Rothrock did say that two suspects "may have been arrested" and in the custody of Mexican authorities.

"It's my understanding that Border Patrol air assets spotted the suspects in Mexico, and the suspects were subsequently apprehended, but I don't know the specifics of how that all came about," Rothrock said.[9]

The *New York Times*, which had sent a reporter to Naco to write a feature on the naming of the Brian A. Terry Station two weeks earlier, published a nine-paragraph story on the Ivie slaying on October 2. Five of those paragraphs included information about the Fast and Furious operation.

After relating the basics of the Ivie case in the first two paragraphs, the story then connected the Ivie slaying to the government's gun-running operation:

> **The shooting occurred near a Border Patrol station in Naco, Arizona, that had recently been named in honor of Brian Terry, an agent whose 2010 murder received national attention because of its ties to Operation Fast and Furious, a botched gun-tracking case.** Two guns found at the scene of Mr. Terry's murder were among hundreds that officials of the Bureau of Alcohol, Tobacco, Firearms and Explosives failed to seize as they hoped to build their case.
>
> Although the authorities said nothing about the weapons used in the shooting on Tuesday, Republican members of Congress who have been critical of the Justice Department issued a statement that tried to tie the shooting to Operation Fast and Furious.

"There's no way to know at this point how the agent was killed, but because of Operation Fast and Furious, we'll wonder for years if the guns used in any killing along the border were part of an ill-advised gun-walking strategy sanctioned by the federal government," U.S. Sen. Charles E. Grassley, Republican of Iowa, said in a statement. "It's a sad commentary."

The *Times* story went on to say that **Turgal "declined to say whether the authorities had uncovered connections between the shooting and Operation Fast and Furious."**

The Times reporter explained that the Fast and Furious operation was an investigation from late 2009 to early 2011 into a gun-trafficking gang connected to a Mexican drug cartel.

The Times story concluded by saying that **officials believed the perpetrators of the attack on Agent Ivie and the other agents "were criminals and that because the shooting had taken place in a rugged area it could take more than a day to collect evidence from the scene."**[10]

The ABC News story posted on its Web site during the day on October 2 also brought attention to the Fast and Furious scandal:

> The last Border Patrol agent shot and killed along the border was Brian Terry, who was killed by bandits in a rugged part of the U.S.-Mexico border. The guns that killed Terry were linked to a disastrous gun trafficking operation run by the Alcohol, Tobacco and Firearms Bureau in Arizona called Operation Fast and Furious. The agents killed and wounded today were assigned to a Border Patrol station that was recently named after Brian Terry.

This story reported that the area where Ivie was shot earlier that day had been a smuggling corridor for many years, which was unabated in recent years.

"The gunshots were possibly fired by drug traffickers, federal and county officials said," the ABC story said.

Probably the biggest splash of all the stories on the agent's murder and its connection to Fast and Furious was made that evening on the nationwide broadcast of ABC "World News with Diane Sawyer."

The 3-minute-long segment included a standup in front of the Brian Terry Border Patrol station, footage of the Mule Mountain region, and photographs of Agents Terry and Ivie.

Here is a partial transcript of the segment:

Anchor Diane Sawyer: "We turn now to a manhunt underway at this hour in Arizona. Helicopters and horses in pursuit along a dangerous stretch of the Mexican border . . . And the question tonight, was this a Mexican drug cartel in action?"

Reporter Cecilia Vega at the border: "This area has earned the nickname as cocaine alley by drug smugglers. It's considered to be one of the most popular places for illegal entries all along the border. But today for the agents who work right here at this station, this is a place of mourning. . . . It was here early this morning on this dusty stretch of land, where Arizona meets Mexico, that three Border Patrol agents were fired on. One made it out safely, another was shot twice and is expected to recover. But the third agent, 30-year-old Nick Ivie was shot dead. . . ."

Acting Sheriff Rexroth, speaking from the lobby of the Cochise County Sheriff's Office, Bisbee: "We suspect this is probably some type of narcotics trafficking event that these agents encountered. But at this time that would be speculative."

Reporter Vega: "As (the three agents) headed up a desert hill, **someone fired right at them, in what is being described as an ambush. The agents work in the very Naco, Arizona station named just two weeks ago for Brian Terry, the last Border Patrol agent shot on duty.**

"His 2010 death from a firearm, sold through the notorious Fast and Furious operation, ignited a firestorm. It is unknown if the weapon that killed Ivie has any link to that now famous controversy. What is clear here is how dangerous life can be."[11]

This was the second day in a row that ABC News had broadcast a story about Fast and Furious. Stories on this scandalous operation had been scarce in the news for the past several months, but now they were proliferating with a vengeance.

What could be done to stop this runaway train—with possible disastrous election results—as more and more follow-up stories on this investigation would certainly surface, along with more news about the prodigious amount of smuggling activity at the border?

The last thing the Obama campaign needed was a gaggle of reporters from Washington, New York, and Los Angeles hanging out near the border, filing stories on what was occurring at ground zero for the prolific, deadly smuggling trade.

As long as this story was up and running, politicians from the opposition party would surely pour gasoline on the media firestorm surrounding the murder of this beloved Border Patrol agent.

On the day of the shooting, Arizona Governor Jan Brewer, a Republican who had previous public confrontations with the president on immigration issues, blamed Agent Ivie's murder on Obama administration policies. This statement, by one of the most outspoken critics of Obama's border policies, accused his administration of lying about the security of the border.

"Arizonans and Americans will grieve, and they should," Brewer said in a statement, which was widely reported in the media. "But this ought not only be a day of tears.

"There should be anger, too. Righteous anger—at the kind of evil that causes sorrow this deep, and at the federal failure and political stalemate that has left our border unsecured and our Border Patrol in harm's way. Four fallen agents in less than two years is the result. It has been 558 days since the Obama administration declared the security of the U.S.-Mexico border 'better now than it has ever been.' I'll remember that statement today."[12]

The CBS national news story that day also spotlighted the Fast and Furious operation, pegging Agent Ivie's death to the gunrunning operation that had already garnered many hours of broadcast time.

CBS News reported:
> **BISBEE, ARIZ.—A Border Patrol agent was shot to death Tuesday in Arizona near the U.S.-Mexico line, the first fatal shooting of an agent since a deadly 2010 firefight with Mexican bandits that spawned congressional probes of a botched government gun-smuggling investigation.**

A few paragraphs later, the story said,
> The last Border Patrol agent fatally shot was Brian Terry, who died in a shootout with bandits near the border in December 2010. **The Border Patrol station in Naco, where the two agents shot Tuesday were stationed, was recently named after Terry.**[13]

The *Washington Post*, the premier newspaper of the nation's capital, also published a story that included information on the Fast and Furious scandal near the top:

The FBI is investigating a shooting in which one Border Patrol agent was killed and another wounded in the southern Arizona desert Tuesday, the first time an agent has been fatally shot since December 2010.

The pair were among several agents patrolling on horseback (*they were actually on foot*) when the shooting occurred near Naco, about 100 miles southeast of Tucson and 50 miles from where Border Patrol agent Brian Terry was killed two years ago. Terry's killing was linked to the flawed 'Fast and Furious' gun-tracking operation, run by the Bureau of Alcohol, Tobacco, Firearms and Explosives, after two guns tied to a suspect in the operation were found at the scene of Terry's death.[14]

Because Ivie was a Utah native, and many of his relatives still resided there, news outlets from the state on Arizona's northern border reported extensively on the case.

The Salt Lake City TV Station, Fox 13, reported in a story posted on October 2 that police "think more than one shooter fired at the agents."

This report included a statement from Lanny Breuer, the head of the criminal division of the U.S. Department of Justice.

"The FBI is at the scene, is investigating, and is going to get to the bottom of this," Breuer said.[16]

Those familiar with the record of partisan behavior by this political operative might have been skeptical of his statement. Some might have wondered why he would be allowed anywhere near an investigation so closely associated with the scandal for which he was already under scrutiny.

Breuer had been in the news a couple of weeks earlier, when Republican lawmakers called for his resignation for his failure to "properly supervise" prosecutors and federal law enforcement officers involved in the Fast and Furious operation."

The U.S. Department of Justice inspector general testified that Breuer and other officials "focused on how they could make sure the media did not find out about it," at a U.S. House committee hearing.[17]

Covering up the Fast and Furious scandal was a priority for Breuer, according to several news reports.

Senator Charles Grassley (R-Iowa), then ranking member of the Senate Judiciary Committee, said of Breuer in 2011 that he had never come across a government official before "who so blatantly placed sparing agencies' embarrassment over protecting the lives of citizens."

Breuer admitted in October 2011 "that he knew federal officials allowed guns to fall into the possession of Mexican drug cartels 10 months before the department denied in February that such an investigative strategy was used." There were calls for his resignation then, but he remained in office until March 2013. He resigned then after a public television exposé showed him to be incompetent in prosecuting Wall Street banks, including one involved in laundering drug money and financing terrorists.[16]

The fact that Breuer was directly involved in the Ivie murder investigation raised a red flag. He was on the hot seat for his involvement in the Fast and Furious operation and its cover-up, but that did not deter him from getting involved in a closely related case.

Breuer, who rose to prominence as the attorney defending President Bill Clinton during his impeachment trial, had a track record of placing politics over justice. Anyone aware of his record would be rightfully concerned about the outcome of this investigation.

Senator Orrin Hatch, R-Utah, one of the longest-serving senators in history, issued a statement the day of the shooting incident that said, "I am deeply saddened and angered by the senseless killing today of Border Patrol Agent Nicholas J. Ivie, who was gunned down by criminals in the Arizona desert as he went about his duty to protect our nation.

"By all accounts, Agent Ivie was a dedicated law enforcement professional, a leader in his church and in the community, and a loving husband and devoted father. . . . **I will continue to press the Administration and do everything I can to ensure our border is secure, our citizens are protected and the perpetrators of this and other violent acts against our Border Patrol agents are brought to justice.**"

One of the most insightful news stories filed on this incident was written by crime reporter Christine Pelisek of the *Daily Beast*, a news Web site then affiliated with *Newsweek* magazine.

"Federal agents and county police are on the hunt for three to four suspects who opened fire on Border Patrol agents," Pelisek wrote in her story.

She quoted several local officials familiar with the case and the territory.

"It is obviously an ambush in my mind," said Commander Marc Denney of the Cochise County Sheriff's Department in Arizona, which is assisting the FBI in the case. "Someone could have been on high ground and had that over them."

Ransom Burke, a Bisbee city council member, said that "This area is completely geographically ready for an ambush" because of its abundance of rocks, cacti, steep canyons, and brush. He said Border Patrol agents were well trained, but the abundance of rocks and brush hampered their ability to detect suspects. "It has perennially been a drug route for a long time."

This story also mentioned the 2010 shooting death of Brian Terry and the fact that guns used in that shootout "were later traced to the Fast and Furious gun-smuggling investigation."

"This is just another reminder of our failed border policy, which is endangering all border residents," said Cochise County Supervisor Richard Searle.[17]

12

Autopsy Shows Ivie Suffered Numerous Wounds

"Nicholas Ivie sustained a 3 cm (1³/₈ inch) linear contusion between the thumb and the index finger on the side of his right hand, with disruption of overlying skin." (Autopsy report on unusual injury, indicating possible struggle to maintain control of his firearm.)

Wednesday, October 3, 8:30 a.m.
Pima County Medical Examiner's Office, Tucson

Even in his death, Nick Ivie continued to serve his fellow man.

Although it is unusual in many jurisdictions for homicide victims to be used for organ donations, Arizona has an aggressive organ donor network which works closely with the offices of medical examiners.

The Donor Network of Arizona requested authorization to remove the heart, in order to obtain valves, as well as some skin, bones, veins and arteries. The medical examiner's investigator informed the network "they are not to touch the head or any other area of apparent injury."

Photographs were taken of Agent Ivie's body after it arrived at the medical examiner's office at 1:30 p.m. Tuesday, Oct. 2, 12 hours after he was killed.

When the body arrived at the office, on the campus of the University of Arizona Medical Center, his body was removed from the sealed body bag in order to secure the organ donations.

Detective Randy Wilson of the Cochise County Sheriff's Office arrived at the office Wednesday morning to witness the autopsy. He had driven FBI Agent Gabriel Maxwell to Tucson from Sierra Vista. Three other FBI agents were also attending the autopsy, as well as members of the Border Patrol CIT Team.

Wilson wrote that Agent Ivie had a U-shaped incision on his chest and several skin grafts "missing from his thighs and legs." His face was covered with dirt and dried blood.

"Agent Ivie also had some minor scrapes on his hands," Wilson wrote.

A "full forensic work up was completed on Agent Ivie, to include swabs and fingernails."

"It should be noted the clothing Agent Ivie was wearing was laid out and photographed. The clothing had been removed from his body when organs and skin graphs [sic] were collected."

"During the course of the autopsy two bullet fragments were removed from Agent Ivie's skull. Those fragments were photographed and turned over to the FBI, along with other items of evidentiary value, for further examination and processing through the FBI Laboratory."[1]

The heart of Nick Ivie, a registered donor, was removed in order to provide valves to help someone with heart disease. However, his whole heart could likely have been used for a transplant if his body had been removed from the crime scene earlier. Medical experts say a heart should be removed from the body within six hours after death to be viable for possible transplant.

The FBI was in charge of the crime scene, including the body. Agents would not be expected to be concerned about organ donations from a homicide victim. But the fact that the body was kept at the scene for 11 hours is not normal.

The autopsy, which began at 8:30 a.m. Wednesday, Oct. 3, was conducted by forensic pathologist Dr. Cynthia Porterfield, with three named assistants.

The witnesses, who observed from a reviewing room, were listed as Aaron Feagley (Border Patrol), Brian Levin and Robert Hickman, (Customs and Border Protection), four FBI special agents: Gabriel Maxwell, Shannon Gonzalez, Carolyn Middleton, and Danica Duclas, and CCSO Detective Randal "Randy" Wilson.

In her written report on the postmortem examination, Dr. Porterfield wrote that Ivie's death was the result of a "penetrating gunshot wound of the head involving the brain."

Dr. Eric D. Peters, Pima County Deputy Chief Medical Examiner, said in a recent phone interview that Nicholas Ivie died "right away" from the gunshot wound.

The manner of death was listed as a homicide.

"His fatal wound was not anything that could have been treated," said Peters, a forensic pathologist for 22 years, who was on the Pima County staff at the time of Ivie's autopsy. Dr. Porterfield has since retired.[2]

Peters, who has performed nearly 5,000 forensic autopsies and has testified more than 200 times as an expert witness in court cases, was asked to discuss several issues connected to this examination, especially the caliber of the fatal bullet and the injuries found on Nick Ivie's body.

The caliber of the bullet is an important factor in this case, especially because that could help determine who killed Agent Ivie.

Peters was asked to explain the difference between the measurement of the entrance wound to the skin, which is listed as 6 centimeters (about ¼ inch) in diameter, and the measurement of the entrance wound to the skull, listed as 1 × 1.5 cm (²/₅ inch by ³/₅ inch).

The smaller measurement of the skin would tend to indicate a small-caliber bullet, such as a .223 or .22 caliber. Caliber is a measurement of the diameter of the bullet, the part of the cartridge that is propelled from the shell. The measurement indicates the percentage of an inch of the diameter of the projectile: a .40 caliber bullet measures 40 percent, or ⁴/₁₀ of an inch in width.

The entrance wound in Agent Ivie's forehead was listed in the report as 3.8 inches below the top of the head and .4 inches to the left of the midline. In other words, in the middle of his forehead, just above his eyebrows.

Peters explained that skin is elastic, like a balloon. If something pierces a balloon, it will collapse and snap back. The hole that was made to deflate the balloon will then become smaller.

"You can have a gun entrance wound that is smaller than the bullet because of the elasticity of the skin," Peters said.

In this case, the written report's description of the skull defect as 1 by 1.5 cm does not necessarily reflect the size of the bullet.

"The hole is an irregular defect," Peters said. "It is not a circle or an oval. It is very irregular in shape."

He explained that when a projectile is fired from a high velocity weapon, it can cause excessive damage to a bone, opening a larger aperture than the bullet's diameter.

"The best way to describe it: If you were cracking an egg, the egg's shell is the skull," Peters said, adding that the frontal skull bone is thin at that point, normally one centimeter or thinner. "The bullet is pushing out the edge of the skull due to its velocity."

When asked if it were possible that the wound was made by a large caliber bullet, he said that because of the elasticity of the skin he would not say with authority that this could be ruled out.

"From the pathologist's standpoint (the pathologist who conducted the autopsy), it was thought to be a small caliber," Peters said.

The distance of fire was undetermined. There was no stippling or soot on Agent Ivie's face, indicating he was not shot in close proximity to the gun barrel.

There has been conjecture about Ivie's wound resulting from a deflected tree branch. The FBI entered into evidence a tree branch with a defect, apparently because of this possibility.

After examining the autopsy photographs, Peters said it appeared to be "an ordinary gunshot wound to the head." He did not observe any evidence of a deflected bullet.

"From the shape of the entrance wound I don't think it was (deflected)," Peters said. "I've had cases of deflections, such as intermediate targets, like through a door or off a pavement. Those bullets cause very irregular entrance wounds."

In addition to the regular shape of the exterior entrance wound, Peters said the penetration of this bullet also indicated an unobstructed shot.

"This bullet went through his skull and into the base of his brain," Peters said.

As a result of his reading of the report, as well as viewing the photographs and diagrams, Peters said he believed the bullet entered at a slightly downward angle.

"There is a purple abrasion, from the 7 to 5 o'clock positions," he said, adding that the abrasion along the margin at the top and both sides of the circular wound indicates the angle of the trajectory. "When bullets enter the skin, they rub raw the skin prior to entering."

A small caliber copper-jacketed projectile was recovered from within the brainstem, Dr. Porterfield wrote in her report. A second fragment exited the skull and fractured the first cervical vertebra. It was recovered from the muscles of the posterior neck.

The photograph of the mangled fragment recovered from the brainstem clearly shows its rounded bottom, which survived the impact as a perfect circle—as if the slug was hit with a hammer straight on its butt end. The photograph clearly shows that, when measured against a metric ruler, the bullet's diameter is about .5 centimeters, which translates to .22 or .223 caliber.

The two bullet fragments recovered from Agent Ivie were turned over to an FBI agent after they were photographed, according to an autopsy document.

There is mystery associated with the bullet fragments.

Some firearms experts say there is no way a .223 bullet shot unimpeded from an M4 rifle would have stayed inside Agent Ivie's head. The bullet has explosive power, and it can penetrate steel and concrete. The .223 cartridge was designed to penetrate. It is a fact that there was no exit wound in this case.

If Agent Ivie were shot to death by a .223 rifle, I do not know how this could have occurred. And after speaking to five different firearms and ballistics experts—who shared with me several conflicting opinions—I readily admit that I do not have all the answers about this aspect of this case.

One expert said the photo of the fragment is definitely a .223 slug, but he does not believe it was actually in Agent Ivie's skull. The .223 cartridge was designed to penetrate a human body with ease. However, the photographs of the bullet fragments, which appear to be from a .223 slug, were clearly taken at the Pima County Medical Examiner's Office after it was removed from the slain agent.

I believe that speculation on this subject will end when a more exhaustive investigation of this case is performed.

Agent Ivie's Numerous Injuries Indicate a Possible Struggle for His Weapon.

EXTERNAL EXAMINATION:

The body is that of a normally-developed, well-nourished, light-complected male measuring 74 inches in length and weighing 126 pounds. The body is cold to the touch. Rigor mortis is minimally present. Lividity is fixed and posterior. Skin slippage involves the right and left lower extremities, the right upper extremity, the forehead and the back. Involving the face, chest, and upper and lower extremities there are multiple areas of tan abrasions/indentations presumably caused by gravel.

In her postmortem report, Dr. Porterfield wrote in the external examination section: "Involving the face, chest, and upper and lower extremities there are multiple areas of tan abrasions/indentations presumably caused by gravel."

GUNSHOT WOUND

On the forehead 9.8 cm below the top of the head and 1 cm to the left of the anterior midline there is a gunshot wound of entry, 0.6 cm in diameter. In the 7 to 5 o'clock position there is a purple abrasion, 0.2 cm. The surrounding skin shows areas of skin slippage and brown abrasion/indentation; however, no definitive stippling or soot is identified. The wound course involves the scalp, the frontal bone leaving an approximately 1.5 x 1.0 cm entrance wound, the medial sides of the right and left frontal lobes of the brain, the brainstem and the cerebellum. Recovered from within the brainstem is a small caliber copper jacketed projectile. A 2nd fragment exits the skull and fractures the 1st cervical vertebra and is recovered from the muscles of the posterior neck. The wound has coursed in a front to back and downward direction. The range of fire is of indeterminate distance.

EXTERNAL EVIDENCE OF RECENT INJURY:

1) On the right lateral hand, between the thumb and the index finger, there is a 3 cm linear contusion with disruption of the overlying skin.
2) Involving the right medial posterior elbow there is a pink contusion, 2 x 1 cm.
3) On the right knee there is a poorly defined area consisting of scattered linear abrasions which covers an area measuring overall 8 x 5 cm.

She added that **"the bony structures of the nose are fractured."**

In the category of "external evidence of recent injury," the pathologist noted that Ivie sustained a **3 cm (1³/₈ inch)** linear contusion **between the thumb and the index finger on the side of his right hand, with disruption of overlying skin.**

This is a very unusual place to receive an injury. When placed in the context of other evidence, this injury tends to indicate that Agent Ivie was in a life or death struggle for control of his service pistol.

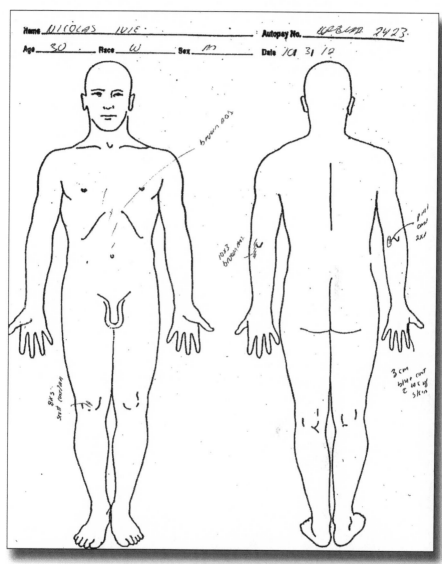

Here we have important evidence of a probable scuffle between Agent Ivie and the smugglers who killed him. If Agent Ivie was just knocked down by a bullet wound to the head, why would he have bruises and scrapes to his elbows, knee, and, most telling, on the area between his thumb and forefinger? Why would he have abrasions on his chest—while wearing a shirt and two undershirts? One fall forward from a single bullet would not cause all that damage.

Other injuries recorded by Dr. Porterfield include a pink contusion 2 × 1 cm (³/₄ × ³/₈ inches) on the inner part of his right elbow, a tan abrasion 10 × 3 cm (4 × 1³/₈ inches) on the outer part of his left elbow, and scattered linear abrasions covering an area on his right knee measuring 8 × 5 cm (3¹/₈ × 2 inches).

Agent Ivie was shot and killed by a single gunshot wound to his forehead. He was obviously murdered by a cold-hearted drug smuggler. The numerous wounds on his body also provide evidence that illegal border crossers most likely attacked Agent Ivie and struggled with him before firing the fatal shot.

Top: Crime scene investigators search for evidence, record their findings, and create a map of the scene. These maps show where Agent Nicholas Ivie's body was found and where injured agent David Johnson was located. Photo courtesy of Cochise County Sheriff's Office.

Bottom: Hundreds of law officers from federal and local agencies rushed to the Mule Mountains to track suspects, search for possible evidence, and establish a perimeter around the crime scene. Photo October 2, 2012, by U.S. Customs and Border Patrol.

Top: The remote terrain of the Mule Mountain Range provides a perfect conduit for the Sinaloa Cartel to transport tons of illegal drugs. At the right is the western edge of the ridge where the Ivie shooting took place. The ribbon of highway in the distance is Route 80, which connects to Interstate 10, a coast-to-coast thoroughfare. Bollek Aerial Photography.

Bottom: An aerial shot from the U.S. side of the border shows the flood gates open on the International Road, just north of where two suspects were apprehended in Mexico the morning of October 2, 2012. Those suspects, arrested in connection with the Ivie murder while in possession of drugs and firearms, were interviewed by the FBI, who obtained their DNA and fingerprints. Bollek Aerial Photography.

Agent Nicholas Ivie, posing on Mouse, the wild mustang he trained, on a slope just west of Remax Saddle, July 2012. Photo by Nick's friend, who wishes to remain anonymous.

A cloud spotlights Nick's Saddle, just beyond the monument built in his honor. The monument is located 1.25 miles south of the mountain and is maintained by the owner of the former Christiansen Ranch. Photo by author.

Top: Christy Ivie, wife of U.S. Border Patrol agent Nicholas J. Ivie, places flowers on the casket of her husband following a graveside ceremony in Spanish Fork, Thursday, Oct. 11, 2012. She is holding her 22-month-old daughter, Presley. Photo by Ravell Call, Deseret News.

Bottom: Monument plaque honors Agent Ivie. The surviving agents referred to Nick by his star number, O-225, throughout their communications during and following the shooting incident. Photo by author.

Top: Agent Ivie parked at this turnaround, at the end of Remax Road, before hiking toward the saddle on a relatively easy climb, ascending 672 feet, from an elevation of 4,862 feet to 5,534 feet, the equivalent of about a 65-story building. Photo by author.

Bottom: Remax Road is a dangerous road. Because of its numerous hazards, agents driving at night must use their headlights, even under a full moon. Ivie had to drive only 1.8 miles, but his speed would be as low as 1 mile per hour at times because of the uneven terrain. Cartel scouts and mules were likely aware of Agent Ivie's movements as he drove and hiked toward the mountain ridge. Photo by author.

The monument at Nick's saddle is believed to be at the spot where he was found, shortly after he was shot to death. This photograph was taken to demonstrate how easily smugglers could have hidden at the saddle, before ambushing the agents. Notice the hand emerging from the top of the stunted mesquite tree at the left. Photo by author, October 4, 2017.

This page
A trail camera captures the image of a train of mules, carrying packs filled with marijuana and possibly other drugs, as it crosses the Mule Mountains, en route to a drop point on the northern side. Cartel scouts on nearby high ground—on both sides of the border—armed with night vision binoculars, sophisticated radios, and cell phones, warn the smugglers of the movements of Border Patrol agents.

Facing Page
Top: One day before the first debate of the presidential campaign, President Obama called the family of Nick Ivie to express his condolences. The murder of a Border Patrol agent was unleashing a firestorm of publicity relating this incident to the Fast and Furious scandal. Failed 2004 presidential candidate John Kerry played the role of Republican Candidate Mitt Romney during debate prep sessions near Las Vegas. Oct. 2, 2012, White House Photo by Pete Souza

Bottom: Agents from the Border Patrol Special Operations Group joined forces with other law enforcement officers to search the Mule Mountains for suspects and evidence. They deployed on helicopters, horses, all-terrain vehicles and foot. Photo October 2, 2012, Courtesy of U.S. Customs and Border Patrol.

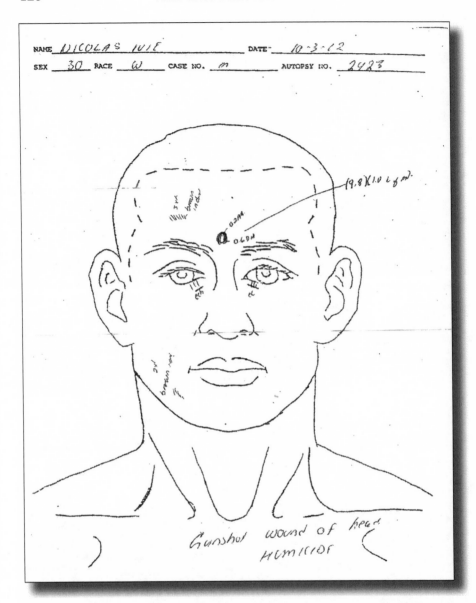

The diagram of Agent Ivie's head shows an entrance wound of 0.6 centimeter in diameter, with an abrasion around the top five-sixths of the rim, indicating a downward gunshot. Was this fatal wound caused by the bullet of an assassin, or was it just the tragic result of gunfire from a fellow agent shooting blindly toward muzzle fire? Diagram courtesy of Pima County Medical Examiner's Office

NCO 50/15.9

U.S. Customs and
Border Protection

October 2, 2012

MEMORANDUM FOR: Richard A. Barlow
                              Chief Patrol Agent
                              Tucson Sector

FROM: Robert J. Edwards Jr.
                              Acting Supervisory Border Patrol Agent
                              Brian A. Terry Station

SUBJECT: October 2nd Remax Saddle Shooting (Nick Ivie)

On Tuesday October 2, 2012, while working in the Brian A. Terry Station Area of Responsibility, I was assigned to work as the Grid 7 Acting Supervisory Border Patrol Agent (ASBPA). Although I was assigned to work to Grid 7, I was assisting other Border Patrol Agents in Hunter Canyon in Zone 28. As the call of shots fired came across my service radio at around 1:30 A.M, I activated my emergency equipment and headed for the scene. Myself and five other Border Patrol Agents met at the trailhead for the Dead Girl Trail north of Gravel Pit Road. I informed each agent of the plan to take the Dead Girl Trail to the ridgeline and once on the ridgeline head southeast towards the shooting scene. Once we got on the ridgeline we headed southeast towards the area of the sensor activation and last known area of the Agents.

As I approached the area around the shooting, the Customs and Border Protection helicopter (Omaha Unit) was being called out by Border Patrol Agent Graciela Borjas. As the Omaha Unit found Agent Borjas in their spot light I approached Agent Borjas and asked her of her condition. She told me that she was ok and unharmed. I then asked the location of the other Agents. She pointed to the Remax Saddle approximately 150 yards northeast of her position. I asked Agent Borjas approximately how many suspected illegal aliens where in the group, if any where armed and if she saw which direction they fled. Agent Borjas told me that she saw three-four individuals in the group and she saw one longarm and was not sure which direction they fled. Agent Borjas then told me she fired an unknown amount of bullets from her service weapon. I told Agent Borjas to insert a fresh source of ammunition and secure the partially used magazine in her magazine pouch since the scene was still unsecure.

Acting Border Patrol Supervisor was the first responder to make contact with Agent Graciela Borjas. She immediately told him she saw three or four illegal aliens, including one with a longarm. Edwards advised Borjas to load a full magazine into her pistol, because the scene was insecure. Edwards found first responder Agent Mc-Whorter with injured agent Agent Johnson, nearby on the south mountain slope. Edwards asked McWhorter where Agent Ivie was, and he pointed to the north. The FBI alleged that Johnson fingered Ivie at his shooter, but Johnson had said the shooters were to his west. This report—filed the same day as the ambush—is another evidentiary document disproving the FBI's finding.

13

FBI Interviews First Responder to the Shooting Scene

"McWhorter picked up Johnson's M4 rifle and began scanning the area for any threats." A statement in the FBI interviewer's report that agrees with the Border Patrol agent's version

Wednesday, October 3
Brian A. Terry Border Patrol Station

As part of the Bureau's investigation, two FBI agents interviewed BP Agent Jake McWhorter. The interviewing agents were listed as Brent A. Templeton and Chad R. Edlund.

When Agent McWhorter was interviewed the day after the shooting by two FBI agents, one of the agents wrote a witness statement summary of that session, known in FBI lingo as a *302*. The report was filed with the FBI on October 11.[1]

Prosecutors frequently tell jurors that there is a puzzle, filled with pieces of evidence, which all fit together to form a clear picture of what occurred. They then tell the jurors that the picture they have presented to them demands a guilty verdict.

Defense attorneys also assemble pictures to present to jury panels. In order to persuade jurors to acquit their clients, defense attorneys figuratively superimpose their pictures over the ones the prosecutors assembled—causing jurors to question the validity of the prosecutors' versions.

In the case of the shooting death of Agent Ivie, the overwhelming evidence pointed to an ambush by illegal aliens involved in smuggling narcotics. There were many pieces of the evidentiary puzzle that fitted together perfectly well, painting a crystal-clear picture of what actually occurred.

However, the lead agency charged with investigating the shooting was piecing together an alternative picture, attempting to obstruct the view of the true accounts of the incident.

The interview report the FBI filed after interviewing BP Agent Jake McWhorter, one of the most important witnesses in the Ivie case, contains some stunning discrepancies from McWhorter's written report.[2]

The FBI report clashes with McWhorter's witness statement—as well as with much other evidence—by indicating that Agent Johnson knew where Agent Ivie was in relation to himself when the gunfight erupted.

It is clear that Johnson did not know where Ivie was when the shooting began. He apparently believed that Ivie was at the saddle, but he did not see Ivie when he arrived there. In fact, Johnson never saw Ivie at all.

The FBI report presents a false picture, saying that, when Johnson was asked where the suspects were, he pointed *in Ivie's direction*. That is a blatant misrepresentation of what actually occurred, according to what McWhorter wrote in his report and what Johnson said in his FBI interview.

This entire FBI report is riddled with inaccurate statements.

According to the FBI report, McWhorter said his partner, Victor Ocejo, talked to Nicholas Ivie on his cell phone the night of the incident. Ivie told Ocejo he was responding to the sensor that went off and was looking for foot signs.

McWhorter said he also heard Gracie Borjas or David Johnson on the radio, saying they were also responding to the "sensors."

Although the FBI report refers to "sensors," McWhorter and everyone else associated with this incident referred to the triggering of *one* sensor as the reason the agents ascended to this saddle. McWhorter, in his written Border Patrol report, specified the identification number, 2453-1, of the one sensor to which Ivie and the other two agents responded.

This is an insignificant detail, but it shows the pattern of inaccurate reporting, which is consistent with the FBI's handling of the case.

McWhorter told the FBI agents that "at some point (he and Agent Ocejo) heard over the radio both Borjas and Johnson say, 'shots fired.'"

The two agents got on their horses and started to ride toward the saddle to assist, the FBI report said.

The FBI summary eliminated the fact that the Border Patrol agents were still sitting in their pickup truck, parked a few miles away, when they first heard the report of "shots fired." Then they drove to a point near the scene and unloaded their horses, before mounting them.

Once again, this omitted detail might seem insignificant, but it helps to paint a false picture of what actually occurred.

When the two mounted agents were about 50 yards from the scene, "located between two peeks [sic] in an area known as a *saddle*, they were told by Omaha (*Omaha* is the U.S. Customs and Border Protection helicopter's call sign) to wait till Omaha cleared the area" (parenthetical in FBI memorandum).

After the helicopter arrived, the two agents resumed their ride to the saddle.

"Once they got to the top, McWhorter saw a Border Patrol Agent (Ivie) laying [sic] face down on the ground," the FBI report said. "McWhorter dismounted from his horse and went to Ivie and turned him over. McWhorter could tell that Ivie was deceased at that time. McWhorter picked up Ivie's pistol that was laying [sic] no more than a foot away and scanned the area."

The pistol was no more than a foot away from what? McWhorter wrote that he found Ivie's pistol near his flashlight. This FBI report contained a mistaken rendering of this significant detail. Even if McWhorter said something a little different in his FBI interview from what he wrote in his report, such as that he found the pistol a foot away from the flashlight, why not say so?

Where Ivie's pistol was located is important, a possible significant evidentiary detail in the case.

According to the Border Patrol crime map, Ivie's pistol was found in a different location from where McWhorter said he found it or later placed it. An FBI agent should have realized this could be important.

"McWhorter stated that Ivie's flash light [sic] was off when they arrived. Then they heard someone yelling for help, who they identified as Johnson. McWhorter had Ocejo stay by Ivie with the horses when he went to check on Johnson," The FBI report said.

Significant Discrepancies

The FBI report on the interview contains a passage that differs in a significant way from what McWhorter wrote about his encounter with Johnson on the slope of the mountain. Especially because this witness interview summary was filed after the FBI revealed its conclusion on the case, I believe the discrepancy was intentional.

"McWhorter found Johnson just on the other side of the hill," the FBI report said. "Johnson was in a seated position with his back leaning against the hill, holding his M4. McWhorter picked up Johnson's M4 rifle and began scanning the area for any threats."

That part meshes with McWhorter's report.

But the line that comes a little later does not:

"McWhorter asked where the suspects were, and **Johnson pointed in Ivie's direction.**"

Two parts of that sentence—the content of the question and how Johnson responded—both differ from what McWhorter wrote about this interaction.

In McWhorter's report, he said he asked this question, which made perfect sense under the circumstances:

"I asked him where the shooters had been when he was shot."

Then Johnson said, "right there," and "pointed toward some bushes, about 10 yards to his west."

After Johnson told him where shooters had been, McWhorter immediately looked over that area to see if those shooters or others were still nearby.

According to the McWhorter report, what transpired between McWhorter and Johnson was a conversation about **being shot at from the vicinity of nearby bushes by unknown assailants.**

"I asked him where the *shooters* had been when he was shot, and he responded saying 'right there' and pointed towards **some bushes approximately 10 yards to his west,"** McWhorter wrote. **"I scanned the immediate area for any threats."**

There was *nothing* **in McWhorter's report about any possibility of Johnson being shot at by Agent Ivie or by any other agent.**

There was *nothing* **in McWhorter's report to indicate that Johnson knew where Ivie was at the time McWhorter asked him where the shooters had been.**

And when McWhorter wrote his report, he was clearly indicating that he was on the mountain when there was still a possibility of an armed threat nearby. **His partner and friend, Agent Nicholas Ivie, would never have been considered a threat.**

When Johnson was shot by the suspects, Ivie was lying face down on the ground about 45 feet northwest of Johnson. **If Johnson did point toward bushes to his west, he was pointing toward bushes that were not near Agent Ivie.**

Agent Johnson was asked by McWhorter where the *shooters* were when they were shooting at him, and Johnson pointed toward where they were when they shot at him, McWhorter said in his report.

In the FBI interview report, McWhorter asked Johnson **"where the suspects were,"** not where they had been at the time they were shooting at him.

So Johnson—who later told the FBI **he never saw Ivie at the scene,** and did not know where Ivie was when McWhorter began speaking to him—somehow **"pointed in Ivie's direction?"**

McWhorter wrote that **Johnson pointed to bushes to the west,** which would have eliminated the possibility of Johnson pointing to where Ivie was found. There were bushes west of the place Johnson was seated, but Ivie's body was not found in that direction.

Agent Ivie's body was found roughly in the direction McWhorter pointed out to Johnson *later* in their conversation, while they were on the southern slope of the mountain.

When McWhorter asked Johnson where the shooters had been, he was likely interested in that **because the shooters could still have been hiding there.**

Neither McWhorter nor Johnson wrote or said anything that indicated that either of them thought Ivie was the shooter, according to McWhorter's report and Johnson's interview.

Why did the FBI report get this important detail wrong? And how did it come about that this glaring error happened to mesh with the FBI's false narrative?

The main point of the FBI report, filed on October 11, based on notes from an October 3 interview, was apparently that Johnson was implicating Agent Ivie as being at the origin point of the gunfire toward him.

By the time they filed this report, the FBI agents would have known exactly where Agent Ivie had been when he was shot and fell face forward. And they would have known that it was not west of the position where Johnson was found.

Agent Johnson had no idea where Agent Ivie was when Agent McWhorter asked him where the shooters had been.

So Johnson would not have "pointed in Ivie's direction," as the FBI report said.

Once again, Johnson said he never saw Ivie at the scene. Ivie's body was lying on the ground, obscured from Johnson's view by thick brush.

Johnson would later tell the FBI he saw toward his left—which would have been to his west—a suspect wearing a blanket, with a smuggler's pack on his back, immediately before the gunfire erupted.

We have to wonder why the FBI agents would write that **Johnson pointed in Ivie's direction when asked about suspects.** There was nothing in McWhorter's own incident memorandum that backed up this statement.

Nick Ivie was not a suspect—he was an agent of the U.S. Border Patrol.

As readers will discover in later chapters, facts that were firmly believed about this incident by law enforcement officers and investigators, as well as by numerous news reporters, were later ignored and even ridiculed—because they did not fit the government's narrative.

It would become obvious to anyone who examined the facts of the case that the FBI did not undertake a normal homicide investigation.

In his report, McWhorter wrote that he found Johnson in a specific place—the same place and defensive posture that Johnson reported to FBI agents during his interview.

The FBI 302 did include the statement by McWhorter that **"McWhorter picked up Johnson's M4 rifle and began scanning the area for any threats."**

By including that statement, the FBI was acknowledging that Johnson and McWhorter both believed there was a strong possibility that there were still suspects in the vicinity.

Johnson also said during his FBI interview that he was concerned about suspects coming toward him while he was wounded, perhaps as many as 50 of them.

Much of the testimony Johnson would give during his interview in the Tucson FBI field office on Thursday, October 4 is corroborated by other evidence. None of it is contradicted by circumstantial evidence or eyewitness testimony.

Many of the details Agent Johnson would relate about the incident match McWhorter's written statement, Agent Borjas's interview transcripts, a statement by the supervisory Border Patrol agent who first found Borjas on the mountain, local law enforcement reports, and the crime scene maps.

But the statement in the FBI report on the interview with McWhorter contradicts much of the evidence, including what Agent Johnson recalled about his interaction with the first responder on the scene.

The conversation between Johnson and McWhorter was remembered slightly differently between the two Border Patrol agents—which is normal—but neither of them reported that Johnson pointed toward the location of Agent Ivie's body.

The FBI report said this about McWhorter's recollection:

"McWhorter asked where the suspects were, and **Johnson pointed in Ivie's direction.** Johnson asked McWhorter if 0-225 (Ivie) was down, and McWhorter told Johnson he was."

But when the FBI interviewed Johnson Thursday afternoon, two days after the shooting, he instead recalled that he asked Agent 190 (McWhorter) where Ivie was. In response to his request, Johnson said that McWhorter did not say anything. "I think he just nonchalantly pointed over the hill."

During Johnson's interview, the FBI interviewer followed that response by asking if Agent McWhorter had asked him where the shooting came from or where the threat was.

"No, no," Johnson replied.

The report written by Agent McWhorter describes the interaction with Agent Johnson regarding the whereabouts of the suspects. That interaction occurred within about half an hour of the shooting. His memorandum was filed with the Border Patrol the day after the shooting. It recalls that Johnson pointed to his west to identify the direction of the shooters.

Ivie's body was found in the approximate direction McWhorter indicated to Johnson, when Johnson asked him where Ivie was. But there was no mention of the location of Ivie's body in McWhorter's written report.

Agent Ivie's body was located north by northwest of Johnson's position—not near the "west" direction McWhorter wrote about as Johnson's perception of where the shooters had been.

McWhorter asked him a specific question: Where were the shooters when you were shot? Then he added that he used that information to scan "the immediate area for any threats."

When Johnson indicated where the shooters had been—without correcting him to say he thought there was only one shooter— McWhorter used that information to check out his close surroundings.

This perfectly matches the evidence, because the shooters had been about five to ten yards away at the time of the shooting, which would cause McWhorter to examine "the immediate area" for threats.

Johnson heard that Ivie was dead—apparently shortly after he was asked where the shooters had been while shooting. The news of his fellow agent's death certainly had a tremendous impact on Agent Johnson.

For McWhorter, who was already painfully aware of the death of Agent Ivie, his attention would have been focused on the whereabouts of the shooters. His focus was on *the threat*—suspects who had already murdered a friend and horse patrol teammate—and who had also wounded another agent.

McWhorter was scanning the area for threats that might come from the direction where the shooters had been. He was absolutely not thinking about a possible threat from his deceased friend.

The FBI version of the McWhorter interview—filed on October 11, nine days after the shooting—does not present a coherent, true story, as do the stories by the two agents who were on the scene.

So Agent Johnson, who did not know whether Ivie was dead or alive when McWhorter first found him—and later told FBI interviewers he never saw Ivie at the saddle—immediately *"pointed in Ivie's direction"* when asked about the suspects?

That makes sense only when you discover what the FBI had already announced about the Ivie case by the time this report was filed, on October 11.

The FBI witness statement on the McWhorter interview is short and concise, just one line more than one typewritten page. But it achieves its goal—to back up the FBI's narrative—by changing the testimony of the agents, who were reliable witnesses.

As this book was about to go to press, evidence about the FBI's practice of tailoring 302 witness statements to fit specific narratives surfaced in another case with obvious political implications. There is more information on this insidious practice in the latter chapter on the FBI.

The discrepancies between Agent McWhorter's written report and Johnson's interview testimony can be explained as two honest officers telling slightly different stories.

Neither mentioned anything about Johnson being shot from the direction of Agent Ivie. Bringing Agent Ivie's name into the story of Agent Johnson being shot has nothing to do with what the agents reported, and everything to do with the FBI manufacturing its own evidence.

14

Wounded Agent Tells FBI He Saw Silhouetted Smuggler

"I kind of had my guard down, and then when I seen a silhouette it was square, it kind of looked like a smuggler with—with a bundle on his back, crouched over." Border Patrol Agent David G. Johnson, on what he saw at the saddle.

Thursday, October 4, 3:55 p.m.,
FBI Resident Agency, Tucson

Agent David G. Johnson, who underwent surgery to treat the bullet wound to his buttock shortly after the shooting, was released from the hospital the same day.

Two days later, he was interviewed by an FBI agent at the FBI resident station in Tucson. The interview lasted for 40 minutes. Also present in the interview room were Sean Chapman, a Border Patrol union lawyer representing Johnson, Michael Kleving, an investigator who worked with Chapman, and Assistant U.S. Attorney Jesse Figueroa.

The timing of the Johnson interview was significant. The same day the interview was being conducted, the FBI released to several news outlets a surprising statement about the Bureau's theory on what had occurred—which contrasted dramatically with what Agent Johnson was reporting.

The day of Agent Johnson's interview—when the FBI would be fully aware of the testimony of both surviving agents—it released its first public statement on its investigation, with full knowledge that the Bureau was disregarding all the eyewitness evidence in the case.

This was not just eyewitness testimony from random passersby. The eyewitness testimony the FBI—and its other federal partner, the Border Patrol—decided to ignore was from trained federal agents.

Both of those agents have worked for the Border Patrol without interruption since then, which begs the question of why they would be retained—without any discipline—if their testimony on a major homicide case was deemed unreliable or dishonest.

But there was no blame assigned to those agents—because they had performed honorably and reported accurately what occurred.

The Bureau assigned no blame to the two surviving agents—while inventing a narrative that implied that their testimony was untrue.

Agent Johnson's testimony would never be addressed by the FBI as part of its public record.

All Border Patrol agents were under threat of discipline or even criminal prosecution if they publicly disagreed with the conclusion of the FBI, which the Border Patrol endorsed. So they would be at risk of losing their careers, their reputations, and possibly even their freedom, if they were to go public with the statements they made in their closed-door FBI interviews.

Both federal agencies were at that time under control of political appointees of the incumbent presidential administration.

Agent Johnson comes across in his interview transcript as someone who was not impressed with himself or his performance while under fire and facing death—yet the way he responded to the ambush was extremely impressive.

Agent Johnson held his fire while he was repeatedly fired upon, with more concern about the possibility of shooting a fellow agent than for his own safety. But after he was injured, he had the presence of mind to fire several suppressive rounds, just enough to silence the suspects who were trying to kill him and his partner.

He deserved to receive the highest commendation for his outstanding performance under fire. Instead he was forced to remain silent, and his brave deeds were swept into the ashbin of history.

When Agent Johnson was interviewed by FBI agents, his account matched the accounts of the first responders who found him shortly after the incident. His statements also meshed very well with the testimony of Agent Borjas and with a tremendous amount of circumstantial and forensic evidence.

There is not one scintilla of evidence in the case that contradicts the statements agents Johnson and Borjas made before the FBI released its astonishing conclusion to the public.

FBI Special Agent Tony M. Taylor Jr. conducted the interview. Taylor, assigned to work out of the Tucson office, had also been involved in the investigation of the shooting of Congresswoman Gabby Giffords and 19 other victims, for which he received a distinguished service award from Attorney General Eric Holder. In that case, the shooter was arrested on the site, immediately after the shooting, pled guilty to murder and attempted murder, and was sentenced to serve seven terms of life in prison, plus 140 years.

Taylor began the interview with Agent Johnson by introducing himself and explaining that the interview was being conducted because the FBI was responsible for investigating assaults on federal officers.[1]

Johnson said he was a line duty agent for the Border Patrol, assigned to the Naco Station. His normal shift was the "midnight shift," from 10:00 p.m. to 6:00 a.m.

Line duty agents from the Naco station are often "forward deployed," patrolling just north of the border fences. If an individual or group jumps a fence or drives through a break they caused, the line agent tries to apprehend them. Line agents—when on duty in a line position—are routinely involved in chases with illegal border-crossers.

Johnson said that on the night of October 1, the agents gathered for muster at the station, where they received their location assignments. He and another male agent were assigned to patrol Seven Alpha within Grid 7. That is the sector in the vicinity of the intersection of International Road, which runs parallel to the border fence and Border Road, which winds down from just south of Highway 80.

After the agents had been dismissed from the meeting, Johnson retrieved his weapons and other equipment and entered his patrol vehicle.

At about 11:00 p.m., Johnson heard over his radio that a sensor had been triggered near Highway 80, in an area with which he was not familiar. He heard Agent Graciela Borjas, an agent with almost two years' experience, respond to the dispatcher. She said she would head toward the sensor, located on a mountain ridge. She would ascend the mountain from the south.

Borjas was assigned to work as a tac agent, patrolling just north of the border. If agents working the line position found signs of illegal aliens at the border, Borjas's job was to provide backup from just north of the line. As line agents pursued border-crossers from the south, she was supposed to help apprehend them as they headed in her direction.[2]

When Johnson heard that Borjas had offered to hike up to the mountain saddle to investigate a likely intrusion by several illegal aliens, Johnson listened to the radio traffic to hear whether anyone else was going to accompany her. Because his duty for that shift was basically to monitor traffic at the border—where his presence in his vehicle would possibly deter traffic in the vicinity—he was hoping another agent would volunteer to go with Borjas, so he could remain on the line.

Johnson had some flexibility while on line patrol. He could decide for himself whether to leave the line in order to chase border-crossers.

If he had been assigned to a Hard X position, he would have had to remain in the same spot near the border.

The Hard X defensive position strategy had been created in the late 1990s, during one of the most prolific periods of illegal immigration in Cochise County history. Because the number of arrests had been so high at the time—with 26,000 illegal aliens arrested in March 1999 by agents from the Douglas Border Patrol Station—the decision had been made by officials in Washington, D.C. to order agents to stand by in one place and do absolutely nothing, as the illegal aliens crossed into the United States.

That way, the arrest statistics—the official way of estimating the number of illegal border-crossers—would be lower. Allowing more illegal aliens in would create a record of fewer coming in. Here you have government math at its finest.[3]

When Agent Johnson did not hear anyone else volunteer to ascend to the saddle with Agent Borjas, he called her on his cell phone.

She told him she would be going up by herself.

"I'll go with you," Johnson told her.

They arranged to meet at the intersection of State Highway 80 and Chisolm Trail, about 17 miles northeast of their duty station, on the north edge of the small border town of Naco. The junction where they would meet, marked by a blue street sign with white lettering, lies about halfway between Bisbee, a picturesque tourist town of about 5,000 residents, and Douglas, a small border city of 15,000.

Johnson drove the Border Road, a two-lane dirt road that wound past an empty ranch house on the right, then onto a short stretch of paved Paul Spur Road, past a towering industrial plant that processed lime from an excavated hillside on his left. He then turned left onto Highway 80, a thoroughfare that winds east to west through the Mule Mountain region, then turns north at both ends, connecting with coast-to-coast Interstate 10 near Tucson to the west, and New Mexico to the east.

Borjas drove a short distance along Highway 80 until she saw the familiar sign for Chisolm Trail Road. She pulled off the Highway, crossed the cattle guard, and parked near the group of rural mailboxes set by the roadway for nearby residents.

On the way to the rendezvous point, Johnson asked a dispatcher at the station to give him GPS coordinates for the sensor, because he was not familiar with that location. The dispatcher gave him the coordinates, as well as "the best route to take up to the sensor."

The two agents met and headed south in their separate patrol vehicles on Chisolm Trail, a dirt road with a few scattered residences on either side, until they reached a location near Dead Girl trail, with the distinct outline of the ridge clearly in sight.

To reach a parking spot below the ridge, they drove slowly across the high desert, beyond the end of a network of dirt roads. They would have to ascend about 1,000 feet from where they left their vehicles. Although neither of them was familiar with that specific territory, they were confident they could arrive at their destination without any trouble, especially with the help of the bright, full moon and their GPS coordinates.

Regular duty agents are rotated from one border section to another, changing beats as frequently as every two weeks. In that way, agents are expected to gain a general knowledge of a wider range of territory.

"We parked just underneath the ridgeline," Johnson told the interviewer. He added that the distance they had traveled from Highway 80 was about a mile.

For the next eight minutes, the two agents retrieved from their vehicles the gear they would carry with them on their midnight hike.

"I always take my M4 with me," Johnson said of his semiautomatic rifle. The M4 featured a 14½-inch-long barrel, weighed seven-and-a-half pounds, and used a 30-round magazine. He was also carrying his H&K P2000 semiautomatic .40 caliber pistol, loaded with a 12-round magazine.

Johnson grabbed some extra batteries for his flashlight, punched the coordinates of the sensor into his handheld GPS, and checked to make sure he hadn't locked his keys in his vehicle.

"For some reason, I left my vest," Johnson told the interviewers.

Agents often choose to leave their vests behind when on foot, because the vests are heavy, retain body heat, and make breathing more difficult. It is more challenging to make a climb in a quiet and efficient way while wearing one. Wearing a heavy ballistic vest is also a handicap in the event of a foot chase.

The temperature was about 60 degrees, with a light breeze. It was eerily quiet, with traffic on the lightly traveled nighttime highway out of hearing range.

Johnson was in the lead. Borjas, who had been a speedy softball player in college just a few years earlier, was having trouble keeping up with him because of her injured knee.

"So I'd go up, I'd stop, and she'd catch up," Johnson said. "And we did the whole accordion thing up the side of the hill."

They would periodically turn on their flashlights to "cut for sign," looking for signs of illegal aliens, such as footprints, but they walked the trail mostly by moonlight. When they did turn on their lights, they cupped their hands and held them against the ends of their flashlights to narrow the beams, to decrease the odds of being detected.

However, it was questionable whether that routine Border Patrol strategy had any effect. Whether or not Agent Ivie was employing that method, the two agents were able to spot him on the north side of the mountain at least twice, as he lit up the ground with his flashlight.

There was no way the agents could sneak up on illegal aliens at night in this area, if the aliens held the higher ground and were awake. From the vantage point of Remax Saddle, the border-crossers could see for miles in almost every direction, including the trails the agents were taking and the roads the agents had taken up to the trailheads.

But there was still the chance that the illegal aliens or their dope could be apprehended by agents approaching from both sides. It was not unusual for smugglers to drop their packs, weighing 50 pounds or more, and take off running.

When Johnson reached the mountain ridge, and Borjas did not arrive shortly afterward, he went back down the mountain to find her.

"I waited for her; she was taking longer than expected, so I went down to look for her," Johnson recounted.

After they had reconnected, they walked along the north side of the ridge.

"There was a ton of trails, and I looked at my GPS—I have a topographical map on my GPS—and the mountain went way around," Johnson said. "I was like, that's going to take too long. So I decided that we needed to take the south side of the mountain, the ridgeline."

As they hiked the trail, they shone their flashlights to "make sure we couldn't see any sign of anything" and "make sure nobody was coming our way."

But mostly they just hiked by moonlight.

"You could see the ground. Every once in a while, you could see Ivie's light in the distance," Johnson said. "He was coming up."

The FBI agent asked Johnson where the starting point of Agent Ivie's ascent had been.

"There's a road called Remax," Johnson replied. "You get off 80 and take Remax up."

Remax Road is a narrow, unmarked road that starts at the highway, less than three miles northwest of the Chisolm Trail junction.

"And it's pretty much a straight climb up," Johnson said, adding that he had first spotted Ivie climbing up when they were about a mile apart.

"So we continued on the trail, occasionally cutting; we'd only turn on our lights here and there. I'd put my hand over my light because I didn't want to give away our position, because the smugglers have an advantage at night.

"So you try to use it to your advantage to sneak up, to where you got to go, cut around and then go from there. Because if they see your light, they're gone. You're never going to catch them."

As they continued walking east along the ridgeline, the two agents were closer than half a mile to Ivie.

"He came on the radio and said he had sign for two, but he wasn't sure if it was new, if it was good, if it was new or old," Johnson said.

Johnson's radio was "acting up," so he took the battery out, put it back into his radio, and it began working again. Meanwhile, his partner remained in contact with Agent Ivie.

"Borjas was the one that was talking to him," Johnson said.

The hike from the south was more challenging than the northern route, with several ascents and descents along the way, as well as more cacti to dodge and more thorny plants lining and intruding on the trail. Even while outfitted with leather gloves and boots, as well as uniform trousers with reinforced knees, a slip or fall into one of those plants could produce painful injuries.

As they walked along an east-west ridgeline, less than a half mile from the saddle, the two agents approached a steep declination, followed by a steep ascent.

"I made a joke to Borjas," Johnson said. The agents were gazing at the challenge before them. They were not as fresh as when they had left their vehicles. Johnson told Borjas, "If I have to go back up that, I'm not going to."

Borjas chuckled at the remark, Johnson said. Then Johnson suggested they take an easier route.

"So we took the ridgeline around and what it did was it met up to that north-south ridgeline. And we kind of side hill it up. There's a saddle, a peak and a saddle.

"We're almost to the south saddle and Ivie got on the radio and said, 'Hey, what's your guy's location?'

"I looked at my GPS and said, 'We're a tenth mile out . . . from the sensor.'"

When Johnson told Borjas they were one tenth of a mile out from the sensor, "she got on the radio and told (Ivie), and that was it."

From what Johnson had heard from Ivie, he believed Ivie had already arrived at the saddle.

"So we continued up. We're at the ridgeline where we hit the saddle. We started making our way up the peak," Johnson said. "As we're coming down the peak, normally what happens is when an agent cuts sign you see a light. We came up; I didn't see any light."

Because Johnson knew that Ivie was nearby—and had not reported any contact with illegal aliens—he believed he would see Ivie at the saddle with his flashlight still on. Ivie had not said a word about seeing any people—just footprints.

"We came up, I didn't see any light. I thought that maybe he was further north of us, so we came down and I was just walking," Johnson said.

Johnson said what usually happens in scenarios such as this one, when agents arrive on a scene as another agent is looking for signs with his flashlight, then the arriving agents also turn on their lights and look for signs.

"I was waiting to see his light."

But there was no light.

Instead, Johnson saw something that put him on alert. He had been "kind of relaxed" as he approached the saddle, because he expected Ivie to be there and nobody else.

"As we were walking down the ridgeline something caught my eye, it was a silhouette. It didn't look right, it just looked out of place from everything else.

"As we're coming down I kind of had my guard down, and then when I seen a silhouette it was square, it kind of looked like a smuggler with a bundle on his back, crouched over," Johnson said.

Johnson immediately thought that this was one of the two smugglers whose footprints Ivie had just seen and reported on his radio.

"I had my M4," Johnson told the FBI interviewer. "I came at the low ready and started walking towards it. And it looked like somebody shoved a blanket off of them, and then I walked two more feet or so and shots rang out. Boom!

"And it was by the third shot, I realized I was getting shot. It was the first three shots; it was a shock. By the third shot I realized I was getting shot at.

"I screamed: 'hey, hey, hey, hey.' I tensed up and then there was like three more shots after that and then there was a brief pause and then it started shooting again," Johnson said. "They started shooting again."

Johnson said he could focus only on the muzzle flashes. He didn't hear the first three shots, just saw the explosions, as bullets came flying out of a gun.

"After that I could faintly hear the actual gun going off."

The FBI agent asked Johnson whether he could identify the kind of firearm he believed was being discharged, by the sound of its firing.

Johnson said it sounded like a handgun. He estimated that he was about 15 or 20 feet from the muzzle flashes, from the shooter.

"So when I went 'Hey, hey, hey,' there was three more shots after that and then there was a pause. And I was still standing there and then I could feel the—they just started shooting again.

"At that point I told myself, 'You know what? You better do something or you're going to get killed up here.'"

Johnson felt rocks hitting his shins, as bullets impacted the ground. He was still standing, an easy target, with a full moon exposing him fully to the shooter. The shooter had a clear view of him, but all Johnson saw were the muzzle flashes. The shooter was likely in a cover position, behind some brush.

"And then my focus went back up and then I got hit in the ankle (by a bullet) and then my focus went back to my ankle. At that point I turned, and I think I got hit in the buttocks. I took a step or two and then I turned around and engaged.

"When I brought my weapon up, it just seemed like forever. I sighted in and I just started shooting.

"I brought it up, I couldn't see anything. I have an EOTech (rifle sight) and I could just see the circle with the dot in the middle. It was dark. And I brought it up, and I just started firing towards where the muzzle flashes were coming from.

Johnson said he did not see any muzzle flashes as he was firing while peering through his rifle sight. He was firing in the general direction of the muzzle flashes that he had just seen moments before.[4]

"I don't know how many rounds I shot. When I was shooting, I could barely hear my M4 going off and then all of a sudden it just got loud, like boom, boom, boom, boom, and then it just went low again.

Johnson stopped shooting, turned around, and grabbed his radio from his shoulder clip.

"I looked to my right and I seen Borjas, she was already going in the direction we came. I took three or four steps and I felt it was like a Charlie horse in my buttocks.

"And I could just feel the blood gushing out."

Johnson told himself: "You're hit; you've got to get down."

"I kind of blacked out a little bit because the shock of being hit, knowing that I was hit I kind of blacked out. I hit the ground."

Johnson regained consciousness when he fell to the ground. Facing the direction of the shooter or shooters, Johnson checked his GPS for his location.

He dropped his radio, lost it, then quickly found it. He pushed open the microphone button and reported his badge number to other agents listening on the frequency.

Then he said, "Eight six nine. Shots fired." The number sequence 869 is the designation of the dispatch control room at the Naco Station.

He heard what he just said, coming from Borjas's radio. She was lower on the slope than he was, toward the west.

Then he heard Borjas also say "shots fired," the sound coming from the spot from which he had just heard his own voice on her radio. That was followed closely by hearing her excited statement coming through his radio.

If any of the shooters were nearby, now they would have a fix on him and his partner.

"I jumped up, and I went south, down the hill a little bit. I took a defensive position and I sat there. I was waiting for someone to come over the ridgeline. Waiting for someone to follow up, and it never happened," Johnson said.

"I didn't know how many people were there, it could have been 50 people, I don't know. I just went down. I got shot. I went down. I held my position to make sure that nobody else was following down.

"I was waiting for somebody to come over the ridgeline. Waiting for someone to follow up and it never happened. I checked my mag (magazine), to make sure I had rounds in it still."

"I got on the radio. I think I called out 225, which is Ivie's number. I called out 358, which is Borjas's number."

Johnson said he thought he later asked for "Omaha," the Border Patrol helicopter that was flying nearby. He realized that he should tend his wound, so he cut fabric from his green uniform pants, loosened his belt, and applied the piece of cloth to his bullet wound.[5]

FBI Agent Taylor asked Johnson whether he heard any commands from the area where the gunshots originated.

In using the word "commands," Taylor was likely inquiring about whether he heard anything from Agent Ivie. Border Patrol agents are under orders to identify themselves and give commands to suspects, such as "show me your hands."

However, there had been no commands.

"It was eerily silent besides the gunshots," Johnson responded.[6]

He had shouted to the shooter, hoping that would stop the firing. In response, the shooter resumed his attempt to take Agent Johnson's life.

"At any point, did you go toward where the threat was?" the FBI agent asked Johnson.

"No. I stayed—I stayed in—where I was—where I set up is where I stayed. I didn't move. I felt 'cause with the bullet wound I wasn't a [sic] 100 percent I didn't want to go out and . . ."

"OK," Taylor said, interrupting Johnson.

". . . so I stayed," Johnson said, completing his sentence.

In response to Taylor's follow-up questions, Johnson reiterated the firing sequence. Three shots were fired initially, followed by a pause and another volley.

"I didn't realize they were shooting at me until after the third round. That's when it dawned on me that I was being shot at."

After the pause, there was a volley that was "a continuous about six to seven rounds."

Johnson probably did not know that 10 shell casings were found at the scene. His testimony as to how many shots were fired at him and the distance between the shooter and himself were remarkably accurate—as recorded on the crime scene map. The approximate distance between Johnson and his assailant could be ascertained by the locations of both of their ejected cartridge casings.

As Taylor interviewed Johnson, asking him to repeat key parts of the narrative, his story was almost exactly the same every time he retold it.

Taylor asked him to describe how he was returning fire.

"Were you facing the threat? Were you moving?" The FBI agent asked.

"I faced, I faced the threat," Johnson said.

Then Johnson said the initial volley was seven shots, slightly different from what he originally said. Taylor asked for clarification.

"Ok. I saw the silhouette, I started going towards it, shots rang out, initially there was three shots. It didn't dawn on me that I was getting shot at. Once it dawned on me, I screamed, 'Hey, hey, hey, hey, hey.' After that there was three more shots. They were all consecutive: It was boom, boom, boom, boom, boom, boom, boom.

"I felt the rounds hittin'—hitting the rocks, the rocks were hitting my—my shins," Johnson said. "I told myself, 'You need to get out of here or you're going to get killed.' I—my focus went to my legs 'cause of the rocks. It went back up to the shooting and then I got hit [with a bullet] in the ankle."

Taylor asked Johnson what direction he was moving on the ridgeline as he approached the saddle where Ivie was located. Johnson said he was moving north.

Then Taylor asked a very important question. With the FBI about to announce something that was unimaginable in light of all of the evidence, the response by Agent Johnson must be considered as a significant piece of the evidentiary puzzle.

Taylor asked, "As you were moving in the direction along the ridgeline, um, did you, um, acknowledge your presence or hear someone acknowledge their presence?"

"No," Johnson responded.

Agents are trained to identify themselves when they approach suspects or fellow agents. Of course, Agent Ivie would have identified himself as soon as Agent Johnson arrived, if there had been no smugglers in the vicinity.

After Johnson responded that there was no identification before the shooting erupted, Taylor changed the subject.

Taylor asked, "OK. Um, where was Agent Borjas at this time when the shooting happened?"

Johnson replied, "When we were coming down the ridgeline, she was behind me. When I caught the silhouette out the—out the corner of my eye, I turned. She was probably six feet behind me, ten feet behind me."

Taylor asked Johnson which direction the silhouette was in relation to him as he approached it.

"It was off, it was off to my left," Johnson said.

It is important to note that the information about the apparent shooter resembling a smuggler did not surface during the questioning by the FBI agent. Although Johnson said that the silhouetted figure flung a blanket off in response to Taylor's question, the information that the suspect also was carrying a smuggler's pack came as the result of a question from Johnson's attorney.

Apparently, the FBI had no curiosity about the individual wearing a blanket, who removed it immediately before someone started firing at Agent Johnson. When someone takes off a blanket in the dead of the night on a mountain, and then firing commences, it is reasonable to believe the two actions are connected. A blanket would be the perfect way to conceal a long arm.

Near the end of the 40-minute interview, FBI Agent Taylor asked Sean Chapman, "Do you have any questions for me?"

Chapman turned to his client and asked, "Just to clarify, because I want to make sure for the record, you've been asked to give distances and estimates of time, lighting, etc. Tell us about your perception of what was going on while this was occurring How were you feeling, what were you seeing and hearing?"

Johnson replied, "Well, initially when we I I was kind of relaxed because I knew Ivie was in the area supposedly, because he did say he cut sign. As we're coming down I kind of had my guard down, and then when I seen a silhouette it was square, it kind of looked like a smuggler with—with a bundle on his back, crouched over, in my mind I was like that's his bodies, that's the two he cut.

"So I started to go investigate a little bit further; that's when the shots ran out, or rang out. And initially, I was-it-I don't-I don't know why I was just was like, stop or just like **'hey, hey, stop shooting.'** And then it kept going, like that pause and then he just kept shooting, and I was like [to himself]: 'You have to do something, you're going to die up here.'

Chapman then asked, "How did it affect what you were seeing and your ability to estimate distances and that type of thing?"

Johnson: "It—it was hard. Like I said, the depth perception was

> JOHNSON: Well, initially when we-I-I was kind of relaxed because I knew Ivie was in the area
> supposedly, because he did say he cut sign. As we're coming down I kind of had
> my guard down, and then when I seen a silhouette it was square, it kind of looked
> like a smuggler with-with a bundle on his back, crouched over, in my mind I was
> like that's his bodies, that the two he cut. So I started to go investigate a little bit
> further, that's when the shots ran out, or rang out. And initially, I was-it-I don't-I
> don't know why I just was like stop or just like hey, hey stop shooting. And then it
> kept going, like that pause and then he just kept shooting and I was like you have to
> do something, you're going-you're going to die up here and I.

all right. A little bit off, a few feet off the trail, it was good. Anything beyond that, it was horrible. I couldn't tell, like I said, when I came down I thought the saddle went further, further north. I guess from the pictures it's not."

Johnson was referring to the crime scene photos, one of which is presented in this book. The saddle is narrow from north to south, measuring about 33 yards.

"But so—it—I don't know—getting shot at and just everything was just, tunnel vision. My hearing went, it came, it came and went."

Taylor then resumed his role as chief interviewer.

He asked Johnson whether he or the other two agents were using any kind of night vision device.

Johnson said he was not, and he did not know whether the other agents were using any night vision devices that night.

During the interview, Johnson revealed how he discovered that Ivie had been killed.

He said that after he was injured, a Border Patrol agent with the star number 190 (Horse Patrol Agent Jake McWhorter) arrived on the scene.

Later, when Johnson ascertained that agents had arrived on horseback at the saddle, he called, "I'm over here."

The agents identified themselves to each other, the normal procedure when agents meet in the bush.

When Agent 190 asked Johnson, "Who is this?" Johnson told him his name and star number.

"I could see him with his lights," Johnson recalled. "They were looking around for awhile actually before they actually got to me."

McWhorter was on the mountain saddle with his partner, and Johnson was downhill from him, out of his line of vision on the southern slope.

"Can you come over here?" Agent McWhorter asked Johnson.

"No, I'm hit," Johnson replied.

Agent McWhorter than hiked several steps down the slope to where Johnson was lying on the ground. He rolled Johnson over, cut open his shirt, and held the shirt fabric against his buttock wound, adding another piece of fabric to try to stop the bleeding.

Johnson asked him where Ivie was.

"I think he just nonchalantly pointed over the hill," Johnson recalled.

FBI Agent Taylor asked Johnson whether he had cell phone contact with Ivie.

Johnson said he did not have phone contact with Ivie, but he did speak with a control agent at their station on his phone.

Johnson: "Control called me to see how I was doing. I think I told them—I asked them where Ivie was at."

When the control agent said he had not heard from Ivie, Johnson reported to control, "I think this might be green on green." (accidental shooting between agents).

Taylor: "And, so you relayed to um, over the cell phone that you thought this might be green on green?"

Johnson: "I thought, I told—I told them, I said, 'If you can't reach Ivie, it's, it's possible it might be green on green.' It's possible. . . . It was chaos, I don't know."

When Agent Johnson said he told the dispatcher that it was *possible* that it was an accidental shooting, he never said that it was possible that *he* shot Agent Ivie.

When Johnson said that he told the control agent that he thought "green on green" was a possibility, the FBI agents did not follow that statement with a question about which agent might have shot Agent Ivie. The details connected to this possibility, and how Agent Johnson's testimony was later used, are essential to unraveling the mystery of who shot Nick Ivie.

15

News Outlets Report on Murder Suspects in Mexico

"The two were in possession of drugs and guns when they were detained." CNN report on the arrest of the shooting suspects near the border.

Thursday, October 4

A report from CBS News, updated at 9:14 p.m. Eastern Daylight Time on Thursday, October 4, about 100 minutes after the Agent Johnson interview, said a law enforcement official had confirmed that "investigators are looking into friendly fire as a possible scenario in the death of Ivie."

The timing of this release from an anonymous official— undoubtedly from the FBI—is very revealing.

The testimony of Johnson would lead an impartial investigator to the understanding that it was more likely smugglers were involved in the shooting than that agents just opened fire on each other.

These initial anonymous *leaks* to news agencies could have been interpreted in this way: agents opened fire on each other accidentally, while engaged in a shootout with smugglers.

That kind of scenario would be understandable, especially in a situation such as an ambush by armed smugglers. Unfortunately, in law enforcement and in war, there have been countless tragic occurrences of so-called *friendly fire.*

In hindsight, however, we can clearly see that the FBI was preparing the press and public for a vastly different finding.

Thus began the press campaign to spin a narrative that flew in the face of all the evidence—especially the testimony of the surviving agents.

It was 4:35 p.m. in Arizona, 7:35 p.m. on the East Coast, when the Johnson interview ended. Because Arizona does not observe Daylight Savings Time, its time in October is the same as Pacific Daylight Time.

This CBS story was posted less than two hours after Agent Johnson completed his testimony in the FBI office in Tucson. Although Agent

Johnson spoke of the possibility of friendly fire—as he had when he spoke to the control agent from the mountainside—he did not present any evidence strong enough to warrant a public statement of this nature.

That same CBS report of Thursday, October 4, carried this lead sentence:

> NACO, Arizona—Mexico arrested two people Wednesday over the fatal shooting of U.S. Border Patrol Agent Nicholas Ivie earlier in the week, a Mexican military official confirmed to CBS News. (*The suspects were taken into custody Tuesday, but were probably officially placed under arrest on Wednesday*).

FBI officials were aware of the arrests of those suspects. Some of the news reports said they were captured with firearms and narcotics. Specific firearms were documented in one news report. So why would the Bureau send news agencies a report of a possible friendly fire incident so quickly?

There was no solid evidence to indicate that either of the surviving agents shot Agent Ivie. Agent Borjas never fired her pistol, and Agent Johnson fired only a short burst of suppressive fire toward the night sky.

Agent Ivie died from a single bullet wound to the center of his forehead.

Anyone with the slightest knowledge of homicide investigations would wonder how someone receives a gunshot wound to the middle of his forehead as a result of fire from fellow agents—at relatively close range under a brilliant full moon—without either agent being aware that Agent Ivie was shot at that time.

The autopsy report stated that Agent Ivie received a gunshot wound in his skull, the size of a large caliber bullet—whereas the only firearm fired by an agent discharged a small caliber slug.

In the heat of a gun battle, anything can happen. But a gunshot wound in the center of the forehead by accident under these circumstances?

Of course, none of those details were ever released to the public. Not one media report I could find revealed the nature of Agent Ivie's wound, or the fact that neither of the other agents even saw him at the scene.

When the FBI announced that Agent Ivie's death was possibly caused by friendly fire, the Bureau had a tremendous amount of evidence that illegal aliens were on the scene, shooting one or more firearms.

Although Agent Johnson said he thought this could have been a "green-on-green" incident, he also clearly reported that he saw no target when he pulled his trigger.

When Johnson said he thought it "could have been" a friendly fire incident, he believed that Ivie was on the scene—although he never saw him at all. When he reported that it was possible that Ivie was killed by an agent, due to the chaotic nature of the situation, he was not aware that Ivie had died from a single bullet wound to the center of his forehead.

Johnson saw Agent Borjas with her gun drawn, apparently pointing it toward the suspects. But he had no way of knowing whether she fired her weapon.

With Johnson firing one burst of six rounds in the direction of the muzzle flashes—without seeing any target in his sight—it is at the very outer edge of the realm of possibility that he could have landed a single shot to the middle of his fellow agent's forehead.

Besides the obvious suspicion that a fatal shot like this would indicate an intentional murder, a burst of gunfire like Agent Johnson's would most likely spray several bullets within a small area. In other words, when Agent Johnson fired several shots within a short period of time—possibly within one second or so—if any of the bullets struck a surface the size of a head, it is likely another shot would have also landed on the same surface.

If Agent Johnson had shot Agent Ivie in the head immediately after Johnson received fire, it is likely that he would have known that he did that. Remember, the two agents were only about 20 feet apart, under a bright full moon. Agent Johnson saw nothing in his sight when he pulled the trigger—no head, no tree branch, just a general target area where gunfire had originated.

If Johnson had seen another agent—and mistaken him for a shooting smuggler—he would have tried to take him down with a bullet to his midsection. Border Patrol agents are trained to aim for critical mass, the larger target of the chest and abdomen—not for a head shot.

The firing toward Agent Johnson ceased when Johnson returned fire. If Agent Ivie had fired all those rounds toward Agent Johnson—supposedly thinking he was a smuggler—why would Ivie then be standing or kneeling without cover, exposing himself to return fire?

As readers will clearly see as this story unfolds, the release on Thursday of the idea that Agent Ivie was killed as a result of a tragic accident was the first public salvo in a barrage of disinformation designed to create a thick smokescreen.

It could be argued that some of the evidence found at the scene could cause investigators to consider that Agent Ivie had been shot by a fellow agent—but there was absolutely no evidence available on Thursday for any responsible law enforcement official to release this statement.

If there was just some slight *possibility* that this beloved Border Patrol agent was accidentally killed—instead of being murdered in the line of duty by cartel smugglers—why release a statement that would cause so much heartache and sorrow to grieving relatives and friends?

If there was just a suspicion of *friendly fire* on Thursday—which is all the evidence would have justified at that time—why not wait until it was actually proven before making such a reckless statement?

The FBI would later claim that it had proved its case by a test—a test that was allegedly administered on Friday. So why release an anonymously sourced statement on Thursday, before this so-called "indisputable" evidence materialized?

The testimony of Agent Borjas was definitely known by the FBI, as well as what she said to first responders after the incident. She never said anything about any possibility of "friendly fire."

The BP CIT crime scene map and the FBI evidence sheet show no evidence of Agent Borjas firing her weapon.

Nothing that Agent Johnson said in his interview would have led well-trained FBI agents to believe there was strong evidence that Agent Ivie was killed accidentally. He said he saw nothing in his rifle sight and fired a few shots toward muzzle flashes.

Would the fact that neither of the surviving agents saw Agent Ivie at the saddle indicate that one of them probably landed a perfect assassin's shot to his head from a weapon neither of them fired?

So why would the FBI hurriedly release statements about the possibility that agents killed and/or wounded each other—without any conclusive evidence?

This would be devastating news to family members and friends of the fallen agent, as well as to the agents who had just survived a murderous attack by smugglers.

That question is especially begged because the FBI normally operates at a glacial speed. Why would the Bureau release this statement, even before the funeral of Agent Ivie had been held?

What was the hurry? Why wouldn't the FBI agents and forensic scientists take their time, sort through and analyze all the evidence, and then issue a complete report about what occurred?

Every bit of information the FBI released to the public, beginning with Thursday— all but one press statement leaked by anonymous sources—totally ignored the testimony of the two sworn federal law officers. It was as if Agents Borjas and Johnson had never been interviewed.

As far as the FBI, the press or anyone else was concerned in the days and years following this incident, their interviews never occurred.

The eyewitness testimony of the two surviving agents was not only ignored by the investigators, but not one report from any media outlet revealed that there were obvious discrepancies between what they said and what investigators concluded.

The transcripts of the interviews with the agents—and their dismissal as irrelevant or worthless by the FBI investigators—provide some of the best evidence that this was not an investigation at all, but plainly a coverup of the true circumstances of the murder of Agent Ivie.

In an ABC World News story, posted at 9:50 p.m. on Thursday—36 minutes after the CBS story—it was revealed that "authorities are looking closely at the possibility that a friendly fire accidental shooting is at the heart of the incident."[1]

Notice the murky language here: The prestigious news network presents a redundancy of synonymous phrases, "friendly fire" and "accidental shooting," followed by a meaningless phrase: "the heart of the incident."

No explanation was given in the ABC story as to why the FBI was "looking closely" in that direction. The FBI also explained in its anonymous statement that it was withholding details "due to the sensitive and ongoing nature of the investigation."

Why not just tell the truth?

The Obama administration was not happy with the idea that smugglers had murdered another Border Patrol agent so shortly before the election—so the FBI should present this unproven theory that agents simply shot each other? The FBI and its political leaders were apparently hard at work manufacturing an explanation to back up this unlikely scenario.

The FBI brass wanted to assure the press and the public that there was genuine evidence behind this ethereal smokescreen, so the ABC story dutifully carried this impressive revelation:

"**Additional forensics are being done on ballistics, and additional interviews are being conducted to determine if the matter can be** *resolved in the coming days*," the ABC story said.

Here we have a statement of exemplary deception.

The phrase "additional forensics" implied that the FBI already had performed significant forensic testing to back its friendly fire accusation. What forensic test did the FBI perform in its lab that proved that both surviving agents gave erroneous testimony about what occurred?

What the FBI did not say on Thursday was that the ballistics testing—which it would present as its indisputable evidence—was not to be performed in its crime lab until Friday.

And what additional interviews were *being conducted*? There were only two eyewitnesses to the murder of Agent Ivie—beside the 3 or 4 or more smugglers who were on the scene. Was the FBI going to try to find other witnesses to contradict the solid eyewitness testimony of the two sworn officers?

Then there was this bit about resolving "the matter" in the coming days. If that didn't raise a red flag for anyone with the slightest suspicion of a political motive, nothing would.

No other complicated homicide investigation conducted by the FBI or any other reputable law enforcement agency has ever been resolved within a few days. The idea that the FBI was working toward a resolution of "the matter" within days provided a stunning clue that the FBI had already reached its conclusion. Politicians and their faithful servants were just hammering out a few more details, which would help complete their narrative.

This homicide investigation involved a tremendous amount of evidence and information, as well as many possible suspects, including the two who were arrested near the scene and remained in custody in Mexico.

It would normally take a significant amount of time to process a stunning amount of potential forensic evidence. This would include six or more firearms—four used by the agents and the two found with the Mexican nationals, 16 or more shell casings, DNA and fingerprints taken from the suspects, testing of numerous items for possible DNA and fingerprints—including three water jugs found with blood on them, two Mexican coins, and a cigarette butt—and shoe prints found at the saddle and on the trail.

It would take more than a matter of days to interview and evaluate the suspects captured in Mexico—of whom it was written in a Mexican newspaper that they were the killers of Agent Ivie. Those two men remained in the custody of Mexican authorities in connection with this murder—at least 13 days after the incident occurred.

So how were the FBI agents going to solve the mystery of who shot Nick Ivie within a few days?

And why would they want to solve it so quickly?

While the FBI was hurrying along to reach its conclusion, its sister law enforcement agency was also looking for answers to come forth as soon as possible—but in an altogether different direction. **Apparently the federal agency that regulates firearms had not yet received the memo that the FBI's investigation was focusing on the activities of the agents.**

The ATF, also under the control of the Department of Justice, was trying to discover information about a revolver recovered from one of the suspects. It was being treated as the possible murder weapon.

The U.S. Bureau of Alcohol, Tobacco, Firearms and Explosives sent out an urgent trace request on a .38-caliber Titan Tiger revolver found in connection with those suspects. The document contained this alert: "Urgent High Profile Border Agent Shot."

This significant detail was carried in an *L.A. Times* story, posted on Friday, October 5. No further information was ever published on those firearms.

The *Times* story on the ATF handling of the two firearms "recovered in the vicinity where Border Patrol agent was murdered," was posted on Friday.

> Gun-trace documents from the federal Bureau of Alcohol, Tobacco, Firearms and Explosives obtained by The *Times* show that a high-powered rifle and a handgun were found near the shooting scene, though it was not clear whether they were connected to the incident.
>
> A .223 Bushmaster rifle, seized on Wednesday, was "recovered in Mexico in the vicinity where Border Patrol agent was murdered," according to one of the documents. It says the weapon was purchased in the United States but does not specify where.
>
> A .38-caliber Titan Tiger revolver was recovered separately Tuesday in Mexico, also near the Naco area, a second document says. That trace record included this alert: "Urgent High Profile Border Agent Shot."
>
> The record says the weapon was originally purchased in February 2009 from the Frontier Gun Shop in Tucson.[2]

The rifle had also been purchased in the United States, but no other information was reported on the rifle in this story.

The story—by the newspaper with the largest circulation of any paper west of the Mississippi River—went on to say that Ivie was killed not far from where "fellow agent Brian Terry was slain" less than two years earlier.

Because both of the Mexican suspects were apprehended on Tuesday, and another news report said those suspects were captured "with drugs and *firearms*," it is more likely both weapons were recovered at that time. There are numerous discrepancies among various news reports regarding the time and place of the arrest of those suspects. The best evidence I found on the time and place of their arrests was the eyewitness testimony of the Border Patrol agent who was on the scene at that time, and was willing to share his observations with the readers of this book.

FBI agents supposedly found a lack of non–law enforcement shell casings at the scene—a detail released to the public through the acting county sheriff. But they conveniently left out the detail that a revolver was found with suspects arrested in connection with the shooting. As every law enforcement officer knows, revolvers do not leave behind shell casings.

The .223 rifle recovered in connection with the suspects was an important find. If Ivie was killed by a .223-sized bullet—which the FBI will later quietly assert—then we have the possibility of this rifle as the murder weapon. Agent Borjas repeatedly said she saw a rifle being fired as soon as the gunfire erupted. It makes perfect sense that Agent Ivie was killed by the first bullet that was fired at the scene, as the other two agents arrived.

I believe it is significant that the rifle found in connection with the two suspects who were arrested just south of the border was not sent to the FBI crime lab. If the FBI believed that Agent Ivie was shot with a small caliber bullet—such as a .223—why was this rifle not tested as the possible murder weapon?

The ATF, the sister agency of the FBI, had possession of this rifle. Agent Borjas told FBI agents she saw the shooters at the scene shooting a long firearm—in an interview just hours before those suspects were taken into custody. The FBI had to be aware that this was a possible murder weapon.

This appears to be a classic case of matching results to a predetermined conclusion.

If there were no shell casings found connected to the Bushmaster rifle, that does not mean that the rifle was not fired at the scene. A nylon bag brass catcher, which collects shell casings as they are expelled from a rifle, could have been attached to that rifle.[3]

The FBI has never told the media that its ballistic test matched a fragment from a .223 slug to Agent Johnson's rifle—probably because that could have caused people familiar with ballistics to challenge that dubious assertion. If there were a piece of a .223 bullet actually found in Agent Ivie's skull it would be more likely to have been fired by the rifle found with the suspects.

FBI: "Murder Weapon Not Found"

Another important detail to emerge from the media reports on Thursday was the release by the FBI—through anonymous sources of course—that they had not found the "weapon used in the shooting."

Almost simultaneous with the first FBI reports that they were "looking into friendly fire" as the cause of Agent Ivie's death, the Bureau told reporters that they had not found the murder weapon.

How could they have it both ways?

Did it make sense that the "murder weapon" had not been found, although the FBI had possession of all the weapons of the Border Patrol agents?

Was this a classic case of the right hand not knowing what the left hand was doing at the FBI?

They had possession of Agent Johnson's rifle the same day as the shooting, which they sent on to the FBI crime lab in Quantico, Virginia, arriving on Friday, according to an FBI document.

So why would government leakers bother telling CBS and CNN, two of the Obama administration's most faithful news agencies, that they had not found the murder weapon?

In the classic style of "plausible deniability" deception—frequently employed by intelligence agencies—they were refuting the news reports that specifically said suspects were found with firearms, and that they "were found near the shooting scene."

Those specific weapons were never directly acknowledged by the FBI. But the FBI would have known that the ATF had possession of those firearms. Neither agency ever publicly acknowledged those firearms—despite the outstanding *L.A. Times* story.

What was the murder weapon that had not been found? Agent Ivie was killed by one bullet. Period.

Weapons *were* found. If the ballistic testing was not to be done until the following day or later, how did the FBI know that the murder weapon had not been found? FBI documents clearly stated that the testing could not have been done before Friday, Oct. 5.

How were the firearms that were found with the suspects ruled out?

This is what two of the news reports of Thursday, October 4, said about the lack of a murder weapon:

In the short CBS/AP story entitled "Possible 'friendly fire' explored in border agent's death," one passage said, "Meanwhile, a law enforcement official confirms to CBS that investigators are looking into 'friendly fire' as a possible scenario in the death of Ivie."

A few lines later, the article said, **"A federal law enforcement** official who spoke on condition of anonymity said investigators who were scouring the area near the shooting had yet to find a gun in their search."[4]

There are layers of deception to be found in this line.

The supposition seems to be that if there were smugglers there shooting at the agents, wouldn't they have surely left a firearm or two lying around right there at the scene?

The investigators "scouring the area near the shooting scene" did not find a gun—except for the firearms belonging to the dead and wounded agents.

So what? Cartel assassins rarely leave their firearms behind, so it was not a big surprise that firearms used by the shooters were not found nearby. Why bother leaking such a bizarre and misleading statement as that?

More importantly, why in the world would a prominent national news organization release this statement as if it were a serious, important pronouncement essential to the understanding of this case. Are reporters and editors really that dense? Did they truly not grasp that it is meaningless to "not find firearms" at a crime scene? As if killers normally leave their firearms right there, in order to help investigators.

This CBS story mentioned that two suspects were apprehended, but it left out the crucial detail that the suspects were armed. With other media outlets covering that significant aspect of this case, apparently FBI officials turned to CBS to blow smoke about zero firearms being found.

It is not clear whether the CBS personnel were aware that firearms were found with the suspects. However, it is evident that the FBI wanted to steer the public away from the fact that firearms were found with the same suspects publicly identified as possible killers of Agent Ivie.

Ironically, just 10 minutes later, at 6:24 p.m. Arizona time, 9:24 p.m. Eastern time, CNN updated its story—which highlighted the fact that suspects detained in connection with the case *did possess firearms.*

The story's lead sentence read, "Two men were questioned Thursday by Mexican authorities about a shooting that killed a U.S. Border Patrol agent and wounded another near the U.S.–Mexican border in Arizona, a source in the Mexican attorney general's office said."

The Mexican Army handed over to local authorities "the two men they had detained near the American border," the federal Mexican source told CNN.

This was one of the first stories to mention that the suspects were armed.

"The two were in possession of drugs and guns when they were detained, added the source," the CNN story said.[5]

This short story included the detail that Ivie was killed near a "border station named for Brian Terry," whose death led to the disclosure of the Fast and Furious operation. It also revealed that Ivie had been the fourteenth Border Patrol agent killed in the line of duty since 2008—and the third in 2012.

In this CNN story, which did not mention "friendly fire," James Turgal, FBI Special Agent in Charge of the Phoenix Division, "declined to say if the Border Patrol agents involved in the incident returned fire."

As the FBI was rolling out its "friendly fire" narrative in a limited way, the local supervisory agent was reluctant to release any information on what actually occurred. In all fairness, decisions were unquestionably being made at a higher level as to how this case was going to be handled.

Turgal could have known as early as Tuesday morning, after the crime scene investigators found shell casings from Agent Johnson's rifle, that gunfire was returned by at least one Border Patrol agent. It is unclear as to whether agents would have understood the facts concerning the discharge of Agent Ivie's service pistol. With reporters still believing in the true story that smugglers had fired on the agents, it was a natural question as to whether Border Patrol agents had returned fire.

But the FBI chose to remain silent about what actually occurred. Everything was being kept tightly under wraps, most likely by order of FBI Director Robert Mueller III, who reported to his boss, Attorney General Eric Holder. Was Obama in the loop all along? We can surmise that the deluge of press reports on the slaying from the most prominent national and international press outlets—and its connection to Fast and Furious—were impossible to ignore.

What a tangled web the FBI and its political overseers were weaving. Fortunately for them, there would not be anyone around for several years to try to hold them accountable for their deception.

Attorney General Holder Announces Involvement in the Investigation

Holder—who was deeply involved in the coverup of the Fast and Furious operation—announced at a press conference Thursday that he was involved in the Ivie case.[7]

Newspapers, including the *Washington Post*, reported on the involvement of Holder in the Ivie case—but not one pointed out the irony of Holder involving himself in a case so closely related to Fast and Furious, the scandal for which he had earned a contempt of Congress citation.

"At a news conference yesterday in Washington, Attorney General Eric Holder said he is getting updates on the investigation's progress and has spoken with Homeland Security Secretary Janet Napolitano about the probe," the New Hampshire paper, *Concord Monitor*, reported, referring to the investigation into the Ivie slaying.

Is it a stretch of logic to believe that Holder was doing a lot more than "getting updates" on the Ivie investigation?

The Holder press conference was held on the day the FBI first leaked information that the agent was possibly killed by friendly fire.

At that time, Holder was the only attorney general in history to have been held in contempt of Congress—by a resolution that passed on June 28, 2012, with the approval of 17 Democratic representatives—for withholding documents about Fast and Furious. That was just three months and four days before the Ivie murder.[7]

The *Monitor* story also revealed that Napolitano would be traveling to Arizona on October 5 "to meet with law enforcement authorities in southern Arizona about the investigation."

Here we have information that two highly partisan cabinet ministers were personally involved in the Ivie investigation, immediately following his murder.

Anyone who held those officials in high regard might have believed that they would have ensured that all stops would be pulled out to discover who killed Agent Ivie, and to bring those killers to justice.

But to astute political observers who had followed recent cases involving the murder of Americans serving in the federal government—Fast and Furious and Benghazi—the involvement of Holder and Napolitano could have instead been seen as a signal that this investigation would be corrupted or buried as soon as possible, by any means necessary.

The shooting case of a young, unknown agent without any political connections—which brought the worst scandal of the Obama administration back into the national news spotlight—would not be a high percentage bet to be resolved by a normal, lengthy, in-depth investigation.

Borderland residents familiar with Napolitano largely despised her for her outrageous statements that the border was now more secure than ever. In 2012, borderland residents were experiencing a high level of traffic from drug traffickers and other illegal immigrants, who burglarized homes, occasionally murdered or kidnapped residents, left behind tons of trash, and caused tremendous financial losses by setting fires and destroying property and livestock.

However, Napolitano scored a few favorable points with Arizonans when she reacted to the murder of Agent Ivie by releasing a strong statement the day it occurred, in which she cried out for justice:

"We are working closely with our federal, state, and local law enforcement partners to track down those responsible for this inexcusable crime, and to bring them to justice."[8]

Like many other Americans, Napolitano was apparently outraged that armed men had taken the life of a brave young Border Patrol agent. She wanted the world to know this crime was "inexcusable." All decent people would agree that there was no excuse for assassinating this kind-hearted young agent. And most Americans would hope that his killers would be captured, tried, and imprisoned or executed.

But despite her political acumen, Napolitano might not have immediately realized that "bringing them to justice" was not necessarily a great idea during this critical election season.

Summary of Information the FBI Released Two Days after the shooting

> • Less than two hours after Agent Johnson told the FBI he fired several shots in the direction of muzzle flashes, after seeing no target in his crosshairs, CBS released a report from the FBI that the Bureau was investigating the possibility of friendly fire in the Ivie slaying.
> • CBS reported that no guns were found near the shooting scene, based on an anonymous FBI source.
> • CNN posted a report 10 minutes later that suspects in the Ivie case were found with guns, from a source in the Mexican Attorney General's Office.
> • An anonymous federal law enforcement source told CNN that no firearms were found connected to the Ivie shooting.
> • The FBI announced its plan to wrap up this "matter" within a few days.

"Nick lived his life as a life of service"
Ivie family holds press conference.
Thursday morning, October 4

At a press conference held on the Sierra Vista campus of Cochise College, Nick Ivie's family memorialized him as a man who was dedicated to the service of God, his family, and his country.

This was the first time the press and public learned some of the details of Nick Ivie's life, including his selfless character. Much more would come out in the days and weeks to come, during which two memorial services would be held.

About 30 members of Nick Ivie's extended family traveled from Utah to Arizona to support Nick's widow, Christy, their two daughters, and Nick's brother Joel. Family members attended the press conference, as well as an ecumenical vigil held that evening at St. Michael's Mission, a Roman Catholic church in Naco.

Nick's other two older brothers, Chris and Rick Ivie, were the only ones who spoke at the press conference and answered questions. Border Patrol Agent Joel Ivie said he was prohibited from speaking by his employer.

When a reporter asked a question about the Ivies' two daughters, the young widow broke down as she stood at the front of the room behind the podium, along with a dozen relatives.

Nick Ivie had joined the Border Patrol in January 2008, at the urging of his brother Joel, who had been serving on the force since 2003. Nick was the youngest of the four brothers, with Joel the brother closest to him in age. Nick loved his fellow Border Patrol agents, Chris Ivie said.

Nick had been a volunteer firefighter and emergency medical technician in the city of Spanish Fork, Utah, at the time when he was accepted into the Border Patrol Academy in 2007. Nick and Joel had worked together during the past few months as members of the horse patrol, Chris Ivie said.

Chris Ivie said Nick was a loving husband and father, as well as a friend to everyone.

"He was a favorite uncle; he was that kind of a person," Chris Ivie said.

Chris and Rick Ivie both said they looked up to their younger brother.

"His real love was the outdoors," Chris Ivie said, adding that he grew up with horses, which he loved. "That kind of transferred over to his work."

Chris Ivie said that working at something you love can take the fun out of it, but that did not apply to Nick's job, which he also loved. When Chris asked his brother whether riding had become a chore, Nick smiled and said, "Riding never gets old."

Chris had been told a detailed account of a story about Nick, which would be retold many times in the days following his death, as an example of his compassionate nature.

"I was actually just made aware of an experience since we've been down here that I didn't even know about, that goes to show how humble Nick was," Chris Ivie said. "There was a time he was on patrol and came across a woman that was with a small group, but she was pregnant, and she had lost her shoes. Her feet were cut up and she had them wrapped in rags. She was in a pretty remote area and couldn't make it any farther.

"He carried that woman a mile-and-a-half to where she could receive the proper treatment that she needed. He really did love the people that he worked with, and he was a hero."

In the aftermath of their loved one's death, Nick's relatives said they had turned to their faith and to each other to stay strong and face the trying times ahead.

"We rely heavily on our Heavenly Father. We know people have been praying for us, and we've passed along an awful lot of prayers ourselves," Chris Ivie said. "We know where Nick's at right now, and that is comforting. We know that he's with loved ones that have passed on before, and we know that we'll be able to see him again, and that definitely is what's carrying us through."

Rick Ivie told reporters that Nick "lived his life as a life of service."

Chris Ivie said, "Nick loved his kids, and it's difficult when they ask for their dad and you can't explain it that well."[9]

16

Agent Ivie's Family Is Told Shocking New Story

"It was really pretty somber," Chris Ivie said, after his family was told that Nick was shot by another agent — after Nick fired at that agent. "Nobody really knew how to take it. It was a lot easier when you thought it was a bad guy out there."

Friday, October 5, Early Morning
The home of Nick and Christy Ivie,
4600 Block of Big Bend Street, Sierra Vista, Arizona

On this momentous day, the FBI would make its final announcement about the Ivie case. But before releasing its statement that afternoon, the story of its finding had to be shared with Agent Ivie's family—in greater detail than the public version.

On Friday morning, federal agents met with Nick Ivie's widow, Christy, and Nick's older brother Joel at the house where Nick and Christy resided, on the southeast side of Sierra Vista.

This meeting was held just before Homeland Security Secretary Napolitano and David Aguilar, acting commissioner of U.S. Customs and Border Protection, were scheduled to arrive at the Ivie house.

Jeff Self, U.S. Customs and Border Protection Joint Field Commander for Arizona, informed Christy and Joel Ivie that Nick was killed because he opened fire on the two other Border Patrol agents, who then returned fire, killing Nick.[1]

Nick apparently thought the other two agents were armed smugglers, Self reportedly told Nick's shocked family members. After delivering this incredible news, Self, along with another Border Patrol official who had accompanied him, departed from the house where Nick and Christy Ivie had been raising their two daughters together.

It is difficult to imagine the level of shock and sadness that Nick's family must have felt when they were the first to hear the news the whole world was about to be told:

Their beloved Nick—an outstanding husband, brother, and father to two delightful little girls—was not a heroic, outstanding agent who was shot while courageously doing his duty. Now they had to live with this strange, unfathomable story, in which Nick—the coolest, gentlest guy that had ever worn a Border Patrol uniform—decided to open fire on his fellow agents way out in the middle of nowhere, for no apparent reason.

This was the conclusion the FBI had reached, and now they were going to have to live with that.

Despite the condolence message the Border Patrol officials conveyed to Christy and Joel—along with this shocking new revelation—Nick's loved ones must have felt as if they had just been punched in their guts with a 10-pound sledgehammer.

Nick's reputation would surely be ruined.

Who ever heard of an agent shooting at another agent? They had been engaged in a routine assignment—agents meeting each other in a remote location to interdict smugglers. Why in the world would they start shooting at each other? They had been on the radio, talking to each other, only minutes before.

All the reports during the first two days after the shooting had said that the three agents were ambushed by drug smugglers from the cartel.

Border Patrol agents never, ever opened fire on each other.

There was no record of another friendly fire incident in the lengthy history of the Border Patrol. It was rare for any law enforcement officer to accidentally shoot another officer—but nonexistent among federal agents protecting the nation's borders.

Agents rarely opened fire even on dangerous smugglers—except in exceptional circumstances, such as when smugglers fired on them or were violently resisting arrest.

The two close relatives of Nick Ivie who were told this story then shared it with other family members, who arrived at the house in time to meet with the high-ranking federal officials who had flown in from Washington, D.C.

Joel and Christy were keenly aware of the stories about Nick confronting smugglers on Remax Saddle three days earlier, and the shootout that resulted in his death. Joel also served on the horse patrol in Naco, and he was friends with the agents who found Nick's body.

Chris Ivie, Nick's brother and the oldest of five Ivie siblings, spoke later to a newspaper reporter about the mood in the room when the extended family members received the news that Nick was shot after shooting at other agents.

"It was really pretty somber," Chris Ivie told the *Deseret News* of Salt Lake City. "It was pretty quiet in the room. Nobody really knew how to take it. It was a lot easier when you thought it was a bad guy out there."[2]

As the family was processing this devastating news, Napolitano and Aguilar appeared at the Ivie house for their visit. News outlets were told that Napolitano and Aguilar were there to pay their condolences.

The two Obama administration officials appeared at the Ivie home in Arizona at about 9:00 a.m., right after the extended Ivie family had received the terrible news.

That same day—at an unknown time, which was not recorded in the FBI ballistics report—Agent Johnson's M4 rifle was received at the FBI Crime Laboratory in Quantico, Virginia.

A fragment of a bullet jacket allegedly removed from Agent Ivie's brainstem during his autopsy arrived at the East Coast lab on the same day.[3]

It is important to note that the widow and brother of Agent Ivie had already been informed on the morning of Friday, October 5, most likely before 9:00 a.m., that Nick's death had been caused by a gunshot fired by a fellow agent. That would have been before noon at the FBI forensic lab in Virginia.

It would be announced later that day that the "indisputable" fact that Agent Ivie was killed as a result of friendly fire was due to ballistic testing that had been performed by the FBI.

The prestigious law enforcement agency—well-known to other agencies as thorough, but normally operating at a glacial pace—would not have ordinarily performed a conclusive ballistic test of this nature within the time span of one morning.

Because we don't know what time of day the lab received the rifle and bullet jacket, we do not know whether the lab had even received those items before the Ivies were told that it was a proven fact that Nick was shot by an agent. But we do know that it is not normal procedure for the FBI to receive items in a high-profile case such as this and produce conclusive results within a matter of hours.

It was not as if there was a serial killer on the loose or a child had been abducted. Rushed results such as this one lay far out of the normal range in a homicide case in which there was no reason to rush to judgment—outside the political realm. Why crush the spirits of family members and friends of a beloved young man without being certain of your conclusion?

The time when Nick Ivie's relatives were being told that Nick had been killed by a bullet from the rifle of a fellow agent—a conclusion allegedly ascertained by a ballistics test at the FBI Crime Lab—was within hours of the lab doing the testing, or even before any testing had been done.

There would be many steps involved in reaching any finding involving a tiny bullet fragment and a rifle, in any kind of homicide case. But to reach an "indisputable" conclusion in a matter of days in a case which was garnering a tremendous amount of national attention, was far beyond the scope of how the FBI—or any reputable law enforcement agency—would normally operate.

And even if it were possible to competently complete the testing in a matter of hours or minutes—which a highly respected forensic expert told me was "unbelievable" during the time frame in question—that would still not explain why the FBI was already leaking to the press the *day before the ballistics test* that friendly fire was being looked at as the cause of Agent Ivie's death.

That advance warning—which was signaling the media to stop talking about smugglers killing the Border Patrol agent—took place the day before the lab had even received any evidence to verify the FBI's theory.

Not one news story ever mentioned anything about the timing of the handling of this critical FBI evidence. Not one news report during the past seven years took into consideration what occurred during this ballistics test—which supposedly provided irrefutable evidence that Nick Ivie was killed by a fellow agent.

Not one news report mentioned that the FBI laboratory had received its evidence to prove or disprove its friendly fire finding one day *after* it had already announced it was looking at friendly fire as the cause of death.

The "Report of the Examination" on the ballistics test that allegedly matched a bullet fragment to Agent Johnson's rifle—which the FBI used as the basis for its "indisputable" conclusion of "friendly fire," is dated October 10, 2012.

On that date—five days after the FBI would release its final statement on its finding in the Ivie case—the FBI Laboratory in Quantico, Virginia sent its report on this ballistics test to the Phoenix FBI office.

The FBI could have sent its investigation partners to tell the Ivies that there were already some indications of the *possibility* of friendly fire.

But that wasn't what Border Patrol officials told Christy Ivie and Joel Ivie the morning of Friday, October 5. Those officials explicitly said that the FBI investigation proved that Nick had fired at other agents and had been killed by return fire.

There is no credible evidence that this ever occurred—and plenty of evidence that Agent Ivie was shot to death by a smuggler.

The Bureau had to wrap up the entire case that day. That meant telling Nick's relatives early Friday morning, and the rest of the world late Friday afternoon. There was no way the Obama administration was going to allow this story to stay alive going into the next week, with the next presidential election debate scheduled for Tuesday, October 16.

Chris Ivie told a reporter from *Deseret News*, Salt Lake City, that Napolitano and Aguilar "assured the family Nick Ivie didn't do anything wrong, and that they would have done the same thing under the circumstances."

Chris Ivie and the other family members were assured that, "It was a tragic accident, nothing more."[5]

The family previously believed—along with everyone else who was following the story—that Nick Ivie bravely went to a remote mountain saddle to try to apprehend illegal aliens—and was then murdered by the smugglers he encountered.

Now Nick's relatives were trying to comprehend this brand-new story, in which there were no other people on the scene at all.

Just three agents—all of whom routinely met with other agents in the dark, while some of them were carrying rifles—but this time they opened fire on each other.

It didn't really make any sense at all, especially because Border Patrol agents had never previously opened fire on each other with fatal results throughout the agency's history, as far as anyone could tell.

More importantly, the eyewitness accounts showed that Agent Ivie was expecting the two other agents to arrive on the scene precisely when they did arrive. And the surviving agents told the FBI they were fired on by *other* people—not by Agent Ivie—when they arrived at the scene.

So here they were, just a group of common people related to a young man who had died in the line of duty, sitting in the Ivie family's starter home in an ordinary working-class subdivision, with two of the nation's top government officials. Those two visitors were the heads of the agencies that oversaw the Border Patrol, the employer of Nick and his brother Joel.

Janet Napolitano, the most notable of the two officials, was famous nationwide. She met with President Obama on a regular basis and made the news just by showing up in the state, where she was formerly its top official. Napolitano had left her position as governor of Arizona at the request of Obama, who appointed her to head the cabinet level department charged with protecting the nation's borders.

It might have been comforting for Nick's relatives to hear such important officials say they would have done the same thing—although Aguilar himself had served as a line agent for about 10 years and never did open fire on another agent. It would take a cynical politician to present an invented scenario—something they possibly realized had never occurred—and then say they would have done the same thing.

Border Patrol agents would *not* open fire on other agents who showed up at a mountain saddle, exactly as expected, under a bright full moon. Nobody would do that.

Chris Ivie told the *Deseret News* reporter that the family was told that all the agents at the scene acted according to their training.[6]

This is a very interesting statement, because there is a grain of truth in it, although ultimately it is an outrageous lie.

If the three agents did approach each other without identifying themselves, and then one agent opened fire on the other ones, the agent who fired first did not act according to his training—or in keeping with the training of any law enforcement officer in the United States.

Border Patrol agents are trained to identify themselves and to fire only when they or others are in immediate danger. And they are not authorized to fire at anyone unless they are certain of their target. Firing on someone up in the mountains because he happens to be carrying a rifle is not acting according to Border Patrol training.

However, I firmly believe that the agents *did act* according to their training, and that they responded admirably when they were ambushed by armed smugglers.

But the story that the FBI and other Obama administration officials were peddling presented Nick Ivie as someone who did not act in accordance with his training—while hypocritically lauding him as someone who had done absolutely nothing wrong.

Nick Ivie was being falsely portrayed as someone who made an innocent mistake that had unfortunately cost him his life.

His training prohibited him from opening fire on a couple of agents—or on anyone—who happened to approach him while carrying weapons in the middle of the night. The fact that the individuals who came under fire were Border Patrol agents in full uniform underlines the depth of the deceptive web the federal officials were spinning.

His training and common sense would have prevented Nick from firing on other agents who approached him under a full moon, just minutes after they told him they were a tenth of a mile away, a distance that would take about three minutes to cover on foot.

Many of the agents who worked closely with Agent Ivie—and knew him very well—never believed he opened fire on anyone. He was too level-headed, cautious, and courageous to make such a costly mistake.

Besides that, he was an excellent marksman. If he had tried to kill an armed smuggler, he would have shot him in the chest with his first or second shot. He would not have missed someone eight or nine times at a distance of 20 feet or so under full moonlight, before striking him in the buttock and ankle.

The statement that Nick acted "according to his training" was obviously made in order to pacify the family, to let them know the Obama administration would do everything possible to get them through this difficult time—as long as they didn't misbehave by publicly challenging the official "investigation" results.

The FBI used other agencies to release strong statements about the validity of its conclusions.

"The Cochise County Sheriff's Office said in a news release that the FBI reached the 'indisputable' conclusion that it was friendly fire after doing ballistics testing," said a story posted October 6 on the Web site of the *Arizona Daily Star*.

The FBI did not present its own information, that it had reached the indisputable conclusion that Nick Ivie died from a fellow agent's

UNCLASSIFIED

FBI Laboratory   2501 Investigation Parkway
                                                           Quantico, Virginia 22135

REPORT OF EXAMINATION

To: Phoenix   Date: October 10, 2012
     Sierra Vista RA
     SA Brent A. Templeton   Case ID No.: 89B-PX-2517028

                                      Lab No.: 121005010 ABL NN

Reference: Communication dated October 4, 2012

Your No.:

Title: NICOLAS IVIE - VICTIM (DECEASED), U.S. BORDER PATROL AGENT;
         DAVID JOHNSON - VICTIM, U.S. BORDER PATROL AGENT;
         GRACIELA BORJAS - VICTIM, U.S. BORDER PATROL AGENT;
         AFO;
         10/02/2012

Date specimens received: October 5, 2012

The following items were received in the Firearms/Toolmarks Unit:

Q1   Metal fragment (1B17, E5077748, Item 3)

Q2   Metal fragment (1B21, E5077746, Item 7)

Q3   Cartridge case (1B30, E5077750, Item 16)

bullet **"after doing ballistics testing."** It gave this information to the sheriff's office, which dutifully released it to the press.

I am convinced that this testing was not done by the time this information was released. According to the unsigned "Firearms Report," which allegedly matched a bullet fragment taken from Nick Ivie's brain to Agent Johnson's rifle, that report was sent to the Phoenix FBI office on October 10, 2012—five days after the FBI asserted by proxy that its friendly fire conclusion was based on this testing.

The only other dates recorded on the FBI's Report of Examination are October 5, 2012, when the rifle and bullet fragments were received at the crime lab, and October 4, 2012, when there was apparently some communication between the lab and FBI personnel involved in this case.

The FBI lab report left blank the spaces at the end of its form requiring the names and dates of those who performed a "Technical Review" and an "Administrative Review." There are no signatures on the "unclassified" version of the report. The only names recorded were that of Erich D. Smith of the laboratory's Firearms/Toolmarks Unit, and of FBI Special Agent Brent A. Templeton, of the Sierra Vista, Arizona Resident Agency. Templeton was listed as the recipient of the report.

K1 Colt rifle, Serial Number   . .   . , with sling and scope (1B45, E5077749, Item 43)

The results of the firearms examinations are included in this report.

Results of Examinations:

Specimen Q1 is a .22 caliber (which includes 5.56mm) copper bullet jacket that was fired from a rifled barrel with six lands and grooves, right twist. The Q1 bullet jacket was identified as having been fired from the barrel of the K1 rifle.

Specimens Q3 through Q8 are 5.56x45mm brass cartridge cases that bear the headstamp of Speer ammunition. The Q3 through Q8 cartridge cases were identified as having been fired in the K1 rifle.

Specimen K1 is a 5.56x45mm Colt rifle, Model M4A1, Serial Number   _ . , with sling and sight. The K1 rifle functioned normally when test fired in the Laboratory using a magazine from the FBI Laboratory's Reference Firearms Collection (RFC).

Specimen Q2 is a lead fragment that has no marks of value for comparison purposes.

Here is the FBI's crime lab document, obtained from the FBI's investigative partner, the Cochise County Sheriff's Department, which allegedly proves that the Bureau tested one bullet fragment and matched it to Agent Johnson's rifle.

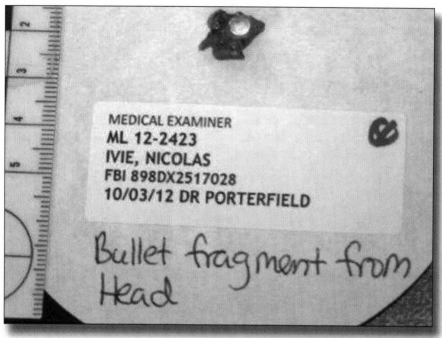

MEDICAL EXAMINER
ML 12-2423
IVIE, NICOLAS
FBI 898DX2517028
10/03/12 DR PORTERFIELD

Bullet fragment from Head

Three photographs of the bullet fragment that the FBI claims was matched to Agent Johnson's M4 rifle. A ballistics expert told the author that he could see in the photographs that this fragment "should have rifling engravings suitable for firearms identification." Photos courtesy of Pima County Medical Examiner's Office.

More importantly, these are photographs taken of the bullet fragment which the FBI claimed that it matched to Agent Johnson's rifle—and this conclusion was "indisputable." There are many unanswered questions about the validity of this finding, including the lack of consideration of any other weapon, as well as the lack of specific times and dates connected to the evidence and alleged test. More importantly, once the smokescreen of this ballistics test is blown away, another question arises: If smugglers fired on agents at the saddle, does it really matter who pulled the trigger of the weapon which killed Agent Ivie? The smugglers who opened fire on the agents would be the only ones guilty of causing his death.

Headline Says It All

The Daily Mail, a London-based newspaper—which at that time had the largest circulation in the world, with about 45 million unique visitors to its Web site each month—posted a story on the Ivie slaying at 3:36 a.m. Arizona time on Friday, October 5.

This story deserved a prize for the most outstanding headline on the Ivie case:

Border agent shot by drug cartel may have been victim of friendly fire.

Let's sort out what this headline is saying:

The Border Patrol agent, Nicholas Ivie, was shot by an operative of a drug cartel.

Although he was shot by a member of a drug cartel, he might have been a victim of friendly fire.

Apparently, the headline writer was trying to reconcile the fact that Agent Ivie was shot by a cartel smuggler with the brand-new information—that the FBI was presenting the idea that he was shot by a fellow agent.

This story was posted after the FBI leaked to its favorite media outlets that its investigation was looking at friendly fire—but before it handed out its official statement.

It comes across as a clumsy headline, yet from the perspective of what actually occurred, it outshines every other headline written during that time frame.

Keep in mind that the most popular news site in the world does not employ amateur headline writers.

Yes, the border agent was shot by an operative of a drug cartel. Despite that fact, the government has a whole other idea to propose. Facts be damned: he might have also been the "victim of friendly fire."

This news story included the information that the agents were fired on in a border section known as "cocaine alley."

It also included information on that significant related story—for its worldwide audience. *The Daily Mail* reported that Border Patrol Agent Brian Terry had been shot to death in an incident that led to the Fast and Furious scandal being uncovered.

The *Mail's* lengthy article also reported that President Obama said his administration was doing everything it could to locate those responsible for "this tragic event."[6]

FBI Issues Press Release, Remains Silent for Seven Years

"The death of United States Border Patrol Agent Nicholas J. Ivie and the injury to a second agent were the result of an accidental shooting incident involving only the agents." This was the "preliminary" finding of the FBI, which has never been amended.

Brief Press Conference
Friday, October 5, about 4:00 p.m.
Tucson Sector Border Patrol Headquarters

During the press conference at Agent Ivie's duty station near the border on the day of the shooting, Jeff Self, Customs and Border Protection (CBP) Joint Field Commander for Arizona, said Ivie died "at the hands of criminals" operating near the border.

"This is a tragic loss for Customs and Border Protection," Self told reporters on Tuesday, October 2, after learning that two Border Patrol agents were shot by smugglers, with one dying immediately.

"We have an unwavering commitment to pursue and bring the perpetrators of this heinous act to justice," Self said.

But just three days later, Self, who would go on to become the chief spokesman for the official government narrative, was already in lockstep with the powerful politicians in control of his agency.

The big news of Friday, October 5, was the release of the statement from the FBI, which would not be a terrific surprise to anyone who was closely following the press reports of the previous day.

FBI Special Agent in Charge (SAC) James L. Turgal Jr., head of the Phoenix-based division covering the entire state, was not present at this press conference. This final press event on the Nicholas Ivie shooting case, well attended by reporters from local and national media outlets, was held at the sprawling Tucson Sector Border Patrol Headquarters, across the road from Davis-Monthan Air Force Base.

Despite his conspicuous absence, the written statement issued in Turgal's name shortly before this media gathering began was the main subject of discussion. Turgal, who released very little information about the investigation officially before this statement was released, has said nothing more to the press or the public in the days and years afterward.

This was the statement issued by the Phoenix Division of the FBI:

"While it is important to emphasize that the FBI's investigation is actively continuing, there are strong preliminary indications that the death of United States Border Patrol Agent Nicholas J. Ivie and the injury to a second agent were the result of an accidental shooting incident involving only the agents."

On this day—just three days after Nicholas Ivie was shot to death while performing his normal duties—the FBI was announcing to the world that this outstanding young agent did not die as the result of an ambush by brutal smugglers.

He died instead because three agents came upon each other during the course of their regular work assignments and opened fire on each other.

SAC Turgal, who had traveled all the way down to the border to pay his respects at the Brian Terry Station near Naco on Tuesday—in order to rightfully involve himself in this important homicide investigation on short notice—was too busy to make the shorter trek from Phoenix to Tucson to take part in the Friday afternoon press conference.

You couldn't blame Turgal and all the other FBI agents for ducking this presser. Why would Turgal attend a press conference—just to duck questions from reporters? Every reporter or editor who had followed this case previously had heard that the agents were shot by smugglers—and two suspects were arrested nearby a few hours later in Mexico with firearms and drugs.

What could an FBI official—who was clearly just an underling regarding involvement in this case—possibly say in response to questions on this stunning new statement? What would anyone in law enforcement do when faced with the dilemma of trying to maintain a reputation of integrity, while being asked to stand behind a false statement concocted for political purposes?

Turgal had already made it clear that he did not want to talk about those suspects—who were being held at that time in a Hermosillo, Mexico jail—and he certainly did not want to answer any possible questions about what the surviving agents might have said in their interviews.

What could he possibly say if a reporter asked him why hundreds of law enforcement officers were sent to the Mule Mountains to search for suspects and collect evidence?

What if one of the reporters asked him about the firearms that were taken from the suspects and processed by ATF?

What would he say if a reporter asked him why agents in radio contact would shoot at each other on a remote mountain ridge with nobody else around?

Turgal, along with many other federal officials, had their orders. They knew they would be rewarded for going along with the official narrative, or they would be punished if they dared to buck the system.

Although there were four FBI agents available to attend the autopsy in Tucson—where the FBI allegedly received a bullet fragment to match up specifically with an agent's rifle—there was not one member of the federal law enforcement agency available to answer reporter's questions on the day the Bureau announced its finding.

Nobody from the FBI was on hand to witness one of the darkest chapters in the Bureau's history—the announcement of a fictional statement, which served to destroy the hope of justice being accomplished in the case of the shooting death of a dedicated, kind-hearted law enforcement officer.

The investigation was over. Those who shot Agent Ivie to death were in the clear. Whatever genuine evidence had been collected would be placed on a shelf. The reputations of the agents who courageously faced a deadly threat were being sullied. The efforts of honest law enforcement officers who wanted to catch the killers and make them pay for their murderous attack were obliterated.

Politics triumphed over justice.

It was Friday afternoon, the traditional time for government officials to release information they wanted to be ignored. Reporters were being counted on to echo the empty words to their audiences and forget about the whole affair by the time they returned to work on Monday.

Which is exactly what they did. All of them. Not one media outlet questioned the validity of the FBI statement.

The statement went on to say that the FBI had not completed its investigation.

"The FBI is utilizing all necessary investigative, forensic, and analytical resources in the course of this investigation," the release said, adding that the Bureau thanked the law enforcement agencies that had assisted in this undertaking. "At the appropriate time, further information will be provided, but while the investigation continues, it would be inappropriate to comment any further at this time."

Although the FBI always keeps its promises in the numerous movies and TV shows that glorify it, the Bureau failed to keep this one. Most of those fictional shows do not reveal that the FBI has failed to live up to its motto of fidelity, bravery and integrity on numerous occasions—especially when its leadership is severely compromised.

The promise that "further information will be provided" at the appropriate time had as much validity as a campaign promise from a two-faced politician. Seven years later, that *appropriate time* has still not arrived.

Instead, the investigation was closed quietly, without any conclusive report given to the press or the public.

"We thank the United States Customs and Border Protection, United States Border Patrol, and the Cochise County Sheriff's Office for the challenging work they do every day and for their ongoing cooperation in this difficult matter," the FBI release said.

Of those investigative partners, all were under the heavy thumb of the executive branch of the federal government, except for one.

The Cochise County Sheriff's Office did a tremendous job of allocating resources on short notice to aid in every aspect of the investigation. Yet when Sheriff Mark Dannels was asked, four and a half years after the incident, what he thought about the results of the investigation, he said he had never received an FBI report.

But in October 2012, there was no public questioning of any report that might be forthcoming from the nation's most prestigious law enforcement agency. Mark Dannels was not yet the sheriff; Acting Sheriff Rexroth was running against him for the recently vacated position. That election was to be held the same day as the presidential contest. Who would question the FBI? Who would want to appear to be some kind of crackpot, for daring to question the greatest collection of highly skilled law enforcement officers on earth?

The press moved on quickly to other stories. After all, it was just an unfortunate accident. Why put salt in the wounds of the agents and their families, who were already undergoing grief and sorrow because of the shooting incident? If they had just accidentally shot each other, there was no good reason to stay on the story.

Border Patrol agents did not believe the FBI report, but they were ordered to remain silent publicly about anything that would contradict the official finding. They were told they could lose their jobs or even face criminal prosecution for speaking out in any way that was not officially approved.

Looking back at the release of the FBI statement six years later, Border Patrol Agent Carlton said that he and other agents whom he knew doubted its validity.

Carlton said that not one agent with whom he had discussed this case said that they believed that "Nick was jumpy" or that they believed this happened the way the FBI said it had occurred.

"Every single person that I talked to about this, that knew Nick, they all say the exact same thing, that Nick's personality was that he was so laid back," Carlton said in an interview. "This situation happening might be a possibility for somebody else. But nobody could see it happening with Nick—that he would freak out and open fire."

Although Border Patrol agents rarely agreed on anything, especially assessments of various agents, all the agents Carlton talked to agreed on these two things:

Number one, Nick would never jump the gun on anything. He was laid back to a fault.

Number two, Nick would not take the first shots and miss.

"From the distances they're talking about, him having a surprise shot, perceiving a threat and having the first move and missing, there is just so small of a chance of it happening that nobody even thinks it's a possibility," Carlton said.[1]

According to Agent Johnson and shell casing evidence at the scene, the shooter fired about eight times before wounding Johnson—at a distance of about 20 feet. Then Johnson was wounded in the buttock and ankle, probably with the ninth and tenth shots.

"Other agents also said he was a good shot," Carlton said of Agent Ivie, adding that he did not have to be an outstanding shooter to hit a man in the chest at that distance.

Carlton said it would have been like hitting the door in the motel room where our interview was taking place.

"And you could pull a gun from a leg holster and hit the door at this distance and not aim. And in stress situations, muscle memory takes over. You would point in that direction and shoot and you're not going to miss.

"None of the Border Patrol agents are going to miss a door-sized target like that. It's not even conceivable to think that Nick would miss from this distance. Johnson was shot twice, but not in areas we would be aiming for," Carlton said. "With no shots close to center mass. . . . all of our shooting is center mass shooting."

None of the shots that were fired toward Johnson "went anywhere close to center mass," Carlton said, adding that indicates that an incompetent shooter was shooting at him.

"I consider a butt shot and a foot shot to be misses," Carlton said. "Because that's not what we're trained for. And to have the first shot, the surprise shot—and then nine follow-up shots supposedly—it really indicates an untrained shooter."

For Nick, it would have been a "huge step" to pull the trigger, Carlton said. To just open fire on someone without a positive identification was totally against Border Patrol training and engagement policy, as well as his character.

"With Nick, he did not get excited. He did not freak out," Carlton said. "But missing? This isn't a guy who is just going to gangster-fire sideways, just start pushing rounds. To miss center target, when the other guy hasn't even identified you as a target yet, I can't see it happening at all."

The veteran agent also addressed the idea that Agent Johnson was the one who killed Agent Ivie, which the FBI has asserted, without naming him publicly. Johnson's testimony and his shell casings show that he fired his semi-automatic rifle six times in rapid succession.

Remember, Ivie was killed by a single bullet to the center of his forehead. Johnson testified at his FBI interview that he fired blindly in the direction of muzzle fire, after seeing no target in his rifle sight. It is more likely whoever shot Agent Ivie intentionally fired at his head.

"He shoots six times in the other direction and only hits with one," Carlton said. "From this distance with a rifle, it's even less (chuckling) of a possibility. It's even less likely that you only get one round on target."

Whether Johnson was holding his barrel steady or panning it, with the bullets flying out at a rate of several shots per second, it would be more likely that more than one bullet would have landed in the vicinity. However, if someone else fired one shot into his forehead, that would fit perfectly with the testimony of the surviving agents and the evidence at the scene.

Carlton said one reason there has never been a "friendly fire" incident in Border Patrol history is that agents train on firearms more than on any other facet of their occupation. They have to take four qualifying tests, or *quals*, every year.

So Agent Ivie would have qualified about 20 times as a Border Patrol agent, after passing about 20 qualifying tests while training in the academy.

"Border Patrol firearms is an eight-hour training day," Carlton said. "That includes policy reviews, our firearms policies, our use of force policies related to firearms."

Training includes running through scenarios, in which agents are instructed as to when to shoot and when not to shoot.

Because of the extensive training, and the fact that those who do not qualify while in the academy do not graduate, Carlton said that all agents are proficient, from the very best to those who are not quite as good.

"Even our bad shots are pretty good shots," Carlton said.

In its concise written statement, the FBI was correct in acknowledging the "challenging work" that the men and women of the Border Patrol, Customs and Border Protection, and sheriff's office performed. And members of those agencies did cooperate at that time with the FBI, providing a mountain of evidence that contradicted the FBI's eventual finding.

Those agencies also deserved the congratulations of the FBI for cooperating in another way: keeping their mouths firmly sealed shut, though many of them knew the FBI's conclusion had to be false, or at least strongly suspected as much.

There was a tremendous amount of evidence that smugglers were involved. Why else were hundreds of officers sent to the scene after the shooting? Why were crime scene investigators ferried by helicopter to the mountain saddle, if three agents just shot at each other—with nobody else involved?

Carlton said another red flag was that no investigations are ever wrapped up that quickly. Especially investigations involving several different agencies: the FBI, Cochise County Sheriff's Office, the ATF, the Border Patrol, and the Pima County Medical Examiner's Office.

"How did they get that done that fast, with multiple agencies involved?" Carlton wondered. "Whenever has interagency cooperation been so good that you can wrap something up (chuckles) on different departmental levels?"

Referring to the ballistics testing, which was purportedly started and finished within a matter of hours on October 5, Carlton questioned its validity.

"An investigation on someone backing their truck into something isn't done in one day," Carlton said.

The FBI Misused Other Law Enforcement Agencies

It was apparent that the statements made on October 5 by other law enforcement agencies who participated in the investigation were spoken on behalf of the FBI—without explicitly revealing the source of their statements.

The FBI brass apparently leaked a steady supply of information to the press about this homicide investigation. If someone else had been leaking that information without the FBI's consent—such as a rogue FBI agent or a member of another agency—there would have been hell to pay.

One of the FBI leaks to news outlets said that it was looking at concluding its investigation within a matter of days after the murder. This shows a reckless disregard for the consequences of clearing a cartel-related assassin and pointing fingers at the Border Patrol agents themselves.

From their perch atop the law enforcement chain, FBI officials did not expect anyone to challenge them for closing out their investigation just three days after a Border Patrol agent was shot to death. There were several FBI agents, and law enforcement officers from other agencies, who knew that the surviving Border Patrol agents said that they saw smugglers at the scene.

But who was willing to withstand the repercussions of speaking out against the Obama administration's FBI?

Whistleblowers are a special breed. There are not many people in any field who are willing to risk their careers—and suffer the retribution that could ruin their lives—in order to set the record straight. Silence was the rule after the FBI released its statement.

In May of 2017, Ed Ashurst, a Cochise County rancher and author, decided it was time to bring public attention to the suspicious circumstances of Nick Ivie's death. Ashurst talked it over with a Border Patrol agent who had worked closely with Nick, and they decided to take their suspicions to a couple of Arizona TV stations. The TV stations brought their concerns to authorities, and a Border Patrol spokesman said his agency stood by the investigation's finding.

The FBI remained silent.

Ashurst had also written about the Ivie case in his book on border issues, *Alligators in the Moat*, released in January 2016. Two months later, he delivered a speech in Animas, New Mexico, in which he asserted that the Ivie death investigation was a politically motivated sham. That speech, part of an event on critical border issues, was attended by several politicians, including a congressman and congressional staff members.

As a result of Ashurst's efforts, this investigative journalism project was undertaken. It became obvious to this author, soon after Ashurst and Nick's former Border Patrol colleague approached the TV stations to try to bring the truth to light, that Agent Ivie's name needed to be cleared of any false accusation of firing at fellow agents.

There is more on the efforts of Ashurst and Nick's friend in the chapter on the author's challenge to the FBI narrative.

When Agent Ivie was killed, reporters from national media outlets flocked to Southern Arizona to cover the story. It has been said that members of the press behave like a string of crows on a telephone wire. They sit on the wire until one flies off. Then the rest of the flock flies off in the same direction.

When the FBI announced that Agent Ivie's death was a case of friendly fire, with nobody else involved, members of the media quietly flew away and returned to perches elsewhere. Members of the local press, as well as media outlets in Utah and other nearby states, followed suit.

Nothing to see here. Excuse us for making a fuss about an unfortunate accident.

All discussion about congressional investigations came to a screeching halt.

The individuals who murdered Agent Ivie would be free to safely slink into the shadows of obscurity.

Anyone with inside knowledge of this coverup who dared to speak out about the administration's phony investigation would certainly be severely punished. Potential whistleblowers would not emerge for several years.

Obama set an all-time-high track record for prosecuting whistle-blowers. Reporters who covered the White House were shocked to discover that Obama's promise of being the most transparent president was followed by practices that proved him to be the exact opposite.

"Over the past eight years, the administration has prosecuted nine cases involving whistle-blowers and leakers, compared with only three by all previous administrations combined," wrote investigative journalist James Risen, in a 2016 opinion piece for the *New York Times*. "It has repeatedly used the Espionage Act, a relic of World War I-era red-baiting, not to prosecute spies, but to go after government officials who talked to journalists."

Risen, a two-time Pulitzer Prize winner, wrote that he experienced firsthand the Obama administration's zeal to prevent leaking and punish journalists, when he tried to shield a source who gave him information in a case involving the CIA and Iran's nuclear program.

"Under Mr. Obama, the Justice Department and the F.B.I. have spied on reporters by monitoring their phone records, labeled one journalist an unindicted co-conspirator in a criminal case for simply doing reporting, and issued subpoenas to other reporters to try to force them to reveal their sources and testify in criminal cases."[2]

How does this record of spying on journalists and punishing whistleblowers apply to the Ivie murder case?

Any Border Patrol agent, FBI agent, or other government official who decided to speak out about inside information on this case could have been subjected to criminal prosecution through Obama's Department of Justice. Any journalist who decided to cooperate with a whistleblower could have also been prosecuted.

An assessment of the Obama administration's aggressive stance against press freedom was published on October 10, 2013, one year after Nick Ivie was murdered. This report by Leonard Downie Jr., former *Washington Post* executive editor, does not address the Ivie case. But it does shed light on why all media outlets quietly went along with the FBI statement.

"In the Obama administration's Washington, government officials are increasingly afraid to talk to the press," Downie wrote, in a special report for the Committee to Protect Journalists. "Those suspected of dis-cussing with reporters anything that the government has classified as secret are subject to investigation, including lie-detector tests and scru-tiny of their telephone and e-mail records. An 'Insider Threat Program' being implemented in every government department requires all federal employees to help prevent unauthorized disclosures of information by monitoring the behavior of their colleagues."[3]

Although the government did not officially classify the Ivie case as *secret*, Border Patrol agents were warned not to speak out on the case. They were aware that any public pronouncements that contradicted the official government statement would bring swift retribution.[4] News reporters had already experienced four years of an administration that routinely objected to any stories that put Obama in a negative light.

The Obama administration was enormously successful in silencing its critics and promoting the idea that all of its scandals were not really scandals at all—just part of a vast right-wing conspiracy.

Where Is the Evidence That Nobody Else Was Involved?

Those who had invented this false narrative made sure it was released late on the day before the weekend began—the classic Friday afternoon news dump, to avoid much coverage and scrutiny. They therefore had to send someone to tell it to the Ivie family ahead of its official release.

The Ivies were informed that "bad guys" were not responsible for Nick's death.

That is the biggest lie of all—the lie at the center of the web of deception, which held together all the other strands. The purpose of the "friendly fire" narrative was not to place blame on Nick for his own death. That was just collateral damage, inflicted by callous politicians.

This web of deception was weaved to steer the press and public away from the truth—that the agents were ambushed by cartel smugglers. Imagine the concern of the Obama campaign officials, when they noticed a horde of members of the national press corps reporting at the border—right before the election. Even the densest reporter might hear from locals about the cartel operatives who were freely bringing drugs, illegal aliens and sex slaves across the southern border on a regular basis.

And more importantly, those smugglers were connected with the cartel which recently received thousands of high-powered firearms through a government program—which resulted in the death of Border Patrol Agent Brian A. Terry, the namesake of the station where the ambushed agents worked.

It wasn't enough to invent a scenario in which an agent accidentally killed Nick Ivie. More importantly, scapegoat agents were badly needed to fill in the blanks on a preposterous story in which no smugglers were on the scene.

The inventors of the Ivie "friendly fire" narrative were the same people who invented the false narrative in which four Americans were killed in Benghazi, Libya, as the result of a protest of an anti-Islam video. And those were the same people who invented a narrative in which Brian Terry and his partners decided to use bean bag ammo when they went out to interdict heavily armed bandits.

However, in every web of deception, it is difficult to keep all the strands together in neat order.

The Obama administration was betting that there would be no significant questioning by the press or politicians into this sham investigation. Anyone who dared to question the investigative integrity of the world's most trustworthy law enforcement agency would be easily dismissed as a "conspiracy theorist."

Once a political leader is able to manipulate the FBI for political purposes, the levers of propaganda production cannot be easily jammed.

In any case, an investigation into this carefully planned coverup would certainly not get off the ground until after the all-important election was in the history books. If any media outlet got out of line, and tried to discover the truth, it would be easily drowned out by the majority media, the Obama loyalists, who understood there would be swift retribution for questioning officially sanctioned coverups.

Time Line of the Day the FBI Said Nick Ivie was Killed for Shooting at Other Agents—with Nobody Else Involved

- At about 9 a.m., Christy and Joel Ivie met with Border Patrol officials in the home of Nick and Christy Ivie. The officials told them Nick was killed, after firing at other agents. They said there was nobody else but agents involved.
- Afterward Nick's widow and brother met with other family members in the house.
- While the whole family was together, U.S. Officials Napolitano and Aguilar arrived at the house to express their condolences. All of this occurred before about 10:00 a.m. Arizona time, 1:00 p.m. Eastern time.
- "She (Napolitano) met with Ivie's family in Sierra Vista to offer formal condolences from her and the government before traveling to the Brian Terry station in Naco," said a story posted on walb.com, a South Georgia TV station, and on the KOLB TV Web site (Tucson, Arizona). "The meeting with the family was a private affair."[5]
- Napolitano traveled from Sierra Vista to the Brian Terry Station near Naco, about 30 miles away. It would have taken about 40 minutes if she traveled by a conventional vehicle

on Highway 92, or about 10 minutes if she was transported by helicopter.
• "She (Napolitano) arrived in Naco at about 10:30 a.m.," The report by the TV station said. "While there she spent four hours with officials from several agencies involved in the shooting probe, including the FBI and Cochise County Sheriff's Department."
• After about two hours of huddling with law enforcement officials, Napolitano was flown over the shooting scene during a 15-minute ride in a Black Hawk helicopter, the report said.
• "Once back at the compound, they (Napolitano and Aguilar) reconvened in a series of offices about 300 yards from a security line keeping reporters and photographers at bay. Napolitano left Naco about 2:30 p.m., without speaking to the media."[5]
• Napolitano left Southern Arizona about the time the FBI was releasing its stunning statement, which would turn the public perception of the case upside-down.

Nobody Else Was Involved—but the ATF

On the same day the FBI released its statement about the agents shooting at each other, with nobody else involved, the *Los Angeles Times* published its story about firearms that were possibly connected to the Ivie incident.

"Gun-trace documents from the federal Bureau of Alcohol, Tobacco, Firearms and Explosives obtained by the *Times* show that a high-powered rifle and a handgun were found near the shooting scene," the *Times* story said. "A .223 Bushmaster rifle, seized on Wednesday, was 'recovered in Mexico in the vicinity where Border Patrol agent was murdered' according to one of the documents. It says the weapon was purchased in the United States but does not specify where."

"A .38-caliber Titan Tiger revolver was recovered separately Tuesday in Mexico, also near the Naco area, a second document says. That trace record included this alert: Urgent High Profile Border Agent Shot."[6]

Apparently, someone at ATF thought this revolver might be the murder weapon. There was no *L.A. Times* follow-up story on these weapons.

It is likely the Obama campaign team was aware of this widely circulated report. This was the day after Obama received the news that he was no longer ahead of Romney in the polls.

18

Female Agent Might Have Fired Fatal Shot?

"_____ just got into a firefight with Ivie." FBI agent leaves a blank in his 302 witness statement, quoting Agent Johnson's phone conversation with Border Patrol dispatcher while he was on the mountain.

Saturday, October 6
Sierra Vista FBI Resident Agency office
Sierra Vista, Arizona

FBI agents interviewed David Thomas Woodbury, the Border Patrol agent who was working as a dispatcher the night of the shooting incident.

The interviewing agents were listed as Brent A. Templeton and Doran C. Anderson. The report was drafted on October 11, 2012.

The interview took place four days after the incident, the day after the head of the FBI Phoenix Division announced the Bureau's shocking finding in the case.[1]

Like other FBI documents, it fits the FBI's narrative, but clashes with other actual elements of the case.

It is unclear whether anything in the FBI documents reflect what was actually said by the people who were interviewed. It has already been shown—in the tape-recorded interview of BP Agent Borjas—that the FBI tended to distort what was said, when the FBI's interpretation of an interview was compared to a transcript of the tape-recorded interview.

The Borjas interview was tape-recorded and transcribed by personnel of the Cochise County Sheriff's Office. The interviews of Woodbury and other Border Patrol agents—with the exception of Borjas and Johnson—were apparently not recorded.

Other evidence has recently surfaced—in another prominent case involving misconduct by the FBI—in which a 302 witness statement was allegedly falsified to level false charges against a retired Army general who Obama viewed as an enemy. More information on this recent development will appear in the chapter on the FBI.

Woodbury, an agent for about four years, said he was a line agent assigned to the control room in the Naco Station the morning of October 2, 2012.

Woodbury said that when the sensor "went off," David Johnson called the control room by phone "to get the long description of the sensor."

This meshed perfectly with what Johnson and Borjas reported during their interviews. Johnson asked control for information on the location of the sensor, including a recommendation for the best hiking route.

Woodbury said that when he heard the report of "shots fired," he called his supervisor Raul De Loera and told him about that.

He said he then tried to call the three agents who were at the scene by radio "with no luck."

When he tried to reach all three agents on their personal cell phones, "the only person he was able to get a hold of was Johnson." This also matched perfectly the testimony of the surviving agents.

But here comes the main part that diverges from what Johnson said during his interview:

Woodbury reportedly told the FBI that Johnson told him on the phone, "that he thinks it *was* a 'green on green'" shooting.

The difference between Johnson's recollection two days after the incident and Woodbury's four days afterward, was that Johnson said he told Woodbury, he thought "it *might* " be green-on-green.

Woodbury reported on Saturday, October 6, that Johnson said he thought "*it was*" green-on-green. There is a difference between those two statements.

Johnson apparently believed that his partner that night "*might*" have fired shots toward Agent Ivie. So when he was interviewed by the FBI the afternoon of Thursday, October 4, he wanted the Border Patrol to know that during the chaotic scene in which the agents encountered smugglers, Agent Ivie "*might*" have died from friendly fire.

However, Agent Borjas never fired a shot, something Agent Johnson apparently did not know when he made that statement.

Agent Borjas herself thought she might have fired shots. She reportedly told the first responder who spoke to her on the mountain slope that she had fired shots.

During Johnson's FBI interview, he explained that it was a chaotic situation, and it was "*possible*" Ivie was killed by a bullet from a Border Patrol agent.

Strangely, there was no follow-up question in the Johnson interview as to which Border Patrol agent might have killed Ivie.

That is especially important, considering the FBI's conclusion. The FBI never publicly declared which agent shot Ivie to death—but its Crime Lab Firearms Report clearly fingered Agent Johnson.

In Woodbury's interview, he allegedly made a startling statement about the nature of the shootout. He allegedly said not only that Johnson told him it *was* "green-on-green," but that it was apparently *someone else* who "just got into a firefight with Ivie."

Although the FBI agent left blank the name of the person who got into the firefight with Agent Ivie, Johnson almost certainly identified Borjas as the one who might have accidentally killed Ivie, according to this FBI statement.

The FBI witness interview report on Agent Woodbury said that Johnson told him while he (Johnson) was on the mountain slope that "_____ just got into a firefight with Ivie."

If Johnson told Woodbury that "*I* just got into a firefight with Ivie," it is improbable that a blank would have been substituted for his admission. The length of the underscoring is five spaces—which would more closely match a name or star number than the single letter "I."

This shows that Johnson apparently did not believe that he was the person who fired the shot that ended Agent Ivie's life.

This is an important piece of the puzzle, because the Bureau's ballistics test clearly blamed Agent Johnson, by allegedly matching his rifle to the bullet fragment that was allegedly removed from Agent Ivie's body.

The FBI never publicly named the other agents in the Ivie case. They also never publicly identified which agent shot Ivie to death—the male or the female.

That left Agent Borjas—who never fired a single shot—vulnerable to the belief among other Border Patrol agents that she was the one who shot Agent Ivie.

I was told in 2017 by a Border Patrol agent, who worked out of the same station as the three agents involved in the incident, that many agents believed Agent Borjas fired that fatal shot. It is possible that this belief by agents, who were hungry to discover the truth, stemmed from Agent Johnson's idea that it was possible that the other agent at the scene shot Agent Ivie.[2]

When I started investigating this case four and a half years after the shooting incident occurred, I was surprised to learn that Border Patrol agents—including some of Nick Ivie's partners and friends—knew very little about what actually occurred. When I later learned the severity of the threat against them for publicly criticizing the official version of events, I understood why they could have lost interest in discovering the truth.

Agent Johnson possibly saw Agent Borjas with her pistol drawn as the gunfire commenced. Because he initially believed that only Agent Ivie was at the scene—before he saw the silhouette of a man with a smuggler's pack, who threw off a blanket—he might have believed that it was possible that Borjas and Ivie were shooting at each other.

However, the evidence clearly showed that Borjas never fired her weapon and that there were multiple suspects at the scene—in addition to the three Border Patrol agents. When FBI officials undertook the task of making the ambush by smugglers appear to be something entirely different, they produced as many strands as possible to strengthen their web of deception.

19

"He Was the Type of Agent Everyone Wanted to Work With."

"He was the type of agent that everyone wanted to work with, because if there was a group to find, he would find it." Nick's friend and fellow agent.

Memorial Service
Monday, October 8
Sierra Vista, Arizona

Nick Ivie was known as a man who loved to serve his country and his family, with a particular affection for the people of Mexico, where he had served as a missionary.

The first of two memorial services was held six days after Nick Ivie's death in Sierra Vista, the largest city in Cochise County, located 10 miles from the international border.

The memorial service at the Church of Jesus Christ of Latter-day Saints Sierra Vista Stake Center on Monday, October 8, was attended by more than 1,000 people, including Governor Jan Brewer, U.S. Representative Ron Barber, and top officials of the U.S. Border Patrol and its parent agency, U.S. Customs and Border Protection. There were also hundreds of federal and local law enforcements in attendance.[1]

Aaron Kerr, a friend of Nick's and a fellow Border Patrol agent, said Nick was an outstanding agent who was widely respected for his skills.

"Nick was a natural when it came to tracking aliens and finding groups," Kerr told the mourners. "He grew up with a hunting background, so he was familiar with tracking and very good at it. Several times with our field training unit, we would be looking in an area for a group, and Nick would be looking in another area, and sure enough, Nick would be the one to come up with the group.

"He was the type of agent that everyone wanted to work with, because if there was a group to find, he would find it."

Nick was an outstanding family man, dedicated to his wife and two young daughters, Kerr said.

When Nick Ivie was not on horseback, he was often seen in his neighborhood riding his bicycle, with one of his girls in tow. He had a bicycle trailer for each of them.

He was constantly playing outside with his daughters, a fact well known to most of his neighbors.

"No child has ever been blessed with a more loving father. He is an example to every man of the joy that comes from righteous fatherhood," Kerr said.

While Nick Ivie was in training at the Border Patrol Academy in Artesia, New Mexico, during the second year of his marriage to Christy, he wrote her a poem, which Agent Kerr read at the memorial service:

There once was a girl who caught my eye,
There was something about her that made me feel I could fly.

In the poem, Ivie was memorializing how he fell in love with Christy Morris, the attractive brunette he first met in Utah. She had moved to Utah with her family from Aztec, New Mexico, during her high school years. Christy had also served as a Mormon missionary. She had been stationed overseas in Berlin, Germany.

Nick, who had three older brothers, could be pushed to try out more grown up activities at a young age.

Joel Ivie told the story of a mishap Nick had while they were growing up in Utah.

"When Nick was 6 years old, his older brother decided it would be about the right time for his first driving lesson. So, his older brother put him behind the wheel of his old Ford Bronco and decided to drive around the work yard by all the construction equipment," Joel Ivie said. "As his older brother sat beside him, Nick was barely able to see over the steering wheel, but maybe through it. He went to turn a corner, and as he boosted himself up to see up higher, he stepped on the gas pedal, and the Bronco went speeding around the corner and right into a classic Mustang."

Years later, Joel would be the one behind the wheel, as they sometimes carpooled from Sierra Vista to Naco while they both worked the day shift on the Horse Patrol Unit.

As an example of Nick's dedication to his family, Joel said he would have to wait in his vehicle some mornings as his younger brother completed chores, in order to relieve Christy of her burdens.

The service was broadcast via closed-circuit TV to four other Mormon meetinghouses: two in Sierra Vista, and one each in Douglas and Bisbee. Hundreds of additional mourners viewed the service via live-feed TV in those nearby Southern Arizona cities.

Before the service began, Agent Ivie's flag-draped coffin was transported on a horse-drawn carriage in a five-mile long procession, from funeral home to meeting house.

The riderless horse in the lead of the somber procession was Nick Ivie's beloved "Mouse," a wild mustang, given that name for its rounded ears. Before its capture, Mouse had lost the tips of his ears when they were frozen, out in the wilderness. Ivie tamed and trained the horse that would serve with him in the ensuing years. As Mouse was walked along the route by an agent, he was followed by 72 Border Patrol agents on horseback.

Joel Ivie delivered the eulogy.

"He was one of the few agents that went up regularly in those hills," Joel Ivie told the large crowd, according to a story in the *Arizona Daily Star*. "He knew all that network of trails up in the mountain there. He died in a peaceful place, and although it may have been a traumatic experience, he did die peacefully."

Nick, the youngest of five children—four boys and one girl—was born in Charleston, South Carolina, then moved with his family to Provo, Utah, when he was 2 years old. He had a happy childhood, despite a serious injury that, for a time, prevented him from participating in contact sports.

After he broke his jaw by smashing his face against the side of a swimming pool, his mother took him to horseback lessons, which opened the door to his passion for horses. He had an exceptional affinity for horses, which extended to a close bond with his Border Patrol steed.

After Nick Ivie graduated from Timpview High School in Provo, Utah, in 2000, he served for two years as a Mormon missionary in Mexico City. After returning to Utah, he served as a paramedic and volunteer firefighter with the City of Spanish Fork Fire Department, before applying to the Border Patrol at Joel's recommendation.[2]

Joel Ivie said that his brother had learned to love the Mexican people during his term as a missionary. He also learned Spanish during his years in Mexico City.

But nothing compared to the love Nick had for his family

"Nick's girls were his pride and joy," Joel Ivie said. "He loved to feed them, bathe them, care for them; he was even known to ride trikes with them."

Nick had a deep faith in his God. His family took comfort in the knowledge that he resides in heaven, where they will all one day meet again.

"Sometimes I have to wonder why Nick was taken at this time, but then I also think, Nick was such a great man that he was ready to enter the kingdom of God," Joel Ivie said. "So as God needed Nick to do work on the other side of the veil, Nick was ready."

Agent Johnson visits Nick's family the day after the FBI announcement

Following the service, there was a brief press conference held, at which Kevin Goates, spokesman for the Ivie family, presented information on events that occurred in the days following Nick's death.

On Saturday, the agent who was injured during the shooting incident visited the family at Christy Ivie's home, Goates told reporters. The story of this momentous visit was carried in the *Benson News*, published on Wednesday, October 10.

Goates said the family had expressed concern for the other two agents involved in the incident and wanted to meet with the injured agent.

When Border Patrol Agent David G. Johnson visited the Ivie home, that was just one day after the FBI announced that Nick was killed by a fellow agent.

"I have to tell you, that was one of the most moving experiences of my life," Goates said of the meeting between Agent Johnson and Agent Ivie's family. "He was welcomed, as he walked into that house, with unbelievable love."

Goates also spoke about the visits by officials to the Ivie family the previous Friday. That was when they first delivered their information about the shooting and presented condolences, in advance of the FBI's statement.

Goates said authorities, who were unspecified in this account, briefed Joel Ivie and Christy Ivie on details on Nick's death, which was the result of friendly fire.

After that meeting, Napolitano, Aguilar, and Self visited with the Ivie family.

Self also visited with Joel and Christy Ivie before Napolitano and Aguilar arrived. Self reported to the press that he was the one who spoke to them about the FBI's "friendly fire" finding.[3]

Goates said that the officials who were there with Napolitano, who was the highest ranking official at the house, presented whatever information they could about Nick's death.

According to Goates, Napolitano did not say much to Nick's surviving relatives.

"She mainly listened to the family and wanted to hear what the family wanted to say and what their thoughts were," Goates said.[4]

20

Did Moon Shadows
Shoot at Agents?

*"And I could distinguish it was a long one," BP Agent Borjas sticks with her
story of seeing a shooter with a long firearm*

Thursday, October 11
El Paso Federal Justice Center, El Paso, Texas

On the same day as Nick Ivie's second memorial service, two FBI
agents from the Tucson Resident Agency traveled to El Paso, Texas,
to conduct a follow-up interview with Border Patrol Agent Graciela
Borjas.

Borjas was driven home to the El Paso area by her family shortly
after the shooting and remained there afterward.

At the time of this interview, she was still listed as an agent
working at the Brian A. Terry office in Arizona. She was on paid leave
following the incident.

The interview was conducted Thursday, October 11, at the El Paso
FBI Field Office. The El Paso Federal Justice Center, which houses
the FBI divisional headquarters, has three-story tall concrete facades,
accented by dark, mirrored glass windows and walls. It is surrounded
by a concrete and steel security fence.

Agent Borjas spent most of her life in the El Paso area before
moving to Arizona to begin her career with the Border Patrol. Five
years earlier, she attended the University of Texas, El Paso, located
just four miles southeast of the FBI's office building. Her alma mater,
set on the east side of Interstate 10, is a short walk from the Mexican
border, just across the highway.

The atmosphere in the room was much different during the second
interview of this important eyewitness to the shooting death of Agent
Ivie. She was no longer distraught, and the FBI agents were no longer
looking for answers.

The interview was conducted six days after the FBI announced
that Agent Ivie was killed as a result of a shootout with another

agent—with nobody else involved except for the agents who shot at each other.

The purpose of this interview was apparently to try to steer Agent Borjas to change her original story. If that failed, the FBI agents could let her know that they were still aware of her—and that the Bureau did not want her to contradict the narrative that was now a matter of the permanent public record.

The transcript of Borjas's second interview showed that many details she already spoke about remained the same nine days later. Once again, what she said meshed with her previous testimony, as well as with the testimony of Agent Johnson and evidence found at the crime scene.

The fact that a female agent was involved in the shooting incident was revealed in many of the early news stories.

None of the news stories revealed whether the male agent or female agent was accused of shooting Agent Ivie to death.

The FBI news release of October 5 specified that "the death of United States Border Patrol Agent Nicholas J. Ivie and the *injury to a second agent* were the result of an accidental shooting incident involving only the agents."

That terse FBI statement did not mention the presence of any other agent. In other words, two agents shot at each other—and nobody else was involved. For anyone who had not read the initial news stories, this statement would mean that no third agent was involved.

It is not clear whether the third agent was intentionally eliminated from that important statement on the incident—or whether that was just an unintended oversight.

Agent Borjas was indeed involved in this incident. An impartial person who knew the facts would conclude that she was nearly shot to death at that time.

The FBI agents who conducted this follow-up interview with Borjas were likely aware of every detail of her short previous interview. They would have been keenly aware that she made statements that sharply contradicted the FBI's final pronouncement on the investigation.

That put Agent Borjas in a precarious position. The FBI, the most prestigious and influential law enforcement agency in America, had publicly proclaimed that what Borjas saw and heard was not true. She had told the FBI in her first interview on October 2 that she saw three or four suspects at the scene, who opened fire on her and Agent Johnson with a long arm and possibly a pistol.

Who was she to contradict the Federal Bureau of Investigation?

After the incident occurred, and after the FBI had released its statement, her employer warned Border Patrol agents not to say anything in public that contradicted the official version.

Would what she would said in this second interview have any effect on her employment?

Now she would have to endure another interview, in the unfamiliar territory of the imposing, gleaming FBI headquarters. There was an attorney with her this time, but she was the one who would be in the hot seat.

In the six days since it had been released, everyone seemed to totally go along with the official FBI statement—although privately, the rank and file agents did not believe the FBI.

Borjas wanted to keep her job, and it had been made clear to Border Patrol agents that the official story was the story they had to stick to in public. However, this was not a public situation. She would tell the truth, something she always tried to do.

Borjas was proud of her ability to perform this challenging job, which few women desired. She had passed the Border Patrol Academy—which did not have separate standards for female recruits. Her excellent athletic and academic background, as well as her bilingual skill, gave her a distinct advantage over many other women.

She would tell the FBI the truth about what had happened. Again. The potential consequences were beyond her control.

During her first interview, the Cochise County sheriff's sergeant had told her that some details would become clearer to her two or three days after the murder of Agent Ivie.

But the FBI had not interviewed her within two or three days.

Why did they wait until nine days later before interviewing her? If she would know more a few days later—when a little more had time passed, and she was no longer distraught—why was there no interview then? It was more common in a law enforcement investigation to follow up a few days later, rather than to wait until nine days later.

And why had they totally disregarded what she had said before reaching their conclusion? How could nobody else be involved? She clearly saw other people at the scene—some of whom were shooting at her.

Despite the challenge of speaking honestly in a way that would contradict the FBI's official version, this interview would prove to be a much more thorough retelling of what Agent Borjas saw and heard on the night she was almost shot to death.

There were some important new details in this interview, including that Agent Borjas said she was just four or five feet away from the shooters when they opened fire on her.

There were four other people in the room during this interview: FBI agents Sonja Frueh and Brian Filbert; Jim Calle, an attorney who represented members of the National Border Patrol Council, the agents' union; and El Paso–based private investigator Mike Briseno.[1]

The tape-recorded portion of the interview would take 57 minutes and 10 seconds. It would be transcribed on October 15 at the Tucson FBI office.

The tone of this interview was different from the first one. During the first interview, Borjas was told that the investigation was about the attack on her and the other agents—not an investigation about whether she performed well.

The first interview was about aiding in a homicide investigation. The transcript of this new interview did not clearly reveal its underlying purpose.

The first thing Special Agent Frueh told her when this second interview officially began was, "I wanted to start by saying the purpose of this interview is to talk about the incident that occurred on October second."

After asking basic questions about her birth date and other identifiers, Frueh asked her how long she had been on the Border Patrol and whether she was still on probation.

Borjas said she had completed her one-year probation period.

This interview was starting with a question on her employment status. This would not have much relevance in a homicide investigation, but it would be a perfect way to try to intimidate a relatively new employee.

Frueh asked her what shift she worked and whether this was her first workstation with the Border Patrol. The question indicated that Borjas was still officially stationed in Arizona at that time.

She would later be transferred to the station in El Paso, Texas— another very busy Border Patrol station.

Borjas was asked what she did at the start of each work shift. She said she got to work about 15 or 20 minutes early and checked her e-mail in a "quiet room." Then she went to the muster room, received her assignment, retrieved her vehicle keys and drove away.

She said she worked five-day weeks, mostly with Sundays and Mondays off, "because I try to come home, and I come to church here."

She was referring to her routine of driving from Arizona to El Paso on weekends. It is a four-hour drive between Naco and El Paso, with most of the distance an easy drive through southeast Arizona and southwest New Mexico on Interstate 10.

She said she usually worked alone in a patrol vehicle, without a partner. She carried an H&K P2000 .40 caliber pistol, with one spare magazine. Each magazine carried 12 cartridges, which would give her a total of 25 cartridges, including the one in the gun's chamber.

Agent Frueh asked her about the sensors, whether "you guys place them out there and move them or? . . ."

Borjas said the Border Patrol had a sensor team, which placed the sensors "where they think a lot of traffic is going on."

She said that when she heard about the sensor hit that night and found the sensor was in her area, she radioed to the control room that she was going to check it out. She heard that there was a sensor hit just as Agent Robert Kristinsson told her that he did not need her help.

Borjas said that she remembered that it "hit for seven."

That was the same number she had given interviewers a few hours after the shooting incident. She said it could mean there were "seven people out there."

FBI Agent Filbert asked her if the seven people could be illegal aliens or drug smugglers.

"Yes, either or," Borjas said.

"Since it was such a large number at that point, did they assign more people to assist you?" Agent Frueh asked.

"Actually, when I got on the radio, and I said I was going to check it out, 341 which is Johnson, he got on the radio and he said he would go with me," Borjas said.

Then Johnson gave her his phone number over the radio so she could call him and they could arrange to meet and go up together, she said.

They met at the intersection of Chisolm Trail Road and Highway 80.

She told the FBI agents that while she was waiting at Chisolm Trail, 225 (Ivie) asked her on the radio where she was located and which route she would be taking to the sensor. She said she told Ivie she was waiting for 341(Johnson) at Chisolm Trail.

Ivie told her, "OK, I'm going to be coming from the north, from the north through Remax."

After Johnson arrived, she asked him, "Did you hear 225 on the radio?"

"Yeah, I did," he told her.

They had an approximate location of the sensor. Agent Johnson told her he would call control and obtain the GPS coordinates. She followed him in her vehicle from the highway onto the grid of graded dirt roads.

As they were driving, Johnson told her on the phone, "We're going to stop here because it gets pretty rough, the terrain gets pretty rough, and we don't want to get stuck." So they stopped their vehicles before driving any farther up the mountain.

They stopped at a spot which Johnson called "Dead Girl Trail." Borjas recalled that she had been there before, during training, but that had been a while ago. That was when they had started walking up toward the sensor.

"And I had never checked that specific sensor before," she said.

When they left their vehicles, "I actually got on the radio, and I told (Ivie) we were going to go through Dead Girl Trail," Borjas said, in response to a question about communication with Ivie. "We were heading that way, and he said, '10-4.' So he knew we were coming from the south, and we knew he was coming from the north."

There was no problem with radio communication between the two agents while they were both beginning to hike toward the sensor. At that point, they were the farthest away from each other, with a mountain between them and no possible direct contact between their radios. The Border Patrol uses UHF repeater towers, some solar powered, to improve agent radio reception in mountainous terrain. Neither of the surviving agents ever complained about radio communication problems, with the exception of a momentary problem with Agent Johnson's radio.

FBI Agent Introduced the Idea That Moon Shadows Might Have Been Involved

In response to a question from Frueh, Borjas said she wasn't sure what time they went up, but she thought it was about 11:30 p.m.

"What was it like that night? Was it pitch dark? Was there a moon out? Were you guys able to see?" Frueh asked.

"There was a full moon," Borjas said.

"OK," Frueh said.

"There was a full moon," Borjas repeated.

"So what could you see with the full moon? Like how was the lighting?" Frueh asked.

"The lighting was OK. We could see where we were going," Borjas said.

"Just the trail basically in front of you?" FBI Agent Frueh asked.

"The trail, I could see the trail and the bushes around," Agent Borjas said.

"Shadows," Frueh said.

It was not a question, just an interjection that was strangely out of place.

Frueh asked how far Borjas could see ahead of her.

Asking for clarification, Borjas asked whether she meant an object or . . .

"Yeah, like if there was a saguaro (cactus) ahead of you, like how far away do you think you'd have to be to see it?" Frueh asked.

Borjas said, "Maybe 20 or 30 feet . . . but I'm not too sure."

Borjas said Agent Johnson was leading as they hiked up the trail. "He put the coords (coordinates) in his GPS, so he was leading the way the whole time," Borjas said. "And he was telling me how far we were and everything."

As they hiked toward the sensor, "we kept checking to see on the trail—to check to see if there was any sign, like foot sign or anything."

"Did you see any signs of footprints or anything?" Frueh asked.

"Not where we were coming from," Borjas said.

"Were you pretty much behind Johnson the whole time as you were walking up within eye—you could see him?" Agent Frueh asked.

"Yes, ma'am," Borjas said.

"At any point, did you ever see Ivie? Or were you only able to talk to him on the radio?" Frueh asked.

Before they arrived at the saddle "there was a point where I told Johnson, 'Oh, he's over there. I saw his flashlight,'" Borjas said. "He was, he was still pretty far from us."

"How far do you think he was?" Frueh asked.

"At that point when I first saw his flashlight, I think he was still around 200, 300 yards maybe," Borjas said.

"That's pretty far," FBI Agent Frueh said.

"He was pretty far, but we could see his flashlight, and Johnson was like, 'Yeah. I see his flashlight.'" Borjas said.

"Were you guys using flashlights as well at that point?" Frueh asked.

"No," Borjas said. "'Cause we could still see, we would only occasionally turn them on and kind of hide the light." She added that they didn't want to give away their position to the suspects.

"And were you still in communication with Ivie at this point?" Frueh asked. "He was coming north [sic] and you guys were coming from the south?"

"Yeah, the last time I had communication with him is when I got on the radio, and it's called 10-18, which means: Do you have anything down there? Is anything going on, or do you need anything?"

Borjas was referring to the Border Patrol "10 code." By saying "10-18" she was asking whether he had knowledge of any illegal traffic and also inquiring about his safety.

"He said, 'I'm checking a wash (creek bed) down here for a sign, or something like that," Borjas recalled. "And I said, '10-4. We're about one tenth of a mile away.' And that was the last communication we had with him."

The distances reported in the recollection of Agent Borjas are important. She and Agent Johnson saw Agent Ivie when he was walking on the north slope of the mountain, 200 to 300 yards away. So that would put Ivie about one city block away.

Later than that—probably 5 to 10 minutes later—Borjas told Ivie she and Johnson were one-tenth of a mile away from their destination. *That is about 176 yards away, a hiking distance of about three minutes.*

If the two agents were about 176 yards away a few minutes later, then when they saw Agent Ivie, he was already close to the saddle, perhaps 25 to 125 yards away.

By the time Borjas told Ivie they were one-tenth of a mile away, Ivie was at the saddle. We know that he was at the saddle, because he reported on his radio that he saw sign of two there—probably the same two whose signs he had seen on the north side of the mountain. Johnson said during his interview that he was somewhat relaxed as he approached the saddle, because he thought Ivie was there. When he saw a man with a smuggler's pack at the saddle, he immediately thought that it was one of the suspects Ivie spoke about.

Of course, Ivie was at the saddle when the two other agents arrived. If both agents had been certain he was not there or nearby, they would have responded to the gunfire by immediately returning fire.

FBI Agent Filbert asked, "One-tenth of a mile away from the sensor?"

"Yes," Agent Borjas said. "That's 'cause I got the information from Johnson 'cause he told me. I asked him, 'How far away are we?' and he told me. He looked at his GPS, and he told me 'one-tenth of a mile.' So I relayed (to Agent Ivie)."

In response to questions from the FBI agents, Borjas said they were walking on the trail at that point; it wasn't steep enough to require switchbacks, and Ivie would have had the same coordinates. Ivie did not tell them how far from the sensor he was when he reported that he was checking a wash.

Note that Ivie had the same GPS coordinates as Johnson and Borjas. This was not challenged. But one year later, when a fantasy story was published to try to explain why Ivie shot at his fellow agents, the heart of that falsification was that Ivie did not know where the other agents were.

"So then what happened?" Agent Frueh asked. "Like—just—you know, try to walk through it best you can remember it at that point what—what [throat clearing] happened."

"OK. So at that point, after I got on the radio, we kept walking, we were going around the actual saddle because that's where the trail was leading us," Borjas said. "We didn't want to go over it 'cause I mean it's really tough terrain, so Johnson said, 'no, we'll just follow the trail.'

"And I followed him—we followed it and that was the last time I—I had seen Ivie's flashlight, when we came around and I said, 'Oh: we're almost there.'"

This is an extremely important detail. Borjas is saying she saw Ivie's flashlight while she and Johnson were almost at the saddle.

"And I had my flashlight in my hand. And I actually stopped for a bit to put it in my CamelBak pack, and I put it in my CamelBak pack, and as we walked a little more, that's when I saw Ivie [sic] turn and I heard a yell and I . . ."

"Who yelled?" Frueh asked, interrupting the flow of Borjas's narrative.

"I don't know," Borjas said.

"OK," Frueh said.

"I don't know. I just heard. I don't know what they yelled. I'm not too sure. I just heard a yell. And I mean everything happened so fast.

"And we were pretty close to it and that's when the shots fired and . . ."

This is another important detail. Borjas is saying she heard someone yell, then shots were fired. Remember that Johnson said he yelled, "Hey, hey, hey, hey!" after about eight shots were fired.

This is likely an indication that Borjas heard Agent Ivie let out a yell right before he was shot to death.

Now it was FBI Agent Filbert's turn to interrupt Agent Borjas's narrative.

"You heard a yell before the shots?" Filbert asked.

"Yes," Borjas said.

"And then shots were fired?" Filbert asked.

"M-hmm (yes). And then shots were fired," Borjas replied.

"As you were walking on the ridge did the shots come from your right or your left?" Filbert asked.

"Our left," Borjas said.

"Your left?" Filbert asked.

"Our left, uh-huh," Borjas reiterated.

"As we were walking, I saw Ivie [sic] something; he turned left right away, and that's when I heard a yell, and that's when everything just happened, and I was behind him," Borjas said.

I believe that Borjas mistakenly named Ivie here instead of Johnson. Later in this interview, Borjas says she was behind Johnson, when he turned to his left. She was behind Johnson at that time, and she was never behind Ivie, according to all the other evidence. It is likely she also mistakenly said "Ivie" instead of "Johnson" in her prior statement, in which she said she saw "Ivie turn." Remember that Borjas did not use the names of the two agents the entire time she was hiking toward the trail. She knew them by their star numbers.

Filbert asked her a series of questions about the yell: "What was the yell?" and "It wasn't a word?" and "It was just a yell?" and "But you couldn't understand what it was?"

Borjas responded that "It was just a yell," and "It might have been a word, I don't recall," and "It might have been a word," and "I don't recall, I don't recall."

There is a sense here of a harassing method of constant interruption, as if the FBI agents want to prevent her from just telling the story of what occurred. Two interrupters working against one young agent who is just trying to tell her story.

"So then you hear the yell and gunfire starts?" Frueh asked.

"Uh-huh," Borjas responded.

"Did you recall in your training what kind of gun did you hear? Did you hear—were you able to decipher whether it was a long gun, a handgun? Or what did you hear first?" Frueh asked.

"Well, from the actual, I saw the—the fire, like the . . ."

"Muzzle flash," Frueh said, interrupting once more.

"Muzzle fires," Borjas said, trying to get out her story.

"Uh huh," Frueh said.

"And I could distinguish it was a long one," Borjas said.

"OK," Frueh said.

So the FBI agent asked her if she "recalled in her training" to distinguish between a long gun and handgun—by sound alone—when suddenly shots were being fired at her on a remote mountain in the dead of night. As if anybody on the face of the earth in this situation would try to think of training—What training?—and try to listen to what kind of firearm was being used to end her life. More on this bizarre question later.

There is no training by the Border Patrol or any other law enforcement agency in which officers under fire at close range should try to distinguish by sound what kind of firearm is being used to kill them.

And Borjas responded by reiterating what she said in her first interview— that she saw someone firing a long firearm. Only now, she was saying the same thing, despite the fact that it contradicted the official FBI version—that there were no other people involved.

Agent Ivie—the one the FBI identified as the only shooter at the saddle who fired on the other agents—did not have a long firearm with him.

So if they could discredit Borjas's account of seeing someone with a long arm at the saddle, that would support the FBI's conclusion.

Borjas continued with her story.

"And as I saw it, I was like 'Oh, my gosh.' I immediately went for my gun. And I pointed it out to the threat, and I do not remember if I did fire or not.

"And all I could think of is 'take cover,' 'cause I mean, I—I, what I saw was I saw three to four people out there. So I just decided to take cover and—and there was like a small little like cactus looking

thing and like a rock, and that's where I hid. I took cover there, and I was still drawn out with my gun."

So now Borjas has succeeded in getting out the other part of her story, which contradicts the FBI official narrative—she saw three or four other people there. Which is exactly what she told the first BP agent on the scene and her interviewers three hours after the shooting.

But this time, the FBI agents cannot let this testimony stand unchallenged. If this interview is to appear as part of the official record, the FBI cannot let the truth stand out there like a spotlight shining on its Big Lie.

"Let's—let's back up a little bit to the first time you see a muzzle flash," Filbert said.

"M-hmm," Borjas said.

"Is that, that's to your left?" Filbert asked.

"That's to my left," Borjas said.

"Right, and you said that—that was ah—you believe a rifle (pause)" Filbert said.

"Yes, uh-huh," Borjas said.

". . . round from your hearing and vision?" Filbert said.

"Yes, and from vision," Borjas said.

"OK, OK, I just wanted to be clear about that," Filbert said.

"Um, you said that you saw—you thought you saw three or four?" Filbert asked.

"Uh-huh," Borjas responded.

"People?" Filbert asked.

"Yes," Borjas responded.

FILBERT:	When you were turning in response to the shots being fired?
BORJAS:	Yes.
FILBERT:	Is when you saw...
BORJAS:	Uh-huh.
FILBERT:	...the three or four...
BORJAS:	Yes.
FILBERT:	...what you believed were people?
BORJAS:	Yes.

Note that Borjas said, "I saw three or four people out there." *The FBI agent followed this just seconds later with, "You said that you saw— thought you saw three or four?"*

So now the interview is about to shift gears deep into the FBI's territory, in which the agents attempt to influence Agent Borjas to go along with the Bureau's artificial narrative.

Borjas plays along—a little bit—with the narrative that the Bureau wants her to articulate. Keep in mind that she wants to tell the truth, but she also wants to keep her job. As we read the transcript, we can feel the tension, as she struggles with proclaiming the truth, while not offending the interviewers.

"OK, and can you describe that a little more, what—what you were seeing?" Filbert asked.

"Well as I—from the actual muzzle, you could see every time, you could, you know, actually see some, and as I was turning that's where I could see some people now. I may have seen shadows, I'm not too sure, but to me it looked like people. It looked like three or four people," Borjas said.

"Right, so at that point you believe it's three or four people. You can't be a hundred percent sure," Filbert said.

"Uh-huh," Borjas said.

"It's, it's dark," Filbert said.

"Yes," Borjas said.

"Maybe shadows," Filbert said.

"Uh-huh," Borjas said.

"OK," Filbert said.

There are several points to be made on this exchange:

Borjas already said and repeated that there was a full moon. Yes, there are shadows from a full moon. If it had been a moonless night, there would have been no shadows.

When a rifle is fired, full moon or not, it will light up the scene, enabling people nearby to see what kind of weapon is being fired.

Most importantly, shadows do not shoot at people. And a Border Patrol agent who did not have a rifle in his possession did not fire a rifle at his fellow agents.

The "shadow" narrative was something concocted by the FBI and told to a group of Border Patrol agents at a meeting in which the "friendly fire" narrative was explained.

Borjas did not see people, just shadows, according to this fanciful narrative. The FBI had to come up with something as an alternative explanation to Borjas's eyewitness account.

Once again FBI Agent Frueh took the lead in questioning.

"Where was Johnson at this point? I know you guys were—he was in front of you at one point, when did—did you hear him fire his weapon before you took cover?" Frueh asked.

"I'm not too sure if I saw him fire," Borjas said. "I might have seen both, but it might have been the one from our left. As I retreated, I don't know exactly; I figured he ran the opposite way that I ran because I never heard him come to my side."

"OK. What was he carrying? What weapon was he using that night?" Frueh asked.

"He was carrying an M4," Borjas said.

"OK. Um did you hear him fire, did you hear any—did you hear him fire then before or after the yelling or was it just sort of . . ."

"No it was just sort of like . . ." Borjas said

"Crazy gun fire," Frueh said, interrupting again. Here it was obvious the FBI agent did not want to hear what Borjas had to say.

"Yeah, m-hmm," Borjas said.

"OK. Um, so he was near you. Maybe you didn't see him fire. And then you just couldn't tell which direction it was coming from," Frueh said.

If there ever was a leading question, that was it: "And then you just couldn't tell which direction it was coming from." But Borjas refused to play along.

"Yeah, I knew it was coming from our left," Borjas said.

Borjas had just said she saw the gunfire coming from her left. So here is another case of Borjas being treated like a suspect.

Either Frueh did not hear what she just said about seeing gunfire from her left, or she heard it and was trying to get Borjas to contradict herself. In either case, this resembles an interrogation of a suspect—rather than an interview of a fellow law enforcement officer.

Zero respect was being shown to this courageous young lady who risked her life on the mountain saddle.

"I could see like the actual, now I don't know if he—he had returned fire because that's when he turned right away," Borjas said.

"OK," Frueh said.

"And I went for cover," Borjas said.

"And then you didn't see him after that?" Frueh asked.

"And I didn't see him," Borjas said. "As I went back to look for cover, I got on my radio and I, I said, 'shots fired,' and then I hid behind that rock."

21

"Those People Are Going to Come after Me."

"Like what if they get me and me and make me go to him and they'd kill us both, or what if they just kill me? . . ." Borjas on her thoughts after surviving gunfire

Part 2 of Agent Borjas's second interview
October 11

Agent Borjas told the FBI agent interviewers she was trying to see "if the threat was coming at me or anything."

Then she heard Agent Johnson say, "shots fired. I'm hit."

"And then what happened after you heard him say he was hit?" Frueh asked.

"I sat there, and I was (thinking) all right; well, I mean these people are going to come after me," she said. "They're either going to run towards me, they're going to go back south, I didn't know what direction they were going to go so I sat there.

"And it became a little quiet, and then I heard people talking, and at that point I was like "oh my gosh. They're coming towards me." So I-I stayed there. I tried to calm myself down, and I made a little noise in the brush and moved a little bit. That's when it stayed real quiet.

"And I turned off my radio at that point because I said, "If I can hear them, they can hear me." So I turned off my radio, and I was just sitting there with my gun out."[1]

FRUEH:	Ok. And then what happened after you heard him say he was hit?
BORJAS:	Um, I sat there and I was like alright well, I mean these people are going to come after me. They're either going to run towards me, they're going to go back south, I didn't know what direction they were going to go so I sat there. And i-it became a little quiet and then I heard people talking; and at that point I was like oh my gosh they're coming towards me. So I-I stayed there I tried to um calm myself down and I made a little noise in the brush and moved a little bit that's when it stayed real quiet. And I had turned off my radio at that point because I said if I can hear them, they can hear me. So I turned off my radio and I was just sitting there with my gun out. And I said you know what like, either I run and go down to the actual like, because you know how it goes down to like a draw?

Borjas would have been aware that the official FBI account was that two Border Patrol agents met each other and began firing at each other—with nobody else involved in any way. So it would have taken considerable courage and integrity to report that there were people there who might be coming after her—people she heard talking, after the shooting ceased.

According to the FBI's narrative, there would be only one other living person up there in the vicinity of the saddle—Agent Johnson. But she heard people—obviously those involved in the attack on the agents—as they were talking to each other.

If the FBI narrative were true, why would Agent Borjas be concerned about her safety? If all that occurred was Agent Ivie accidentally shooting at Agent Johnson, and then Johnson shooting Ivie to death, why would Agent Borjas be hearing multiple people conversing? If Agent Ivie was dead, and her partner was injured—and nobody else was nearby—why would she have her gun out, concerned about other people who might come after her or run toward the border?

Shadows do not talk to each other. Despite the fact that the FBI agents wanted Borjas to affirm their bizarre theory that she saw shadows rather than people, they never accused her of hearing voices in the night that did not exist.

Borjas told the FBI agents that she wanted to head down to a nearby gully, so she could go around from there to help Agent Johnson, because he had been hit.

She went down the side of the mountain and toward her left, which would have been southeast. She said she did not hear or see Johnson, so she figured that he went the opposite way. She said that when she heard him on the radio, saying "shots fired," she heard him only on the radio, but not otherwise. She said she had the radio turned down "real low" and on her "actual ear."

"So I ran, and I ran east, and I was trying to make my way down. . . . I think I ran about 200 yards; I'm not sure how far I ran. And when I got there, I sat there again. I was trying to be very quiet, trying to hear if they were coming my way, where they were going.

"I didn't hear anything at that point. I sat there for awhile, and I could see the agents on Highway 80. . . . I could see a bunch of vehicles with their lights on, with their overheads on.

"And I couldn't get out on the radio because I don't know how far they are from me."

Agent Borjas said she was considering which way to travel to make her way to Johnson's location, when she heard a helicopter.

"And that's when I turned on my radio and I directed, which is Omaha, we call (helicopters) Omaha; I directed him to where I was at, and I said, 'I'm east of you,'" Borjas said.

Borjas then recounted how the Customs and Border Protection Black Hawk circled around, as the crew searched for her with its searchlight on.

She made it back up the hill, got close to the searchlight, and waved her hands. Then she was spotted by someone aboard the chopper.

"And I got on the radio and I said, 'Go find Johnson. He's toward my west, because he's been hit. . . . I'll be fine. Just go and find him.'"

When a helicopter crew member asked how far away Johnson was, she said told them she was not sure, maybe 200 or 150 yards away. Then a crew member told her, "you have some agents coming towards you."

Then she saw a couple of flashlight beams nearby on the ground and saw several agents approaching on foot. When they reached her, she told them she was fine.

"And we were making our way toward the west, and I kept telling them, 'be careful, this is where it happened.'"

If this were just an unfortunate accidental shooting, with one agent dead and another injured, why would Agent Borjas be telling the first responders to be careful? Why would they be concerned about their safety, if only Border Patrol agents were on the scene when they arrived?

Borjas Recalls Details That Are Corroborated by Other Evidence

She said Agent Edwards, a temporary Border Patrol supervisor, told her to remove the magazine from her pistol and top it off, so she did that.

"I put the actual mag that was in my gun, I put it in the bottom, and I topped off, and we were heading west, and then that's when some other agents actually found Johnson," she said.

Borjas recalled that Johnson was later walking toward the landed helicopter, with the assistance of other agents. While he was walking, he was "holding his butt area.

"And that's all I remember. They just put us in the helicopter, and they took us down to where there was an ambulance, and they asked me if I was shot, and I was like, 'I don't think so.' And they took him—and they took him back to the station."

The FBI agents then asked her to point out on a map where she had been at various times.

She said they were on level terrain when they came under fire.

"It was like a flat. We weren't going down, and we weren't going up. It wasn't like a slope," she said.

Filbert asked her to estimate the distance between her and where the shots were being fired.

"From what I remember, we weren't too far," Borjas said. "I was like maybe four to five feet away."

"Four to five feet?" Filbert asked.

"Yeah. We weren't far, I mean," Borjas said.

While Johnson estimated that he was 15 to 20 feet away from the shooter or shooters, Borjas was in a different position. She had been behind him, but also to his left.

When someone is shooting in your direction—or shooting a firearm in any direction—from such a close range, is there any way you would not see them? Is there any way you would mistake inanimate shadows for human shooters that were four or five feet—or even 25 feet away from your face?

Borjas said that Johnson was closer to the shooters than she was, "'cause I was at an angle."

About halfway through the interview, the Border Patrol union attorney spoke for the first time.

"Take a second to describe that triangulation that you had described to me in the sense of how far away you were from Johnson," Jim Calle said. "And then when the shots fired the angle that you believe the shots were coming from Johnson and the angle in reference to you. I think that helps explain how close you perceived it to be."

FBI Agent Filbert asserted his own authority by interjecting, "Please do."

A map was placed in front of Borjas, which she pointed to as she explained the logistics of the shootout.

"Johnson was about right here. This is the trail. This is the hill right here," she said. "And we went around the hill. We were coming this way. This is the area that I said was flat.

"Johnson was right here. This is the trail we were on. We were in the middle; I was about four, five, six feet away from him, not too far. It was right here. He was like across when he actually turned to the left."

Borjas pointed to where she was when the shooting began. Recalling the situation in the context of being behind Agent Johnson, she thought she might have been a little farther away.

"I don't know how far, maybe ten feet away from it, from what I can recall. We were extremely close to it," Borjas said.

"OK. To where the muzzle flashes were coming from?" Filbert asked.

"To where the muzzle flashes," Borjas said. "Johnson was the closest one. He's the one that actually turned."

Apparently Borjas is correcting her earlier statement about Ivie turning. During both interviews she said she never saw 225 (Ivie) at the saddle.

Borjas said that she was not sure where she was in relation to the map when the shooting began.

"And the map is just simply an aid to get your bearings, but if you can't tell from the map, that's fine," Filbert said.

Frueh returned to the subject of the yell Borjas heard before the shooting began.

"So then you heard yelling first, and you don't—do you recall? Maybe you don't recall what was said?" Frueh asked.

"No," Borjas said.

"As far as language that was being spoken, or?" Frueh asked.

"It was just like a yell, I don't . . . " Borjas said. "And all I could see was Johnson turned, he turned, and that was when the yell was, so he turned before the actual yell."

"OK. So he heard something, saw something," Frueh said.

"And he turned, and that's when everything just started," Borjas said.

This testimony perfectly matched what Johnson said during his interview and also what I believe occurred in relation to the shooting of Agent Ivie.

Johnson said he saw the silhouette of someone with a smuggler's pack. When the shooting began, it came from Johnson's left and front. He returned fire toward his left.

It made sense that Johnson turned toward his left, just before the shooting began.

A yell just before the shooting began could have been the final utterance of Agent Ivie. All was quiet before that, with Ivie probably involved in a struggle with several suspects. When he yelled in order to warn the other two agents, Agent Ivie was shot in the head by an assassin, as another shooter unleashed a couple of volleys with Agent Ivie's pistol toward Agents Johnson and Borjas.

FBI Agent Filbert asked Borjas, "Could you tell who shot first?"

"I could see from our left the shots," Borjas said.

"So in your mind, the shots were coming from the threat?" Filbert asked.

"From the threat," Borjas said.

"First," Filbert said.

"M-hmm," Borjas said, answering affirmatively.

"Did you hear Johnson yell anything or say anything?" Frueh asked.

"No, the only time that I heard him was after I said, 'shots fired' on the radio, and I heard him say, 'shots fired. I'm hit.' That was the last time I had any communication, because like I said, I heard something, and I had to turn my radio off for my own safety because I would have given up my position."

Filbert asked Borjas if she was also concerned about giving up Johnson's position when she turned off her radio.

"I don't know where he ran, so I didn't know his position either way," Borjas responded.

Filbert asked her if it "crossed her mind" that his radio "going off" would give away his position.

Then Borjas did something that was quite remarkable. The young Border Patrol agent admitted the depth of the fears she experienced as she crouched on the side of a mountain slope, hoping the smugglers would not find her. She was afraid of what they might do to her, and what she might do under pressure from them.

As she tried to make herself invisible behind a rock and a plant, she was keenly aware of the kind of people who had just opened fire on her and her partner. A cartel smuggler who had just shot and wounded her partner would not hesitate to murder both of them.

If three or four of them came looking for her, she would not be able to shoot her way out of that situation.

"Yeah, I'm like, if—if they hear anything then you know I'm out of luck," Borjas said. "And they're going to come towards me and—and they're maybe—I don't know, just a lot of thoughts were going through my head. Like what if they get me and make me go to him, and they'd kill us both, or what if they just kill me, or? You know, just so many thoughts in my head."

"And at this point how far do you think you were from your car?" Frueh asked, adding, "How long had you been walking?"

"I think we walked about maybe 45 minutes," Borjas said.

"So you were far from any . . ." Frueh said.

"Yeah, there was no way we could have ran to our vehicles," Borjas said.

Borjas said she could see the highway, or what appeared to be the highway. She was not sure whether it was the highway (State Route 80) or another road.

"But all I could see was a bunch of agents when everything happened," she said, apparently referring to the agents rushing to the scene with their emergency lights on after the *shots fired* reports were relayed to law enforcement on the Border Patrol frequency.

Filbert asked Borjas whether her concern for Johnson being wounded was based on there being "a good chance that he had been hit" because of the "shots going back and forth."

"No, I heard him on the radio," Borjas said, referring to what she just told the FBI agents a few minutes earlier.

"You heard him on the radio?" Filbert asked.

"He actually said—" Borjas began to say.

"I've been hit—" Filbert said, interrupting after apparently remembering what Borjas said earlier.

"I've been hit," Borjas said. "And I automatically thought it was him because I never thought Ivie was near us at all. From the last time I saw his flashlight I never even thought he would be near where we were.

"I actually thought he didn't even make it to the shootout, our shootout."

At that time, Borjas believed the shootout was entirely between a group of smugglers and the two Border Patrol agents who encountered them, Johnson and herself.

Later that morning, she heard that Ivie had been shot to death during the encounter.

Filbert returned to the subject of Borjas's encounter with Acting Border Patrol Supervisor Edwards, the first responder on the scene to contact her. He found her on the side of the mountain 20 to 30 minutes after the shooting. Filbert asked her whether Edwards directed her to exchange magazines for her pistol. She said that he had done that.

After the Shooting, She Wondered Where the Shooters Were

In response to Filbert's questions, Borjas said she placed a new magazine in her pistol to "top it off," that is to have a full magazine in place.

"So at that point I mean you didn't know if the threats were still in the area?" Filbert asked.

"Yeah, I didn't know," she said.

"You wanted to make sure you were completely topped off just in case the threats were still around?" Agent Frueh asked.

"Yes," Borjas said.

Filbert asked her whether she told the responding agents to be careful for the same reason that she exchanged her magazines—that she believed the threat was still in the area.

"Yes," Borjas said. "I kept telling them, 'be careful, this is where I saw them and I heard them.' I kept telling them, 'be careful, be careful.'"

Knowing that the FBI had announced that nobody else was there, Borjas was boldly proclaiming that she believed otherwise. She knew that their narrative was inaccurate. A lesser person would not insist that she saw and heard people who, according to the FBI scenario, officially never existed. A Border Patrol line agent was sticking to the truth, despite the pronouncement from the leading law enforcement officials of the United States.

Filbert said he wanted to talk about intel reports about this area.

"You'd gotten intel reports prior to the night of October second, the morning of October second about this area? About smuggling in this area?" Agent Filbert asked.

"There's always smuggling there," Borjas said. "That's where most of our traffic, narcotics traffic, is at."

She clarified that this was not just in the specific area of that mountain saddle, but that the narcotics traffic was heaviest in Grid 7, rather than in other districts.

Grid 7 is a district designated by the Border Patrol that includes the Mule Mountains. It is patrolled by agents from the Brian Terry Station. Agents are assigned to patrol specific sections of Grid 7, or other grids, on each shift.

Filbert asked Borjas whether she had in mind that she was covering a heavily used smuggling area when she was assigned to Grid 7.

"Yeah, there's probably more than likely you're going to encounter drug smugglers, more likely in that specific grid," she said.

Changing the subject, FBI Agent Filbert returned to questions concerning her reaction to the shooting. He asked her to perform an analysis on the state of her senses and other physiological systems immediately after she was nearly shot to death.

"Once the—the shots had been fired—um—and you had started—um—when you started—um—when you sought cover—ah—do you recall like having—ah—tunnel vision? I mean, what did you—were you having trouble hearing? Was there—what was your physiological reaction to what was going on?" Filbert asked Borjas.

"Ah, I was scared," she said.

"Sure," Filbert said.

Once again, we have to notice the raw honesty of Agent Borjas. Not every law enforcement officer would want to go on the record as being "scared."

Now that Filbert had brought up the painful subject of her reaction to being shot at by cartel smugglers on a desolate mountain ridge, Borjas took the opportunity to articulate more details of what had occurred. Instead of performing a useless self-analysis of her psychological condition, Borjas took the opportunity to place on the record more of what actually occurred. She was a law enforcement officer, not a psychologist.

She was brilliantly declining to help the FBI dig up grounds to discredit her. In other words, she was outsmarting them.

"To Me It Sounded Like Spanish"

Borjas continued to recount what was taking place near her, as she hid on the side of the mountain, after nearly losing her life.

FILBERT:	...Um, you once the-the shots had been fired um and you had started um when you sought cover ah do you recall like having ah tunnel vision? I mean, what did you-were you having trouble hearing? Was there-what was your physiological reaction to what was going on?
BORJAS:	Ah, I was scared.
FILBERT:	Sure.
BORJAS:	Um, and I could hear talking but I could not make it out. I could not make out what was said and I mean I immediately thought that's them, they're still here and that's when I was like I have to turn off my radio.
FILBERT:	And you couldn't tell the language that was being spoken?
BORJAS:	No, it to me it sounded like Spanish but I mean, I can't because I'm pretty fluent in Spanish and it sounded like Spanish to me but I couldn't make it out. I could not make it out. So I don't know if it was because I was like in shock and you know everything my adrenaline was going and everything I don't.

"And I could hear talking, but I could not make it out," Borjas said. "I could not make out what was said, and I mean I immediately thought, that's them, they're still here. And that's when I was, like, 'I have to turn off my radio.'"

"And you couldn't tell the language that was being spoken?" Filbert asked.

"No, it to me **it sounded like Spanish**," Borjas said. "I'm pretty fluent in Spanish, and **it sounded like Spanish to me,** but I couldn't make it out. I could not make it out."

Borjas added that she did not know whether she had trouble making out the language because she was in shock and her "adrenaline was going."

"And that's right after you took the initial cover is when you heard that?" Filbert asked.

"Yes, that's the first time I took cover, and I heard them, and that's when I turned off my radio," she said. "'Cause I figured they're going to keep calling me on the radio."

Filbert told Borjas and her attorney that he wanted them to look at a "FD-302," a FBI witness statement summary, which was written after the shooting. It was based on the interview Borjas underwent a few hours after the shooting with FBI agents and a Border Patrol supervisor.

That FBI document distorted what Borjas said in her initial interview. So this is a dirty trick, to try to get Borjas to base what she would say nine days later on what she did not say at her previous interview. Once again, this shows that Borjas is being treated like a suspect. It is legal for law enforcement officers to lie to suspects during interviews, in order to elicit information. To use this tactic on an honest Border Patrol agent is a despicable abuse of power. However, these agents were not successful in steering Borjas to comment on the contents of the false FBI statements.

"I want (you) to look at it and understand that this interview is really a continuation of what you said right after the shooting, OK?" Filbert said.

Borjas responded affirmatively.

Border Patrol union attorney Calle said to Borjas, "Before we look at that, there is one question I want to ask you: You're sounding like you're more certain about who was firing first?"

"Yeah," Borjas said.

She had said on the morning of the shooting that she did not recall where the shots were coming from.

"I mean, it looked like it was to the left but I'm not sure 'cause everything just happened so fast," Borjas said.

Calle reiterated his question.

"Not only the direction, but who fired first," the attorney said.

He asked her if she recognized where the first shots originated at the time she was first interviewed.

"No," Borjas said.

"Have you now ended up hearing some additional information that may have solidified in your head who may have fired first?" Calle asked.

"Yeah, I may have," Borjas said.

Calle asked her if this contributed to the answer she gave to the FBI in this second interview. She said that it did.

"OK, now we'll look at this," Calle said, referring to the FBI's document.

Before Borjas could tell what kind of additional information she received and from whom—which influenced her answer about who fired first—an FBI agent butted in to once again change the subject and remove her lawyer from his position as interviewer.

"So you understand that this, what we're doing today with this interview today, is just to follow up on the initial—ah—contact that was made, the initial questions that were asked, and ah get more of the story?" Filbert said, repeating an expanded version of what he had just said one minute earlier.

Calle asked the FBI agent for clarification.

"(It was) my understanding ultimately that there were FBI agents sitting in on the eight firearms questions?" Calle asked, referring to the fact that the initial interview on October 2 had been a question-and-answer session focusing on a series of standard questions for agent-involved shootings.

Both FBI agents answered affirmatively.

Frueh went on to give a lengthy explanation as to why they were interviewing Borjas again. Nobody ever returned to the subject of what additional information Borjas had heard.

"And we—we know that after a shooting incident I mean you're in shock, it's not really, that's why we wanted to come you know after you know give you an opportunity to really think I mean things like anything happens right then and there we know that that things," Frueh said.

"M-hmmm," Borjas said.

"You remember things slightly differently and you kind of replay things in your mind and you just we felt we wanted to give you a chance to just actually talk to us not immediately following," Frueh said, her role switching from interviewer to filibusterer.

"M-hmmm," Borjas said.

"You know um which is what we're here for um so you can think of anything else that maybe we didn't ask that would help shed light on the whole incident?" Frueh asked.

It was apparently important for the FBI to put on the record that the first shots came from a shooter at the saddle. This fit the FBI's narrative of Agent Ivie causing his own death by firing at the other agents. This was apparently one of the goals of this interview.

At her first interview, Borjas was not asked who fired the first shots or their points of origin. She said she heard yelling and gunshots, saw three or four suspects, and they were firing a long arm and possibly also a pistol.

Nine days later, we have FBI agents trying to put words into a young Border Patrol agent's mouth.

Apparently, the FBI did not want it to come out in the interview that Borjas had learned—like everybody else who was following the case—that investigators told the Ivie family on Friday, October 5, that Agent Ivie fired first at his fellow agents.

The story of investigators concluding that he fired first— "and then (he) was killed when they returned fire"—was carried in an article posted by the Deseret News on Sunday, October 7. It was entitled "Slain Border Patrol agent Nicholas Ivie opened fire first, investigators say." That story said that "they returned fire," which is an inaccurate statement. Only one of the two surviving agents fired a weapon.[2]

With not one media outlet that I could find challenging the veracity of the "friendly fire" narrative, most people would naturally accept it without question. There were Border Patrol agents and borderland residents who privately expressed disbelief, but most Americans at that time believed that the FBI was a rock-solid, nonpolitical agency that should be believed at all times.

After Frueh asked Borjas whether she had any more information on the incident, Borjas said she did pull her gun from its holster.

"So you didn't pull it in reaction to Johnson's perception that something was to the left?" Calle asked.

"No, it was after I had heard the actual gunshots," Borjas said.

Frueh said, "So you pulled your—you drew your weapon after—"

Borjas responded, "I drew my weapon after—"

"—you heard the gunshots," Frueh said, finishing Borjas's sentence for her.

"—I heard the gunshots," Borjas said, finishing her own sentence despite the interruption.

Borjas Saw People Sitting on the Ground— as Gunfire Erupted from That Place

Then Borjas reiterated the main discrepancy between her eyewitness account and the FBI's conclusion—with a new wrinkle to it.

"And like I said I saw, I actually did see people and I saw like on the actual ground sitting on the ground," Borjas said.

"Those were the three to four?" Frueh asked.

"Yeah, that I had seen. Like they—they were all on the ground," Borjas said. "Like I never saw anyone standing."

This was brand new information. There was nothing in the transcript of her October 2 interview, or in the first 35 pages of this 40-page October 11 interview transcript to indicate that the three or four suspects at the shooting scene were on the ground.

If this is accurate, and you add in that Johnson said he saw one man standing—who was wearing a smuggler's pack and removed a blanket from himself—this paints a different picture of the scene. If three or four were sitting, and at least one was standing, this would mean that there were a total of four, five, or more people on the scene.

Nevertheless, it contradicts the FBI allegation that there was nobody else involved but the two agents. But it tends to place the three or four individuals Borjas saw in a more passive role.

Were they shooting from a sitting position, or did she just see these people sitting, while not clearly seeing the people who were shooting? The FBI agents did not ask whether Borjas saw the seated people firing weapons.

Calle then asked his client for another clarification.

"But just to reiterate what you already said, that you saw something there, you thought they were bodies (illegal aliens) but they could have been shadows, you just you're not precisely sure," Calle said.

"Yes," Borjas said.

"And were they in the direction of where the shots were coming from?" Filbert asked.

"Yes," Borjas replied.

"Very near?" Filbert asked.

"Yeah, 'cause like when I was turning that's when I saw and recovered and then I went to go look for cover, that's when I heard like those actual voices," Borjas said.

"When you were turning in response to the shots being fired?" Filbert asked.

"Yes," Borjas said.

"Is when you saw the three of [sic] four you believed were people?" Filbert asked.

"Yes," Borjas said.

"OK, near where the shots were coming from?" Filbert asked.

"Correct, yes," Borjas said.

After other Border Patrol agents arrived on the scene on foot and horseback, the two agents were flown down from the mountain in a Black Hawk helicopter. Borjas was then driven by a Border Patrol agent to her station. She did not learn what had happened to Agent 225 (Ivie) until she arrived at her station.

"And (the chaplain) told me Ivie didn't make it," Borjas recalled.

She said that when the chaplain told her Ivie died, at first she thought that it was her partner, 341, "'cause I really don't know their last names—I'm fairly new, so I just know them by their star numbers."

After the chaplain told her that Agent Ivie died, she asked the agent who had driven her to the station, "Who's Ivie? Is he 341?"

The agent who drove her to the station is referred to in the transcript as having a last name that sounded phonetically like "Signs"

"And he told me, 'No, that's 225.' And I couldn't believe it because I never . . .I didn't think he was in the area. He to me, he never actually was there where we were.

"And I mean just started crying and that's when I broke down," Borjas said.

She said she did not believe he was nearby when the shootout occurred, "based on the last time I saw his flashlight."

Her attorney asked her if she remembered making statements to the other agents who arrived at the scene, shortly after the shooting, regarding whether she fired her weapon.

"I don't recall," Borjas said. "Agent Edwards kept telling me, 'just relax, just relax.'" Borjas said she must have been "really nervous, and I think I was talking a lot."

"But I do remember telling them, 'Be careful, be careful, they were right here, this is where it happened,'" Borjas recalled.

With the interview nearing its end, Agent Frueh reminded Borjas once again that there were shadows out there.

"And on a full moon in the desert I know that we-we've had a lot of rain this year so all the trees and shrubs are pretty tall," Frueh said.

"Um, and the shadows, I mean a full moon here can cast shadows."

"M-hmm," Borjas said, agreeing with the obvious.

"Which is, I know something maybe people don't, can't imagine, but I mean you—you can cast a shadow of yourself pretty easily of yourself [sic] and you can see it, I mean is that an accurate description of what it was like that night? Where you could see shadows pretty clearly and you—" Frueh said.

"Yes," Borjas said.

Frueh had one more thing to say, which did not surprise Borjas.

"Because it was—," Frueh said.

"—it was a full moon," Borjas said, finishing the FBI agent's sentence.

For anyone trying to believe the FBI agent's logic, we must accept this premise: Because a Border Patrol agent working the midnight shift could see her own shadow under a full moon, she could therefore mistake the shadows of "pretty tall trees or shrubs" for several people shooting at her and her partner with a rifle—and then talking to each other.

There is no confirmed account of a moon shadow firing shots at anyone at any time or in any place. Neither of the agents who saw people on the saddle who were firing gunshots at them thought that they were under attack from a group of moon shadows.

Moon shadows also do not leave behind evidence, such as Mexican coins, water jugs containing moisture, shoe prints, cigarette butts, and impressions of marijuana bundles. Neither are moon shadows normally apprehended by agents who spot them from a helicopter after the sun rises.

The Borjas interview ended with the two FBI agents—who had traveled from Tucson, Arizona to El Paso, Texas, for the occasion—discussing whether the time of day was this or that, because they had undergone a one-hour time change.

22

"We Called Nick the Neighborhood Dad."

"He is remembered for his selflessness and his absolute commitment to family, country, and faith," U.S. Representative Jason Chaffetz.

A second memorial service
Thursday, October 11
Provo Metropolitan Area, Utah

Nine days after his death, Agent Ivie was honored once more at a funeral service held at Utah Valley University, in Orem, just north of Provo. He was buried in the Spanish Fork City Cemetery, just south of Provo, in the city where he first lived with Christy, before joining the Border Patrol.

The service was attended by hundreds of mourners. A section set apart on the floor of the UCCU Center auditorium was filled with law enforcement officers from local, state, and federal agencies.[1]

A Border Patrol color guard and bagpipe and drum corps preceded Ivie's flag-draped coffin as it entered the room.

Ted Stanley, a Border Patrol agent and neighbor of the Ivies, was tasked with leading Mouse by his reins, as he carried Agent Ivie's cowboy boots backwards in his stirrups. One of the most poignant moments of the day was when Mouse was led past the fallen agent's casket at the cemetery.

"Nick loved that horse," Joel Ivie said at the service that morning. "He was always hugging that horse."[2]

Stanley, who lived across the street from the Ivies in Sierra Vista, said his children and Ivie's children played together, and Nick Ivie "was usually in the middle of it."

He said that Nick Ivie "actually took the time to get to know my kids' likes and interests inside and out. We called Nick the 'neighborhood dad.'"

Stanley said Ivie was the one who encouraged him to join the horse patrol, although Stanley had no previous experience with horses.

When they were on a shift together, Ivie had shown him his favorite spot in the mountains, close to the border. When he showed him the trails and shared his knowledge of the area, he convinced Stanley to give the horse patrol a try.

David V. Aguilar, acting commissioner of U.S. Customs and Border Protection, spoke at the Utah service.

Aguilar publicly addressed the daughters of the slain agent, saying that their daddy was a good man, a patriot who was admired by others. He wanted them to know what kind of man he was when they would "look around the country" later on in their lives.

"I want you to know your father was a big part of that way of life, that American way of life," Aguilar said.

Border Patrol Chief Michael Fisher said he "said a prayer for Nick and for the family" when he and other agents hiked up to the mountain saddle where Agent Ivie had been killed.

Fisher addressed Christy Ivie during the service, as she sat by the coffin, holding her two young daughters.

"Your husband died in service to his country. He did so with pride, and he did so with distinction," Fisher said.

After the ceremony, as the lengthy procession made the 15-mile trip between the university and the cemetery, hundreds of area residents stood along Main Street to pay their respects. Many of them held American flags.[3]

The cemetery where Agent Ivie was buried is located between the Wasatch Mountains to the east, crowned by 10,000-foot-high Spanish Fork Peak, and scenic Utah Lake to the west.

At the graveside service, seven honor guard members fired three rifle volleys in unison. Helicopters flew overhead, and two buglers played "Taps."

Mouse was led past the casket by Agent Stanley. Agent Ivie's badge number, 225, was announced over a radio, with the declaration that he was "10-7," law enforcement code for "out of service," or deceased.

Douglas Ivie, Nick's father, delivered a graveside prayer. Then many family members embraced and sobbed.

Christy Ivie held her 22-month old daughter Presley in her arms as the young widow placed a dozen red roses on her husband's casket, after receiving the flag that had graced his wooden casket. She then lifted 3-year-old Raigan, so she could also place a rose on her father's casket.

Nick and Christy Ivie were wed in 2006, the same year they met. The following year, Nick Ivie was accepted to train at the Border Patrol Academy in Artesia, New Mexico. After his training was completed in January 2008, the couple moved to Sierra Vista from Spanish Fork, Utah.

Both of their daughters, Raigan, 3, and Presley, 22 months, were born in Arizona. Sierra Vista, the largest city in Cochise County, in the southeast corner of the state, had about 43,000 residents at that time. Sierra Vista is home to many Border Patrol agents who serve at the Brian A. Terry Station.

The Ivies lived in a brand-new ranch house on the east edge of a subdivision overlooking the high desert, between the Huachuca Mountain Range to the west, and the San Pedro River to the east. The San Pedro, flowing north from Mexico—remains viable longer into the dry seasons than other watercourses in the region.

The San Pedro, lined with towering cottonwood trees, creates lush green ecosystems that attract hummingbirds and other avian species that are followed by bird-watchers from around the world. The Mule Mountain range rises from the valley floor about 10 miles east of the Ivie home. The Mule range, formerly considered the southern part of the Dragoon Mountain range, was named after the numerous wild mules found there after prospectors abandoned them in the 1880s.

The Ivies were enjoying their lives in their new community when the tragedy struck. They had many friends throughout Sierra Vista because of Nick's law enforcement career, as well as their fellow worshippers in the Church of Jesus Christ of Latter-Day Saints.

Not long after Nick Ivie's death, his widow and their two daughters moved to Massachusetts.

"The Ivie family has endured a terrible tragedy and made an extraordinary sacrifice on behalf of all Americans, and we are forever thankful," U.S. Representative Jason Chaffetz, during a tribute in the House Chamber

Friday, October 12
House of Representatives, U.S. Capitol, Washington, D.C.

U.S. Representative Jason Chaffetz, R-Provo, stood in the historic House chamber to honor Nicholas Ivie, who had previously resided in the Third Congressional District that Chaffetz represented.

Chaffetz delivered a eulogy that recounted many biographical details of the agent's life and lauded him for his service and dedication to his family, community, and nation.

The remarks by Chaffetz were entered into the Congressional Record.

Chaffetz said he was honoring a dedicated Border Patrol agent and American hero who died tragically while working to keep America's southern border secure.

"In the early morning hours of October 2, 2012, 30-year-old Border Patrol Agent Nicholas J. Ivie died near Bisbee, Arizona, while responding to a sensor in a remote border region," Chaffetz said. "He died in the line of duty of injuries sustained from a gunshot wound. We honor his service and sacrifice to the security and safety of the American people."

Chaffetz said that Ivie had spent two years as a missionary in Mexico, where he developed "a great love for the Mexican people." Ivie later gained certification as a firefighter and emergency medical technician, before serving as a Border Patrol agent, along with his brother Joel, near Naco, Arizona.

"After joining the Border Patrol's horse patrol, Agent Ivie was assigned a new mustang that had been captured in the wild," Chaffetz said. "The horse's ears were rounded because the tips had been frozen off in the cold, so he named it *Mouse*. Nick loved horses and had a special relationship with Mouse.

"He died in a beautiful place among rugged terrain, which he had frequently patrolled on his beloved horse and companion, Mouse," Chaffetz said.

The Congressman never said anything about the allegation that Agent Ivie's death was the result of a friendly fire incident.

"Agent Ivie was an outstanding agent, and, according to his family, a compassionate man. He once carried a pregnant woman with bare, badly-battered feet for a mile and a half, after she and her group of illegal border crossers became lost in the dessert," said Chaffetz, a second-term Congressman at the time. He would go on to win his third term in the upcoming election.

"He took his obligations to his family, [his] friends, and his church very seriously," said Chaffetz, who also was a member of the Church of Jesus Christ of Latter Day Saints. "He is remembered for his selflessness and his absolute commitment to family, country, and faith. He also distinguished himself as a dedicated and accomplished agent who loved his job, his coworkers, and his service to his fellow man."

Chaffetz said that honor was due to members of Agent Ivie's family for their tremendous personal sacrifice.

"He leaves behind his wife, Christy Lyn, and two daughters, 3-year-old Raigan and 22-month-old Presley. Those around him knew he had a deep love for his wife and called his daughters his pride and joy. We also recognize his mother, Cheryl, father, Doug, four siblings: Chris, Andrea, Rick and Joel, and his stepmother Donetta.

"The United States was a beacon for freedom and liberty around the world because of the honorable and dedicated service of agents like Nicholas and his brother Joel, Chaffetz said.

"The Ivie family has endured a terrible tragedy and made an extraordinary sacrifice on behalf of all Americans, and we are forever thankful."

Chaffetz concluded his speech by asking members of Congress to join him in honoring the life and legacy of Agent Ivie, as well as every man and woman in the Border Patrol, who "toil daily to secure our borders and maintain our safety."

In the ensuing years, Chaffetz would become prominent as the chairman of the House Oversight and Government Committee, which investigated the Obama administration's handling of the terrorist attack on the U.S. compound in Benghazi, Libya, in which four Americans were killed.

On the day Agent Ivie was killed, Chaffetz said he expected "a full and immediate investigation into the incident," said a story in the *Deseret News*.

"As the facts come to light, we must take measures to ensure the safety and security of our Border Patrol and our residents in the region," Chaffetz said in his statement.[4]

23

Murder Suspects Remain in Custody in Mexico

"That after the FBI announced that they turned out to be innocent, they were still detained by Mexican authorities with a number of charges. . . .'"
Facebook post by relative of the two suspects arrested for agent Ivie's murder

October 15, 2012
Agua Prieta, Sonora, Mexico

The two main suspects in the murder of Agent Ivie remained in custody in Mexico for at least 13 days after they were arrested. A relative of the suspects wrote a message to a Mexican TV station via Facebook, asking why they were still being held, after the FBI had cleared them of involvement in the Ivie murder. The FBI never revealed any of this to the public.

What has become of those two murder suspects?

According to Facebook posts, Durazo was residing in Hermosillo in September 2019: Soto was in Reynoso, Tamaulipas in 2017.

Both suspects, apparently first cousins, had been residents of Agua Prieta, Sonora, at the time of the Ivie slaying. Aqua Prieta is the border city just south of Douglas, Arizona, about 15 miles east of where they were arrested the morning of October 2, 2012. Agua Prieta had a population of about 79,000, according to the 2010 census.

Although the FBI never publicly acknowledged the arrest of any suspects in connection with the shooting death of Border Patrol Agent Nicholas J. Ivie and wounding of Agent David G. Johnson, FBI agents did interview two men arrested near the scene and took their fingerprints and DNA samples as evidence.

Those two men, Martin Amando Enriquez Durazo and Victor Manuel Durazo Soto, were arrested just south of the border on the morning of October 2, in possession of firearms and drugs, according to news sources and Border Patrol agents who were on the scene.

There were numerous news reports about the arrests of two suspects in Mexico, by both U.S. and Mexican media outlets. Most of those reports were published within a few days of the incident, with

(U) One Mexican Peso
(U) USBP Hat
(U) Empty Nana plastic bottle
(U) Camelback containing reddish brown substance.
(U) Fingerprint card for Martin Armando Enriquez-Durazo.
(U) 2 buccal swabs of Martin Armando Enriquez-Durazo.
(U) Fingerprint card for Victor Manuel Durazo-Soto.
(U) 2 buccal swabs of Victor Manuel Durazo-Soto.

The FBI evidence sheet for the Ivie case included fingerprints and DNA swabs taken from suspects apprehended south of the border.

practically no follow-up by media outlets on what later happened to those men.

I could not find the names of the suspects published by any U.S. media, but one Mexican news site did publish their names.

The FBI evidence report also recorded their identities in its case file, which matched the names published by the Mexican news site.

It is not clear whether any other suspects were arrested in connection with this case. An article published one year after the shooting by a former Border Patrol official mentions three other suspects, who were arrested near the shooting site a few hours later. There was no other mention of those three suspects, who remained unnamed, in any other media report I could find.

A blog covering the Mexican cartel drug wars, *Borderland Beat*, reported that Mexican soldiers arrested the two named suspects in an operation that involved the military, as well as federal and local police. Citing sources including a Mexican Army officer and police official, the story refers to the two men as "alleged perpetrators" who were "arrested in the killing of a U.S. Border Patrol agent and the wounding of a second officer in Arizona."[1]

The FBI evidence report on the Ivie case, obtained along with other "unclassified" documents from the Cochise County Sheriff's Office, showed that evidence was obtained from Martin Amando Enriquez-Durazo and Victor Manuel Durazo-Soto (hyphens added by the FBI): A fingerprint card and two buccal swabs were collected from each suspect. (A buccal swab, similar to a Q-tip, is used to collect saliva cells containing DNA from inside a person's cheek. This method is commonly used by law enforcement.)

It should be noted that on the two pages entitled "Acquisition Event" within the FBI Evidence Report, all the evidence collected in connection with the Ivie murder case shows the details of where and when the evidence was obtained—except for the fingerprint cards and buccal swabs of the two Mexican suspects.

For example, evidence obtained on the day of the autopsy was catalogued as "Evidence obtained from Pima County Medical Examiner's Office on 10/03/2012." Evidence found at the shooting scene was catalogued as "Evidence obtained on 10/02/2012 at GPS Coordinates N 31 23.772; W 109 49.098."

However, evidence listed from Enriquez-Durazo and Durazo-Soto are lacking the details as to where and when they were collected.

Why would the normally methodical FBI—which listed the dates and locations of 89 evidentiary items in the same case—fail to include the date and location of potentially important evidence obtained from two suspects in the shooting of a federal agent?

When the FBI announced that no other people were involved in the shooting of Nicholas Ivie, had they already processed all the DNA and fingerprint evidence found at the scene and compared it to the DNA and fingerprints of those suspects? Had they submitted any DNA or fingerprints they found at the scene to national databases to discover whether anyone else was at that scene?

Had they received information as a result of the processing of the DNA and fingerprints as to the criminal records or lack thereof regarding the suspects who were being held in a Hermosillo jail? Had Mexican authorities shared information on the suspects with the FBI?

The timing of when the FBI statement was released, stating that "only the agents" were involved, was just three days after the shooting—normally too early for that conclusion to have been established.

By the time the two suspects were captured, about seven hours after the shooting, the word would have spread into Mexico about the shooting of a Border Patrol agent. Hundreds of law enforcement officers had already flooded into the area, including agents who were on or near the border roads when tactical Border Patrol agents took the suspects into custody.

Almost all of the border fences in that immediate area allowed for visibility between the two nations. They were constructed that way so American authorities could see what was going on across the line. Of course, that also allowed people in Mexico to observe activities, such as an enormous ongoing operation by U.S. law enforcement.

In addition to the visibility through the border fences, Border Patrol agents were standing up on platforms above the tops of the fences, peering into Mexico. This would have been easy for anyone in the vicinity to see, especially after sunrise.

Although it is possible that those suspects were not connected with the shooting incident, this matter does leave some unanswered questions.

Why would anyone be hanging out near the border on the Mexican side—with firearms and drugs—who had no connection with this shooting?

"It was fully daylight," said a Border Patrol agent stationed about 50 yards away at the time of the arrest. "These guys weren't sneaking anywhere at that point. I don't know if they were trying to move away at all.

"Seeing people in Mexico, on the south side of the fence, anywhere near the fence, we always kind of assume that they're going to try (to cross), or they just returned to Mexico."

That agent, who had been on the scene since about 5:30 a.m., said it was not common to come across suspects that far out in the desert with firearms.

"When we catch groups, very rarely are they armed," the agent said. "And you don't see armed people too often in Mexico, either, unless they're military. Especially with a rifle, with an AR. That was an oddity, that those guys were right there, and they were armed."[2]

The weapons that were seized in connection with the suspects were identified as a .38 caliber revolver and a .223 Bushmaster rifle.

The agent said he was later told by Border Patrol officials that there was no evidence found at the shooting scene of any ammunition other than what agents were using. However, a revolver does not leave behind shell casings, which are retained in its cylinder.

One of the weapons captured from the suspects had a revolver capable of producing an entrance wound that possibly matched the size of the one in Agent Ivie's skull. The other weapon fired the same caliber bullets as the rifle fired by Agent Johnson.

Remember that Agent Borjas reported seeing someone firing a long arm from the saddle.

"It's coincidental, if you believe in coincidences," the Border Patrol agent said, adding that the Bushmaster .223 rifle is not a common rifle to be found south of the border. "It's a common rifle here. Having that style rifle in Mexico is not common at all. So for it to be in the exact same location at the same time is a fairly large coincidence."

The cartel that controlled the Mexican side would not have been sending anyone into that area at a time when hundreds of law enforcement officers were nearby. It was more likely those suspects were resting after fleeing for their lives from the shooting scene. Perhaps they thought they would be safe on the Mexican side, as it was a rare occurrence for American law enforcement to cross the border to apprehend suspects.

If those suspects were involved in shooting the agents, they might have felt safer out in the desert, knowing that the cartel bosses for whom they worked might deal harshly with them if they returned to their nearby hometown. The cartel normally prohibited their mules and coyotes from causing harm to gringo officers and civilians. Cartel bosses hate the unnecessary attention that incidents like this automatically bring to their territory. Killing an agent could bring repercussions that would diminish their profits.

Even if those suspects were not tied to the shootings by their DNA and fingerprints, that did not conclusively eliminate them as suspects. Many guilty parties leave no DNA behind. However, in this case, there were some excellent possibilities to collect DNA evidence. Water jugs found at the scene—which had fresh blood droplets on them—most likely had DNA saliva samples at their mouth openings. A forensic scientist told me there was about a 90 percent probability of finding DNA that would yield a profile on a water jug such as that.

Those jugs were collected by the FBI as evidence. Their placement at the scene, in close proximity to where Agent Johnson was when he was shot, indicated a strong possibility of their connection to the crime. It was noted by a crime scene investigator that they still contained water condensation, indicating that they had been left at that scene recently.

There were many news stories published, broadcast, and posted on the Internet that included information on the arrests of the suspects—although the FBI repeatedly declined to answer any questions about their arrests. An FBI official acknowledged that the Bureau was aware of *reports* on the suspects, while never publicly acknowledging their arrests.

One Border Patrol agent, mentioned earlier in this chapter, said he was on patrol near the border, south of the mountain saddle where his friend had been killed a few hours earlier. He noticed several aircraft overhead, including helicopters and a drone.

The suspects were named in a Mexican news report as Martin Armando Enriquez Durazo and Victor Manuel Durazo Soto. The two men are cousins, according to a Facebook post later that month from a woman who claimed to be the sister of one and the cousin of the other. In that post, she inquired of a Mexican TV news station, asking why her two relatives were still in custody 13 days after their arrest.

The message was tagged onto the page of Victor Manuel Durazo Soto. Translated to English, the post directed to Noticieros Televisa said,

We are relatives of the two detainees in the case of Nicolas [sic] Ivie, and we would like you to contact us, because we are very concerned about the situation of our family members Martin Amando Enriquez Durazo and Victor Manuel Durazo Soto, they are my brother and cousin. That after the FBI announced that they turned out to be innocent, they were still detained by Mexican authorities with a number of charges that at any time did not mention the FBI or any of the means of communication.[2]

In Hispanic culture, each person has two family names, or surnames. The first surname is the same as the first surname of the person's father. The second surname is the same as the first surname of the person's mother. So Martin's father's first surname was Enriquez, and his mother's was Durazo. Victor's father's first surname was Durazo, and his mother's was Soto. Martin's mother and Victor's father both had fathers surnamed Durazo, so those two parents of the suspects were likely siblings.

The woman listed her e-mail address and telephone number.

She wrote that if the TV station followed up on this news, it would discover in Arizona "that it will be solved according to the FBI, but here in Mexico we still do not solve the situation of our relatives being innocent."

The FBI never publicly elaborated on its allegation that nobody else was involved in the shooting incident. I could locate no news reports in which the FBI revealed that its agents had interviewed suspects and obtained their DNA and fingerprints.

To whom did the FBI announce "that they turned out to be innocent?" Why didn't the FBI announce this to the U.S. and international press, which had reported in many stories that two suspects were arrested in Mexico?

The Mexican news story that named the suspects contained more details on the arrest of the suspects than most other stories.

The headline of the Spanish language story posted on October 7, 2012, on proyeccioncannanea.com, a news site then covering the Mexican state of Sonora:

Detienen a los asesinos de agente de la Border Patrol de Naco.

English translation: **Naco Border Patrol agent killers arrested.**[3]

The first six paragraphs roughly followed the American accounts, with details about Agent Ivie and the fact that he had been the first Border Patrol agent shot to death since Brian Terry.

Then the Mexican media outlet added some details, many of which were not included in stories in the U.S. press:

> **The suspects were arrested by members of the Army and "placed at the disposal of the Attorney General's Office to carry out investigations into the case," said the report by the news outlet based in Cananea, a mining town located about 50 miles southwest of Agua Prieta.**

Then it provided the names of those "suspected of involvement in the murder, Victor Manuel Durazo Soto and Martin Armando Enriquez Durazo."

There was no mention of U.S. Border Patrol agents involved in the arrest. Mexican citizens are known to generally oppose involvement by American law enforcement on their soil, which might explain why the Border Patrol agents were not mentioned by Mexican officials who spoke with various media outlets.

> **Sources close to the case, in the City of Agua Prieta, unofficially revealed that military personnel during the early morning hours had obtained the arrest of two people, who were located in the immediate vicinity of the events.**
>
> **It was also said that one of the suspects had been in possession of a firearm, which is being analyzed to verify their criminal history, in addition to possible involvement in a crime.**
>
> **The PGR (Attorney General of Mexico) continues investigations to determine whether or not there was any involvement in this and other crimes of the accused.**

On the Facebook page of Victor Manuel Durazo Soto, these photos were posted in 2011: photos of AK-47 rifles, hand grenades and hunting rifles, a bearded man being arrested by Mexican soldiers wearing ski masks, convoys of Mexican military vehicles carrying heavily armed soldiers, along with police vehicles apparently involved in a joint operation, a rodeo rider on horseback, and two mating horses.

There were no posts by Durazo Soto after November 2011.

Martin Armando Enriquez Durazo also has a Facebook page, which recently listed his residence as Hermosillo.

Details about the arrests of the two suspects varied in American news reports. Some said the two suspects were arrested after Tuesday,

October 2, and others said they were arrested in Agua Prieta.

The Utah media closely followed developments in the Ivie case. The *Deseret News* of Salt Lake City published a story on October 3, dateline Sierra Vista, Arizona.

The headline read: "He was the best dad that you could ever be."[4]

The lead sentence related details about uniformed Border Patrol agents standing vigil outside Ivie's family home in Sierra Vista. One agent told a reporter he would be there as long as the family wanted him there.

The story then shifted to the latest development in the homicide case:

> **Two suspects were detained and later arrested in Mexico in connection with the death of Ivie, a former Provo resident, according to Mexican officials quoted by the Reuters news agency. But few other details were released on a day when members of this small border-area town rallied to the aid of a grieving family.**

The newspaper, with the second highest daily circulation in Utah, said authorities declined to provide details on what prompted the shooting and whether the agents were ambushed.

> **"Still they suspect that more than one person fired on the agents," the *Deseret News* story said. "The area is heavily used by drug smugglers and offers many hiding places and is close enough to Mexico for them to make a quick getaway in the sparsely populated southwestern Arizona desert."**

This story included the Reuters report, which cited an anonymous Mexican Army officer who said, "Mexican troops arrested two men in a military operation in the city of Agua Prieta, in Mexico's Sonora State, a few miles from where Ivie was killed."

A story posted by CNN Thursday, October 4, carried this headline:

Source: 2 questioned in Mexico over fatal shooting of U.S. Border Patrol agent.

> Two men were being questioned Thursday by Mexican authorities about a shooting that killed a U.S. Border Patrol agent and wounded another near the U.S.-Mexican border in Arizona, a source in the Mexican attorney general's office said.

The Mexican Army handed over to local authorities in Sonora two men they had detained near the American border, the source in the federal department said Thursday. **The two were in possession of drugs and guns when they were detained,** added the source.

"Local authorities are investigating if the pair had anything to do with Tuesday's shooting near Naco, Arizona, where Border Patrol agents came under fire after responding to a sensor that had gone off nearby."[5]

The CNN story goes on to say that Agent Ivie "was killed near a Border Patrol station recently named for Brian Terry, whose 2010 death led to the public disclosure of the botched Fast and Furious gun-smuggling stint."

That passage is followed by a link to another CNN story, originally posted two weeks earlier, summarizing the "long-awaited" report by the Department of Justice inspector general, about the "controversial gun-trafficking operation known as Fast and Furious." That story said the operation traced weapons sold to buyers who were turning them over to Mexican drug cartels. "Nearly 2,000 firearms from the program went missing, some turning up at killing scenes in Mexico—and at the site of a gunbattle in Arizona that left U.S. Border Patrol agent Brian A. Terry dead."

There is also a link to a timeline on "Fast and Furious," which showed that the death of Border Patrol agent Brian Terry had led to the uncovering of the government operation. The timeline included details potentially embarrassing to the Obama administration, such as that the House of Representatives had voted just a few months earlier to hold Attorney General Eric Holder in contempt of Congress, the first attorney general to be dishonored in this way.

On June 20, 2012, President Barack Obama responded to a House committee subpoena for documents about the operation by asserting executive privilege, preventing some documents from being examined.

"The White House move means the Department of Justice can withhold some of the documents," The CNN timeline story said.

To summarize the importance of this CNN story: On the same day when the Obama campaign was reeling from the loss of the first presidential debate, the TV network known for its support for the president was connecting the slaying of a Border Patrol agent two days earlier with the "Fast and Furious" operation. Obama had done everything in his power to tamp down this scandal, including invoking executive privilege—the only time he did so during his entire White House tenure.

This was the same day major news outlets were releasing the stunning revelation—likely leaked by the FBI—that Agent Ivie might have been killed by friendly fire.

CNN was focusing instead on the story of Mexican suspects being questioned in connection with Agent Ivie's death, while also returning its spotlight to the "Fast and Furious" scandal.

The BBC, Great Britain's premier broadcast station, also posted a story on Thursday, October 4, which ignored the U.S. government's "friendly fire" narrative and instead focused on the arrest of the Mexican suspects.

The story carried the headline: "Two men held in Mexico for US agent Nicholas Ivie death," followed by the lead sentence: "Two men have been held in Mexico over the death of a US border agent shot near the US-Mexico border in the state of Arizona, Mexican officials said."[6]

BBC reported that the suspects were "arrested during a Mexican military operation on Wednesday in Agua Prieta," information that was relayed to the Reuters news agency by a Mexican official.

Many American news outlets carried this information—apparently also obtained from the Reuters report—which placed the arrest one day later and about 10 miles east of the time and location originally reported. The probable explanation for this is that the suspects were taken into custody on Tuesday out in the desert near the border fence, then formally arrested in nearby Agua Prieta the following day.

After a line that said, "it was not clear if strong evidence linked the men to the killing of Nicholas Ivie," and one that reported that another agent was treated for his injuries, BBC also connected the shooting incident to the "Fast and Furious" scandal.

"This is the first such incident since 2010, when an agent's murder led to a review of a botched US-run operation," the prestigious international news outlet reported. "In Operation Fast and Furious, US agents lost illegal guns from Arizona that were allowed into Mexico to track dealers."

The BBC story carried a quote from George McCubbin, president of the Border Patrol agents' union, which helped to explain why the suspects were captured in Mexico.

McCubbin said that "it was likely the gunmen had time to cross the border into Mexico before escape routes could be sealed off," the BBC story said, adding that McCubbin doubted that "anybody would be laid up and hiding" on the American side after the incident.

That story said the Cochise County Sheriff's office reported that "They found tracks heading south from the scene of the shooting."

What is interesting about this statement is that some of the best trackers in the area said they found evidence of humans heading from the vicinity of the shooting to the Mexican border. Was this just a coincidence, or more evidence that there were border crossers at the scene at the time of the shooting?

"Agents Radioed That They Had Come Under Fire . . ."

One of the earliest stories verifying the suspect arrests was by the *L.A. Times*, which published several in-depth stories in the aftermath of the incident. That newspaper had at least five reporters involved in coverage.

In a story posted on Wednesday, October 3, 2012, the *Times* reported that Commander Mark Denney of the Cochise County Sheriff's Office said two suspects **"were detained Tuesday in connection with the shooting."**

However, the *Times* reported in that same story that "a Mexican military spokesman said no arrests were made" though dozens of soldiers and police scoured the border area.

That story went on to explain that the area is in a border smuggling corridor favored by Mexico's Sinaloa Cartel, which runs a distance of about 120 miles, from Nogales, Arizona, to the New Mexico border.

Denney told a *Times* reporter that when the agents arrived on the scene after a sensor had been triggered, they were ambushed.

"The agents *radioed* that *they had come under fire* from three or four people, he said, but by the time the deputies responded, the gunmen had disappeared, apparently fleeing on foot into the rocky hills," the *L.A. Times* story said.

Here we have a published account that added an important detail: Border Patrol agents involved in the shooting incident (or possibly one of the agents) had reported via radio that there was gunfire originating from three or four people. This matched perfectly with what Agent Borjas told the FBI in her post-incident interviews, as well as what she told the supervisor who arrived on the scene shortly after the shooting. Of course, it does not match the notion that only agents were on the scene. The L.A. Times was reporting what was universally believed about the incident before the FBI abruptly changed the narrative.

Denney said the sheriff's department had "worked that area pretty significantly over the years," describing it as a known smuggling area, mostly for drugs, but also for smuggling illegal immigrants.

"You never know what you're going to run across out there," Denney said. "It's a very rough area—it's mountainous, rocky, loose rock, low vegetation. It's hard terrain to maneuver around."

The Concord (New Hampshire) *Monitor*, one of many newspapers to cover this case nationwide, posted a story titled "2 held in border shooting," on Friday, October 5, 2012.

Lydia Antonio, a spokeswoman for the Mexican Embassy in Washington, confirmed the detentions of the two suspects, said the story by the daily paper of the state's capital city.

"Authorities have declined to provide details about Tuesday's shooting, including what they believe prompted the shooting, whether the agents were ambushed, and whether any guns from the shooting were recovered."

"Still They Suspect That More Than One Person Fired on the Agents."

Law enforcement officials and news reporters heard about leaks and rumors of friendly fire—rumors apparently orchestrated by the FBI—the day before the official narrative was released on Friday. However, the reporters at this newspaper did not hear about the "friendly fire" narrative or chose to ignore it.

Instead, shortly before the FBI's official friendly fire announcement, the *Concord Monitor* reported that authorities suspected that more than one person had fired on the Border Patrol agents. Those authorities were not identified. They could have been FBI officials who were not aware that the political appointees in charge of the Bureau were crafting a totally different story.[7]

As mentioned earlier in this book, the contradictory idea that Agent Ivie was killed by a fellow agent—although suspects had been arrested in connection with his death—was a fascinating aspect of the media coverage.

Many of the stories posted Friday or Saturday included the two seemingly contradictory narratives, that two suspects who were not Border Patrol agents were arrested for their possible involvement in the shooting and that the FBI announced that nobody but Border Patrol agents were involved.

This is a peculiar challenge for journalists—something which most of us will never encounter during our careers.

The media outlets I found that reported on both developments in the same story, in addition to the Daily Mail, all handled this challenge in the same way. The conflicting possibilities were presented as if they were perfectly compatible.

Which begs the question: How could anyone be killed by suspects who were in custody, but the agent was also killed by a fellow agent, without the involvement of any suspects?

In other words, how did a suspect and a Border Patrol agent both fire the exact same bullet?

This is a sign of the times. During this specific time period—during which the presidential administration exerted relentless pressure on news outlets to refrain from criticism—many obediently published whatever the government fed them. Questioning the validity of any government statement was considered verboten in some newsrooms. With that in mind, why would a reporter or editor bother to question the government when it announced that it was "definitive" that nobody else had been involved in this incident? The traditional American journalism watchdog was enjoying a deep slumber.

Although several reporters had asked the FBI Phoenix division head about the two suspects, earlier in the investigation, there were no more questions asked on that subject after the pronouncement of friendly fire was handed down from the Bureau.

In all fairness to the reporters and editors involved, the FBI said there would be later revelations about the case. Despite the pronouncements from other agencies that the FBI results were "indisputable" and "definitive"—all apparently acting as mouthpieces for the Bureau—the FBI promised to tell more about the case later on.

But nobody from the press bothered to dig deeper into the case, with so many other stories commanding attention. Just reading the transcripts from the interviews with the surviving agents would have provided glaring clues that the FBI report was a fabrication—even to a reporter for a junior high school newspaper. Those transcripts were readily available to the press and the public.

The earliest mention of suspects by the press that I could find was in a story by the *Tucson Sentinel*, updated at 2:11 p.m. on October 2, shortly after the FBI held its initial news conference.

The headline on that story, originally posted at 9:12 a.m. local time, said that Border Patrol agent Nicholas Ivie was killed, and another agent was wounded near Naco.

Here is the subhead, placed just below the main headline in bold type:

The FBI won't comment on reports that suspects detained in Mexico.

The third paragraph said that James Turgal, FBI agent in charge of the Phoenix division, "refused to release specifics on the case; he declined to comment on the reports that two suspects in the shooting have been detained in Mexico."

"I'm not going to talk about any issues regarding suspects at this time," Turgal told reporters at 2:00 p.m., the Sentinel said.

The FBI never changed its tune on this subject.[8]

The following day, October 3, there was a trickle of more stories published that mentioned the arrest of suspects.

In an article mentioned earlier in this chapter, an *L.A. Times* reporter wrote, "Two suspects were detained by Mexican officials Tuesday in connection with the shooting, according to Cochise County, Arizona Sheriff's Commander Marc Denney.

> However, a Mexican military spokesman said no arrests were made, even though dozens of soldiers, federal, and state police officers and investigators fanned out across the border area on foot and in vehicles.

So here we have a story in which an American sheriff's command officer said his information was that suspects were detained, whereas a Mexican military spokesman said no arrests had been made.

Those are not contradictory statements. Even in America, a suspect can be detained for questioning for a period of time before he is either placed under arrest or released.

The spokesman who said no arrests had been made could have known that two suspects were in custody, yet the men had not been placed under arrest at that time. As stated earlier, some stories based on Mexican sources said they were arrested on Wednesday.

The *L.A. Times* story pointed out that the Border Patrol agents were shot "while patrolling a troubled stretch of southern Arizona favored by Mexican drug cartels. The fatality was the agency's fourth in that area in the last two years."[9]

This story also captured a very interesting quote, especially in light of the source, Jeff Self, who has become the designated Border Patrol spokesman for insisting that nobody else was involved, except for the agents.

Self, then Arizona joint field commander for Customs and Border Protection, told a reporter that Agent Ivie was survived by his wife and two small daughters.

"This is what's going to strengthen our resolve to bring these people to justice," Self said of the suspects in Ivie's killing, the Times reported.

Why would a high-ranking Border Patrol official speak out about those specific suspects? Did Self have some inside information on the suspects? Why would he say that they needed to be brought to justice?

Had Self not yet heard that the FBI was remaining silent about the suspects? He obviously did not know that a total reversal was right around the corner.

The Huffington Post, a left-leaning online media outlet, posted a story datelined "Mexico City," with the headline, "Arizona Border Shooting: Mexican Police Arrest 2 in Connection with Killed Border Patrol Agent, Nicholas Ivie."

The story, datelined Mexico City and posted on October 4, 2012, said that federal police arrested two men "who may be connected with the fatal shooting of a U.S. Border Patrol agent just north of the Mexico/Arizona border."

This story also connected the Ivie and Terry slayings. "Terry's shooting was later linked to the government's 'Fast and Furious' gun-smuggling operation, which allowed people suspected of illegally buying guns to walk away with weapons, rather than be arrested."

The *Huffington Post*, using only anonymous sources in its story, also reported that authorities said that "they suspect that more than one person fired on the agents."[10]

An *Arizona Star* story focusing on Agent Ivie's family press conference on Thursday, October 4, said, "Separately Thursday, a Mexican law enforcement official confirmed Mexican authorities have in custody two men who could be connected with Ivie's killing."

"The anonymous official said it was unclear whether there was 'strong evidence' linking the men to the shooting," the story said.

The writer for the Tucson-based newspaper related information from Radio Sonora, an FM station based in the Sonoran capital city, Hermosillo, about 175 miles southwest of Agua Prieta.

Radio Sonora reported Thursday that the two are young men from Agua Prieta, sister city of Douglas, who were arrested about 5 miles south of the shooting scene in Mexico early Tuesday. They had a gun and 10 kilograms of marijuana, and they're being held now by Mexican federal police in Hermosillo, the radio network is reporting.

It is important to note that the actual shooting scene is about 4.3 miles north of the border. So when the radio station says the suspects were arrested "about five miles south of the shooting scene," it is placing them just south of the border.[11]

The *Borderland Beat* story, posted on October 4, carried the headline: **"Mexico Arrests 2 for Murder of Border Patrol Agent."**

Directly beneath the headline was inserted an italicized update, with the date of October 5:

Investigators are preparing to announce that the death of Border Patrol Agent Nicholas Ivie in Arizona earlier this week was the result of friendly fire—accidental gunfire from another agent who responded to the same scene, state and federal officials told NBC News on Friday.

This is followed by the main story, which obviously clashes with the update.

> Mexican troops have arrested two suspects in the killing of a U.S. Border Patrol agent and the wounding of a second officer in Arizona, Mexican security officials said on Wednesday. The two suspects were detained in a Mexican military operation in the city of Agua Prieta, in Mexico's northern Sonora state, a few miles from where Nicholas Ivie was shot dead early Tuesday while responding to a tripped ground sensor, (said) a Mexican Army officer, who declined to be named.[12]

If those suspects were cleared of involvement in those crimes by the FBI, as their relative wrote to a Mexican TV station, the Bureau has an obligation to publicly declare that they were wrongfully arrested.

Anyone who is wrongfully arrested for a crime, and his name is publicized as the perpetrator of that crime, is entitled to a full public vindication. If the FBI found out that those suspects were innocent, they should say so.

24

Widow Speaks Out
One Year Later

"That's what I'm fighting for. I want them to release it, and I want them to tell (everyone) what happened," Christy Ivie, on the FBI report on what happened to her husband

October 2, 2013 — one year after the murder of her husband Sierra Vista, Arizona

In an interview with CBS5, a Phoenix TV station, Christy Ivie revealed that she was still adjusting to her life without Nick and that she questioned the initial report, which said Nick fired the first shot, which led to his death by gunfire from another Border Patrol agent.

The story on the station's Web site, posted on October 3, showed deference to the official version of the shooting incident.

Its lead sentence showed that the station's personnel did not question the FBI's finding:

"One year ago, Border Patrol Agent Nick Ivie believed he was tracking Mexican drug smugglers," the story said.

It went on to say that "Ivie thought two other responding Border Patrol agents were smugglers. A shootout unfolded, and Ivie was shot and killed."

Christy Ivie, obviously still in the throes of deep grief, told the TV reporter that she was still coming to terms with the fact her husband would not be coming home.

"Sometimes I still wake up in the morning and I have to remind myself that this is my reality," said the young widow and mother of two young daughters.

After the initial shock of the news that her husband had been killed early on the morning of October 2, she later learned that he had "died after being shot by a fellow Border Patrol agent," the TV station reported.

That was difficult for her to accept.

"I think it's harder because I don't have someone to be angry at," Christy Ivie said. "I don't have someone to blame. It wasn't a bad guy that he was up against. So that's hard."

Christy Ivie told the TV reporter that she questioned the initial reports, "which say her husband fired the first shot. "She said she hoped the Border Patrol would release "the full, final report."

"That's what I'm fighting for," she said. "I want them to release it, and I want them to release it and tell (everyone) what happened."

She told the interviewer that "(Nick) felt threatened, and there was a lot of miscommunications that happened."

Those details, that Nick had "felt threatened" and "there was a lot of miscommunications" had not been released to the public, but they would be contained in an article with an unofficial explanation of the case, which would be published nine days later, on October 11, 2013.

It is not clear whether the article was specifically a response to the concerns of Christy Ivie and other family members.Christy Ivie said that she was raising her two daughters by herself, while she was missing Nick.

"He was a wonderful father and husband, and he loved spending every second he could with the girls and me. I think that's what I miss. Just the family life."[1]

October 11, 2013

"Walk a Mile in His Boots," an article by a retired Border Patrol official, was published in order to provide an explanation of what allegedly occurred.

That article, endorsed by the Border Patrol, was filled with inaccurate statements.

It asserted that Agent Ivie shot at other agents, bringing about his own death—but absolved him of any wrongdoing.

Released as a substitute for an official FBI report, this article praised Agent Ivie, while accusing him of shooting at other agents without any reasonable cause, bringing about his own death.

The article is a masterpiece of deception, especially effective because of the author's outstanding credentials, which he thoroughly presented. When this article came out, Border Patrol agents who did not believe it was true remained silent, as they remained under a gag order that prevented them from speaking on the case.

"Like it's hunting season on dope smugglers. Just because someone is committing a crime doesn't give you the right to shoot them. It's a ridiculous concept to think that is how any professional person is going about their job." The response of a Border Patrol agent, a friend of Nick's, to this article's assertion that Agent Ivie was justified in

shooting at a fellow agent, because he thought he was an armed
smuggler. This agent does not believe Nick shot at anyone.

There are so many unusual aspects of the Nick Ivie case, but the
article that lists as its author Ron Colburn—a highly respected former
Border Patrol agent, with a sterling resumé including a stint in the
White House—is high up on the list.

The stated goal of this article was to combat the "finger pointing
and misinformation in the press and news media," which has "been
the rule, rather than the exception."

That sounded like a noble goal. However, there never was any
"finger pointing or misinformation in the press." The press was silent
after the FBI released its report on October 5, 2012, a report that said
Border Patrol agents shot at each other, with nobody else involved.
There is no evidence that anything written or broadcast prior to that
was not factual or involved "finger pointing"—whatever that was
supposed to mean.

What we have here is a frequently used Obama administration
tactic: invent a straw man, an imaginary enemy who did something
outrageous, and then knock him down. In this case it was "the press
and news media" that were the culprits. "The press" and the "news
media" are synonymous terms, so this was a clumsy way of letting
the public know that everything they read *before* the FBI revealed its
version of events was simply part of a "misinformation campaign."

This was just another way of saying that anyone who dared
to challenge a government pronouncement — *even before that*
pronouncement was made—was simply a conspiracy theorist. In this
case, the Colburn article implied that the members of the "press" and
"news media" who covered this incident were nothing but purveyors
of a false campaign.

In retrospect, it is easy to see how the Obama administration—
which was undoubtedly reeling as one story after another linked
this shooting incident to Fast and Furious—would perceive it as a
campaign aimed at its heart. Colburn, who was closely associated
with key members of the Obama administration at that time, could
have seen it as a malicious operation, designed to destroy the
president's reelection campaign.

The "misinformation" that was reported by media outlets throughout
the nation and the world was that Agent Ivie was shot and killed
by suspects—possibly cartel smugglers—in an area known for its
smuggling activity. This was being reported because that is exactly what
law enforcement agencies were saying about the shooting incident.

It was a bit odd for so many media outlets to write so many stories
that were potentially damaging to President Obama's campaign,

at a time when almost every major media outlet endorsed Obama and stood behind him in countless ways. But there simply were no contradictory facts to write about after the shooting occurred. The media agencies that were reporting the facts on the shooting of Agent Ivie in the days after he was killed were simply doing their jobs.

One year later, with stirring from the Ivie family about seeing an actual FBI report, it was time to blast another cloud of smoke into the eyes of anyone who still cared to discover the truth.

It would be a positive outcome for the Obama administration if the president and federal law enforcement agencies could continue to keep the family and friends of Agent Ivie quiet, by convincing them that the shooting really had been an accident.

The Obama camp was already dealing with challenges from the family of slain Border Patrol agent Brian Terry and ATF agents concerning its denials about the administration's involvement in the Fast and Furious operation and the subsequent coverup.

There were also challenges from the CIA contract agents who had battled against terrorists in Benghazi, to correct the Obama administration's false narrative of what occurred during the battle they waged for 13 hours to save American lives. Family members of the murdered Americans who died in that planned attack were also complaining about the lack of honesty from Obama, Former Secretary of State Hillary Clinton, and their subordinates.

It would be advantageous to release an unofficial explanation about what had supposedly occurred in the Ivie case, with the hope it would keep this cold-blooded murder and its successful coverup from emerging as yet another scandal.

This article, titled "Walk a Mile in His Boots," was released for publication on October 11, 2013. At that time, Coburn was working as a private consultant on border issues. According to a speech Colburn would later give to a group of ranchers, he worked closely with Obama's cabinet-level officials, specifically Holder and Napolitano.

Colburn's article was first published on the Web site of the Southern Arizona Cattlemen's Protective Association. It was also posted on KSL.com, the Web site of the NBC TV affiliate in Salt Lake City. The following month, it was published by the *Provo Herald*, the daily newspaper of the city where Ivie had grown up.[2]

"Walk a Mile in His Boots," contains a mixture of a false narrative and some apparently accurate information. It was ostensibly written by Colburn, who claimed to be privy to inside information from the FBI, Border Patrol, and other investigative agencies. It was riddled with misstatements and errors, including misrepresentations of the statements surviving agents gave during their interviews.

Colburn's story parroted the FBI line that there was nobody else involved in the shooting incident.

The main fabric of this story quickly unravels in light of the actual evidence in the case. However, it has apparently been accepted as a true version of events among some interested people.

Many of the statements contained in the article are glaringly false.

"There was no physical evidence, such as foot sign, to indicate that other people (Spanish-speaking) were there," the article claimed.

This was contradicted by reports by Cochise County sheriff's personnel, who recorded that there were footprints at the saddle from someone who was not law enforcement, as well as reports from a surviving agent that Ivie reported that he saw foot sign at the saddle. If Colburn had really examined the reports on the case, he would have been aware of the plethora of evidence that there were other people there, including freshly discarded water jugs with blood on them, Mexican coins, and impressions from marijuana bundles.

It is bizarre that the story would explicitly exclude the possibility that Spanish-speaking people were there. Was there a forensic test available that would identify the language spoken by the people who dropped the water jugs at the saddle? Or did the writer or writers of this article assume that readers were so stupid that they would believe that the FBI could tell the language of individuals by their footprints? Were the pesos found near the shell casings from Agent Ivie's pistol dropped by English-speaking people? Was there some mystical test the FBI had developed that could ascertain the language abilities of suspects by evidence left at a crime scene?

The article claimed to clear Agent Ivie and the other agents of any wrongdoing—while painting a picture of agents who acted against their training and Border Patrol policy. The Colburn article claimed that they did absolutely nothing wrong, as they exchanged gunfire with each other after Agent Johnson walked past Agent Ivie on a quiet moonlit night—before either of them ever uttered a word.

This article stated that nobody, except the third agent, was around when two agents opened fire on each other.

There was no explanation as to why Agent Ivie would have fired 10 shots at Agent Johnson at close range—firing many of the shots after Agent Johnson had shouted loudly in response to the first three shots—wounding Johnson only in his ankle and buttock.

The article also failed to mention that Agent Johnson told FBI agents he returned fire toward a shooter or shooters at a range of 15 or 20 feet—after seeing nothing in his rifle sight.

There was no explanation as to why hundreds of law enforcement officers were sent to the scene to perform an intense manhunt—if two agents had shot at each other at close range—with nobody else involved.

Common sense would tell you that honest agents—and Colburn's story affirmed that not one of the surviving agents uttered a false word about what occurred—would have immediately reported that this was a tragic accident.

The fact that both surviving agents blamed the shooting incident on armed smugglers says all we need to know about the depth of deception of this article.

Although this unofficial version of what occurred was released under the name of a private citizen, it is likely that the FBI was complicit in its production. Hopefully, we will one day find out the identity of the person or persons who decided to release this atrocious article to the public. Although the FBI was probably involved, it is also possible political officials directly oversaw the article's production.

The Border Patrol went on record as saying "they stood behind" Colburn's story in a TV newscast by the Salt Lake City ABC affiliate, ABC4, on October 24, 2013.

That statement put an exclamation mark on Colburn's fictional "Walk a Mile in his Boots" story!

An agency normally "stood behind" its own pronouncements, not something that was written and released by an independent source. An article supposedly written by an unbiased citizen, free of interference by any interested agency, would not normally elicit a response of standing behind it.

Remember that, in 2013, both the Border Patrol and the FBI remained under the control of administrators appointed by Obama. Those two agencies—which were able to decide within three days the final outcome of a complicated homicide investigation—had a vested interest in keeping the web of deception intact.

Before I examine this article, apparently intended to be the last word on the investigation into the fatal shooting of Agent Ivie, readers should have some background on the individual listed as its author. Colburn's resumé includes a "special tour of duty" at the White House in 2002 and 2003, as a member of the Homeland Security Council. He had retired from the Border Patrol in 2009, after 31 years on the force, with his final posting in Washington D.C., where he served as deputy chief.

After retiring from the Border Patrol, Colburn began a career as a consultant with Ron Colburn Consulting, LLC, and Command Consulting Group, two companies specializing in border security issues. He began turning up in media stories as an expert source in controversial cases—in which he often expressed views favorable to the government's side. Colburn was the government's go-to guy, when they wanted someone to be its unofficial mouthpiece, to express its viewpoint, truthful or not.

Colburn had been involved in the initial phase of the coverup of the Brian A. Terry slaying, which occurred on December 14, 2010. In the Terry incident, the government initially also tried to blame the death of Terry on the actions of Terry and his team.

That failed because Terry's fellow agents and family members insisted on telling the truth in public about what had occurred and on discovering everything they could about the government's actions.

As one Border Patrol agent familiar with both cases told me, that was the main difference between the success of the coverup of the Ivie case and the failure of the coverup of the Terry murder: Terry's friends and family members refused to remain silent.

Within two months of the death of Brian Terry, his death had been connected to the government's Fast and Furious gunrunning scandal. Firearms found at the scene of his slaying had earlier been shipped to drug cartels through the intentional actions of agents of the U.S. Bureau of Alcohol, Tobacco and Explosives (ATF), who were acting under orders of the Department of Justice.

In February 2011, ATF Agent Jon Dodson broke the story wide open when he told CBS News reporter Sharyl Attkisson that the agents were ordered to allow straw buyers to cross the border into Mexico with firearms purchased from Arizona gun stores.

After it was revealed that the agents on Terry's BORTAC team fired first at the bandits in a remote canyon near Nogales with beanbag ammunition, Homeland Security officials remained silent on that issue for several months. In March 2011, Alan Bersin, commissioner of U.S. Customs and Border Protection, announced that the BORTAC team had decided *on its own* to first use nonlethal force.

In other words, Terry's team fired beanbag ammunition before he was killed because he and other BORTAC agents wanted to confront lethal force with nonlethal force.

"There is no policy and [there] was no standing policy regarding the use of nonlethal force as a prelude to the use of lethal force," Bersin said at a Tucson press conference, according to a *Tucson Weekly* article of March 24, 2011.

Homeland Security Secretary Janet Napolitano backed up Bersin's comments, saying that agents were allowed to use lethal force if "under threat of serious injury of death."

But T. J. Bonner, then the recently retired president of the National Border Patrol Council, the agents' union, said he did not believe that the agents made up their own minds to use nonlethal force.

"It makes absolutely no sense that someone trained in tactics would opt for less than lethal force when facing bandits with rifles," Bonner said. "The intelligence was solid that these guys operated in that area with rifles."

Colburn, then a retiree from the Border Patrol, turned up as a government spokesman, supporting the idea that the BORTAC agents—not their leaders—had decided for themselves to use nonlethal ammunition.

"Bersin's comments ring true," Colburn said, according to the *Tucson Weekly* story.

Colburn, who had served as one of the original BORTAC agents in the 1980s, was quoted as saying, "The team chooses their method for challenging those dark silhouettes in the night. It's entirely up to them."

So here we have Colburn, a government consultant, promoting the government's lie—that agents in the field decided on their own to use bean bags when fighting against killers with live ammunition.

There was no mention in this article as to whether Colburn was ever on a team that was given the choice of whether to shoot bean bags against bandits armed with live ammunition. Colburn publicly supported the false government version instead of the testimony of the line agents who risked their lives in the field. Common sense would tell you that no law enforcement officers—especially those working in cartel smuggling territory—would ever think of firing bean bags.There are several similarities between the attempted coverup of the Terry case and the successful coverup of the Ivie case. Here, Colburn brings up the idea of "dark silhouettes" in the night— who were actually bandits who opened fire on Terry and his fellow agents. In the Ivie case, the FBI tried to convince Agent Borjas that the smugglers shooting at her were really shadows.

Although Bersin said he had no direct information from the BORTAC agents, because they were "lawyered up," Brian Terry's brother, Kent Terry, told a reporter that he did have direct information from the BORTAC agents.

"The other agents who were there that night told him that they were instructed to use the nonlethal beanbags first," said an article in the March 3, 2011, issue of the *National Review*.

As Colburn was trying to help bolster the government's false argument in the Terry shooting, he made an important statement that would contradict his future effort to aid in the coverup of the Nicholas Ivie shooting 19 months later.

Colburn: Officers Do Not Shoot First, Ask Questions Later

Colburn said that a key point in the Terry case was that no law enforcement agency in America shoots first and asks questions later, according to the *Tucson Weekly* article of March 24, 2011.

But that was exactly what Colburn would say occurred between agents Ivie and Johnson, when he was called on once again to support the government's position, to cover up the cause of the death of a field agent.

In the article with his name attached, Colburn shamelessly accused Agent Ivie of shooting first, without giving any commands or asking any questions.

If law enforcement officers don't ever shoot first without regard to the consequences, why did Ron Colburn put his name on an article accusing a Agent Ivie of doing just that—resulting in his death? And why would he try to fool the public into believing that doing that would be considered an acceptable action?

Another interesting element of the October 2013 article, ostensibly penned by Colburn—which connects the narrative's origin to information from the FBI—is that Colburn referred to the site of Agent Ivie's death as a "canyon saddle" on page 6, after referring to it as a "mountain saddle" on page 1.

A saddle—defined in the dictionary as a "pass in a mountain range"—resembles a horse rider's saddle. It is a flattened point on a mountain ridge, with higher features on two sides. There is no such thing as a "canyon saddle," but if that phrase were to be used, it would refer to something deep in a canyon—which would not resemble the site where Agent Ivie was killed.

In all the hundreds of reports from law enforcement and media reporters on the incident, Colburn's story is the only place I found that referred to the site of the shooting in the Mule Mountains as a "canyon." However, there was one other place in which it was reported that "several U.S. Border Patrol agents rushed to the remote canyon."

Colburn also contributed to story blaming Ivie's death on faulty sensor

That was in an *L.A. Times* story of October 19, 2012, which quoted unnamed government officials—who blamed the entire fatal incident on a faulty sensor.

"Officials say a false alarm from a ground sensor in southern Arizona was to blame when several U.S. Border Patrol agents rushed to the remote canyon on horseback October 2, shortly after midnight," wrote Brian Bennett, *L.A. Times* Washington Bureau reporter.

In other words, Colburn—who was apparently assigned to represent the entire government apparatus one year after the shooting—was in agreement on an erroneous detail with the people assigned to promote a unique coverup story 17 days after the shooting. It brings up the question of whether Colburn, who claimed to be familiar with the territory where Ivie was shot, was the one who made the same mistake twice. Or was there an anonymous source involved in both articles that made that same error on two occasions—in two of the most misleading articles which were part of the government's elaborate coverup?

The shooting did not happen in a canyon—it occurred on a mountain ridge. It is a strange coincidence that two stories—both with involvement from Ron Colburn—contained the same exact erroneous detail.

The October 19, 2012, *L.A. Times* report contained other mistakes. Despite dozens of news reports that correctly related that the three Border Patrol agents approached the mountain saddle on foot, the *L.A. Times* report said they "rushed to the remote canyon on horseback."

The *L.A. Times* Washington Bureau reporter, who did not bother to check basic facts about the incident—while faithfully relaying the government's narrative—included Colburn as his second named source. This was a curious journalistic move, considering this was supposed to be an authoritative piece on the failure of a specific Border Patrol sensor.

Colburn had retired from the Border Patrol three years earlier. In Colburn's explanation in the *Times* article, he did not offer any solid evidence that this particular sensor—which Agent Ivie himself had placed at the saddle—was actually defective.

No active member of the Border Patrol commented on this brand-new idea—that the only reason Nick Ivie answered the call to check out the sensor alarm was because the sensor itself was faulty.

Here we have another wrinkle in this elaborate coverup—which was also hastily released to the public in advance of the presidential election. Just in case anyone would ever question why the three agents found absolutely no smugglers there after the sensor was triggered—there it is, an even better explanation. The darn thing never worked.

Apparently, with the election still ahead, someone got nervous about the idea that the Ivie case could still surface—perhaps an October surprise from the enemy camp.

What if one of the surviving agents decided to tell someone what really happened, and explained that it made no sense that they had responded to a sensor alarm and were then ambushed by smugglers—but nobody was there but them?

So someone thought it would be a good idea to tell the *L.A. Times* this fabricated story about a sensor on an Arizona mountain that went off only because it was broken.

When was this faulty sensor discovered? Why didn't it work? Who said it didn't work? None of those questions were asked or answered. There was no Border Patrol testimony to that effect. Instead, the story delivered a bushel of gibberish about Congressional funding that was not utilized.

So here was Colburn, a consultant who earned part of his livelihood by working with the federal government on border issues, acting as a faithful "expert" to tell the public whatever the government wanted to say about two deaths it tried to cover up. He was involved as a minor player in the coverup of the Ivie slaying just 17 days after the shooting incident—and involved more deeply one year later.

The *L.A. Times* quoted Colburn—who would never officially be connected to the FBI—as affirming that it was just a government glitch of underspending funds that caused the death of the young agent.

"They are experiencing delays," Colburn told a reporter about the upgrading of technology at the border. "It is taking longer than they hoped."

The paper's readers were being led to believe—less than 3 weeks before the election—that "a deteriorating network of more than 12,800 ground sensors, as well as other outdated technology, could endanger the lives of those who police the long border with Mexico."

This entire article, shifting blame far from the actual killers to a widespread technological challenge, **cited no report that showed that this specific sensor was faulty**. Are we to believe that Agent Ivie, who was involved in installing the sensor, never bothered to check out whether it was working?

Known as a diligent, hard-working agent, who liked to apprehend smugglers, Ivie would have wasted part of a shift responding to a sensor that was out of order?

Why blame a "deteriorating network" of ground sensors for a specific shooting incident involving several agents—including two survivors—without any evidence that the sensor had misfired? Would a fatal train wreck be blamed on a deteriorating nationwide track network without any evidence of the condition of the specific tracks where the train had derailed?

But with less than three weeks to go before the election, it was time to blow some more smoke in the eyes of potential voters—just in case someone got wise to the fraudulent handling of this case.

The first named source in that October 19, 2012, article was a Democratic politician, Representative Bennie Thompson, the minority party leader on the Homeland Security Committee. His response shed light on the purpose of this article.

U.S. Customs and Border Protection "must replace outdated sensors with more modern, effective technology that can assist Border Patrol in securing our border **while not sending agents into the field unnecessarily**," said Thompson, the representative from Mississippi's second congressional district, a rural area located hundreds of miles away from any U.S. border.

How would Representative Thompson know that Agent Ivie and his fellow agents were sent to apprehend illegal aliens by mistake? Why was he chosen to speak on behalf of Congress on the issue?

In this overheated political season, a loyal ally of President Obama was relied on to validate the false narrative—without offering a scintilla of evidence to back up his statement.

Because the incident actually occurred on a mountain ridge—which would not be referred to as a "canyon ridge" by anyone familiar with mountain terrain—it is possible that a portion of Colburn's narrative was written in the same office, or even by the same person, which authored this other false story one year earlier.

Border Patrol agent debunks L.A. Times *story on faulty sensor*

I asked Agent Carlton to comment on the *L.A. Times* story, which went largely unnoticed at the time it was published. If any Border Patrol agents who patrolled the southeast corner of Arizona at the time had read the story, they would have been amazed at how it clashed with what they knew about the actual situation.

Carlton noticed that the article's second sentence contained two bits of false information, saying that agents "rushed to the remote canyon on horseback October 2."

"Nobody rushed there on horseback because of the sensor. The horse patrol agents were still in the truck," Carlton said. "They rushed to a hill, the exact antithesis of a canyon. The only thing they got right was the date."

Now that it was established at the outset that facts were optional, Carlton examined other erroneous information.

Carlton said that nobody familiar with how the sensors functioned in that area was quoted in the article. "Because they would tell you that the sensor did its job," Carlton said. "The sensor went off."

He said the article, which had a lengthy discussion on the general state of the "deteriorating network of more than 12,800 ground sensors," was "just crap."

"A lot of our sensors are Vietnam-era tech sensors. But the reason they use them is because they still detect vibrations," Carlton said, adding that those sensors are durable and would not misfire in the way the article says this one did. "The technology is old, but so is the table. We still use tables. The sensors are fairly reliable for what they do."

Carlton disagreed with a statement, which was published in the story without attribution, which said "agents often find that wires have been eaten through by ants or the batteries corroded by rainwater."

"So this whole section is just crap," Carlton said, chuckling. "Since when have you seen an ant eat through a metal wire?"

He said the sensors are enclosed in Pelican cases, which prevent corrosion and insect damage.

"If the cases were intact, I would find it hard to believe any of the batteries were corroded by rainwater," Carlton said. "They are air- and water-tight cases. Ants don't eat through the cases. There's nothing in it that would attract ants. Ants would go around it. That's just stupid."

The idea that Ivie was killed because he answered the report of a faulty sensor—which backs up the FBI narrative that no people were there—makes no sense, in light of the fact that sensors do not give false signals of that nature.

"The sensors, when they fall into disrepair, it's usually that they aren't giving a signal, not that that they 'false' and go off," Carlton said. "Now, they do sometimes false and go off for no reason. They top out at 99 hits. So if you have a sensor that is topping out at 99 hits every five minutes, then our sensor crews go out and they check them. That is not usually a problem. They would fix them if they could."

But if a sensor went off for seven hits—as it did in the Ivie case—that would not be considered a false alarm.

"It would be a very high number, not seven. Seven indicates some kind of traffic," Carlton said. "Depending on the area and what they could set the sensor for, seven might for that particular sensor, mean seven contacts. Or it might mean there was one guy walking around. Seven doesn't necessarily mean anything. It just means there was an activation."

Carlton said writing an article that said the sensor triggered a false report "is grossly misleading because the sensor itself wasn't falsing in the sense that it was outside of its normal reporting capabilities."

The article—published as part of the media campaign to support the FBI's false finding—was filled with irrelevant statements about more recent technology and the Department of Homeland Security's plan to purchase more up-to-date equipment. None of this proved that the sensor to which Ivie and the other Border Patrol agents responded did not work properly.

"D.C. has no knowledge of our day-to-day operations," Carlton said. "They have no idea of the work at a specific location. They would have no knowledge that a sensor is faulty. They would have no knowledge that an area is heavily trafficked or not heavily trafficked. There would be nobody who could say that a single activation could be a false report. How would they know one sensor, in the middle of the mountains, was a false report?"

Carlton said the agents were doing their jobs when they responded to the sensor alert.

"If the sensor is set up to cover this whole area here, you don't necessarily need to go to right where that sensor is," Carlton said, explaining how the agents respond to a sensor alert. "You have to cut the area around it to read that sign."

I believe members of the Obama administration were responsible for both stories on the Ivie slaying with which Colburn was involved. He contributed to the *L.A. Times* story of October 19, 2012, which blamed Ivie's death on a faulty sensor, and he supposedly wrote the story published on October 11, 2013, which placed the blame on a faulty radio and miscommunication between agents.

It was a clever move to assign someone to these false stories with a long list of credentials in federal law enforcement, who would seem to be an objective, reliable source. In the story he supposedly wrote, "Walk a Mile in His Shoes," Colburn proclaimed himself an expert on "the rough terrain and area where Nick was assigned." He proclaimed that he had many other "bona fides," which included his work as a "professional consultant, working with the US government, as well as the public and private sector."

Colburn said he had "spent a lot of time speaking to reliable sources and reviewing the case." However, the information is not presented with any specific sourcing. In other words, Colburn has been assigned to be the only source fully responsible for every word. For example, when the article said that Ivie shot at another agent after that agent walked by him, it did not reveal the source of that information. It was just something Colburn discovered along the way.

Because the agents never actually walked past each other, who would want to take credit for giving Colburn that information, which flies in the face of every shred of evidence. But Colburn was willing to include that glaring lie under his name, in an article in which there were numerous verifiably false statements.

The most ironic entry on Colburn's resumé is his involvement with a "nonprofit organization that supports the families of the fallen in law enforcement," which he said he cofounded. He helps the government to cover up the murders of two Border Patrol agents, but then works with a group that assists with providing aid to the people most profoundly hurt by the government's actions. There are no words to explain this.

Colburn's most recent project is to assist in the production and fundraising for an effort to make a film about what happened to Agent Brian Terry. Colburn took the government's side, to deceive the public on the use of bean bag ammunition, which played a role in Agent Terry's death. But now he has taken on the role of helping a filmmaker tell the story of what really occurred, when Agent Terry was shot to death in Peck Canyon. Will Colburn's role in helping with the initial coverup be revealed in this documentary film? That is extremely unlikely.

The Colburn article of 2013 clashes wildly with the testimony of the surviving agents and the actual facts of the case. The article stands in stark contrast to the crime scene maps produced by the Border Patrol for the FBI-led investigation, as well as other evidence found at the scene. Colburn also claimed to have met with sources connected to the CIT, the Border Patrol group that produced the crime scene map. However, the crime scene map that the CIT produced provides some of the best evidence that Colburn's narrative is outrageously false.

Why would a man with some of the most sterling credentials in the agency's history get involved in something as nefarious as coverups of the murders of two Border Patrol agents?

Colburn worked closely with the Obama administration. At a stakeholder meeting at the Nogales Border Patrol station, Colburn spoke of his close relationship with two top officials overseeing the Agent Ivie homicide investigation. Stakeholder meetings are held to foster positive relationships between the Border Patrol and local ranchers and other residents.

Colburn told the story of traveling to a meeting in Mexico with Eric Holder and Janet Napolitano, after Mexican officials discovered that the U.S. government had been complicit in arming cartels with thousands of high-powered firearms. Colburn said that when the meeting was about to begin, Holder and Napolitano entered a room, and the door was closed in his (Colburn's) face, leaving him outside.[3]

The Mexican government was kept in the dark during the entire U.S. government's Fast and Furious gunrunning operation. The meeting Colburn was apparently referring to was to smooth things over after the scandalous operation came to light, following the death of Agent Brian Terry. Mexican government officials have said that they knew nothing of the operation—which funneled high-powered firearms to Mexican cartels in 2009 and 2010—before it was exposed by media stories in 2011.

At the meeting in the Nogales station in 2016, Colburn confided with attendees about inside information on the Terry case. He said that the firearms found at the scene of the Brian Terry slaying were sent to a forensics lab in Florida. Colburn said that two of the rifles were excluded by the lab technicians from identification as Agent Terry's murder weapon.

"The other one vanished from the earth," said Carlos Sanchez, a Nogales area resident, recalling what was reported by Colburn at that meeting.

Sanchez said that when Colburn announced the details of the coverup of the Terry slaying, he noticed that Border Patrol agents in the room appeared to be very angry, as they stood around the conference room, with their arms crossed.

"They looked ready to kill," Sanchez said, adding that he understood they were hearing this information for the first time.

Sanchez also recalled that Colburn's wife was in attendance, sitting near Colburn as he spoke. She was also not happy about what was being said, but for a different reason.

"She was saying, 'You'd better quit; you'd better stop,'" Sanchez recalled.

Colburn's wife was apparently aware that he was implicating himself by having inside knowledge of government mischief—which had never come to light.

At the Nogales meeting, a short video was shown about the Terry incident, which was part of the project with which Colburn has been involved as a consultant. The video showed a reenactment of the Brian Terry shooting, with actual Pinal County deputies portraying the Border Patrol agents who were involved with the case.

"Pinal County detectives had trained with Brian Terry," Sanchez said. "They all knew each other."

The video showed that the suspects who attacked Terry and other agents were part of a rip crew, a group of illegal border crossers who robbed other illegals.

"They were packing weapons from Fast and Furious," Sanchez recalled.

He said the video showed that the Border Patrol agents were under orders to fire only nonlethal ammunition before they were fired on by lethal ammunition. The surviving agents did wound and apprehend several of their assailants, while others got away.

Some of the facts that Colburn revealed during the Nogales meeting were not known to the public. However, the fact that Agent Terry fired nonlethal "bean bag" ammunition became public information shortly after ATF agent whistleblowers broke open the scandal in 2011.

This fact, that elite BORTAC agents were under orders to fire nonlethal projectiles, could have influenced the shooters in the Agent Ivie slaying. The cartels—which have plenty of intelligence operatives on both sides of the border—undoubtedly knew about this directive.

This author could find no mention in any news story in which the Border Patrol released information saying it would no longer be ordering agents to use nonlethal force. If cartel leaders believed that they were fighting agents who would be shooting bean bags, that could have emboldened them in their approach to agents.

Although Sanchez could not recall whether Colburn had revealed a specific date of that meeting in Mexico involving U.S. cabinet ministers, it most likely occurred between February 2011, when the Fast and Furious scandal became a headline news story, and August 2013, when Napolitano resigned as head of Homeland Security.

Colburn, whose 2013 article claimed to be based on inside information from people connected to the FBI and other law enforcement agencies, did not mention in that influential article that he was closely associated with Holder and Napolitano—whose positions in Obama's cabinet placed them over the FBI and Border Patrol.

Instead, Colburn's article was presented from the position of an impartial insider, sympathetic to the slaying victim and his family, who just wanted to tell the truth about an unfortunate accident.

Border Patrol agents eager to find out the truth about this case received some of their information from this untrustworthy document. One of Agent Ivie's relatives said on social media that this article was the place to find out what had actually occurred.

The Colburn article blamed the shooting on an unfortunate mixture of circumstances—none of which ever occurred: the breakdown of communication between the agents, and Agent Ivie being surprised by the arrival of the other agents.

And even if those things had occurred—which were the exact opposite of what the surviving agents reported—there is no way that they would have led to Agent Ivie shooting at the other agents that night.

An Article Riddled With Disinformation

The Colburn article claimed that the agents had poor communication because Agent Johnson's radio was not working.

However, Agent Johnson said in his interview that his radio had stopped working for only a moment, then began working again, once he had reinserted the battery. Besides that, the two surviving agents kept in touch with Agent Ivie mainly by using Agent Borjas's radio, which had no problem whatsoever.

The Colburn story claimed that Agent Ivie thought the other two agents were far away when they told him they were just one-tenth of a mile out. Agent Ivie misunderstood what they were saying, thinking that they said that they were one-tenth of a mile from another ridge, the Colburn story reported. Therefore, when the two agents arrived on the scene, Agent Ivie was surprised and started shooting at them.

There is no indication contained in any of the postincident interviews with the surviving agents that any of the agents were confused about where the others were. When Borjas told Ivie that she and Agent Johnson were one-tenth of a mile out from the sensor, he said "10-4." Then the two agents arrived on the scene minutes later, and they were immediately fired on by unknown assailants, including one wearing a blanket and carrying a smuggler's pack.

If Agent Ivie did not know what Agent Borjas meant when she said they were one-tenth of a mile away, he would likely have said so. They were supposed to meet at the saddle, then Agent Borjas told him that they were close by, and Agent Ivie responded that he heard and understood.

Colburn offered no evidence in his article to support his theory that Ivie thought the other two agents were farther away. Once again, even if they did show up ahead of when he believed they were going to arrive, there is no way he would have opened fire on them. No way!

Not only did Agent Borjas tell Agent Ivie they were one-tenth of a mile away from the sensor a few minutes before the shooting started, but Agent Johnson said he saw Agent Ivie when they were about a half mile from the sensor, and Agent Ivie was almost there.

It is likely that Agent Ivie also saw agents Johnson and Borjas at that time, because if Agent Ivie was in their line of sight, they were also in his. They were "walking along the ridgeline," at the time when Agent Ivie reported being "almost at the top."

When Agent Ivie was near the top of the ridge, and the two other agents were "walking the ridgeline," he would have had a clear view of the man and woman walking toward him in the moonlight.

Colburn also presented a brand-new scenario on where the two agents were when they opened fire on each other—which is contradicted by everything the two surviving agents said, in addition to the crime scene maps, the reports of the first responding Border Patrol agents and common sense.

Although both surviving agents said that, as they arrived at the saddle, gunfire broke out, Colburn presented an alternative narrative. Colburn's article succeeded in fooling many people for a sizeable length of time by making no direct references to the testimony of the surviving agents—or to any other actual evidence.

In Colburn's story, Agent Johnson was identified as Agent #1, and Agent Borjas was Agent #2. The information on their actual names, though not revealed in any media stories, has been readily available in public records, on the Internet, and to anyone filing a Freedom of Information Act request with law enforcement agencies. This is how the Colburn story described the incident:

> *I conclude that when Nick saw there was an armed subject approaching down the trail (Agent #1 carrying a rifle), he tried to get as low as possible to the ground and let the threat pass by, a common tactical practice in the brush, in order to minimize the risk of a close quarters gunfight. Agent #1 did take a few steps past Nick before realizing something, or someone, was there.*
>
> *When Agent #1 said he saw what looked like someone coming up and throwing a blanket off their shoulder, I believe that was Nick rising up and drawing a weapon. The motions are similar, and bandits are well known to use blankets, or wear serape type attire in order to camouflage themselves at night, and to conceal weapons.*

A man removing a blanket from his shoulders bears no resemblance to someone who does not have a blanket on his shoulders drawing a gun from his holster. Conveniently missing from this sentence is the fact that Agent Johnson also saw that the man with the blanket was wearing a smuggler's pack. Strangely enough, the Colburn story admits that "bandits" wear blankets, while trying to establish that the figure Johnson saw was Ivie, not a bandit. Border Patrol agents never wear blankets.

Here we also have the idea that Ivie was crouching, Johnson walked by him "a few steps," and Ivie stood up and shot him.

This fictional scenario does not hold up for a variety of reasons:

Both surviving agents said the gunfire erupted in front of them. They never walked past anyone.

The evidence on the crime scene map shows that the shooter was about 20 feet away from Agent Johnson, just as Johnson said. If Johnson had just walked past Ivie a few steps, and Ivie had opened fire, the shell casings from the two firearms would have been found much closer together, and in totally different locations in relation to each other.

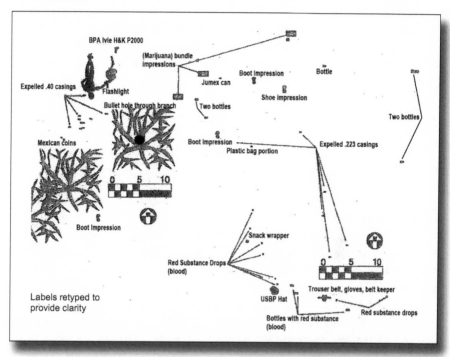

On this crime scene map, it clearly shows where Agent Ivie's body was found, in the northwest corner. In the southeast corner are shell casings from Agent Johnson's rifle, indicating the area he was standing while he was shooting. Immediately to the south of where he had been standing are items of his clothing, including his USBP hat, belt and gloves. This verifies what Johnson said: He came from the south and never walked past Ivie. The location of the shell casings clearly verify that Johnson never walked past Ivie.

If Ivie were crouching and saw Johnson walk past him on a moonlit night, he would have immediately recognized him as a Border Patrol agent. A "few steps" would mean they were about five feet away from each other when the shooting broke out.

Agent Johnson said he was shot at about 10 times before he returned fire. If they were just about five feet apart, why would they have both failed to notice that the other guy was also a Border Patrol agent. And, how do you fire shots that kick up rocks and hit someone in the ankle at a distance of about five feet?

Agent Johnson said that after the first few shots, he yelled, "Hey, hey, hey, hey!" If they were about five feet away, a little more than an arm's length away, how in the world would they have both missed that the other was a Border Patrol agent?

Especially if nobody else was there.

There are many people, law enforcement agents and residents of Cochise County, who believe that perhaps a Border Patrol agent killed Agent Ivie—during a shootout involving illegal alien drug smugglers.

But practically nobody who has any knowledge of the case believes that the agents walked up on each other, did not say one word, then opened fire.

Strangely enough, a former Border Patrol agent with experience working in this area stepped forward to try to persuade everyone that this totally unbelievable scenario actually occurred.

If the Colburn story were correct, Agent Johnson and Borjas would have been on opposite sides of Agent Ivie when the gunfire occurred. But both of them said they approached the scene, the gunfire broke out, and they were both together on one side of the saddle, with the shooter or shooters on the other side. And they both were found by the first Border Patrol agents who responded to the scene on the south slope of the saddle—with Agent Ivie's body north of both of them.

If Agent Johnson had walked past Agent Ivie a few steps, received fire from him, then returned fire with his rifle, all the evidence would have been vastly different. If he had aimed his rifle from a distance of five feet or so at Agent Ivie's head and pulled the trigger six times, Ivie would not have received just one bullet wound to the center of his forehead.

With both agents trained to shoot at center mass—the chest and abdomen area—why would they both miss their targets with a total of 16 shots from a distance of about three paces?

Agents Johnson and Borjas were on the south side of the saddle, whereas Agent Ivie was on the north side of the saddle. The surviving agents approached from the south, and all the evidence showed that they never made it far enough north to walk past Ivie.

According to the reports by Border Patrol agents Jake McWhorter and Victor Ocejo, the first responders on the scene, they found Agent Ivie's body on the north side of the saddle. They then heard Agent Johnson shouting from just south of the saddle, down the sloped trail.

No Evidence Supports the Idea That Johnson Walked Past Ivie

There is absolutely no evidence of any kind that Agent Johnson ever walked past Agent Ivie. All evidence points to the fact that no agent ever walked past Agent Ivie. That includes eyewitness testimony, reports from the first responders, the crime map placement of shell casings, Agent Ivie's body, items left on the ground by Agent Johnson, and the blood trail left by Agent Johnson.

If Agent Johnson shot Agent Ivie up on the saddle after walking past him — with no smugglers around — why was he on the south slope of the mountain, still concerned about the armed smugglers coming after him? Why did he ask the responding agents about the location of Agent Ivie?

If he walked past Agent Ivie and shot him dead, he would have known exactly where Ivie was and what had happened to him.

If Agent Johnson had shot Agent Ivie and then lied about it, that would have been cause for termination from the Border Patrol and criminal prosecution. But because he told the truth, and all of his testimony was backed up by evidence, he was treated very well by the Border Patrol after the incident.

When Supervisory Agent Robert Edwards Jr. arrived a few minutes after the horse patrol agents, he found Agent Borjas also on the south side of the mountain, west of where Agent Johnson had been found. Both were farther south of the positions where they had been when they first arrived at the saddle, and gunfire erupted.

Both surviving agents said they never saw Agent Ivie. If Agent Johnson had been shot at close range by Agent Ivie, and then he returned fire, Johnson would have seen him.

Readers might want to try this experiment. Crouch down on a bright moonlit night and have another man walk past you, wearing a uniform and a full duty belt, carrying a rifle pointed at the ground. See if you could recognize whether the man walking past you resembles a Border Patrol agent, or some kind of law enforcement officer — or a smuggler wearing a cubical pack and a blanket.

Then reverse roles.

Walk past a crouching man in a full uniform, who is wearing a duty belt with a sidearm, who pulls a gun and fires a few shots at you (toy gun recommended).

Notice whether he resembles a man throwing off a blanket, with a large cubic burlap backpack on his back. When he starts firing, you yell "Hey, hey, hey, hey!" at him.

He says nothing, but shoots several more times as you stand there. He misses with 10 shots at close range, but kicks up some rocks which hit your shins, and he lands a shot to your buttock. You bring your rifle up to your shoulder, look through your sight (even though you are just a few feet away), pull the trigger, and squeeze off six shots.

Would you see that the guy in the uniform was a guy in a uniform? If you shot him smack dab in the middle of his forehead, and he fell face forward onto the ground right after you shot him, wouldn't you notice that?

The scenario presented in the article makes no sense, especially in light of the evidence. It actually makes no sense even if there were absolutely no evidence.

But there is much evidence found in this article—of purposeful deception.

"The physical evidence does not indicate who fired first," Colburn wrote. "Agent #2 (Borjas) stated that she did not know who fired first, and Agent #1 (Johnson) stated that Nick fired first, and that he returned fire."

In his postincident interview, Agent Johnson *never* stated that Nick fired at all. He said he saw someone wearing a smuggler's pack, then someone opened fire on him. He *never identified* Ivie as the one who had been firing at him.

Agent Borjas did not say *she did* not know who fired first. She said that when she and Agent Johnson arrived on the scene, people began shooting at them.Borjas *did* say who fired first—the people who were on the scene when she and Agent Johnson arrived. That testimony matched the story that Agent Johnson told *and* all the physical evidence.

She knew exactly who fired first—the suspect who was shooting a long arm and possibly another suspect shooting a shiny pistol. And Agent Ivie had neither a long arm nor a shiny pistol.

The implication in the Colburn story—that Borjas knew that Ivie and Johnson were firing at each other—was totally false. People at the saddle were firing at Borjas and Johnson as they arrived. That was what she reported about the shooting.

Agent Borjas also said that she never saw Agent Ivie at the scene, let alone see him firing a weapon.

By saying that Agent #2 did not know who fired first, the article implied that Agent Borjas affirmed that those two agents were shooting at each other. In her interview, she never said anything about Agent Ivie shooting at all.

She said in her October 11, 2012, interview that she had not believed Agent Ivie was there. She was shocked when she was told later that Agent Ivie had been killed—because she did not know he had arrived on the scene before she and Johnson arrived.

It was a great leap of creative storytelling from what Agent Borjas said—that she did not know Ivie was even at the scene—to the Colburn article interpretation that she did not know which agent fired first.

There is much more in this article that clashes with the testimony of the surviving agents and the evidence found at the scene.

The article is disjointed and contradictory, with digressions to irrelevant points, such as that Border Patrol agents were excellent marksmen.

If those two agents shot at each other right after walking past each other, what outstanding marksmanship would be required?

If Agents Are Superb Marksmen, How Did Ivie Fail to Shoot His Target 10 Times?

If Agent Ivie was such a great shot—as the Colburn article implied—how did he manage to shoot his target only in the buttock and ankle from close range, while squeezing off 10 rounds?

If Colburn meant to imply that Agent Johnson was also a great shot, that was missing the mark by a long shot from what actually occurred. Agent Johnson fired a burst of suppressive fire from about 20 feet away toward bright muzzle flashes, after seeing nothing but sky in his rifle sight.

There is no way he would have shot at Agent Ivie at close range—and there is no way that he landed a perfect assassin's head shot on a fellow agent.

Whether or not Agent Johnson was an excellent marksman, Johnson did not shoot Agent Ivie in the head, as the Colburn article and an FBI report concluded.

Once again, this article filled the bill of plausible deniability. Colburn claimed that he was "briefed" for this article by the FBI, Border Patrol, and Cochise County Sheriff's Office. But the FBI never confirmed or denied that this version was accurate. Only the Border Patrol publicly announced its support for this article.

An FBI official or Attorney General Holder might have enlisted Colburn to write this article, but officially they had nothing to do with it.

The fact that it was not repudiated by the FBI—which would easily be able to distinguish this fiction from the facts in the case—tends to confirm that this was part of the FBI's coverup.

Why would Colburn, a former top Border Patrol official with a pedigree of service to that agency—including a father, grandfather, and son who have served on the force—suddenly decide he was the one to set the record straight? He was a recognized expert on the border, who was working as a consultant for the government at the time the article was published in October 2013. Why would he want to get involved in this case, taking the side of those who were backing a false narrative?

Many other assertions in this article clashed with the evidence, and they are obvious to anyone familiar with what actually occurred.

If Colburn had just gathered information from three law enforcement agencies as part of a truly independent inquiry, and then released this particular account, the Border Patrol would most likely have issued a statement distancing itself from the results. The disclaimer might have said something like: "This story is the work of a private party and is not the official account of the Border Patrol or any other investigative agency associated with the Nicholas Ivie case. The Border Patrol does not endorse the views expressed therein."

I believe the Border Patrol instead released a public statement that the agency "stood behind it," because the Border Patrol and the FBI were actively involved in its production, with some assistance from Colburn.

In the TV news show that affirmed Border Patrol support for this narrative, several of Agent Ivie's family members were interviewed. The picture painted by the story was that the relatives said they were glad to receive this news, because it showed that Nick did not do anything wrong. One relative said it showed that Nick acted properly, according to his training.

Although I believe Agent Ivie did act properly, in accordance with his training, this article showed him doing the exact opposite.

Border Patrol agents are not trained to open fire on other Border Patrol agents who walk past them on a bright moonlit night, from a distance of a few feet away. Neither are they trained to open fire on anyone without announcing who they are and making sure that the target is posing a threat.

Agent Johnson was not posing a threat to Agent Ivie when he arrived on the scene. He was planning to cut sign with Agent Ivie. If Agent Ivie were alive and alone at the moment the two other agents arrived, he would not have opened fire on them.

It compounds the tragedy to see relatives of a courageous agent with a spotless record being purposely misled by the agency he was serving at the time of his death.

As we have noted earlier, the FBI made no official statement in response to any element of its coverup—including the Colburn article. Despite its promise to release more information later, the Bureau has remained perfectly silent since it declared Agent Ivie's death a case of accidental discharge.

Gleaning Truth from Deception

There are some statements in the Colburn article that are possibly true, and they can be offered here as additional information that will help readers understand the entire scenario. They do not necessarily support the FBI's conclusion, but they were included in that article.

The Colburn article includes this passage, which could open a whole new window for any future investigators of this case:

"There were, however, three Mexican nationals discovered and arrested within a few hours of the incident, and only about 1.5 miles south of this saddle, where the incident occurred. They were walking southbound, back toward Mexico, at the time."

If this is true, this is a significant detail that is not mentioned in any other media report. Remember that there were other Border Patrol agents at the saddle within 20 minutes or so of the shooting. At the same time, there was also a helicopter with a powerful spotlight, carrying a crew of agents up there.

A short time later, there were dozens, then very soon, hundreds, of law enforcement officers swarming over the area.

Who were these Mexican nationals, who were in the middle of this scene "a few hours after the incident?" Where were they at the time of the shooting? What were they doing in the area? Were they aware that a Border Patrol agent had just been shot to death? Did they know the smugglers who were at the saddle a few hours earlier?

If they were 1.5 miles from the saddle a few hours later, it would be likely that they would have had information pertinent to the case or concerning other illegal activity in the middle of the night, in the same immediate area.

If this really occurred, why was there no mention of it in any other news report?

How were they all cleared of any involvement? If they were there a few hours later, they would have been in that area at the time of the shooting. They would have not entered an area that was swarming with law enforcement agents. The agents were saturating that area well ahead of the published time of their arrest.

Colburn mentions their arrests in passing, without any explanation as to what happened to them. This information tends to confirm Agent Borjas's testimony of seeing three or four suspects at the scene.

If there were three arrested a short time later nearby, and two more arrested a few hours after that, those facts would fit her assessment of the number of people on the scene.

The Colburn story also mentions the two suspects who were arrested in Mexico, but dismisses them as of no consequence.

"They were in possession of a pistol, at the time. They could not be connected to the shooting scene by any physical evidence, and investigators dismissed their presence as coincidental and not associated with the case," Colburn wrote, citing no specific source or agency.

The handgun that was seized when the two Mexican men were arrested just south of the border was a revolver, not a pistol. It was traced by the ATF in connection with the murder of Agent Ivie.

The distinction is important, because pistols expel shell casings, often leaving behind evidence at the scene of a crime. A fired revolver retains its shell casings. As a career law enforcement officer, this would be a detail of which Colburn would be keenly aware. Did someone withhold the truth from him? The *L.A. Times* published a story about the kind of handgun found with the suspects arrested in Mexico.

Had Colburn seen this news story? Had he heard from the FBI that the Bureau interviewed those suspects in Mexico and retrieved DNA and fingerprints from them?

Here is more information from the Colburn story that tends to collaborate my conclusions, more than the conclusions drawn by Colburn's article and the FBI's final statement:

"According to Agent #2 (Borjas), as she walked behind Agent #1 (Johnson), shooting suddenly erupted. She looked down to the left, where Nick would be, and believed she saw 3–4 people sitting, or in some kind of low position. Agent #2 then ran a short distance and took cover."

Here we have Agent Borjas saying she saw several people, a sharp contrast with the "nobody else involved" statement.

She never said anything about looking toward where Nick would be, but in her second interview she did say this: "I saw three to four people out there. So I just decided to take cover and—and there was a small like cactus looking thing and like a rock where I hid." Following that she said she saw a muzzle flash to her left from a rifle.[4]

The Colburn article continued:

"She stated that she then heard voices in Spanish and she thought they might come after her. Agent #2 then turned off her radio so that transmissions would not give away her position. She relocated to another ridgeline some distance away," the Colburn article said.

In her second interview, Borjas did say she heard voices that sounded like they were speaking Spanish.

How Does This Match a Conclusion of "Nobody Else" Being Involved?

If Agent Johnson was the only other person in the vicinity—someone who spoke English except in exceptional circumstances—who were those people who were speaking in Spanish who might come after her?

Was Johnson speaking back and forth to himself in Spanish, while sitting still and bleeding, in order to threaten his partner?

Many people involved with the investigation would have known that this article was a combination of outright lies, half-truths, and a few facts. But with nobody speaking up to contradict this false story, it would be understandable that those who knew little about the evidence, but were hungry to hear the truth, would accept the article as factual.

Although this article accuses the media of spreading misinformation and finger-pointing—by reporting honestly on what occurred on Remax Saddle—the article itself is a barrel of disinformation designed to point fingers at those who spent a few days telling the truth.

25

Borderland Author Presents Public Challenge to FBI

"Several Border Patrol agents I interviewed knew Ivie well and swore that under no circumstances would he have opened fire in the direction of other agents." From **Alligators in the Moat,** *by Ed Ashurst[1]*

May 2017
Cochise County, Arizona

Many national, international, and local news stories told millions of viewers and readers that illegal aliens had ambushed and killed Agent Ivie, early in the morning on October 2, 2012, on a remote mountain ridge in the Mule Mountains.

That was the accepted narrative all law enforcement and political leaders agreed on—until the FBI made a surprise announcement three days later that its investigation showed that Agent Ivie's death was the result of agents shooting at each other.

Nobody else was involved in the shooting death of Agent Ivie, the FBI said. The FBI did not answer any questions from the press after that announcement was made.

The FBI sent out a press release, and that was that. The Bureau presented no facts to back up this statement—which stood in sharp contrast to the evidence in the case.

At some point, the investigation was officially closed. We know it was closed because a Border Patrol agent who knew Agent Ivie found shell casings several years later at the saddle—now known as "Nick's Saddle," in his honor. That agent was told by his superiors that no new evidence was being collected because the investigation was closed.

It is not known whether those shell casings were related to the Ivie case. Firearms might have been fired at that location for several different reasons during the ensuing years, or for no reason at all.

More importantly, the investigation was actually closed the day the FBI announced that Agent Ivie was killed by another agent.

You might say that the investigation was closed before it began—

as soon as news reports of the death of a young, highly respected federal agent were perceived as a possible political threat during the 2012 presidential election campaign.

Then Attorney General Eric Holder—who on June 28 of the same year had been held in contempt of Congress for lying about the Fast and Furious operation and withholding documents—was involved with the Ivie investigation.

Holder was a self-proclaimed "wingman" for President Barack Obama—rather than an unbiased chief federal law enforcement officer—and his involvement in this case would immediately cast a shadow of suspicion over the integrity of the investigation. The Ivie case was linked to the killing of Agent Brian Terry and the Fast and Furious operation, both mentioned in many national and international press reports about Nick Ivie's death. That deadly government gun-running operation was administered by the Phoenix ATF office, with the full knowledge of Holder, whose department oversaw the ATF.

Holder should have recused himself from the Ivie investigation, which was compromised by his involvement. Once media outlets began linking the Ivie slaying to Fast and Furious, Holder had a vested interest in interrupting the flow of news stories.

Instead, Obama's wingman got involved within a short time—before the FBI had even issued its final statement.

The shooting death of a dedicated young Border Patrol agent—a beloved husband, father, son, brother, colleague, neighbor, and friend—was not considered worthy of a genuine investigation, which would normally have lasted for weeks, months, or years. An investigation into the ambush of three Border Patrol agents—resulting in the death of one and the injury of another, would ordinarily be executed with the kind of depth and tenacity that every fallen law enforcement officer deserves.

Why allow the killers to get away with murder, while pinning the blame for the brutal attack on agents who were out on a mountain ridge, courageously doing their jobs?

Agent Nicholas Ivie was declared guilty of shooting at other agents in the dark, causing one of those agents to shoot him dead. No evidence would ever be presented to the public—or even to the Border Patrol agents who served alongside Agent Ivie—to substantiate this conclusion.

Although the FBI has not honored its promise to present a report on the investigation, members of other law enforcement agencies, which were initially involved in the investigation, have spoken out on the case. At least one investigative partner expressed skepticism about the FBI's silent treatment.

In May 2017, the Border Patrol responded to a TV news report by Fox 10 Phoenix, which reported that one man, Ed Ashurst, a Cochise County author and rancher, did not believe the FBI report. Ashurst raised the question of the accuracy of the FBI's conclusion in *Alligators in the Moat*, his 2016 book on border issues.

"Ashurst and many others believe the Border Patrol agents stumbled upon a drug smuggling operation, and it was the smugglers who opened fire first," a FOX 10 reporter said, during a broadcast aired on May 20, 2017.[2]

Ashurst referred to a report from Detective Sergeant Sean Gijanto of the Cochise County Sheriff's Office, which said that the surviving female agent saw three or four people at the scene. She also said that the people who attacked her were firing a long arm, and that she heard people whispering in Spanish or English after the shooting stopped. Gijanto was one of the questioners at Agent Borjas's initial interview, just three and a half hours after the incident. He recorded the interview on the tape recorder that was used to produce the official transcript.

The FBI did not respond to this public challenge to the Bureau's conclusion, after four years and seven months of silence. Once again, the Bureau instead let officials from other agencies speak on the issue, despite the fact that the FBI had been the lead agency in the investigation. The FBI had brought down the curtain of silence on the case, and it maintained its resolve to keep it in place.

When Ashurst aired his suspicions on this news show and on a subsequent broadcast on a Tucson NBC affiliate, those appearances brought media attention to the case for the first time since the Colburn article was published in October 2013.

With the FBI exercising its right to remain silent, the Border Patrol responded by bringing Jeff Self back to Arizona to answer this vigorous accusation. This was an acknowledgement that the Border Patrol remained in lockstep with the Bureau in clinging to the original FBI narrative. In 2017, Self was serving as sector chief in El Paso, Texas, where Agent Graciela Borjas has been employed since shortly after the incident.

Self was speaking for the Border Patrol as he answered the allegations of Ashurst and an anonymous Border Patrol agent, who had also spoken out against the FBI's conclusion. Jeff Self had been the commander of the U.S. Customs and Border Protection Arizona Joint Field Command at the time of the Ivie slaying. Although he had passionately insisted that the killers would be brought to justice when the facts about the ambush first came out, he later changed his tune to speak just as passionately for the FBI's official explanation.

Self's main argument in defense of the FBI conclusion was centered on the unreliability of Agent Borjas, whom he did not name. By discrediting her testimony, Self was callously impugning the reputation of a courageous, honest agent, who nearly gave her life while serving our nation.

Borjas did not allow that near-death experience, nor the blatant disrespect of her superiors, to interfere with her career. She has remained on the border protection force since then. She was recently recommended by the Border Patrol to appear in a Fox TV news report in El Paso on outstanding women in the force. [3]

"My brothers, cousins, they were the ones that influenced me," Borjas said of her decision to join the Border Patrol during the news segment. "It's been a good journey so far."

In the TV news show which aired on March 8, 2018, Borjas urged other women to join the Border Patrol.

"If you're up for the challenge, I would say 'Come and join.' This is a very good job; I'm blessed to have this job."

It is too bad that the Border Patrol did not show her the respect she deserved in 2012, when they totally dismissed her testimony.

The testimony Borjas gave to investigators several hours after the incident perfectly matched Agent Johnson's testimony and the other evidence in the case. Self was not able to point out a single inaccurate statement that Borjas had made in her interviews. Her testimony was consistent throughout her two FBI interviews, and matched what she told a Border Patrol acting supervisor just minutes after the attack occurred.

In his 2017 TV interview, Self did not provide any information about what the female agent said in her post-incident interviews or what she told the Border Patrol supervisor on the mountain—but simply dismissed her testimony as untrue. He did not address Agent Johnson's testimony at all.

As the chief spokesman for the investigation, Self must have known more about the case, including what Agent Johnson said in his interview and how Borjas repeatedly stuck with her story.

But instead of presenting any evidence to back his statement, Self instead accused Ashurst, and the anonymous Border Patrol agent who challenged the official version, of speaking out of ignorance.

Self told the TV news reporter that the female agent at the shooting scene was traumatized. That implied that anything she said was null and void.

He conveniently failed to report that when she was found on the mountain slope by the Border Patrol acting supervisor, she was found to be stable enough to handle a loaded firearm. Acting Border

Patrol Supervisor Robert Edwards made sure she had a fully loaded service pistol, because he believed she was fully competent to take part in a shootout with murderous smugglers, in case they decided to attack again.

Nothing in the report by Edwards indicated that she was upset or unreliable. There was nothing in any of the numerous reports on the case to indicate that anything that Borjas said was inaccurate.

What stood out in all the reports involving Borjas was her consistency and honesty. She freely spoke about running from the saddle immediately after the gunfire ceased. She admitted that she was scared. Any honest investigator would call her a very reliable witness. Any prosecutor would be thrilled to put her on the witness stand.

Self also failed to say that the female agent underwent an extensive FBI interview nine days after the incident, when there was no recorded sign of any emotional trauma. She was admittedly distraught at her first interview because of the shock and grief of hearing of the death of a fellow agent. But the shock of hearing that Agent Ivie had been killed—news she received only after she was airlifted down from the mountain—had zero effect on her overall ability to accurately report on the circumstances surrounding the shooting incident.

In responding to Ashurst's statement about the female agent seeing three or four people—based on a police report from the sheriff's office—Self said that conclusions about the incident should be based on all the evidence.

"They are taking that one piece and drawing a conclusion—there was some kind of conspiracy or cover-up as a result of this one report," Self said on the air on the Phoenix TV station in 2017.

However, Self offered no information to contradict that important piece of evidence. The evidence Ashurst presented was strong enough for any objective person to question the FBI's conclusion.

By pointing to "all the evidence" in the case, Self was accusing Ashurst of possessing only a superficial knowledge of the evidence, which was not true.

Self focused on the one piece of evidence that Ashurst presented, which the author presented, with the hope that it would help spark a deeper investigation to uncover the true story of what occurred. Self tried to discredit Ashurst and Borjas by attacking their credibility.

It was not accurate that Ed Ashurst drew his conclusion from one report. Ashurst, an authority on border issues, had read many pages of reports and talked with several law enforcement officers involved in the case. He presented the best evidence he had at that time, which he rightfully believed blew out of the water the FBI conclusion that nobody else was involved but the agents.

The testimony that Borjas delivered while she was upset—shortly after hearing about Agent Ivie's death—matched the accounts she gave before and after that interview. Self never mentioned the fact that Agent Borjas's three accounts—at three different times and locations—all matched. It is well known among law enforcement officers and military interrogators that a story staying essentially the same during several retellings is a strong indication of its veracity.

Even when FBI agents tried to persuade her to change her story to match theirs on October 11, 2012, she bent a little bit, but ultimately did not break. She insisted that she saw three or four people on the scene.

In its May 2017 story, Fox News TV reporters said they contacted the U.S. Department of Homeland Security, as well as the two chief officials who were active in the case in 2012, Janet Napolitano and David Aguilar. The station received no responses. The U.S. Department of Homeland Security, Napolitano, and Aguilar all declined the opportunity to present evidence to back up the FBI's case.

KVOA, the NBC affiliate in Tucson, broadcast a similar story on May 25, which also focused on Ashurst's allegations of a cover-up. It was entitled: **"Questions remain about what happened the night of Nick Ivie's death."**

That story reported that Mark Dannels, who was elected Cochise County sheriff one month after the Ivie incident, said he believed the reports written by members of his department. Those numerous reports, including the one about the testimony of Agent Borjas, repeatedly affirmed that there were suspects involved in the shooting of the Border Patrol agents.

All of those reports were based on the events that occurred the morning of October 2 in the vicinity of the mountain ridge where Agent Ivie was gunned down.

Sheriff Dannels said in a May 2017 interview that he had never received an FBI report, "and questions of what happened that night still remain."

He said he saw the ballistics report, which indicated that it was a "blue-on-blue shooting."

That report, which indicated that a bullet fragment taken from Agent Ivie's skull was matched to Agent Johnson's rifle, was performed after the FBI had already released to media outlets the conclusion that Agent Ivie's death was being investigated as a "friendly fire" incident.

Dannels said, **"What I don't have is what happened that night when it comes to, were there smugglers in the area. It seems like that's the big question here."**

In response to a request for a comment from the Tucson TV station, the Border Patrol released this statement:

"A thorough investigation was conducted by the federal Bureau of investigations [sic]; it concluded this was a tragic case of friendly fire. Unfounded conspiracies are not based on facts and based on theory and not a complete view of the investigation. If there were criminals that perpetrated the death of Agent Ivie, I assure you that the U.S. Border Patrol would not rest until their killers came to justice."

It was understandable for the government agency to label legitimate questions about this tragic death as an "unfounded conspiracy" that was not based on facts. This reaction—accusing those who question government officials about their conspiracy of themselves being conspirators—is a ploy that has been around since government officials began conspiring against their subjects.

It is easy to throw mud at honest questioners, but it would be far more difficult to actually prove that highly trained agents shot at each other, after they met at a predetermined rendezvous point.

The proof behind the FBI's conclusion has never been presented to the public or to any outside agency.

The Border Patrol failed to present any facts to back up its assertion that the FBI had conducted an honest investigation, free of political bias. Not one scintilla of evidence has ever been presented to the press or the public to support the Bureau's conclusion that nobody else was at the scene when two agents were shot.

That is the essential lie that can never be transformed into truth.

Far from being a "conspiracy theorist," Ed Ashurst was instead trying to expose a genuine conspiracy to deprive the public of the truth about the slaying of Agent Ivie.

There are many unanswered questions about what really occurred. A conspiracy, by definition, is a secret plan by a group to do something unlawful or harmful. Clumsily accusing Ashurst of theorizing that a conspiracy existed does not add one iota to the public's knowledge of what occurred.

Instead of trying to silence someone who stuck his neck out to reveal the truth of what occurred in this case, why haven't government officials pressured the FBI to keep its word and reveal the true results of its investigation?

26

Just One More Corrupt FBI Operation?

"But the reality of the job is that, as head of the FBI, you have such great power for good or ill." Louis J. Freeh, FBI director before Robert Mueller.

The successful Ivie case cover up of 2012 emboldened the FBI to spy on the Trump campaign in 2016

"The Justice Department and the FBI are allowed to go to a secret court that Congress created in 1978 and present an application that says the person they want to surveil, or the person they want to monitor, they want to *spy on*, is an agent of a foreign power. . . . You have surveillance going on against people who are presumed innocent and who have a full array of constitutional rights, and they never find out about it (that the FBI is spying on them).

"What we found out in this investigation, that was precisely what they did, but they did it for the purpose of monitoring a political campaign." Former federal prosecutor Andrew McCarthy, on the clandestine surveillance of the Trump presidential campaign by the FBI in 2016.[1]

When the FBI went to bat for Obama during the 2012 presidential campaign, by covering up the true cause of Agent Ivie's death, that operation was a total success. That could have emboldened Obama and his new FBI Director Jim Comey, a close friend and longtime associate of Mueller's, to indulge in other election-related operations during the 2016 campaign.

If there had been a congressional investigation into the FBI's phony findings in the Ivie case during the 2012 election campaign, perhaps Obama's FBI would not have been so enthusiastic in undertaking bigger and better dirty tricks four years later.

The motto of the Federal Bureau of Investigation is *fidelity, bravery, and integrity*. Thousands of agents have lived up to this motto.

Director Louis Freeh, predecessor to Robert Mueller, wrote an FBI Core Values code, in order to impress the importance of ethical behavior on his agents:

Those values are rigorous obedience to the Constitution of the United States, respect for the dignity of all those we protect, compassion, fairness, and uncompromising personal and institutional integrity.

Freeh also wrote this statement on the importance of the FBI's independence from political influence:

"Lockstep, blind obedience by the director to an attorney general, without questioning potentially unlawful or even dumb orders, is a formula for disaster—both for the FBI and the nation." Louie Freeh, on rejecting "marching orders" from the attorney general as one of the FBI's priorities.[2]

Freeh lived up to this statement by keeping a distance from the White House. Although Clinton had appointed Freeh as director, the Bureau he directed found evidence that President Bill Clinton had sex with intern Monica Lewinsky, after the president had publicly denied doing so. That was the only time in history when the FBI was involved in the successful impeachment of a president.

However, Freeh's successor, Robert Mueller, did not maintain a distance from President Barack Obama. In fact, the two men enjoyed a close relationship, meeting almost every morning in the White House during Obama's presidency, according to an article published three weeks after the Ivie slaying. The article, which was favorable toward Obama and Mueller, was written by Tim Weiner, an author who penned a book on the FBI.[3]

In order to understand how the FBI allowed itself to be used for political purposes in the case of the murder of Border Patrol Agent Ivie, it is important to look at the evidence of a pattern of similar incidents involving the Bureau—especially under the extended tenure of FBI Director Robert Mueller III, who served from 2001 to 2013.

"Robert Mueller has a long and sordid history of illicitly targeting innocent people that is a stain upon the legacy of American jurisprudence," wrote U.S. Representative Louie Gohmert, R-Texas, a former judge, who is an outspoken Mueller critic. "He lacks the judgment and credibility to lead the prosecution of anyone."

Gohmert was referring specifically to Mueller's role as Special Counsel, in which he led a team that included FBI officials, to investigate possible Russian collusion with the Donald Trump presidential campaign. Mueller became one of the most well-known public figures because of this appointment.[4]

Mueller's investigation—which lasted for two years, before concluding there was no evidence of collusion—also exerted influence over an election. Many observers believe the Democrats took control of the House of Representatives due to this highly publicized investigation, which was still in progress during the 2018 mid-term election. There is much evidence that this investigation was nothing but a politically motivated operation, based on the foundation of a fictional dossier about Donald Trump, funded by the Democratic National Committee and the Hillary Clinton campaign. The FBI was involved in every phase of the Russian collusion anti-Trump operation.

It is not this author's intention to impugn the reputation of the FBI, for which I have deep respect. I have been personally acquainted with several agents and was privileged to attend the FBI Citizens' Academy in 2011, which gave me a close look at the agency's inner workings.

The outstanding work of the FBI in setting high standards for law enforcement worldwide, while performing the gritty daily work of investigating and apprehending criminals, should not be overshadowed by the relatively few incidents of corrupt practices by a small number of its leaders and individual agents.

However, it is disturbing that many agents will play along with a dishonest investigation, rather than expose it as an outright deception. If all FBI agents were bursting with integrity—as the Bureau's motto boasts and former FBI director Freeh apparently strove to achieve—the deception of the Ivie investigation would have been prevented or exposed long ago.

The history of the Federal Bureau of Investigation, from its complicity in the Watergate scandal in the early 1970s, to its spying on Donald Trump's presidential campaign, is riddled with true stories of corrupt practices, some of which directly influenced elections.

Some of those cases of FBI corruption are presented here as examples of FBI operations similar to the coverup of the slaying of Agent Ivie. If the FBI had never before or since engaged in a corrupt operation—as some naïve people might believe—it would be understandable to believe that this allegation of the coverup of the Border Patrol agent's murder is nothing but a "conspiracy theory."

In fact, this situation differs from similar FBI operations only in the stunning nature of its success. Seven years later, the bogus investigation and phony conclusion have gone largely unchallenged. Every official account of the Ivie slaying says it was from "friendly fire."

Unlike his predecessor, FBI Director Robert Mueller III did the bidding of the president. When Obama asked him to fly to Tucson in January 2011 to oversee the investigation of the attempted assassination of Congresswoman Gabrielle Giffords, an incident in which six other people were murdered, Mueller jumped on a plane.

The shooter was arrested at the scene, later pled guilty to 19 felony counts, and was sentenced to life in prison.

So why was Director Mueller sent to Arizona, except for political showmanship? Everyone knew who committed this heinous crime. The Mayberry Police Department could have executed a successful investigation—with Barney Fife as its leading homicide detective.

When the murder of a Border Patrol agent occurred the following year—a murder that demanded an honest investigation after the shooters escaped to Mexico—Mueller was nowhere to be found. Why didn't Obama send him to Tucson then to oversee an investigation that genuinely required honest leadership for justice to be accomplished?

We can surmise that FBI Director Mueller was also involved in the Ivie case, which involved the president, the attorney general, the criminal division chief, and top officials of Homeland Security. But Mueller, who would later be tapped to lead the most partisan, politicized Department of Justice investigation in U.S. history, remained behind an opaque curtain during the incredibly brief Ivie homicide probe.

Once again, let us turn to the words of Freeh to understand the power of an FBI director to oversee investigations:

"But the reality of the job is that, as head of the FBI, you have such great power for good or ill. Directors of the FBI can launch an investigation or stop one, or they can influence the drift of an ongoing one if they choose. Careers can be made or undone in the process."

Although Mueller shunned all publicity as the FBI released its "friendly fire" narrative before Agent Ivie was buried, there is no question he was involved in this politically charged case. You might say his modus operandi was to work quietly behind the scene, letting others step into the spotlight—and taking the heat, if the operation should later go south.

After 9/11, when the FBI made counterterrorism its top priority, Mueller sent mixed messages about his dedication to that goal.

When Mueller served under President George W. Bush, the FBI shielded Saudis living in Florida who had ties to Osama bin Laden and Al Qaeda, apparently because of the Bush family's ties to the Saudi royal family. He later went along with Obama's focus on investigating potential "Islamophobes," while handcuffing the FBI from preventing Islamic terrorism.

Mueller had FBI training materials purged of anything that might offend radical Islamic terrorists, which put the FBI at a disadvantage in trying to prevent terrorist attacks, Gohmert wrote in his column.

"The blinding of our FBI agents to the domestic threat of radical Islam is part of the beguiling damage Robert Mueller did as FBI director," said a 2016 article in PJ Media. An antiterrorism expert pointed out that most attacks by Islamic terrorists were executed by individuals already known to the FBI as potential threats.

Obama Keeps Mueller in Office Beyond His 10-year Term

When Mueller's 10-year term expired in 2011—in accordance with a federal statute enacted to prevent a director from wielding too much power—Obama asked Congress to extend his term for two more years. This would keep the director Obama trusted in power during the 2012 election campaign. Mueller was the only FBI director to complete a 10-year term, after J. Edgar Hoover's 48-year reign gave him unlimited power, which he abused by keeping files he could hold over the heads of significant political leaders.[6]

FBI director Robert Mueller had already established a record of using the Bureau as a political tool to influence the outcomes of elections—long before the Ivie case came to his attention. And though Mueller remained in the shadows of the Agent Ivie case, the markings of his leadership were familiar to those who followed his career. Mueller's willingness to use his positions of power for political and other unethical purposes would later be widely recognized as his trademark. He especially exhibited insensitivity to prosecuting innocent people and running a tight ship that punished those who would expose corruption within the Bureau itself.

The names of countless government leaders have surfaced for their involvement in this case, including President Barack Obama, Attorney General Eric Holder, Homeland Security Secretary Janet Napolitano, Customs and Border Protection Acting Commissioner David Aguilar, and many others.

But there is no mention of FBI Director Mueller in any press report I could find.

Lesser agents took the blame in earlier cases in which inappropriate behavior was made public, but those high-profile investigations would likely not have gone forward without the knowledge or direction of Mueller. In every case of government corruption exposed during Mueller's tenure, he remained silent about his personal involvement. Subordinates were rightfully accused of wrongdoing in many cases. But Mueller—who would have signed off on every case involving politicians or other highly publicized cases—always stayed in the background.

Some writers who covered the FBI have pointed out that Mueller tended to be a loyal soldier of the presidents under which he served, regardless of whether they wanted to protect Saudis related to Osama bin Laden or prevent the FBI from flying to Benghazi to protect American lives.

For Mueller to order an investigation by the Bureau to be concluded quickly—in order to help the president who had just extended his term in office—fits this profile.

There have been several other operations in which Mueller and his FBI showed their lack of integrity, as well as political bias, including some that directly influenced elections:

- Curt Weldon, an 11-term Republican Congressman representing Pennsylvania's Seventh District antagonized the FBI by delivering numerous speeches in which he said the Bureau's actions had failed to prevent 9/11. Weldon had easily won previous elections and was up in the polls just two weeks before the 2006 election. FBI agents raided his daughter's home, sparking media stories implying that Weldon was also under investigation.

  Weldon and his daughter were never charged with any crime, but the FBI hit job cost him the election. "The early morning raid by Mueller's FBI, with all the media outside, obviously alerted by the FBI, had achieved its goal of colluding to abuse the federal justice system to silence Curt Weldon by ending his political career. Mueller's FBI worked it like a charm."[7]

- Ted Stevens was the longest-serving Republican U.S. senator in history when Mueller's FBI manufactured a criminal case against him, alleging he had not disclosed on Senate forms the cost of a cabin renovation. In 2008, he was indicted during his reelection campaign and convicted just eight days before the election. Stevens, a pioneer instrumental in Alaska's achieving statehood, lost the election by less than 2 percent of the votes. Because of massive FBI improprieties, the conviction of this man, known for his integrity, was later overturned. Four years later, the FBI investigator accused of wrongdoing in the case was still investigating cases; the whistleblower who revealed that the FBI used false evidence to frame an innocent man was demoted and subsequently resigned.[8]

- As another example of how Mueller's FBI enforced silence about the Bureau's wrongdoing—ironically rewarding dishonesty— former FBI agent Jane Turner was mistreated after she reported that fellow agents took valuable souvenirs from the rubble of the World Trade Center following the 9/11 terrorist attacks. She won a jury trial against the FBI, after alleging that FBI supervisors forced her to quit because she blew the whistle.[9]

With Mueller remaining in power for 11 months after the Ivie slaying, to be succeeded by Comey, it is understandable why no whistleblowers have surfaced in the Ivie case.

• Mueller's FBI also mishandled the famous 2001 Anthrax mail case, which had cost the lives of five people and injured 17 others. An innocent man, research scientist Dr. Steven Hatfill, was singled out as a suspect by the FBI, based on shoddy evidence—that two bloodhounds sniffed the anthrax-carrying letters and "alerted' on him. Mueller assured the attorney general that Hatfill was the guilty party. Hatfill's reputation and career were ruined by the FBI's highly publicized, erroneous case.

Mueller later announced that the FBI had not made any mistakes in the case. However, the Justice Department exonerated Hatfill and paid him $5.82 million in a settlement of his legal case against the government. The FBI ignored leads about a more plausible suspect, Dr. Bruce Ivins, who committed suicide when Mueller's Bureau turned its attention to him. Once again, Mueller showed he was callous toward ruining the lives of innocent people.

• A scandal that should have rocked the entire world—if not for the highly partisan media and political environment of the twenty-first century—was the Obama administration's use of the FBI and other government agencies to spy on the Trump presidential campaign. Trump campaign aides were surveilled in an activity called *Operation Crossfire Hurricane.*

The FBI obtained a wiretap on Carter Page, who had served as a confidential source for the FBI and CIA, by submitting a salacious, fictional dossier about Trump's activities in Russia to the Foreign Intelligence Surveillance Court. This operation, activated while Jim Comey was FBI director in 2016, has been covered in thousands of news stories, as well as in several books. It is mentioned here as another stunning example of the willingness of the FBI to be used for political purposes during the Obama administration.

• Three weeks before Agent Ivie was murdered by Mexican smugglers near the southern border, Obama was faced with a much larger threat to his reelection campaign. On September 11, 2012, a large contingent of terrorists attacked the U.S. diplomatic mission compound in Benghazi, Libya. Ambassador Chris

Stevens and about 30 other Americans were in immediate danger of losing their lives. Highly trained diplomatic security agents stationed at the C.I.A. Benghazi Annex, one mile from the main compound, drove to the compound to fight off the terrorists and rescue a group of Americans.

CIA and Defense Department officials quickly assembled a counterterrorism force to fly to the aid of the embattled Americans, according to an eyewitness account by Robyn Gritz, then serving as an FBI supervisory special agent. Gritz was asked by Department of Defense officials to put six FBI agents on a plane of the Foreign Emergency Support Team (FEST), an elite unit tasked with responding to terror incidents worldwide. Gritz and other veteran FBI agents were shocked to hear assistant director Andrew McCabe give an order for the FBI to stand down, rather than assist in the rescue.

FBI agents later learned that Mueller approved this order to ground the FBI agents. The FEST mission was then scrubbed, on orders from the White House. Other U.S. forces available to combat the terrorists were also ordered to stand down, as a handful of courageous American defenders battled a host of terrorists for 13 hours. Four Americans lost their lives in this terrorist attack, while Obama sent zero assistance.

Although Mueller and other FBI officials knew that Americans were killed in Libya because of a planned terrorist attack, none of them spoke out when Obama officials lied afterward, saying the murders were caused by a spontaneous demonstration resulting from a video that painted a negative picture of Islam.[10, 11, 12]

- Mueller's FBI failed to investigate any corruption as then Secretary of State Hillary Clinton turned the U.S. State Department into her own personal pay-for-play piggy bank, while using an unsecured private computer server to conduct government business, including the storage and transmittal of classified information. When the Clinton email scandal came to light after she left office in 2013, Mueller's friend Comey, was the FBI director. The FBI investigation of Clinton was a farce. Clinton was exonerated before she was interviewed. When her emails were subpoenaed, she deleted more than 30,000 messages and had cell phones destroyed. Mueller was the FBI director during Clinton's entire term as Secretary of State.

- Under Obama, the FBI was used as a political apparatus in a manner unprecedented in history. While Hillary Clinton was under investigation by the FBI, Bill Clinton had a private meeting with Attorney General Loretta Lynn, an Obama appointee, on the tarmac of Phoenix Sky Harbor International Airport. Comey would later say that this meeting between Lynch and Clinton led to his decision that he would have to be the one to publicly clear the former secretary of state of criminal charges. FBI agents were serving on Lynch's security detail, but apparently were not in that 20-minute meeting.

The FBI later conducted an investigation to discover who leaked to the press the information that the private meeting had occurred. With Hillary Clinton expected to win the presidency, there was speculation that an offer had been made to Lynch about a future position in the administration, in exchange for favorable treatment by the FBI. Because FBI investigations routinely include wiretaps, it is possible that the airplane meeting was considered the safest way to hold a meeting.

When Comey announced that the FBI found Hillary Clinton had not broken the law, but her handling of classified information was "extremely careless," there was a tremendous outcry from political leaders and pundits of every political stripe. The FBI was then viewed by many as a biased agency, with loyalty to the Obamas and the Clintons—rather than to the rule of law.[13]

The FBI, which is tasked with investigating public corruption, played along with the Obama administration's corrupt practices. Mueller, who was appointed in 2001 by President George W. Bush, proved to be the opposite of his predecessor, Louis Freeh, who kept his distance from President Bill Clinton, under whom he served for more than seven years. Freeh clashed with Clinton on several issues, including the president's reluctance to aid in the prosecution of the Iran-directed bombers of the Khobar Towers, which claimed the lives of 19 U.S. service members in Saudi Arabia.

Mueller instead went along with the agendas of the presidents under which he served. After his extended term ended, and he was replaced by James Comey, it was not long before he returned to public life.

After Comey was fired, Mueller was appointed as special counsel of the Justice Department. He built on his record of political partisanship, hiring a team of Democratic Party–connected attorneys to investigate the recently inaugurated Republican President, Donald Trump. For 22 months, Mueller's office sought evidence of collusion between Trump's presidential campaign and the Russians. The investigation, which produced no evidence of collusion between Trump campaign officials and Russian agents, was based on a fictional dossier about

Trump misdeeds in Russia, written and paid for by the Hillary Clinton election campaign and the Democratic National Committee.

Once again, Mueller was involved in a bogus investigation that influenced an election. Although there was no evidence to support the allegation of collusion or obstruction by Trump, the investigation dragged on through the 2018 election. With many media outlets constantly releasing information alleging that Trump would be found guilty of collusion or obstruction, the Democrats won back the House of Representatives in that election. Many analysts concluded that the false allegations kept alive by the Mueller probe influenced that election.

The abuse of the FBI's power during and after the 2016 election clearly showed a willingness to use extreme measures for political purposes. The success of the coverup of the Ivie case during the previous election cycle—along with other scandals that were ignored or spun by the media—emboldened the Obama administration and Mueller to continue to abuse law enforcement powers.

As this book was about to be published, stunning new revelations came out about how the FBI used manipulation of 302 witness interview forms. I have shown examples in this book of how the FBI created its own evidence to prove that Agent Ivie shot at other agents, thereby causing his own death. Anyone examining the FBI file on the Ivie case would find it filled with 302 forms with false information, as I have pointed out throughout these pages.

It has recently surfaced in numerous news reports that the FBI manipulated the interview testimony of Trump's National Security Advisor, Lt. General Michael Flynn, causing him to lose his job, his reputation, and to plunge him into enormous debt from legal expenses. Flynn pleaded guilty to lying to the FBI, as part of a plea deal. He reportedly agreed to the plea under threat of a federal prosecution of his son. Flynn agreed to meet with the FBI on January 24, 2017, after agents led him to believe the Bureau just wanted to talk to him because of his new position, and it was not a big deal requiring a lawyer. They did not tell him he was being interviewed as a suspect in a counter-intelligence investigation.

Flynn's attorney, Sidney Powell, wrote in a recent legal brief that the FBI changed its 302 report on the interview with Flynn, to make it appear that he had lied. He was asked whether he spoke with the Russian ambassador about sanctions, which had been put in place against Russia by Obama after Trump won the election. Evidence showed that top FBI officials discussed a strategy in which to interview Flynn, in order to entrap him. FBI agent notes discovered by Powell showed that Flynn said he was not even certain he spoke with a Russian ambassador on the issue of sanctions. But in order to make a case against the highly respected military veteran the FBI turned Flynn's testimony upside-down.

"Overnight, substantive changes were made to the Flynn 302," the legal filing said. Instead of Flynn's actual response, as reflected in the notes, the 302 report was changed so that it reported that Flynn denied speaking about sanctions. Because the FBI already had a transcript of the phone call, which had not been previously revealed to Flynn, he was easily framed.

There was no tape recording of the interview. Unlike other law enforcement agencies, which routinely tape record or videotape interviews, the FBI does not normally record its interviews. That way, FBI agents can freely manufacture evidence in any cases in which they care to determine outcomes which would not otherwise go their way. Their 302 reports are accepted as evidence in courts of law, and are used to intimidate defendants in order to obtain plea deals or to convince judges and juries of their guilt.

The FBI wields enormous power. A suspect interviewed by the FBI will normally not be able to prove that he did not say what the FBI says he said. Even in the case of a high-ranking public official such as Flynn, it took almost three years and a brand-new, first-rate attorney to finally find evidence that the FBI fabricated its case against him.

Although the FBI agents who interviewed Flynn said they believed he was not lying, lies were written about him in order to damage the newly installed Trump administration. Evidence surfaced that those who were directly involved in this conspiracy against Flynn and Trump were determined to overturn the results of the 2016 election.

Flynn's attorney compared the notes of the agents who interviewed Flynn with the 302 that later became part of the record.

That final 302 in the Flynn case had another inconsistency from the notes turned over to Powell, Powell wrote in the brief. Both agents' notes stated that Flynn said he did not remember making four to five calls to the Russian ambassador from the Dominic Republic, but if he did that was because he repeatedly called because of the lousy phone service. But Powell discovered that the final version of the 302 said the exact opposite: "Flynn remembered making four to five calls that day about this issue, but that the Dominican Republic was a difficult place to make a call as he kept having connectivity issues."

"When they couldn't trip him up, somebody manipulated the 302 report of their interview with him," said investigative reporter Sara Carter, in a post on her blog on October 25, 2019. "Even though they had no evidence Flynn had lied, they didn't care. The prosecutors and FBI have the power of the purse and the ability to threaten and strong arm those they want to prosecute. That's what they did. [14]"

Flynn's 302 was entered into a file on May 31, 2017, "for Special Counsel Mueller to use." In other words, twisting the words in a 302 was part of something bigger than just ruining the life of a man who had devoted his life to serving his country. It was part of the plan, orchestrated by the highest officials of the FBI, to try to destroy the presidency of the man who had defeated the Democratic candidate. The FBI was using its falsified investigation to influence the 2016 election—even after it had been decided.

The Flynn case is related to the Ivie case, because they are both examples of corrupt, biased FBI leadership using agents for political purposes. In the Flynn case, the FBI was trying to tie Flynn to a Russian conspiracy to influence the 2016 election. A few months later, after Flynn was ensnared in this web of deception, Robert Mueller was appointed special counsel to find more evidence of the ties between the Russians and the Trump campaign. The entire investigation was built upon a false salacious dossier paid for by the Democratic Party and the Hillary Clinton campaign, and was ironically aided by some Russian participants.

The FBI does a tremendous job of investigating thousands of cases involving terrorism, sex trafficking, kidnapping, child pornography, murder and organized crime. But when politicians exert undue influence on the FBI in cases with political implications, the reputation of the entire Bureau suffers.

To help summarize this chapter, we turn again to Andrew McCarthy, who successfully prosecuted the terrorists who committed the first bombing of the World Trade Center in 1993. He recently delivered a speech about how Obama used the FBI and Department of Justice to try to influence the 2016 election, and then incited unprecedented harassment of the election's winner.

> The Obama administration had an eight-year record of politicizing intelligence and using law enforcement processes to punish political enemies and scapegoats. So when it got to the Hillary campaign losing ultimately to Trump, and they needed a rationale for why they lost, why did anyone think that they wouldn't be able to come up with one? Because this is what they do.[15]

Four years earlier, Obama was exerting the same kind of corrupt influence over the presidential election that was held during his first term in office. In the autumn of 2012, Obama successfully shielded the public at large from the truth about all his scandals—including the murder of Border Patrol Agent Nicholas Ivie.

27

Eyewitness Account of Arrest of Suspects

"I really hope that someday if something happens to me, somebody will put out whatever they think is the truth of the situation." Border Patrol agent, on why he spoke out on the life and death of Nick Ivie

2017 to present
Interviews conducted in Cochise County, Arizona
For the first time in his career, he heard that agents were being hunted

Andrew Carlton, who knew Nick Ivie as a fellow agent who had a profound influence on his career, was on duty at the border the morning of the shooting incident. He arrived at the border after the fatal shooting incident—as a large contingent of law enforcement officers searched for suspects and evidence.

Carlton said there were many reasons he and other agents did not believe the narrative that the FBI presented. One of the principal reasons was that agents—especially Nick Ivie—would always exert extreme caution rather than shoot a fellow agent.

In interviews for this book, Carlton revealed new information about the shooting incident, some of which is being released to the public here for the first time.

Carlton said one of the most stunning elements of the Ivie case was that Agent Gracie Borjas reported on her radio that after the smugglers shot at them, they were then hunting for the Border Patrol agents.

Carlton heard information on this rare scenario from other agents when he came on duty. Hearing that report from an agent who came very close to being killed pushed the manhunt up to the highest level of urgency.[1]

"Gracie heard people talking in Spanish—that they were looking for her now. And she turned off her radio and hid," Carlton said, recalling what he heard from other agents, as he arrived at the scene.

"So we had agents in the area with the mindset that we have agents that are being hunted by whoever was up there. We were assuming they were the drug cartel, the smugglers, and that they were trying to find the agents so they could finish them off."

On the morning of Tuesday, October 2, Carlton was driving in to work to begin his shift.

"I texted my supervisor and asked him what was going on, because I got passed by a bunch of undercover vehicles running with their lights on," Carlton recalled. "So I sent my supervisor a text and asked him what was going on, and he called me and told me that it was Nick and that he was gone."

He then called a couple of his friends who had been working that night and asked them whether they had heard anything.

"And everybody was responding to the area," Carlton said, adding that agents from the Naco station, to the west of the shooting scene, and, the Douglas station, to the east, were rushing to the area where the shooting had occurred. "We were flooding it with as many people as we could because we had been told that there were still bodies in play that they were looking for."

After picking up his green-and-white patrol vehicle and speeding down Highway 80, Carlton turned off the highway onto Paul Spur Road, headed south on the road that runs along the prominent limestone quarry, then onto Border Road, an unpaved roadway.

The agents turned north from the border onto a set of tracks running north of an east-west railroad bed, formerly carrying Southern Pacific tracks.

"We parked it out there, out in the desert," Carlton said. "We parked in the smuggler's tunnel area, west of the Christiansen ranch and almost directly south of Nick's saddle."

The ground where Ivie was killed has been known as "Nick's Saddle" since that night. There is a memorial to the slain agent on the mile-high mountain ridge, with his name and the date of his death stamped in a white metal cross.

The Christiansen ranch house, lying just north of the border and southeast of the saddle, was unoccupied at the time of this incident. It was the only structure on the south side of the saddle in the immediate area.

Carlton said the radio transmission from Agent Borjas was a highly unusual element to this incident, unlike anything he had encountered in his career.

"For most of the agents, it was surreal," he said. "There are shootings on the border on a fairly regular basis, but this idea that there were Border Patrol agents up there, they were being hunted, that part was surreal for a lot of agents."

By the time Carlton arrived on the scene, the two surviving agents had been airlifted off the mountain.

But law enforcement officers on the scene had heard that the female Border Patrol agent had radioed in that unusual alarm. She said suspects were hunting for her. Members of BORTAC, the Border Patrol tactical unit he met on the ground, confirmed to Carlton what he had already heard from other agents.

"The way the radio traffic went out was that the people who were shooting at Nick, Dave, and Gracie were trying to locate the other agents. That's the way they took it from what Gracie said.

"So we had agents in the area with the mindset that we have agents that are being hunted by whoever was up there. We were assuming they were the drug cartel, the smugglers, and that they were trying to find the agents so they could finish them off. That's the way the Border Patrol agents were responding."

Carlton said that agents from Douglas, who were outstanding trackers, were tracking suspects from the saddle in a south to southwest direction.

"They were pushing sign and they would update on the radio every so often that they were still on sign or which way it was heading," Carlton said.

Carlton witnessed the arrest of the two suspects on the south side of the border, an incident covered briefly in an earlier chapter.

He said the apprehended suspects were found in the general area where the trackers were working.[2]

"It's a very big area. From the area where Nick's saddle is, saying that the suspects went southwest, you could throw a lot of things into that area. There wasn't one direction they had to take. It isn't like they popped up in a different area altogether. But it wasn't the line agents or the agents that were pushing sign that led to these people. They were picked up by aerial surveillance."

Carlton said he never heard whether those suspects were connected with the shooting or whether they just happened to be in the area at the time.

"The Border Patrol never denied that two guys were arrested," Carlton said. **"They just denied that they were involved."**

It was widely accepted within the agency that the suspects were apprehended by BORTAC agents, members of the Border Patrol tactical team, and turned over to Mexican officials. Despite later denials that the BORTAC helicopter had ever landed in Mexico, it would make no sense for U.S. federal agents to arrest Mexican nationals on American soil, then hand them over to Mexican law enforcement authorities for detention and arrest.

This agent's account of their capture meshes well with news accounts and other information obtained by this author.

"Our station management told us they were being interviewed by U.S. officials," Carlton said, adding that was about one week after the shooting—after the FBI released its statement that nobody else was involved but agents.

The FBI was the lead agency in the investigation, so it is reasonable to believe they conducted that interview. It would also follow that the FBI would have obtained fingerprints and DNA from the suspects at the time the interview or interviews were conducted.

"The Border Patrol itself has a Mexican liaison unit, the Border Patrol agents that work with Mexican officials," Carlton said. "So they go down to Mexico on a fairly regular basis. So it wouldn't be outside my expectations for our Mexican liaison officials to be involved either."

But Carlton said he and other line agents were never given information on the suspects or on anyone else who might have been involved.

After the station manager reported that the suspects were interviewed about one week after the shooting, Border Patrol officials denied that those suspects were involved in the incident.

"They said nobody else was involved," Carlton said. "There was nobody else present up there, and it was an agent-on-agent shooting."

Carlton said he believes there has to be a coverup because they're not giving out some of the information on the case.

"There are pieces of the puzzle missing," Carlton said.

Agents would rather die than kill another agent

It did not make sense to Border Patrol Agent Carlton that Nick Ivie would start to shoot blindly at anyone—when he had known that other agents were coming up to meet him at that location and had just been in radio contact with them.

"That doesn't make any sense to any agent, let alone agents that know Nick personally," Carlton said. "That would never happen. That could never happen.

"Because most people I know who do this job would rather die than kill another agent or have another agent killed because of them. I don't know how I could live with myself if I shot and killed another agent."

Carlton said he could accept that it was a friendly fire situation between Nick and Dave under other circumstances.

"I could easily see it if there was a crossfire. But saying that they opened fire on each other and there's nobody else there, I can't

believe that. Not with knowing the distances they were using and the amount of light that was out there."

Carlton said it did not make any sense that Nick would just blindly start firing—especially at a distance at which he should be able to identify people under a bright full moon. Border Patrol agents were easy to distinguish from smugglers, because they wore uniforms, specific kinds of hats, carried sidearms, and were not particularly quiet because of their gear."

As for the two other agents, Johnson and Borjas, they were not trying to conceal themselves.

"You could see up there. If I could see from here to there (pointing from one end of a large motel room to the door), I could see who it is."

Carlton was asked about one possible scenario that was presented to the public in the form of an article by former Border Patrol official Ron Colburn. In that article, in which the retired official said he had access to materials from the FBI and other law enforcement sources, the theory was advanced that Ivie had been hiding when Johnson walked right past him. Then they started shooting at each other.

According to that article, initially published in a trade journal and a newspaper, Ivie was surprised by the other agents, because he did not expect them to arrive so soon. So when they arrived unexpectedly, they began shooting at each other.

"That doesn't make any sense," Carlton said. "I always go back to a very simple thing. I put myself in the situation. This isn't the first time I heard Nick was hiding, that he took a position of cover. And that he opened fire. But at 30 feet, 25 feet, 15 feet, and you don't know I'm there. There's no way I miss."[3]

But Carlton said he does not believe that Nick would have shot at anyone and missed at close range, as reported in the Colburn article.

"He has qualified with his weapon," Carlton said. "He has been in over four years and has had a minimum of four quals (qualifying tests) a year. So that's 16 quals plus basic qual in the academy; and we shot hundreds of times in the academy. So you have a competent shooter at a close range and he's not able to kill him with the first surprise shot.

"That's just not believable at all."

In the government's unofficial version of what happened—which has been published instead of any official word from the FBI—Nick is hiding when Agent Johnson walks straight toward him, without seeing Nick. Then Nick opens fire, without either agent saying one word.

Carlton said that in another version he heard, Dave was walking away, but turned around and still didn't see Nick.

"So Nick waits and waits and pulls the trigger and misses?" Carlton said. "Or he shoots him in the butt? He is coming toward him, and he shoots him in the butt?"

Law enforcement officers are trained to shoot to kill. So how does this story fit in with the way Border Patrol officers actually operate?

"First of all, every Border Patrol shooting is deadly force. With American law enforcement, we don't shoot to wound people," Carlton said. "You hear all the time from the people who are armchair quarterbacking about law enforcement: Oh, he could have shot him in the arm or the hand, or he could have shot him in the leg.

"Then you are talking about a much smaller target than shooting at center mass, which is where we are taught to shoot. So you're giving yourself a very big target, rather than a very small target."

Officers are taught to shoot at the "center mass" of the body, roughly from the shoulders to the navel.

"You have to be in fear of your life or the life of another or of grievous bodily injury to shoot somebody. But you can't just shoot somebody to wing them."

Because of the ballistic evidence found on the scene—and the theory that nobody else was involved but agents—Ivie is accused of shooting at a fellow agent 10 times, from a distance of 15 to 20 feet. Those 10 shots resulted in two wounds, one to the agent's buttock, another to his ankle.

Carlton said he does not believe that scenario, that Ivie would be such a poor shot with his pistol.

"So if Nick was hiding, I have to assume he was low. And you're aiming for center mass in the chest, so you're aiming up. So you're not going to shoot down here. From the angle of what you're shooting at, you're not going to hit that low."

During qualification tests with pistols, agents shoot at distances of 25 yards, or 75 feet, roughly the distance from a free throw line to the distant backboard on a basketball court.

"So you're aiming at center mass of the target," Carlton said. "And you'll see people miss about a foot low. You could draw a circle and about a foot or so outside the center mass is where most of those rounds are going.

"And that's at 75 feet. If at 75 feet, you're missing by about a foot, maybe a little over a foot. If this is your point of aim, and you hit someone in the butt and the ankle, you're talking about two or four feet, the distance that you missed by from 20 feet. That is a huge, huge miss."

The Border Patrol-supported article published in 2013, which offered an explanation of the shooting, put Agents Ivie and Johnson even closer than that. The article said that Johnson walked by Ivie, and Ivie opened fire.

The scenario published under Ron Colburn's name does not make sense to Carlton.

"So Dave's just a big walking target, and Nick's got that first surprise shot. And close. I don't see it happening, if you get that first shot. Especially if you fire three off in rapid succession."

Remember, in his FBI interview two days after the incident, Agent Johnson said the shooter fired three shots in rapid succession from 15 to 20 feet away. Then Johnson yelled, "Hey, hey, hey, hey!" at him. Then the shooter fired about seven more shots, including two that hit him, in the buttock and the ankle.

"Keep in mind, Border Patrol agents don't hide under blankets," **Carlton said. "Border Patrol agents don't carry blankets around** **with them to cover themselves up. It's just one of those things that** **just doesn't happen. Nobody has a blanket with them."**

Johnson told the FBI agents he saw someone flip a blanket off of himself right before the firing started. He was on the edge of the saddle and never walked by anyone.

Carlton said that it is not unusual for an agent to work alone, as Ivie was doing as he hiked toward the saddle. In this case, Ivie had been running a little late to the station, so rather than leave on patrol with other horse patrol team members, he drove out to the field in a green-and-white Border Patrol SUV.

"We very often have to work by ourselves," Carlton said. "They like you to take a partner when it's feasible. It's just not always feasible."

Carlton said the Mule Mountain territory near the border was an area Ivie liked to work.

"He heard that bug (motion sensor) go off, so he went and responded," Carlton said. "That happens. That happened to me just the other night. My team was tied up with something. I responded on foot and helped out some other agents."

Carlton explained how the radios were working between Agent Ivie and the other two agents. Basically, when you have line-of-sight, with no obstruction between two agents, then the radios go line-of-sight.

"If I am on one side of the mountain and you are on the other side of the mountain, the mountain is between us, there is no line of sight," Carlton said. "That's when the radios use the repeaters. My radio has to talk to a repeater that is over here, then your radio talks to a repeater on this side. Then the signal gets bounced together."

Carlton was asked to address the allegation that the friendly fire incident arose partly from poor radio communication between the two agents. Carlton was aware that Johnson said in his FBI interview that his radio was working, except for one momentary failure.

"Generally in the Border Patrol, radio communication is a problem," Carlton said. "But in that area, from that night, the guys who I talked to who were on, were talking about listening to the radio communications. And they said it was kind of surreal. So how could they say that it was surreal to hear what was going on if they can't hear the radio communications?"

Carlton said the officials who advanced the friendly fire narrative used the momentary problem and "spun it into something bigger."

Carlton was reminded that Agent Borjas informed Agent Ivie that she and Agent Johnson were one-tenth of a mile out from the sensor, to which Agent Ivie responded, "10-4." She relayed the information from Agent Johnson to her partner.

"And a tenth of a mile is not that far," Carlton said. "And up there you can see for a tenth of a mile. You can see for quite a way.

"It doesn't make any sense when you go out there and see. The only way he knows he's a tenth of a mile is that he's using GPS coordinates. Tenth of a mile is very precise.

"So it seems like everything was working. If things aren't working, that would add to the confusion. When everything is working, I know exactly where this guy is. It's a very precise measurement."

Carlton said Nick knew where the sensor was.

"He was right there. He knew: I'm going to be seeing these guys any second. Any second, these guys are going to be right here. And then to start shooting in that direction. You wouldn't."

As an example of how Border Patrol agents operate, Carlton said he was out recently with some of the mountain team agents.

"There was nothing going on at the mountain, so they came out to the river where we were at, on horses," Carlton recalled. "We had guys walking north and I'm walking south. And there was some confusion about if they were on the correct sign, where exactly they were."

Carlton knew exactly where he was, because he had just exited a road at a specific intersection. Then the other agents told him their GPS coordinates. He told them, "I am directly north of you, this far, and I am headed south." They responded that they had heard his message.

One of the main reasons agents constantly share their locations with other agents is to *prevent* friendly fire situations.

"When they give out an affirmative that they understand, that this guy is a third of a mile north of us, if something spooks between us, you have to be careful of how you respond," Carlton said. "Because you know for sure there's an agent right there."

Carlton said the fact that Agent Borjas informed Agent Ivie as to the location of the two agents strips away all credibility to the theory that "Nick just didn't know where they were."

Carlton was asked whether he would coordinate an operation in which two groups of agents were approaching a single destination in order to arrive at the destination at about the same time as other agents.

"Not necessarily try to coordinate so we arrive there at the same time," Carlton said. "But if you have people (illegals) coming in, you try to squeeze them in. These two agents came in from the south, and he came in from the north. That way, if they run, you have more of a chance to catch the group, or at least some of the group."

As the illegal border crossers in this case were being "squeezed in" from two directions, they had several distinct advantages, including the high ground, from where they could see the approaching agents.

Nighttime Favors Those Who Operate Without Light

The smugglers also had another advantage, which might have played a key role in the outcome of this encounter.

When Agent Ivie arrived at the saddle, he was using his flashlight to look for signs of recent human activity.

"It is nighttime, and the eyes of the illegals are already adjusted to the dark," Carlton said. "So you're walking around with a flashlight, and you're one guy, and your cone of visibility is just where that light is shining. And now you have people that are moving outside that arc of light."

As Agent Ivie was ambushed by one or more illegal aliens, and he still had his flashlight on, he would be able to clearly see only what was in that cone of light.

"He can't see anything else around him, because his eyes are blinded by his own light," Carlton said. "If he still had his flashlight on, he could see only what is in that cone of light."

With multiple suspects at the scene, they would have seen his flashlight beam and easily attacked him from outside of the light.

"We all know this. When you're working with a flashlight at night, you're supposed to be scanning all over the place, because once your eyes are dependent on that light, you can see only what's in that actual beam of light. And even if it was a moonlit night, his vision is dependent on his flashlight until his eyes adapt to not having the flashlight.

"And he is trying to find guys who are moving around in the dark, who are not using a flashlight. They are not dependent on that light. Their ability to see the entire scene is not restricted to that cone of light. That might be a reason they were able to get the drop on Nick, because he just wasn't able to see outside the frame of his own flashlight.

"I don't know about this specific time, but I know that happens all the time. When you are using a flashlight, when you turn it off, you are essentially blind for a little bit."

Carlton was asked whether it could also have been a factor that an agent would not be expecting to be attacked by smugglers. There was a possibility—however unlikely—that Ivie confronted the smugglers before they attacked him. In most cases, illegal aliens do not react violently when confronted by Border Patrol agents.

"I think that goes agent to agent. When you're up there, for me, I always try to come out more aggressively. You can bring it down. If I see somebody, and you are giving them commands, and they are obeying your commands, you can always bring the level down.

"But if you start out, 'Hey buddy, show me your hands,' it takes too long to react to somebody."

Carlton said the best way to handle an arrest scenario is to cause suspects to react to you.

"If I think that he is being a nice guy, so I'm going to be a nice guy, and he has already made up his mind that he's going to fight—then he is acting, and I'm reacting to him," Carlton said. "For law enforcement, that's not a good situation to be in. You want to come in and control the situation.

"You want them to react to you. You're acting; they're reacting. That means you act faster, and they have to react to it."

People will often say: "The cops came out, and they were being too aggressive," Carlton said. They don't realize the reason you do that is so suspects have to react to how you are acting.

"With Nick's personality, Nick was almost always reacting," Carlton said. "Nick was a very laid-back person.

"This is just conjecture. But he might have seen one, focused on that one, and not assumed it was a dangerous situation, not assumed that there were other people right there [and] that they were going to jump him."

Agents who have been on the force for three or four years have made hundreds or even thousands of arrests, with few turning into physical altercations.

"So you get into the bad habit of thinking: He is just an alien, he's going to do whatever I say," Carlton said. "It's all very possible,

if you're considering different scenarios, that they did take away Nick's gun. That they attacked him and forced his gun out of his hand. It's all very possible.

"Maybe their intention wasn't to shoot him. Maybe their intention was to escape. Then those other agents closed in on him, and then they felt trapped. Who knows? It's all very possible."

Border Patrol Agents Don't Aim for the Head — But Cartel Killers Do

American law enforcement agents are trained to aim for the chest and abdominal area in most cases. But it is not uncommon for homicide victims to die from head shots.

Agent Carlton was asked whether cartel operatives were known to shoot people in the head.

"Generally speaking, if it is a point-blank thing, and they are assassinating the person, they shoot you in the face," Carlton said. "If it's a shootout, whether it's a Mexican, an American, or anyone else in the world, anyone who's received training through the military or law enforcement, they shoot center mass. Because that's the largest probability of hitting your target.

"And there is plenty of evidence to suggest that a lot of drug smugglers are ex-military. There is plenty of evidence to suggest that they are at the very least competent with weapons, have some sort of training. So if it is a situation where it's a shootout you'd expect to see center mass shots.

"If it was an assassination, I would expect to see a head shot."

Carlton said it is not uncommon for an agent to encounter a drug smuggler by training his flashlight and gun on him, as was possibly done in this case. Ivie was found dead with his flashlight near his hand, and his pistol near his flashlight.

"If they're close enough to grab the gun from him, they're close enough to shoot him in the face," Carlton said. "If I'm 25 feet away, I can't grab your gun from you. I might be able to shoot you in the head, but I'm not going to be able to get the gun from you.

"It's kind of a likely scenario. The way things likely worked in this area. He sees one (smuggler). He's focused on that one. And the others took advantage of that fact. It's opportunistic."

Carlton said he had no information to suggest that smugglers "operate with tactics in mind of ambushing us."

"Most times when we have agent assaults or agent-involved shootings, it's all based on whatever presents itself in that situation," Carlton said.

Carlton was shown the Facebook pages of the two suspects who were arrested in connection with the Ivie killing. Most of the entries on their pages were made before the incident. The pages displayed photos of AK-47 rifles and arrests of suspects by Mexican military forces. Mexican civilians are prohibited from owning firearms, with few exceptions.

These were the social media pages of the men who were arrested by the Border Patrol agents who landed the helicopter just south of the border. As reported earlier in this book, a woman reported in a Facebook post that those two men, both relatives of hers, were still being held in a Mexican jail 13 days after they were arrested in connection with the murder of Agent Ivie.

When asked his response to the Facebook posts, Carlton said it was likely that those men were engaged in some illegal activity on the border, since they were caught at that spot. However, he said that would not directly tie them to the saddle where Nick was shot.

"The fact that the Mexican authorities aren't releasing them (supposedly after they were cleared of charges in the Ivie case), Mexican authorities don't do things like we do," Carlton said.

However, Carlton also said those two men *could* have been involved in the shooting.

"It is just as likely that these guys were involved and it's a coverup as it is that these guys aren't involved, but they're involved in some other illegal activity, and that the Mexican government was holding them for that illegal activity," he said.

The fact that those men were being held in custody in a Mexican jail did not necessarily indicate anything.

"The fact that the Mexican government is holding them and not letting them go, that's kind of a Mexican government thing," Carlton said.

He said one possible scenario was that the suspects were running dope without the permission of the cartels.

"The cartels run the local Mexican governments," Carlton said. "These two guys, if they were running stuff without the cartel's permission, they're going to be punished by the government in place of the cartels for running stuff when they shouldn't have."

It was also possible that they worked for the cartel, but the cartel was not happy with them. The cartel leaders do not appreciate mistakes. Shooting at Border Patrol agents could be considered a grievous mistake, because of the unwanted attention it brings to the cartel.

"We've caught mules and guides before that have told us they get beat up and threatened and their families get beat up if they lose a load or get caught. So there are a lot of possibilities."

Carlton was asked what he thought about the fact that the FBI never released any information on the suspects, despite the fact that many media outlets reported that two suspects were arrested, and that the FBI collected DNA and fingerprints from them.

"If it is a government coverup, they don't gain anything by releasing information clearing these guys any more than saying these guys were involved," Carlton said. **"If it is a coverup, they want to put out no information whatsoever.**

"If these guys were involved, that ruins their narrative that there was nobody else up there. If they weren't involved, it's going to get people asking more questions again. If they stay quiet, their hope is for people to stop caring, to move on."

Carlton said that he personally wanted the FBI to release information on what really happened, based on all the evidence that they had.

"I want to know the truth. If these guys aren't involved, cool— say it. If these guys are involved, let's move forward and deal with it. That's the way I look at it. There is only one reason to put out no information whatsoever. And that's to get people to forget."

Supervisor to Agents:
Keep Quiet or Lose Your Job and Face Charges

Carlton said the first thing his supervisors officially told the line agents, shortly after the incident, was to order them to refrain from giving their opinions on the incident to reporters.

"We were told to wait for the official story to come out, wait for the official party line," Carlton recalled. "That was given in our musters, our preshift musters, where they disseminate information. They had several people come in through our musters. At my station, it was the station management. PACs and APACs, the agents in charge at the station and his assistants, second and third in command.

"Any time there's an incident like this, they come out and say not to say anything against what's handed down, the official version. I don't believe they ever issued a memo. They like to keep things like that word of mouth. That way we can't track it back to anybody.

"And they try to come at it with an angle that 'You don't know the facts.' Then they won't give you any facts. They say, 'Wait for the facts to come out.'"

This keeps a cold, wet blanket on any conversation about the incident—especially with the media or any investigative authorities—such as Congressional committees.

"When things first come out, and you're waiting on them, and you're counting on them to learn in an honorable fashion the right thing to do, they give you something that is just a big book of lies."

In response to questions from line agents, Border Patrol leaders told them to not spread rumors and to not to question their version.

"They threaten you with not being promotable, and they threaten you with that you could lose your job. They always throw in that it could contain criminal consequences."

Although there was no word to the public about the supposed ongoing investigation, supervisors told Border Patrol agents that the FBI was hard at work uncovering the facts.

"At the station level, people kept asking questions," Carlton said. "So regardless of how long the official investigation took, they tell us at the station level that things are still ongoing. That they are still looking at all the data, things like that.

"They absolutely were not giving us information. It was a process of telling us: 'Wait for all the facts to come out. Wait for all the facts to come out. We'll give you all the information.' It begins to look like a stall tactic, so people just get bored of it.

"At that time, we were waiting for information to come out. And when they finally did release information, everything they released was that Nick overreacted, that Nick shot without seeing what was going on around him, and that Nick shot first. Nick opened fire on the other two agents, who didn't even know exactly where he was yet.

"And for a lot of us, that just didn't make any sense. And then, when they gave us their official story, and people started saying that it didn't make any sense.

"Then they just went back to, 'This is what we're saying. And don't contradict what the official investigation says.'"

Carlton said one reason some agents believe the official narrative is a coverup is because when Brian Terry was killed less than two years earlier, the government came out "very quickly" with a false narrative.

There was one important difference between the Terry case — which led to the exposure of the Fast and Furious government gun-running scandal — and the Ivie case. Terry had other agents with him who stood up for him and told the truth about what occurred.

"Because the rest of his team stood up and said: 'No, this is *not* what happened. *This* is what happened.'

"And that was hard to refute. They had already started the coverup. They had already put out this huge narrative that it was Brian going off and trying to be a Rambo and a hero and all this other stuff. They were already pushing that, all the way down to the station levels.

"Then when his team came out and said, 'That was not it at all,' there was no way for them to backtrack. They were too deep into the coverup. It was a blatant coverup at that point."

So when the government released a false narrative on Ivie, that was already familiar to many of the agents.

"And then with Nick, all these same things started happening. They blamed the one guy who can't say anything to defend himself. And everybody else for the most part has hushed up on it.

"The difference between the Terry incident and the Ivie incident was that the other people involved with the Terry incident had the strength to stand up and say, 'No, that's not what happened.'"

Carlton said he understands why people who have information on the Ivie case that contradicts the official narrative have remained silent for several years.

"I would be able to look at someone and say, yeah, they were afraid for their jobs," Carlton said. "But if there are people who have information, they need to come forward."

Carlton said he had reached the point where he felt free to speak about what he knew about the Ivie case.

"My view on it is that after they've given you an order to lie, that's not a legal order and you're no longer obligated to follow that order."

28

"That's Just Not Believable at All."

"Until you can see that guy and know that's a bad guy, you just cannot shoot."
Nick's friend tells why he does not believe the FBI's story

Part 2 of Carlton's testimony on the life and death of his friend.
2017 to present
Cochise County, Arizona

Carlton said that Border Patrol agents have been trained to perform only in a way that they could justify afterward.

"You aren't going to be able to justify shooting at a sound you can't identify or a shape you can't identify. You would not do something like shoot at something you can't identify."

Agents have been continually reminded of this policy.

"It's drilled into you in the academy," Carlton said. "It's drilled into you in all our firearms training, that you will have to justify what you do with your firearm, in particular. No Border Patrol agent is ever going to want to go to court and be grilled on the stand for your firearm use when you can't identify what you're shooting at."

In response to TV news stories presented in May 2017, which questioned the veracity of the original government statements, the Border Patrol has issued public and in-house responses to those allegations, including details of the shooting incident that have surfaced.

Agent David Johnson's statement—in which he cried out "Hey, hey, hey, hey!" after hearing three shots, and then was shot at several more times—was explained away by the Border Patrol brass, in order to fit the narrative of Ivie as the persistent shooter.

One Border Patrol agent, not Agent Carlton, was told that Agent Ivie was probably deafened by his first shots and did not hear Agent Johnson yelling at him.

But Agent Johnson said in his FBI interview that he was just about 15 or 20 feet away from whoever was shooting at him. Johnson said in that he saw the silhouette of a man with a smuggler's pack before the shooting started, and never saw Agent Ivie at the scene.

Carlton said he does not believe that Agent Ivie would have been unable to hear someone yelling at him after firing his pistol a few times.

"There's a phenomenon when you are under a high-stress situation: auditory exclusion," Carlton said, adding that he understands that there is a drastic difference between the way people respond to live shooting incidents, compared to training sessions.

He has read accounts of law enforcement officers involved in live shooting incidents.

"I've read several of these interviews, and they all say the same thing: If you're out practicing, you'd better have ear protection, because it's going to be the loudest thing in the world.

"And when you're in the middle of a gunfight, it just sounds like 'pop, pop, pop.' There's no ringing in your ears, there's no anything, although you have no ear protection. Your body just shuts down that portion of your hearing."

In many cases, including Johnson's, officers involved in a shooting later say they can't even remember how many rounds they've fired.

"That's partly because they're not hearing that gun go off. It tends to be a much more subdued sound," Carlton said. "In training, if you shoot a .40 cal. out in the desert, your ears are going to ring; it's going to be really loud. And you go into a real-life situation and have to shoot it, and you barely hear a thing."

Carlton believes the scene actually could have played out in a variety of ways. Perhaps one of the illegal aliens decided he was not going to be arrested.

"It might have been that the others were willing to go along with whatever happened, but one guy decided: 'No, not today'. And he decided to fight, and everybody else was like 'Well, we're in it now.'"

"So it became a brawl. That is the easiest way I see that it happened.

"There are probably 10 different scenarios that are more believable and more probable than the narrative that they put out. I can't emphasize enough that nobody would shoot at something that they can't see for no reason.

"So where Dave [Johnson] started shooting, he couldn't really identify, he knew where the shots were coming from. . . . You shoot at the flash at that point. That's perfectly reasonable; that's well within tactics and training.

"But from Nick's perspective, where there's no threat, there's no immediate danger, he would not open fire."

"This isn't an active combat zone. . . . We see people with rifles."

Carlton was reminded that the unofficial story was that Nick saw someone with a rifle. So naturally, he shot at him. Agent Johnson did have a rifle.

"Right, but we see people with rifles. That isn't something that is completely foreign for Border Patrol agents out there. Just seeing someone with a gun—and I think this is why their narrative starts to fall apart.

"Because every lie depends on a previous lie. He didn't know they were coming, so then he saw a guy with a gun. And that's why he freaked out."

But the true record showed that Agent Ivie was communicating well with Agents Borjas and Johnson—up until a few minutes before Agents Johnson and Borjas arrived on the scene.

"So if we already know that they've been communicating with each other, and then he sees a guy with a gun, you're going to call out; you're going to identify.

"You might not say, 'Hey, Border Patrol,' but you are going to say, 'Who are you?' or 'Hey, Dave.'"

If he said 'Hey, Dave,' and doesn't get the response he intended, then he would try something else.

"But you are going to try to get some type of communication before you start shooting," Carlton said. **"This isn't an active combat zone, where it's just triggers free, and you can shoot whatever you want whenever you want."**

Although the Mule Mountains and other desert wilderness areas are known for their smuggling routes, there are other people who still use them for legal purposes—including many who carry firearms.

"We know that people hike around these places. A lot of them come armed. I think it would be a poor idea for you to go hiking through these mountains at night with a long arm. But just a few weeks ago we had some hunters who didn't get out of our area before dark. So they were still walking back to their vehicle with the long guns."

"And the agents in the area were very, very careful to identify who they were. Before they even went in to make contact with the hunters, they made sure they weren't walking into something ridiculous."

"They gathered all the information they could before they drove in toward these people, and then they were very aware of how these guys were responding. That's just part of what you do. You can't just start shooting at people."

Seeing an Armed Man in Arizona Is Not an Excuse for Shooting Him

Andrew Carlton said that, in the state of Arizona, you might as well assume that everyone has a gun.

Carlton was asked: If you saw someone at night, up there in the mountains with a rifle, what would you do?

"If you see a guy with a rifle, and you don't have a rifle, you might choose to stay quiet right then," Carlton said. "Because you're automatically going to be outgunned getting into a firefight."[1]

Carlton said he found it "real hard" to believe Nick would open fire, just because he saw someone with a rifle.

"Even at night, even if he thought (the suspect) was working a dope load, until you can identify him, you can't shoot."

Carlton knew his friend as "a very tenderhearted guy."

"He was not one of these guys who was a hardened combat vet who might shoot and deal with the consequences later. I don't think Nick could have pulled the trigger like that and dealt with the consequences."

From his knowledge of Nick's character, he believes he was much more likely to get shot because he reacted too slow, or he underreacted to the suspects at the saddle.

"I think if it were me, and I saw somebody who had a rifle, I would wait until I were in a position so the rifle is not aimed at me, and I would get real loud. I would go lights on and tell him, 'Drop it.' All the cop things you see in every movie.

"You get loud, you get aggressive, you try to dominate the situation so that they feel overwhelmed. It's something we call officer presence. But in none of those situations do you just start shooting.

"Until you can see that guy and know that's a bad guy, you just cannot shoot."

Border Patrol agents carry their M4 rifles slung in a downward position, the barrel facing the ground, where it can be raised quickly to a firing position.

"Where the barrel is, is very important. If the barrel is pointed in your direction, even if it's low, all you've got to do is bring it up. If it's low, but it's pointed in your general direction, it would be a smarter thing to stay quiet till the guy moves.

"Nick would have to be on that side of the rifle to have an immediate threat."

The body position of the armed subject is very important, when assessing the threat level.

You would have to assume in the hypothetical situation set forth in the official narrative that Nick felt threatened.

"If Nick started yelling, and the subject brought his rifle up, that would have changed the scenario again, and an agent might start shooting. But none of that has been reported by anybody to be facts in this scenario."

Remember, Agent Johnson reported that he was carrying his rifle in the downward pointing position at the time someone opened fire on him. It was not until after he was fired upon about 10 times—and was wounded in two places—that he lifted his rifle to his shoulder and fired in the direction of the muzzle flashes.

Agent Carlton was asked, "In a scenario such as the one that occurred at the time Agent Ivie was killed, if you saw one or more illegal aliens at the saddle, what would you say to them?"

"I always start with, 'Border Patrol.' In Spanish it's *'Patrulla Fronteriza.'* Then in Spanish I say, "I'm a Border Patrol agent. Don't move. Show me your hands."

Would you have your light and gun out?

"Generally, no. If I'm cutting sign, I've got my light. I'm looking around. And you see somebody.

"Before you do anything, you say, 'I'm a Border Patrol agent. Don't move. Show me your hands.'

"Generally, when somebody's hiding, you want to see their hands right away, because when they're hiding, their hands are hidden. A lot of times, they are lying down, with their head on their hands, or their hands under their chest, or their hands under their shoulders, like in a pushup position.

"And you want them to show you their hands, and you want them to not get up. So you'll shine your light on them and generally, you'll have your hand on your gun, and you're watching what they're doing, and if they're following your commands.

"For instance, if a guy has his hands underneath him, and you say, 'show me your hands,' and he doesn't, he might be hiding something. Or he might be getting ready to spring up.

"So, you want him to put his hands up so he can't react as fast, and he can't hide whatever he has in his hands. He might have something concealed on him. Generally, you ask after that if he has any weapons.

"Everybody always says 'no'. Every guy I've ever pulled a knife off of has said, no, he didn't have any weapons. Part of that is if they're just a regular alien and part of a farming community, they don't consider their pocketknife to be a weapon.

"They could be not registering at that moment that what they have is a weapon. Or if he's a criminal doing bad things, he's going to lie."

At what point would you withdraw your gun from your holster?

"I've pulled my gun right from the beginning during scenarios, and I've let it stay in the holster during the entire time. It's a feel-by-feel thing.

"In each scenario, you go by the information you've been given. If you have any inclination that it's related to narcotics, you assume that they're going to be armed. So as soon as I see somebody that I think is involved with narcotics smuggling, generally, I'll pull my gun out.

"When you draw, you don't draw with your finger on the trigger. You're giving yourself that time to assess the situation, so that you don't do something stupid and overreact. Or as you're drawing, [you might accidentally] squeeze off a round. There's no safeties on the pistols."

Border Patrol agents carry thumb-break holsters, safety devices that keep weapons in place. This prevents accidental dropping of the weapon and makes it more difficult for anyone other than the agent to withdraw it.

"I have a Black Hawk holster, so on mine it has a thumb release and then a release that's up on the slide. It's called a trigger release, but it's on the slide portion of the gun. So you have two things that you have to unlock. As you're putting your hand over it, it has a button on the side that drops the bail, and then you pull your gun out.

"But you always pull your gun out with your finger along the slide, not in the trigger well. Because there is a good chance you'll put a round through your own leg if you do that. So, it is our training to not have our finger on the trigger yet."

Carlton said there is no hard and fast rule as to when to draw one's gun.

"I've seen people arrest the load drivers, with the drug loads that come over, without ever drawing a weapon. I've seen people draw their gun out for just a regular alien, and they're not wrong to do that either.

"I have done that many times myself, especially when they have that hesitation. If I'm out there, especially if I'm out there by myself, and I say, 'Show me your hand,' and they either pull their hands in tighter, or they reach for anything, I'm definitely going to draw my gun.

"But there's nothing that says you have to. It's all on your own instinct. It's all on your own personal assessment of whatever scenario you're in. But there is not one policy on when you can or cannot have your gun out."

"Nick was very laid back. Everybody that knew Nick kind of agreed that Nick reacted too cautiously to things."

Nobody just starts shooting. Agents do not want to end up in court.

Carlton said Border Patrol agents and law enforcement officers in general are not looking to kill anybody.

"If we can deescalate, we will. Generally speaking, in my opinion, shooting is the result of the other person's actions, not yours.

"You're responsible, but somebody else gets to decide if you acted reasonably or not.

"**So, if you're not absolutely sure that you should be pulling the trigger, you don't pull the trigger. Because somebody else gets to decide if you go to prison or not. Nobody wants a court case with their name on it versus the United States.**"

Carlton was asked, "When they say it was Nick Ivie who shot and wounded another agent, they are saying he was intending to shoot someone else, possibly a smuggler or some other illegal alien. Could you explain why he would most likely not shoot at a smuggler, even if the smuggler were carrying a rifle?"

"**With a shooting, everything is going to come down to your perception of it,**" Carlton said. "**All of your training gears you to being able to testify at some point as to what you did. You have to be able to take responsibility for what you've done. You have to be able to justify your actions.**

"**So on some level, every time you got your gun out, every time you're considering, Do I need to shoot somebody or not?—at that time you're trying to figure out if you could justify, even to yourself, why you need to shoot.**

"**So in asking about this case specifically, I don't know without any kind of announcement, without any kind of threat directly toward you, if any agent would want to take the risk to shoot somebody, if they haven't been able to articulate a threat or an aggressive act toward them.**

"**You definitely don't have to wait to be shot at before you can shoot. But at the same time, you have to be able to say something to justify your action later.**

"**Not just that there was somebody there with a gun. If they haven't made any kind of aggressive act toward you, it's not going to look good.**"

If an agent has taken cover, and someone is approaching with a firearm, is there any reason an agent would open fire on that person?

"I will give you one scenario. If you're lying in hiding, and there was already a prior shooting, and the subject was running away from the other shooting and running toward you, you wouldn't need to necessarily notify them of your presence. You could just take action.

"Because they've already shown they're willing to shoot, and they're a risk to people. But we're still obligated to identify ourselves if it doesn't put us at an increased risk.

"So if you can't point to a reason that you're at more of a risk, you still have to identify yourself. You still have to give some kind of a command. And not just opening fire on people."

It has been established through the interviews with the surviving agents that none of the agents identified themselves. This makes perfect sense if smugglers suddenly opened fire on all three agents, killing Agent Ivie immediately and wounding Agent Johnson soon after that. It does not make sense in connection with the scenario invented by the FBI.

Carlton was asked, "In your years in law enforcement, have you ever heard of any incident like this, which occurred in the way the FBI said it occurred? Is there any incident that you know about that went down the way they say it went down?"

"No, absolutely not. This is a nightmare scenario for anyone in law enforcement. I never heard of a situation where a police officer took a position of cover and opened fire on someone he hadn't identified, nor identified himself to.

"That's not a tactic that's taught to law enforcement under any circumstance. We do see rare cases where there is a traffic stop, and an officer shoots somebody as he runs away, and there is a video, and it is apparent that is not a good situation for a law enforcement officer.

"In those instances, those police officers are responding to something. They may have responded incorrectly, but they are responding to an action. Somebody who was running away from them, someone who was fighting, but stopped.

"The situation with Nick, according to the official narrative, he was initiating the contact *before* any kind of situation. So he wasn't reacting; he was initiating the contact instead of reacting to a situation. And that's a pretty big difference.

"Nick was very laid back. Everybody that knew Nick kind of agreed that Nick reacted too cautiously to things. So to have a scenario—knowing how laid back Nick was and how slow he was to react to situations—where he initiated the contact, is so far from the character of Nick. It's basically unfathomable."

Bruising Near Nick's Trigger Finger Indicates a Possible Struggle

Carlton was asked about a key piece of evidence, which tends to indicate that Nick was involved in a struggle before he was shot:

Nick had a bruise between his thumb and forefinger, according to the autopsy report. Could that be a sign of a struggle?

"I've drawn my gun hundreds of times, thousands of times. I've never had a bruise from drawing my gun.

"But we do something we call weapon retention. If someone grabs your gun while its holstered, the first thing you do is you sit your hand over the grip of the gun, and you push down and back. Because to draw the gun, it has to come straight up.

"So you're putting pressure down and on it. And a lot of guys, if you have both hands free, will cover their first hand with their second hand."

Carlton said it would also be possible for an agent's hand to be bruised during a fight, if he hit his hand down on the gun very hard as he went to draw it.

"You can feel there is not a whole lot of cushion (in the crook of the hand between the thumb and forefinger). Guns are not soft. So if you're really putting pressure down, it wouldn't take much to bruise it there.

"There shouldn't be any bruising from drawing your gun or shooting. I can't think of a time I ever had bruising there."

Carlton said the indication of bruising to Ivie's knee and elbow in the autopsy report could also indicate a struggle, especially because of the rocks on the ground at the saddle.

One of the sheriff's deputies wrote in his report that the Mexican coins, the pesos, were found mingled with the bullet casings. How often would you find coins on the ground? Do you usually tell suspects to empty their pockets?

"For Nick, especially where he was right then, he wouldn't have had them take stuff out of their pockets."

Carlton said that if Nick encountered one of the illegals, he could have had him stand up and patted him down for weapons and a cell phone.

"We take from them if they have a lighter, any kind of weapon, or a cell phone. We take those things right away. The rest of their stuff, they can keep that until we get down to a vehicle. Then we have them wear only one shirt and one pair of pants. Everything else they have to take off.

"We take their belts, rosaries, necklaces, rings, earrings—elastic hair ties for women. They're allowed to keep their paper money, but any coins go into their property bags. We do all that as we're writing them up.

Carlton said agents will remove shoelaces from the illegal aliens so that they can't run away as well.

"If they're committed to it, it doesn't stop them. We've had guys run away barefoot before. But you take their shoelaces away so they're less likely to run, less able to run.

"And some guys will make them take their belts off. I don't like to make them take their belts off. This is a personal preference. If they remove their belts in the field, before we walk them out, then they have something with some weight to it. They could start swinging it.

"Me, personally, I like them to keep their belts around their waist. Some guys like their belts to come off, because if they run, they are messing with loose pants. I'd rather them have their hands more empty. That is up to each agent. There is no hard and fast rule on what you have to do."

Border Patrol Agents Don't Carry Mexican Coins

Carlton was asked to comment on how pesos could have ended up on the ground, very close to where the shell casings from Nick's pistol were found. How would you explain how those coins could have landed there?

"Well, number one, somebody else had to be there. I don't know any Border Patrol agents that carry around Mexican coins. You can't buy anything with them here. There's no point to carry them. One of my good friends goes back and forth to Mexico all the time. He's got family there. But he doesn't carry Mexican coins at work. You can't do anything with them. Why have them?

"They're only going to be there if there is an alien there. And they would have to come out in some kind of a struggle.

"Maybe the guy was pulling his own little pocket revolver out. Maybe the guy was pulling a knife out. Maybe he had his hands in his pockets.

"It could even be as simple as Nick asking him if he has anything in his pockets, and he reaches into his pockets and then pulls his hands out and starts fighting.

"Or maybe Nick's standing here, and the guy is lying down in front of him and he says, 'No, I don't have anything in my pockets,' and another guy comes from behind and starts a fight. Now the alien who had his hands in his pockets is reacting. Now he's going to fight, too, and everything comes out.

"And the coins would be right where Nick fell.

"I could see a couple of different ways the coins come out of somebody's pockets, or out of their bag, if they're carrying them in their backpack or something like that, in a struggle.

"But the coins aren't there if there are no people there. There are lots of different ways that they could have come out of somebody's pocket, but what you can't get past is somebody had to be there for those coins to be at that one spot. It takes a person to be there."Their narrative was 'Nobody was there.'"

Government tried to cover up Brian Terry's death. Why believe them now?

With all the eyewitness and circumstantial evidence that point to suspects on the scene when Nick was killed, why do you think the FBI would issue a statement that nobody else was involved?

"I think it's part of a larger coverup that comes from the top down. I don't think many Border Patrol agents or law enforcement people trusted that administration to begin with. They started moving people around at the top, and unfortunately a lot of guys at the bottom who would be your stand-up good guys would go along to get along.

"In an organization like the FBI, a lot of the guys have goals; they have ambitions. To me it shows that this particular administration was willing to cover up these types of shootings, because it was all tied to the gun-running operation.

"They were willing to cover up the Brian Terry killing. That got blown open, but now we know they're willing to do it.

"I think most of us are willing to give an administration a chance until we start seeing their pattern of behavior. I don't think you can totally discount the way somebody previously handled something, when considering how they're going to handle the next situation."

Blaming the Victim

Carlton said the authorities are blaming the victim, especially because he is dead and cannot defend himself.

"If there's no other witnesses that are willing to come forward, then it kind of ends there," Carlton said. "What that administration already showed was a willingness to blame the victim and try to intimidate other witnesses."

Carlton said the strategy of intimidating other witnesses eventually failed in the coverup of both the Benghazi and Fast and Furious scandals.

"But it's the exact same scenario with what they're doing with Nick Ivie," he said. "With Brian Terry, they said it was his plan to try to take down this organization with less than lethal ammunition. That was put out there for about two weeks, before his team was able to put out the truth, that this was an order that was given to them, a directive."

"You don't ever have *Bad shoot, good guy.* That doesn't work for law enforcement."

Carlton said that, by presenting a narrative in which Ivie shot at other agents—whom he had not identified—the government was saying he operated outside of his training and policy.

"They say he fired without identifying the target or himself."

But at the same time, the Border Patrol announced that he did nothing wrong, and he was a hero.

"They are trying to placate people," Carlton said. "It's pandering. It's talking out of both sides of your mouth. They're saying it was his fault, but we loved the guy; he was a hero. He did great things. But it's his fault that this situation happened. So they're placing the blame anywhere but themselves or where the blame happens to belong.

"And they're saying good things about him so people who like him won't cause a big fuss. But you can't talk out of both sides of your mouth."

Carlton pointed out that within the law enforcement tent, every shooting is broken down into a good shoot or a bad shoot.

"It's either justified or not justified," he said. "If it was a good shoot, people talk about what a good guy the officer was, a hero, all the adulation that comes with doing a heroic deed.

"If it's a bad shoot, they don't talk about that guy being a hero. He screwed up. He did something that was bad. Now, it doesn't matter if the good shoot resolved the situation in a positive way or not; if the shoot was good, the guy's actions were good.

"In this case, they're saying it was a bad shoot, but he was a good dude. But that's not how law enforcement classifies shootings. Law enforcement classifies shootings only as good shoots or bad shoots.

"Good shoot, the guy did the right thing, the guy's a hero. Bad shoot, the guy did a bad thing, and the guy's at fault. He's culpable for the shooting. Those are the only two breakdowns.

"You don't ever have *Bad shoot, good guy.* That doesn't work for law enforcement. If it's a bad shoot, it's a bad action. Now you could have a good shoot, but the guy's a jerk or a bad guy. He happened to do the right thing, but he's morally decrepit. But you don't have a bad shoot and a good guy."

Putting aside the government's hypocrisy of branding Agent Ivie as someone who made the outrageous mistake of shooting at fellow agents, thereby causing his own death—while heaping praise on him — Carlton said he agrees with the positive things that have been said about him.

"I absolutely believe Nick was a good guy. I've never heard anybody say a bad thing about Nick. But he's an innocent guy, and he's being blamed for something, and his family's paying the price for it."

Carlton was asked, "Do you think Nick's family members deserve to hold their heads up high, knowing Nick did his job honorably— and not the way they said he was performing when he was shot?"

"I really hope that someday, if something happens to me, somebody will put out whatever they think is the truth of the situation. That's why I'm here, doing what I'm doing, because what they said is not the truth. It can't possibly be the truth.

"And somebody, or in this case a bunch of somebodies, need to get together and get the real truth out. I would hate the thought of anybody's kids going through life, anybody's wife going through the rest of her life, with that baggage.

"Knowing that they have this visual of who this person was to them and the public persona of who this guy has now become. Nick's family, they already know who he was. It's the false narrative that's being spun that is wrong."

"Then you have two other agents who did the best they could according to their training and the circumstances of this ambush," I said to Agent Carlton. "Agent Johnson withheld fire until he was fired on repeatedly and finally hit. Then he realized he couldn't just stand there until they killed him, so he put down suppressing fire.

"As a result of the false narrative, it is widely accepted that one or both of those agents wrongfully killed Nick. And some agents believe Agent Borjas shot Nick, despite the fact that she never fired her weapon. So don't those two agents need to be exonerated also?"

Carlton responded, "I think a lot of agents who knew Nick think that they're not coming out and giving a full account of what happened. And it might not even be their fault, but it's our harsh perception, Monday morning quarterbacking the situation. It might not even be fair to them.

"But if they could come out and give accounts, not just their previously recorded testimony, I think that would go a long way with other agents towards them. Until all the pieces are fit together, it is really hard to be angry with or judge anybody. They were put in a really bad situation. I don't think anybody holds them responsible."

Carlton said he believes the Obama administration didn't want to tell the truth about a law enforcement death at the border, especially after that incident caused more publicity on Fast and Furious and the cover-up of that government-initiated gun-running operation.

"And that will inevitably bring up all the deaths in Mexico," Carlton said. "A couple of cops got killed here, but hundreds of people were killed on the southern side of the border. They gloss over that."We know the FBI is compromised," Carlton said, adding that many cases have been mishandled in recent years.

"They have covered up other deaths of agents, including the one who was killed in Mexico. One was killed, and the other survived. You never hear anything about that."[1]

Carlton said he believes most of the Border Patrol line agents "are not pushing one conspiracy theory or the official government line." Seven years after Nick Ivie lost his life on a moonlit mountain saddle, most of his fellow agents know no more about what happened than what they were told in 2012.

"They just want the truth," Carlton said. "They just want to know what happened."

Carlton believes a full revelation of what actually occurred would bring peace of mind to him and other agents. He said too much of the information put out by the Border Patrol "just doesn't make sense."

"If something like this happens to me, are people going to keep pushing until they know the truth? The truth is more important than any particular narrative or agenda."

Epilogue

The Final Chapters of This Story Have Not Yet Been Written

A terrible injustice has been done. Those who care about the safety of law enforcement officers and the integrity of our political system need to help write the final chapters.

Nick Ivie is no longer with his family, friends and co-workers, but the memory of this kind-hearted, dedicated public servant lives on in their hearts and minds. For some who were close to Nick, there is a mixture of grief and anger, because of the uncertainty about how and why he was killed.

There has been much speculation about what actually occurred, but no final report was ever released by the FBI. The announcement made by the Special Agent in Charge of the Phoenix Division three days after Nick Ivie was shot to death was the final word from the Bureau.

As a police reporter who has covered dozens of murder cases for a daily newspaper, I decided to take a look into this case, to see whether there was any validity to what skeptics were saying. After author Ed Ashurst told me what he knew about the case and showed me some documents, that piqued my interest.

In examining documents from the Cochise County Sheriff's Office, FBI, Border Patrol and Pima County Medical Examiner's Office, it became apparent that something the government had done was stinking like a high hill of rotting alewives. There was enough evidence to fill a prosecutor's file drawer—all clearly showing that several suspects were on the scene when Agent Ivie was killed.

But somehow the FBI reached the conclusion that Border Patrol agents shot at each other when nobody else was around.

As I began digging deeper and deeper into the evidence in this case, I found stunning irregularities at every turn. When I shared this evidence with friends and acquaintances in law enforcement, they let me know I was *not* traveling on that infamous road to becoming a crazy "conspiracy theorist."

The evidence points away from the FBI's hasty conclusion and toward something more complicated and sinister. Could it be possible that the FBI would lie about its findings?

Would the FBI accuse Border Patrol agents of accidentally engaging in a deadly shooting, knowing that this false conclusion could cause great pain and shame to those who were involved and to their families?

Was the FBI capable of allowing the actual killers to go free, while framing fellow law enforcement officers?

The Smugglers are Responsible for the Murder and Attempted Murder

When a crime is committed, such as the shooting of law enforcement officers or a bank robbery, the individuals involved in the crime are legally responsible for the shooting death of anyone who dies during the commission of that crime.

After I learned numerous details of this case—including the placement of the entrance wound and the fact that Agent Johnson saw nothing in his rifle sight—I was convinced that Agent Ivie was not shot by a fellow agent.

But in the larger legal picture, whether agents accidentally shot each other is almost totally irrelevant.

The most important evidence in this case shows that the three agents were ambushed by smugglers, who fired at them with one or more weapons.

The other facts in this case fall into the shadows, behind the pillars of evidence that reveal the presence of other shooters at the scene.

I do believe the smugglers killed Nick Ivie with the first shot, and Agent Johnson did not shoot anyone.

But even if Agent Johnson were guilty of committing "friendly fire," as the FBI alleges, the smugglers are the ones who are responsible for the death of Agent Ivie.

I asked a legal expert to explain the felony murder rule, which allows prosecutors to charge suspects with first-degree murder if someone was killed during the commission of a serious crime.

"It wouldn't be a problem to prosecute them for murder for the death of the agent," said the law professor, who requested anonymity because he was not familiar with the entire case. "Even though someone else ended up firing the fatal bullet doesn't change the fact that they were trying to kill the Border Patrol agents, which is the required intent.

"There is the question if they had the required mental state. If you're shooting at Border Patrol agents, you're trying to kill them.

If you're trying to kill them and one of them ends up dying through some unexpected means, not being struck by their bullets, but instead being struck by friendly fire, that would not break the chain of causation.

"They would still be responsible for causing the death because they started the shootout.

"This is called the felony murder rule. It means if you're committing a felony and somebody winds up being killed it doesn't matter that you weren't the one who fired the bullet. You'd still be guilty."

As part of this investigation into Agent Ivie's death, it was necessary to not only present and analyze as much of the evidence as we were able to uncover, but also to present an assessment of the possible motives behind the failure of the FBI to conduct an honest and complete investigation. I have tried to remain objective in examining the motives of the FBI and its political leaders, based on information about similar activities before and after this incident.

Agent Ivie's death was declared an incident of friendly fire—an "accidental shooting incident"—with nobody but agents involved.

The "friendly fire" scenario is preposterous. If three agents came upon each other on a remote mountain ridge under a full moon and accidentally shot at each other, they would have known about it immediately. If that was what actually occurred, and then the two surviving agents made up stories about there being other people involved, their careers with the Border Patrol would have ended.

The two surviving agents told the truth about what occurred. What they said was never revealed to the public. They said they were ambushed by multiple people—and hundreds of law enforcement officers were sent to the scene to rescue them and apprehend their assailants. They were believed because they told the truth.

But after they told the truth in multiple interviews, they were silenced. All Border Patrol agents were threatened with firing and possible criminal prosecution if they spoke out about this incident.

The Border Patrol—which won the award as the least transparent government agency in 2013 from Investigative Reporters and Editors, Inc.—would not allow the surviving agents to tell their stories to anyone in the media.

The narrative that the U.S. government broadcast to the public did not ring true to many people. It immediately came into question by those who knew the character and skill of the deceased agent, as well as the deceptive practices of the administration that was in power at that time.

The overwhelming majority of law enforcement officers would do anything in their power to avoid shooting another officer. Some say they would rather die than kill a fellow officer.

It is rare for a Border Patrol agent to shoot an illegal border crosser, and unheard of that an agent with the sterling character and compassionate disposition of Agent Ivie would engage in reckless conduct.

Long Odds Against Landing an Unlucky Shot Like This One

The idea that Agent Ivie shot at another agent—because he mistakenly believed he was an armed smuggler—lies outside the realm of credibility.

The assertion that Agent Ivie and Agent Johnson had a shootout with each other, on a windless night on a silent, remote mountain saddle, flies in the face of common sense and all the evidence.

If this unlikely event occurred, wouldn't the three agents on the scene—with nobody else involved—immediately know exactly what happened?

Why would one of the agents be running for cover if the only one shooting at her and her partner was lying there stone-cold dead?

Why would the injured agent be sitting there—clutching his M4 rifle—waiting for another possible deadly attack by those who just shot him?

If there were only two other people around—and one was just killed by a Border Patrol agent's bullet—what in the world would he be doing sitting there like that?

Why would the agents who arrived on the scene about 20 minutes later be concerned about the danger of nearby killers if the only ones involved in the shootout were their fellow Border Patrol agents?

Why would Border Patrol ask for backup from the Cochise County Sheriff's Office and other law enforcement agencies if this was just a terrible mistake, with only the three agents involved?

Why would multiple aircraft be deployed to the scene, as part of a massive manhunt for suspects, if two agents shot at each other by mistake, but nobody else was involved?

Why would the Border Patrol deploy their best trackers to hunt the suspects if nobody else was involved in this tragic accident?

Why would two trained Border Patrol agents—one with military training in addition to law enforcement training—give detailed accounts of the incident that matched each other's—but that clashed wildly with the conclusion of the FBI?

If only Agent Ivie was present on the saddle—while carrying only a sidearm—how in the world did one agent see three or four people there, with one suspect shooting a long firearm?

If only Agent Ivie was at the saddle, why did an agent who arrived on the scene say he saw someone wearing a smuggler's pack remove a blanket right before the shooting began?

The FBI apparently convinced members of every media outlet covering the case that the "ballistics testing" it performed on or before Friday, October 5 conclusively proved its case.

My research showed that October 5 was the same day the FBI crime lab in Quantico, Virginia, received a rifle belonging to one agent and a bullet fragment allegedly extracted from the brainstem of the deceased agent. The FBI document on its ballistics test shows that it reported its results to the FBI in Arizona on October 10.

Details about the ballistics test were never released to the press. There was just a statement—from an anonymous source within the FBI—that a test was performed and that it proved that Agent Ivie was shot to death by a fellow agent.

No other details were ever released.

For anyone familiar with how the FBI normally operates, the statement that it had done its testing and reached an "indisputable" conclusion the same day it received its evidence begs for it to be disputed. The FBI is known for its thoroughness, not for its speedy lab work and lightning-fast conclusions.

Compared to normal FBI standards—in which results are stringently checked and rechecked in order for them to be ascertained as correct and to withstand opposing viewpoints—the release of the proclamation that its lab had proven that one federal agent killed another appeared at the speed of light.

Leaks and second-hand statements were employed by the FBI throughout the days following Agent Ivie's death, as the Bureau remained officially silent, but released authoritative statements through various news outlets and law enforcement agencies.

That time-tested method left plenty of wiggle room for the FBI, in case anyone uncovered the real evidence, which showed that neither of the Border Patrol agents were shot by the other agent—and there were definitely other people involved.

The FBI released only one official statement. And then said nothing else.

FBI agents were actively involved in the post-incident interviews with the two survivors.

The interview with Agent Johnson, the man who stands accused by the FBI of accidentally killing Agent Ivie, was conducted the previous day, Thursday, October 4, at the FBI office in Tucson.

FBI agents were keenly aware of the tremendous amount of evidence collected at the scene which indicated the presence of possible suspects, including the specific information that one of the suspects was carrying a standard smuggler's backpack.

The idea that Border Patrol agents who were expecting to meet each other at that location—at that specific time—opened fire on each other without identifying themselves is so far beyond the realm of believability that a scenario involving aliens from outer space would be just as credible.

The FBI's truncated investigation proved absolutely nothing. That is why the FBI leaders had practically nothing to share with their investigative partners.

The eyewitness, forensic, and circumstantial evidence presented in these pages clearly shows that there were armed smugglers at the shooting scene when Agent Ivie was killed.

The FBI had to ignore an enormous amount of evidence to reach the conclusion that nobody else was involved.

In order to try to massage the feelings of the aggrieved, while sticking with a totally false narrative, the agents involved in the shooting incident were not criticized for their actions.

Knowing that most journalists and citizens are not familiar with law enforcement policies and procedures, the government officials concocted the lie that it would be perfectly fine for one agent to shoot at another, without identifying himself, if he came across an unidentified individual with a firearm at night in a mountain range.

The actions of Agent Ivie would have been terribly wrong if the incident actually occurred that way.

So the FBI and its political leaders had to invent an explanation as to why Agent Ivie did nothing wrong by accidentally shooting at agents— without identifying himself or his targets. All they had to do to justify that lie was to lie about what is acceptable under those circumstances.

By adding one lie about how it was just fine for Agent Ivie to shoot at Agent Johnson if he thought he was a smuggler, to the lie that it was Agent Ivie who was shooting at Agent Johnson, the FBI created a smokescreen that has stayed in place for several years.

Who was harmed, if everybody involved was patted on the back as if nobody had done anything wrong?

As in most cases of government dishonesty, there were consequences to this deceptive scheme.

All three agents should have received commendations for their actions in response to an armed ambush by smugglers. The three agents bravely ventured into the remote mountain range to interdict an unknown number of smugglers in the middle of the night.

They were attacked by desperate suspects, dangerous criminals who surprised the agents by greeting them with extreme violence.

Instead of being commended for their actions—which would have shown the world the potential dangers Border Patrol agents are constantly confronting—the agents were portrayed as victims of their own inability to distinguish between armed smugglers and fellow agents.

The evidence presented in this book shows that Agent Ivie never fired a shot at anyone and that Agent Johnson bravely stood his ground and fired his M4 carbine in the direction of the smugglers who had killed Agent Ivie.

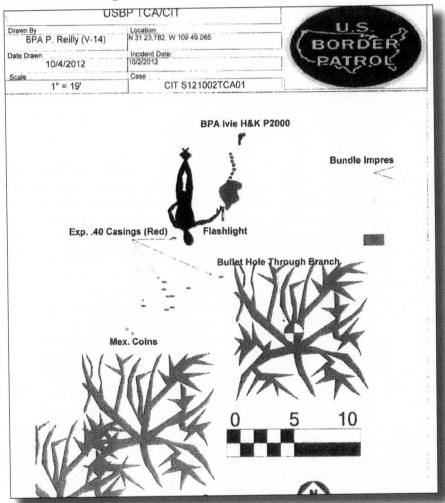

When a Border Patrol agent shoots his government-issued pistol next to other agents at the firing range, the shell casings fly backwards toward the agent at his right hand. Notice where the shell casings were located in relation to Agent Ivie's body. He was found *face down where we now see a pool, which was revealed after he was flipped over and pulled toward the south. Notice the little blood trail north of the pool, indicating the location of his head before he fell forward. If Agent Ivie had been firing his weapon before he was killed, the shell casings would be in the vicinity of where his feet are on this map. Whoever was shooting Agent Ivie's weapon was south of his body, shooting his pistol after he had been killed.*

Agent Johnson displayed extraordinary restraint and courage by holding his fire while ten shots were fired in his direction—most likely because of his concern that Agent Ivie was somewhere on that mountain saddle.

Though Brian A. Terry is rightfully celebrated as a hero who died in a gunfight with armed illegal aliens, the memory of Nick Ivie is not celebrated. I would like to see a statue of Nick Ivie cast and set near the magnificent one that honors Brian Terry.

There is a dignified, poignant monument to Agent Ivie on a ranch road just south of the saddle where he died. There is also a simple cross on Nick's Saddle to memorialize his sacrifice.

But the memory of this outstanding young agent is overshadowed by the Big Lie that was devised for political reasons—with no respect for the honor due to Nick Ivie for his courageous, selfless service.

To this day, almost nobody in the United States has any association with the name "Nicholas Ivie." Even in Cochise County and the rest of Arizona, Nick Ivie is largely unknown outside of his circle of family, friends and fellow law enforcement officers.

Some of his fellow Border Patrol agents want to see Nick Ivie's name cleared so that he will not go down in history as being the only Border Patrol agent killed in a friendly fire incident.

It is important that Nick Ivie instead be remembered as a courageous soul who was willing to hike by himself to a remote mountain ridge to confront an unknown number of drug smugglers in the middle of the night—even if he had to encounter them while he was still alone.

That is the way he actually died, and the way he should be remembered by his widow, daughters, parents, siblings, fellow law enforcement officers, and the grateful citizens of the United States.

These are the final chapters that I would like to write:

Chapter 29
FBI agent blows whistle on phony investigation.

Chapter 30
Killers of Nick Ivie convicted of first-degree murder.

This book was written so that those chapters could be written.

I do not believe officials at the agencies involved in this terrible episode are going to say: "Well now that this guy has written this book about what really happened, let's just admit what we did and let Nick Ivie and the other agents receive the honors they deserve."

It is up to officials at those agencies, lawmakers charged with overseeing them, squeaky wheels in the public, and the law enforcement community, to pitch in to right these wrongs. There needs to be a thorough investigation of how this case was mishandled, as well as an honest investigation of the crimes.

What Firearm Was Used to Shoot Nick Ivie?

Rancher Ed Ashurst recently set out to prove that Agent Ivie was not shot to death by another agent wielding an M4 carbine. An avid hunter, Ashurst said every person he knows who is knowledgeable about firearms agreed that a .223 round would penetrate a shooting victim's head. The .223 cartridge was designed to cause maximum penetration and bodily damage, when it was first manufactured in the early 1960s, during the Vietnam War.

Nick Ivie had only an entrance wound in his forehead; there was no exit wound, because the bullet remained in his body.

To prove his hypothesis, Ashurst performed a series of ballistic tests with semi-automatic rifles and 55 grain soft nosed, copper-jacketed bullets—the same kind of ammunition used by the Border Patrol. He wanted to demonstrate the penetrating power of a .223 bullet, which travels from the 14-inch barrel of an M4 carbine at 2,878 feet per second—almost 2,000 miles per hour.

After shooting one round through two half-inch thick conveyor belts and 1/16-inch sheet metal, Ashurst fired another slug through 4-inch-thick concrete, then another through two sidewalls of a semitruck tire. Then he set up the ultimate test. He placed two inflated 20-inch truck tires eight feet apart, a few inches from a piece of 1/20-inch-thick sheet metal, followed by a corrugated metal roofing sheet and a steel oil drum. The bullet penetrated all of the above, including one side of the steel drum. Then it bounced off the other side of the drum and dropped.

"It went through four sidewalls and four pieces of metal," Ashurst said. "A .223 round would not have stayed in Nick Ivie's head."

One ballistics expert suggested to me that the bullet that killed Nick could have been deflected. With the FBI entering a branch into evidence, that is apparently also one of the Bureau's theories.

But it is extremely unlikely that a bullet shot from 20 feet away by someone who saw nothing in his rifle sight—and never saw Nick Ivie at the scene at all—would hit a branch and then fly straight into the center of his unintended target's forehead. There is a very slim probability of that occurring. The most scientific way to describe the odds of that occurring would be slim to none.

Which is probably why the FBI never explained to the press or the public this important detail—or any of the details that would make people with normal intelligence doubt its story.

The odds of someone shooting toward flashes in the night sky and shooting an unintended target right in the middle of his forehead would be much higher than scoring a hole-in-one, which many avid golfers never achieve. It would be closer to this occurrence: A golfer hits a long, high tee shot off of tee box number one on a windless day. The ball strikes a tree branch, goes way off course, but drops softly into the cup on the back edge of a green—on hole number two.

Was Nick shot by a suspect shooting a .22 caliber round, possibly a revolver?

After consulting with several ballistics and firearms experts, I have not reached a conclusion about which firearm was used, or even the caliber of the fatal bullet.

Hopefully, the entire file the FBI has on this case will be made available for investigation one day. Then and only then will we have all the answers to the mysteries in this case.

I do not know which suspect shot Nick Ivie to death, or whether the suspect who shot him was ever arrested. But I believe there was enough evidence gathered in this case to determine which smugglers were at the scene at the time, and possibly to obtain convictions for their involvement.

During two and a half years of working on this book, I obtained much evidence on what occurred on Remax Saddle, and events associated with the shooting and its coverup. However, there is much evidence I have not uncovered. Hopefully this book will provide a starting point for other researchers interested in finding out exactly how and why the truth about this incident was concealed.

The evidence presented in this book clearly shows that the three agents were ambushed by armed smugglers, who shot at them. It is those smugglers who are totally responsible for the death of Nick Ivie, the wounding of David G. Johnson, and the harm caused to all three agents and their families and friends.

I believe that smugglers shot and killed Nick Ivie and shot and wounded David Johnson. But there is much greater evidence that shows that—regardless of which shooters fired bullets that caused harm to the agents—it was the smugglers who fired shots at the mountain saddle resulting in Nick Ivie's death and Dave Johnson's injuries.

I do not know which suspect shot Nick Ivie to death. But I believe there is enough evidence available to determine who was at the scene at the time, and to obtain a conviction for their involvement in his murder.

Afterword

I have invented a story to illustrate what occurred, to enhance the understanding of readers who might not be familiar with the southern border, mountainous terrain and the work of federal agents who cover vast stretches of dangerous, cartel-infested territory.

A city police department receives a tip that some local gang members are making a drug deal in the middle of a remote park on the edge of town. Three officers are dispatched to the scene. One is heading to the scene from the north, the other two travel together from the south.

The lone officer arrives at the park, looks around, doesn't see anything. He radios the other two, who tell him they are a few minutes away.

"10-4," the lone officer says.

When the two officers arrive at the park, they walk toward the place they believe the lone officer will be located. Immediately someone begins shooting in their direction. One of those officers is wounded. He immediately returns fire, but sees nobody in his rifle sight.

The other officer hides behind a shrub and calls in, "shots fired." She tells first responders she saw three or four people, with one shooting a long arm. The lone officer was only armed with a pistol.

Dozens of police officers head for the scene, to render aid to their comrades and apprehend the shooters. The lone officer is found lying face down in the middle of the park.

The whole town hears the news that one officer was killed and another wounded by the gang members.

Two suspects are located nearby, with drugs and firearms. They are arrested and booked into jail in connection with the murder and attempted murder of officers.

The city's mayor is up for reelection in five weeks. Part of his platform is that he has kept the city safe. His opponent says the city is not safe at all. The mayor and the city prosecutor have been shipping firearms to gang members, as part of a bizarre plan to shut down gun shops and change gun laws. Many have been killed with those weapons. The mayor denies all involvement in that scheme.

The police chief announces that the officer was killed by friendly fire, with nobody else involved. He orders all the police officers to keep quiet about what happened, under threat of firing or criminal prosecution.

All the local media outlets report on what the police chief announced. They accept as fact that this was all just a tragic accident, and dutifully report exactly what they were told to report.

The mayor gets reelected, remaining in control of the police department, while wielding even more influence over the media.

Acknowledgments

In a time when powerful government agencies have been deployed for partisan political purposes, this book has benefitted from the contributions of many courageous people.

Ed Ashurst started me on this trail and used his wagon boss skills to help complete the long drive.

Nichole Kroncke provided invaluable expert advice and unending encouragement from start to finish.

Jimmy Owens exceeded the call of friendship by conducting ballistic tests to help me understand what occurred on Remax Saddle.

Border Patrol agents who were friends and co-workers of Nick Ivie provided a tremendous amount of information, as well as inspiration. They have chosen to remain anonymous.

Other outstanding individuals who also assisted tremendously will also remain nameless.

Editor extraordinaire Rob Siedenburg helped carry the book to the finish line, taking on an enormous workload as if it were his own book. A tremendous joy at the end of the journey.

Cheryl Taylor, artist and page designer, used her impressive skills to transform a boatload of words and images into something much greater than it was.

Jim Hart, Hartline Literary Agency, poured his heart and professional expertise into helping with this project.

Other contributors: Jean Ann Ashurst, Amber Bates, Howard G. Buffett, Dr. Mary Case, Ken Chumbley, Jim and Sue Chilton, Michael E. Day, Tom and Diane Denning, Chuck Edenfield, Richard Fairburn, Larry Foster, Ed German, Lucien C. Haag, Pamela Hulme, Lori Hunnicutt, Lynn Kartchner, Marvin Kouza, Sue Krentz, Bill Kroncke, John Ladd, Jack Levine, David Mabe, Lori Martinsek, Dr. Eric D. Peters, Rev. Darrell C. Porter, Mark Rigel, Sheriff Billy Darnell, Thad Smith, Bob Thorpe, Jean Zerfowski.

This book could not have been written without the love, assistance and encouragement of Katie, my amazing wife and soulmate.

Bibliography

Acosta, Hipolito. *The Shadow Catcher: A U.S. Agent Infiltrates Mexico's Deadly Crime Cartels*, Atria Books, Simon & Schuster, Inc., New York, 2012.

Ashurst, Ed. *Alligators in the Moat: Politics and the Mexican Border*, Ed Ashurst Publishing Co., Douglas, Arizona, 2016.

Attkisson, Sharyl. *Stonewalled: My Fight for Truth Against the Forces of Obstruction, Intimidation and Harassment in Obama's Washington*, HarperCollins Publishers, New York, 2014.

Buffett, Howard G. *Our 50-State Border Crisis: How the Mexican Border Fuels the Drug Epidemic Across America*, Hachette Book Group, New York, 2018.

Daniel, William R. and Larry Dempster. *Dever, The Life and Death of America's Sheriff*, Cochise County Productions, Benson, Arizona, 2015.

Daniel, William R. *One if by Land: What Every American Needs to Know about our Border*, Wheatmark, Tucson, Arizona, 2012.

Detty, Mike. *Guns Across the Border: How and Why the US Government Smuggled Guns into Mexico*, Skyhorse Publishing, New York, 2013.

Di Maio, Vincent J. M. *Gunshot Wounds: Practical Aspects of Firearms, Ballistics, and Forensic Techniques*, CRC Press, Boca Raton, Florida, 1993.

Dodson, John. *The Unarmed Truth: My Fight to Blow the Whistle and Expose Fast and Furious*, Simon & Schuster, Inc., New York, 2013.

Dudley, Steven. *Transnational Crime in Mexico and Central America: Its Evolution and Role in International Migration*, Migration Policy Institute, Washington, D.C., November 2012.

Fairburn, Richard. *Police Rifles: Selecting the Right Rifle for Street Patrol and Special Tactical Situations*, Paladin Press, Boulder, Colorado, 1994.

Freeh, Louis J. *My FBI: Bringing Down the Mafia, Investigating Bill Clinton, and Fighting the War on Terror*, St. Martin's Press, New York, 2005.

Giffords, Gabrielle & Kelly, Mark, with Jeffrey Zaslow. *Gabby: A Story*

` *of Courage and Hope*, Scribner, New York, 2011.

Haag, Michael G. and Haag, Lucien C. *Shooting Incident Reconstruction*, Academic Press, Elsevier Inc., San Diego, 2011.

Kessler, Ronald. *The Bureau: The Secret History of the FBI*, St. Martin's Press, New York, 2002.

Kirkpatrick, Terry. *Sixty Miles of Border: An American Lawman Battles Drugs on the Mexican Border*, Berkley Books, New York, 2012.

Limbaugh, David. *The Great Destroyer: Barack Obama's War on the Republic*, Regnery Publishing Inc., Washington, D.C., 2009.

Longmire, Sylvia. *Cartel: The Coming Invasion of Mexico's Drug Wars*, Palgrave Macmillan, New York, 2011.

McCarthy, Andrew C. *Ball of Collusion: The Plot to Rig an Election and Destroy a Presidency*, Encounter Books, New York, August 13, 2019.

Morgan, Lee II. *The Reaper's Line: Life and Death on the Mexican Border*, Rio Nuevo Publishers, Tucson, September 2006.

Malkin, Michelle. *Culture of Corruption: Obama and His Team of Tax Cheats, Crooks, and Cronies Scandal*, Regnery Publishing Inc., Washington, D.C., 2009.

Pavlich, Katie. *Fast and Furious: Barack Obama's Bloodiest Scandal and Its Shameless Cover-up*: Regnery Publishing Inc., Washington, D.C., 2012.

Powell, Sidney. *Licensed to Lie: Exposing Corruption in the Department of Justice*, Brown Books Publishing Group, Dallas, 2014.

Strassel, Kim. *The Intimidation Game: How the Left is Silencing Free Speech*, Hachette Book Group, New York, 2016.

U.S. Government Accountability Office. *Border Patrol: Key Elements of New Strategic Plan Not Yet in Place to Inform Border Security Status and Resource Needs*, U.S. Government Accountability Office, Washington, D.C., December 2012.

Wolffe, Richard. *The Message: The Reselling of President Obama*, Hachette Book Group, New York, 2013.

Zuckoff, Mitchell with the Annex Security Team, *13 Hours: The Inside Account of What Really Happened in Benghazi*, Hachette Book Group, Inc., New York, 2014.

End Notes

Chapter 1

[1] Interview with John Ladd, September 29, 2017.

[2] Carlton interview.

[3] "Fast and Furious Scandal: New Details Emerge on How the U.S. Government Armed Mexican Drug Cartels," ABC News/ Univision, September 30, 2012. www.abcnews.go.com/ABC_ Univision/News/fast-furious-scandal-details-emerge-us-government-armed/story?id=17352694.

[4] "Furious' guns tied to 2010 Juarez massacre, other murders in Mexico, Fox News, October 1, 2012. www.foxnews.com/politics/furious-guns-tied-to-2010-juarez-massacre-other-murders-in-mexico.

[5] Obama says Romney is "a good debater. I'm just OK." *L.A. Times* 9/30/2012: http://articles.latimes.com/2012/sep/30/news/la-pn-obama-seeks-to-lower-debate-expectations-20120930.

[6] "Migrants are forced to serve as mules and prostitutes," *Transnational Crime in Mexico and Central America: Its Evolution and Role in International Migration*, by Steven Dudley, Migration Policy Institute, November 2012.

[7] Borjas interview, October 2, 2012.

[8] Ocejo Shooting Incident report, October 3, 2012.

[9] Interview with Border Patrol Agent Andrew Carlton.

[10] Interview with Border Patrol Agent Andrew Carlton.

[11] Ed Ashurst. *Alligators in the Moat,"* 2016, Ed Ashurst Publishing Co.: Douglas, Arizona, pp. 73–81

[12, 13] William R. Daniel and Larry Dempster. *Dever, The Life and Death of America's Sheriff,"* Cochise County Productions: Benson, Arizona, 2015.

Chapter 2

[1] Borjas interview transcript, October 11, 2012.

[2] "New Border Patrol station named for Brian A. Terry opens," U.S. Army Corps of Engineers, posted October 2, 2012: www. spl.usace.army.mil/Media/News-Stories/Article/477151/new-border-patrol-station-named-for-brian-a-terry-opens/.

³"Agent Pulled into the Fray over an Agent's death," *New York Times,* September 20, 2012.

⁴Borjas interview.

⁵ Magliano, Carlton interviews; Border Patrol statistics.

⁶Carlton interview, Magliano interview.

⁷Carlton interview.

⁸Johnson interview.

⁹ Johnson interview.

¹⁰Johnson interview.

¹¹Borjas interview.

¹²Johnson interview.

¹³Conversations with law enforcement and area residents.

¹⁴"El Chapo Found Guilty on All Counts; Faces Life in Prison," *New York Times,* February 12, 2019: www.nytimes.com/2019/02/12/nyregion/el-chapo-verdict.html.

¹⁵"Joaquin 'EL CHAPO' Guzmán, Sinaloa Cartel leader, convicted of running a continuing criminal enterprise and other drug related charges," U.S. D.E.A., February 12, 2019: www.dea.gov/press-releases/2019/02/12/joaquin-el-chapo-guzman-sinaloa-cartel-leader-convicted-running.

Chapter 3

¹Borjas interview 2, October 11, 2012.

²Borjas interview 2.

³Ron Colburn. "Walk A Mile in His Boots," p. 4, first published on Southern Arizona Cattlemen's Protective Association Web site, October 11, 2013; This article was also posted on KSL.com, NBC TV affiliate in Salt Lake City. The following month, it was published by the *Provo Herald:* www.heraldextra.com/news/local/new-info-released-about-death-of-border-patrol-agent/article_cee515c3-023a-5e9c-88c5-70e7c6043c7f.html.

⁴Borjas interview.

⁵Borjas interview.

⁶Johnson interview.

⁷Johnson and Borjas interviews.

⁸Johnson interview.

⁹Borjas interview.

¹⁰Borjas interview.

¹¹Borjas interview.

¹²Johnson interview.

¹³Borjas interview.

¹⁴Borjas interview.

¹⁵Borjas interview.

Chapter 4

[1]Johnson interview.

[2]Ron Colburn. "Walk A Mile in His Boots," p. 4

[3]Borjas interviews.

[4]Johnson interview.

[5]Summary of FBI interview with Border Patrol Agent David T. Woodbury, October 6, 2012, drafted October 11, 2012.

[6]McWhorter BP Shooting Incident memorandum, October 3, 2012.

[7]McWhorter BP memorandum.

Chapter 5

[1]Johnson interview.

[2]McWhorter BP memorandum.

Chapter 6

[1] BP Acting Supervisor Edwards shooting incident memorandum, Oct. 2, 2012.

[2]"SHOOTING, Border agent slain; partner wounded," *Arizona Daily Star*, October 3, 2012: tucson.com/news/local/border/border-agent-slain-partner-wounded/article.

[3]tucson.com/news/national/photos-arizona-border-agent-killed/collection_20eda728-0cd2-11e2-b06d-001a4bcf887a.html#18BP agent interview, January 11, 2019.

[4]Carlton interview.

[5]Carlton interview.

[6]Border Patrol Agent Kyle Babbie shooting incident memorandum, Oct. 3, 2012.

[7]Marc Lacey. "Evidence Points to Methodical Planning," *New York Times*, January. 9, 2011: www.nytimes.com/2011/01/10/us/10giffords.html.

[8]Deputy Arthur Estrada officer incident, filed Oct. 13, 2012.

[9]Deputy Guy Hudson officer incident report, filed Oct. 4, 2012.

[10]Hudson incident report.

[11]"SHOOTING, Border agent slain; partner wounded," *Arizona Daily Star* October 3, 2012: tucson.com/news/local/border/border-agent-slain-partner-wounded/article.

[12]"Slain Border Patrol agent's wife speaks for the first time," October 3, 2013: www.azfamily.com/story/2306032/slain-border-patrol-agents-wife-speaks-for-the-first-time.

Chapter 7

[1]CCSO Sgt. Sean Gijanto officer incident report filed October 8, 2012.
[2]Sgt. Gijanto report.
[3]FBI "302" Borjas interview report by Special Agent Chad Richard Edlund, filed October 5, 2012.

Chapter 8

[1]CCSO Detective John Monroe officer incident report, filed October 8, 2012.

Chapter 9

[1]Ron Colburn. "Walk a Mile in His Boots," p. 5:
[2]"Fatal shooting of border agent likely friendly fire, FBI says.": http://archive.azcentral.com/arizonarepublic/news/articles/20121005arizona-border-shooting-possible-friendly-fire.html.

Chapter 10

[1]CCSO Detective Randal Wilson officer incident report, filed Oct. 2, 2012.
[2]Wilson report.

Chapter 11

[1]"U.S. Border Patrol agent saluted for selfless service," *Washington Post*, Oct. 3, 2012.
[2]"Slain Border Agent Identified, Drug Traffickers Suspected," *ABC News*, October 2, 2012: abcnews.go.com/US/slain-border-agent-identified-nicholas-ivie-drug-traffickers/story.
[3]"Bodies of 4 Americans killed in Libya returned to U.S.," *CNN*, September 15, 2012: www.cnn.com/2012/09/14/world/africa/libya-us-ambassador-killed/index.html.
[4]Richard Wolffe. *The Message: The Reselling of President Obama*, 2013: Hachette Book Group, NY.
[5]Andrew McCarthy. *Ball of Collusion, 74*, Encounter Books: 2019, New York; p. 74. McCarthy, a former chief assistant U.S. attorney for the Southern District of New York, successfully prosecuted the 1993 bombers of the World Trade Center.
[6]National news broadcast on ABC's "World News with Diane Sawyer," evening of October 2, 2012.
[7] "Border Patrol Agent Nicholas Ivie Killed, another wounded near Naco," *Tucson Sentinel*, October 2, 2012: www.tucsonsentinel.com/local/report/100212_bp_shooting/border-patrol-agent-nicholas-ivie-killed-another-wounded-near-naco/.

8, 9 "Border Patrol Agent Fatally Shot in Southern Arizona," October 2, 2012, KPBS, San Diego.

10 "U.S. Agent is Killed and Another is Injured in Shooting at Mexican Border," *New York Times*, October 3, 2012: www.nytimes. com/2012/10/03/us/one-border-patrol-agent-killed-another-injured-in-arizona.html.

11 "Arizona Border Patrol Shooting Leaves Agent Dead," *ABC News*, October 2, 2012: abcnews.go.com/WNT/video/arizona-border-patrol-shooting-leaves-agent-dead-17379996.

12 "Border Patrol Agent Nicholas Ivie killed, another wounded near Naco," *Tucson Sentinel*, October 2, 2012: http://www. tucsonsentinel.com/local/report/100212_bp_shooting/border-patrol-agent-nicholas-ivie-killed-another-wounded-near-naco.

13 "Border Patrol Agent Killed in Arizona," October 2, 2012, 5:00 p.m., CBS/AP: www.cbsnews.com/news/border-patrol-agent-killed-in-arizona/.

14 "Border Patrol agent killed, another wounded in Arizona, October 2, 2012: www.washingtonpost.com/world/national-security/border-patrol-agent-killed-second-wounded-in-arizona/2012/10/02/

15 "Border Patrol agent, a Utah native, dies in AZ shooting," *Fox 13 TV*, Salt Lake City, 10:51 a.m., October 2, 2012: fox13now. com/2012/10/02/border-patrol-agent-killed-in-arizona/.

16 Fast and Furious Report Lands DOJ's Breuer in Hot Seat, *Law360*, New York September 20, 2012.

16 "Frontline Gets Its Man: Lanny Breuer Leaves DOJ After Expose," January 24, 2013: www.prwatch.org.

17 "Was Shooting of Border Patrol Agents in Arizona an Ambush?" *The Daily Beast* 10/03/ 2012.

Chapter 12

1 CCSO Detective Randal "Randy" Wilson officer incident report 2, filed October 3, 2012.

2 Interviews with Dr. Eric Peters, Oct. 9 and 15, 2019

Chapter 13

1 McWhorter BP memorandum, October 3, 2012.

2 McWhorter BP memorandum.

Chapter 14

1 Johnson interview.

2 Carlton interview.

3 Lee Morgan II (former U.S. Customs special agent). *The Reaper's Line:*

Life and Death on the Mexican Border, pp. 330–332: Rio Nuevo Publishers, Tucson.

Chapter 15

[1]Jack Date. "Border Patrol Agent Killing: Friendly Fire?" *Good Morning America*, World News, [originally posted October 4, now listed on Web site as October 5, 2012]: abcnews.go.com/blogs/headlines/2012/10/border-patrol-agent-killing-friendly-fire/.

[2]Richard A. Serrano and Cindy Carcamo. "Friendly fire likely killed Border Patrol agent, FBI says," *L.A. Times*, October 5, 2012: www.latimes.com/nation/la-xpm-2012-oct-05-la-na-border-patrol-shooting-20121006-story.html.

[3]https://www.gunmann.com/ar-15-brass-catchers/

[4]"Possible 'friendly fire' explored in border agent's death," CBS/AP, October 4, 2012, updated 9:14 p.m. Eastern Time: www.cbsnews.com/news/possible-friendly-fire-explored-in-border-agents-death/.

[5,6]Rafael Romo. "Source: 2 questioned in Mexico over fatal shooting of U.S. Border Patrol agent," CNN, October 4, 2012, updated 9:24 p.m. Eastern Time: www.cnn.com/2012/10/04/world/americas/mexico-arizona-border-violence/index.html.

[7]"2 held in border shooting," *Concord Monitor*, Concord, New Hampshire, October 5: www.concordmonitor.com/Archive/2012/10/999640622-999640623-1209b-CM.aspx.

[8]Homeland Security Web site: www.dhs.gov/news/2012/10/02/statement-secretary-napolitano-death-border-patrol-agent-nicholas-j-ivie.

[9]"Family members grieve BP agent's death," *Sierra Vista Herald*, October 5, 2012: www.nogalesinternational.com/news/family-members-grieve-bp-agent-s-death/article_654d4f1e-0f01-11e2-9939-0019bb2963f4.html, and another outlet.

Chapter 16

[1]Brady McCombs. "BORDER, FBI: Friendly fire killed Arizona Border Patrol agent," *Arizona Daily Star*, October 5: 2012tucson.com/news/local/crime/fbi-friendly-fire-killed-arizona-border-patrol-agent/article_249eb3fb-9a53-5a6a-87f0-e2d885ffc86e.html.

[2]Dennis Romboy. "Slain Border Patrol agent Nicholas Ivie opened fire first, investigators say," *Deseret News*, October 7, 2012:

[3]Report on Postmortem Examination at Pima County Medical Examiner's Office, examination performed October 3, 2012; and FBI Firearms Report, date of ballistic test unknown, Report of Examination October 10, 2012, sent to FBI office in Phoenix on that date.

[5]*Deseret News*, October 7, 2012.

[6]Alex Ward. "Border agent shot by drug cartel may have been victim of friendly fire," *Daily Mail*, October 5, 2012, 6:36 a.m. EDT: www.dailymail.co.uk/news/article-2213285/Nicholas-Ivie-U-S-Border-Patrol-Agent-possibly-killed-friendly-fire.html.

Chapter 17

[1]Carlton interview.

[2]"If Donald Trump Targets Journalists, Thank Obama": www.nytimes.com/2016/12/30/opinion/sunday/if-donald-trump-targets-journalists-thank-obama.html.

[3]Leonard Downie Jr., with reporting by Sara Rafsky. "The Obama Administration and the Press, Leak investigations and surveillance in post-9/11 America," A CPJ special report: cpj.org/reports/2013/10/obama-and-the-press-us-leaks-surveillance-post-911.php.

[4]Carlton interview.

[5]Bud Foster. Napolitano flies over shooting scene, *WALB.com*, South Georgia News, October 5, 2012.

[6]"Friendly fire likely killed Border Patrol agent, FBI says," *L.A. Times*, October 5, 2012.

Chapter 18

[1]FBI "302" BP Agent Woodbury interview report by Special Agents Brent A. Templeton Chad, Doran C. Anderson, conducted October 6, filed October 11, 2012.

[2]Interview with Border Patrol Agent Sal Magliano, June 2017.

Chapter 19

[1]Brady McCombs. "More than 1,000 join to remember fallen Border Patrol officer Nicholas Ivie," *Arizona Daily Star*, October 9, 2012: tucson.com/news/local/border/more-than-join-to-remember-fallen-border-patrol-officer-nicholas/article_91c485b0-bc98-5e04-b980-b05a7b3ea801.html.

[2]Obituary of Nicholas James Ivie, *Salt Lake City Tribune*, October 10, 2012: www.legacy.com/obituaries/saltlaketribune/obituary.aspx?n=nicholas-james-ivie&pid=160337042.

[3]Rebekah Zemansky & Dylan Smith. "FBI: BP Agent Ivie likely killed by friendly fire," originally posted October 5, 2012, 4:19 pm TucsonSentinel.comhttp://www.tucsonsentinel.com/local/report/100512_ivie_friendly_fire/fbi-bp-agent-ivie-likely-killed-by-friendly-fire/.

[4]"Family, friends share cherished memories of Nicholas Ivie," *Benson News*, October 10, 2012, www.bensonnews-sun.com/news/article_f8a61a98-126c-11e2-a6b2-0019bb2963f4.html.

Chapter 20

[1]Borjas interview, October 11, 2012.

Chapter 21

[1]Borjas interview, October 11, 2012.

[2]"Slain Border Patrol agent Nicholas Ivie opened fire first, investigators say," *Deseret News*, October 7, 2012: www.deseret.com/2012/10/7/20507795/slain-border-patrol-agent-nicholas-ivie-opened-fire-first-investigators-say#rick-ivie-and-his-brother-chris-talk-to-the-media-about-border-patrol-agent-nicholas-ivie-at-cochise-college-in-sierra-vista-ariz-thursday-oct-4-2012-ivie-was-killed-while-on-a-regular-patrol-near-the-arizona-mexico-border.

Chapter 22

[1]Kimball Bennion. "Utahns bid 'Auf Wiedersehen' to slain Border Patrol agent," *The Salt Lake Tribune*, October 12, 2012: archive.sltrib.com/article.php?id=55061105&itype=CMSID.

[2] "Friends, family, colleagues honor fallen Border Patrol agent Nick Ivie," *Deseret News*, October 11, 2012: www.deseret.com/2012/10/11/20508273/friends-family-colleagues-honor-fallen-border-patrol-agent-nick-ivie.

[3]Dennis Romboy. "Friends, family, colleagues honor fallen Border Patrol agent Nick Ivie," October 11, 2012: www.deseret.com/2012/10/11/20508273/friends-family-colleagues-honor-fallen-border-patrol-agent-nick-ivie.

[4] "Honoring the Life and Service of U.S. Border Patrol Agent Nicholas J. Ivie," from the Congressional Record Online, U.S. Government Printing Office, Friday, October 12, 2012.

Chapter 23

[1]"Mexico Arrests 2 For Murder of Border Patrol Agent," *Borderland Beat*, October 4, 2012: http://www.borderlandbeat.com/2012/10/mexico-arrests-2-for-murder-of-border.html.

[2]Carlton interview.

[3]"Detienen a los asesinos de agente de la Border Patrol de Naco," published October 7, 2012, *Policíacas, Internacional*: www.proyeccioncananea.com/vernoticia.php?fn_mode=fullnews&fn_id=3449.

[4]Dennis Romboy. "He was the best dad that you could ever be," Family and friends rally to aid of fallen agent," October 3, 2012, 9:11 p.m.: www.deseret.com/2012/10/3/20507662/he-was-the-best-dad-that-you-could-ever-be#aaron-kerr-holds-back-the-tears-as-he-talks-about-his-friend-and-home-teaching-companion-nicholas-ivie-outside-of-ivies-home-in-sierra-vista-ariz-wednesday-oct-3-2012-ivie-was-killed-in-a-shootout-tuesday-while-on-patrol-near-the-mexican-border.

[5]"Source: 2 questioned in Mexico over fatal shooting of U.S. Border Patrol agent," CNN, October 4, 2012.

[6] "Two men held in Mexico for US agent Nicholas Ivie death," October 4, 2012: www.bbc.com/news/world-us-canada-19835173.

[7]"2 held in border shooting," *Concord Monitor*, October 5, 2012.

[8]Dylan Smith and Rebekah Zemansky. "Border Patrol Agent Nicholas Ivie killed, another wounded near Naco." FBI won't comment on reports that suspects detained in Mexico, *Tucson Sentinel*, updated October 2, 2012, 2:11 p.m., originally posted October 2, 2012, 9:12 a.m.: www.tucsonsentinel.com/local/report/100212_bp_shooting/border-patrol-agent-nicholas-ivie-killed-another-wounded-near-naco/.

[9]Richard Marosi. "Border Patrol agent is slain in Arizona, October 3, 2012, 12 a.m.: www.latimes.com/archives/la-xpm-2012-oct-02-la-na-border-agent-shooting-20121003-story.html.

[10]Ethan Fedida. "Arizona Border Shooting: Mexican Police Arrest 2 In Connection with Killed Border Patrol Agent, Nicholas Ivie, October 4, 2012, 01:42 pm ET, dateline Mexico City: www.huffpost.com/entry/arizona-border-shooting-mexico-arrest_n_1939921?utm_hp_ref=crime.

[11]Tim Steller. "Slain agent's brother: 'He lived his life as a life of service,'" *Arizona Daily Star*, October 4, 2012: tucson.com/news/local/border/slain-agent-s-brother-he-lived-his-life-as-a/article_d2641f12-0e41-11e2-94d3-001a4bcf887a.html).

[13]"Mexico Arrests 2 For Murder of Border Patrol Agent," October 4, 2012, update October 5, 2012: http://www.borderlandbeat.com/2012/10/mexico-arrests-2-for-murder-of-border.html.

Chapter 24

[1]"Slain Border Patrol agent's wife speaks for the first time," posted October 3, 2013, updated October 17, 2013, CBS5 (KPHO Broadcasting Corp.), Phoenix. *Web link no longer active.*

[2]*Provo Herald*: www.heraldextra.com/news/local/new-info-released-about-death-of-border-patrol-agent/article_cee515c3-023a-5e9c-88c5-70e7c6043c7f.html).

[3]Information from interviews with area resident Carlos Sanchez, August 2017.

[4]Borjas interview 2.

Chapter 25

[1]Ed Ashurst. *Alligators in the Moat: Politics and the Mexican Border*, p. 186: Ed Ashurst Publishing Company, Douglas, Arizona, January 2016

[2]"FOLLOW-UP: Border Patrol sticks to its guns, says Ivie shooting was not a cover-up," FOX 10 broadcast, May 20, 2017: www.fox-10phoenix.com/news/arizona-news/follow-up-border-patrol-sticks-to-its-guns-says-ivie-shooting-was-not-a-cover-up.

[3]Claudia Tristan .Women share experiences in male-dominated U.S. Border Patrol," KFOX TV, El Paso, Texas, March 8, 2018: kfoxtv.com/news/local/women-share-experiences-in-male-dominated-us-border-patrol.

Chapter 26

[1]Speech at The Liberty Forum of Silicon Valley, August 13, 2019, on the day his book *Ball of Collusion* was released. www.c-span.org/video/?463427-2/ball-collusion.

[2]Louis J. Freeh. *My FBI: Bringing Down the Mafia, Investigating Bill Clinton, and Fighting the War on Terror*, pp. 38–39: St. Martin's Press, New York, 2005.

[3]Tim Weiner, "No, Mr President—how the FBI bosses the White House," *The Guardian*, October 24, 2012: www.theguardian.com/world/2012/oct/24/how-fbi-bosses-us-presidents.

[4]"Robert Mueller: Unmasked by Congressman Louie Gohmert," op-ed, *Judicial Watch Inside Report*, June 18, 2019.

[5]"Robert Mueller: Unmasked by Congressman Louie Gohmert," *176–177*.

[6]Documented by many writers, including Ronald Kessler, in *The Secrets of the FBI*, Crown Publishers, New York, 2011.

[7]"Robert Mueller Unmasked by Gohmert," and "The Clinton-directed FBI hit job": www.wnd.com/2016/11/the-clinton-directed-fbi-hit-job/.

[8]"Why is lead FBI agent in botched Ted Stevens case still employed?": www.adn.com/alaska-news/article/why-lead-fbi-agent-botched-ted-stevens-case-still-employed/2012/06/07/).

[9]"Why is lead FBI agent in botched Ted Stevens case still employed?"

[10]Though FBI Director Mueller loyally played the role assigned him by the White House, then CIA Director David Petraeus later threatened to expose details about Benghazi, which would "soil"

Obama's legacy, according to Department of Defense sources. Three days after Obama was reelected, Petraeus was forced to resign. His extramarital affair with an author was exposed, and he was indicted for leaking classified information to her.

[11]"FBI's McCabe and Mueller ordered FBI Benghazi stand-down": www.galtreport.com/index.php/politics/item/2301-fbi-s-mc-cabe-mueller-ordered-fbi-benghazi-stand-down

[12]"Under Obama and Secretary of State Hillary Clinton, FBI Director Mueller and CIA Director Petraeus Grounded Critical Benghazi Rescue Operation": truepundit.com/obama-secretary-state-hill-ary-clinton-fbi-director-mueller-cia-director-petraeus-ground-ed-critical-benghazi-rescue-operation/.

[13]"Report reveals details of the Sky Harbor meeting between Clinton and Lynch"; www.azcentral.com/story/news/politics/arizo-na/2018/06/14/bill-clinton-and-loretta-lynch-meeting-phoenix-airport-details/703771002/.

[14]FBI Agents Manipulated Flynn 302 Interview. His Case Must Be Dismissed By Sara Carter. https://saraacarter.com/fbi-agents-manipulated-flynn-302-interview-his-case-must-be-dismissed-it-was-a-setup/

[15]Andrew McCarthy, Speech at The Liberty Forum of Silicon Valley, August 13, 2019, on the day his book *Ball of Collusion* was released: www.c-span.org/video/?463427-2/ball-collusion.

Chapter 27

[1]The information from Agent Carlton was gleaned from author interviews held in Arizona.

[2]This could be an indication that the apprehended suspects had recently been at Remax Saddle.

[3]As was reported earlier in this book, the Ivie family was told that Nick shot at the other agents first. Then another agent returned fire and he was killed.

Chapter 28

[1]ICE Special Agent Jaime Zapata was killed in Mexico by suspected drug cartel members in February 2011, with firearms linked to an ATF operation in Texas. Victor Avila, Zapata's partner, survived that attack.

Index

About The Author

This is the third book by Huey Freeman, a former police reporter for a daily newspaper in Central Illinois. He became interested in border issues a few years ago, after visiting with ranchers, law enforcement officers and other residents of Southern Arizona. Freeman, who holds bachelor's and master's degrees in journalism from the University of Illinois, has served as an adjunct journalism professor at Eastern Illinois and Millikin universities. Freeman is working on a book of oral histories of borderland residents. He is married to Kate Freeman.

Made in the USA
Columbia, SC
24 September 2023

23301061R00221